The Siege of Fort Cumberland, 1776
An Episode in the American Revolution

Focusing on the revolutionary movement in the Fort Cumberland region of Nova Scotia in 1775–76, Ernest Clarke explores why supporters of independence did not prevail in this British North American colony. He reveals how the siege of Fort Cumberland shaped the attitudes of Nova Scotians to the revolution and their place in the North American world.

Clarke describes events in Nova Scotia leading up to the siege of Fort Cumberland in 1776 and argues that from the beginning of hostilities Nova Scotians' primary loyalty was to Britain. He examines the attitudes of the various players in the region – New England planters, Acadians, Native peoples, Yorkshiremen, and Scots-Irish – and their responses to the call to arms issued by the revolutionary forces in the thirteen colonies. Clarke is the first to take the Nova Scotia patriots seriously and explain their motives instead of damning them as rebels.

The Siege of Fort Cumberland is a valuable study of divided loyalties at the beginning of the American revolution, not only in Nova Scotia but also in the other colonies.

ERNEST CLARKE is an architect, town planner, and independent historian.

The Siege of Fort Cumberland, 1776

An Episode in the American Revolution

ERNEST CLARKE

McGill-Queen's University Press
Montreal & Kingston • London • Buffalo

© McGill-Queen's University Press 1995
ISBN 0-7735-1323-X

Legal deposit 4th quarter 1995
Bibliothèque nationale du Québec

Printed in Canada on acid-free paper

This book has been published with the help of a grant from the Social
Science Federation of Canada, using funds provided by the Social Sciences
and Humanities Research Council of Canada.

McGill-Queen's University Press is grateful to the Canada Council for
support of its publishing program.

Canadian Cataloguing in Publication Data

Clarke, Ernest, 1939–
    The siege of Fort Cumberland, 1776
    Includes bibliographical references and index.
    ISBN 0-7735-1323-X
    1. Fort Beauséjour (N.B.)–Siege, 1776. I. Title.
    FC2321.35.C53 1995   971.02′4   C95-900761-X
    F1038.C53 1995

This book was typeset by Typo Litho Composition Inc.
in 10/12 Baskerville.

To Ralph Birden Clarke

Contents

The Nova Scotia Rebellion... the most unthinkable one Eric Morris before in the World

Saul and Smith, Port Laforest, 1997

The siege of Fort Cumberland, which began in late October 1776 and ended a month later was the climax of a "most unreasonable" rebellion. It had been planned in American and local patriots as a bold attempt to add Nova Scotia to the thirteen colonies of the newly independent United States of America, or as one patriot remarked, "to add another stripe to the American flag." The siege failed and while the defence of the fort by provincial troops and royal marines was militarily unspectacular, but their victory marked a turning point for loyal Nova Scotia, made a strong impression on the native nations, and signalled the end of local republicanism. In public terms the siege was a watershed for the colony soon to win fame as "New Brunswick's Oxford."

Today the ruins of Fort Beauséjour (Fort Cumberland's original name) occupy a place among one of the Tantramar marshes that mark the boundary between the Maritime provinces of Nova Scotia and New Brunswick. Built by the French in 1751 in an attempt to limit the area that had been ceded to the British – in particular Nova Scotia, Beauséjour was captured by an Anglo-American force in 1755. The fort was renamed Cumberland and maintained by the British until 1835. As an operational fort, therefore, it was Beauséjour for four years and Cumberland for eighty years; it was during the much longer British period that the fort was besieged, attacked first by another New England force. These two military events were quite different in nature. The siege of Fort Beauséjour in 1755 was part of a war between two nations, France and Great Britain, while the siege of Fort Cumberland in 1776 was part of a civil conflict. In the context of the American Revolution, New Englanders were

Preface: Tantramar Revisited

The Nova Scotia Rebellion: the most unreasonable one Ever Known
before in the World.

Nathaniel Smith, Fort Lawrence, 1777[1]

The siege of Fort Cumberland, which began in late October 1776 and
ended a month later, was the climax of a "most unreasonable" rebellion.
It had been planned by American and local patriots as a bold attempt to
add Nova Scotia to the thirteen colonies of the newly independent
United States of America, or as one patriot intimated, "to add another
stripe to the American flag."[2] The siege failed and while the defence of
the fort by provincial troops and royal marines was militarily unspectacular, their victory marked a turning point for loyal Nova Scotia, made a
strong impression on the native nations, and signalled the end of local
republicanism. In political terms the siege was a watershed for the colony known formerly as "New England's Outpost."

Today the ruins of Fort Beauséjour (Fort Cumberland's original name)
occupy a ridge arising out of the Tantramar marshes that mark the
boundary between the Maritime provinces of Nova Scotia and New Brunswick. Built by the French in 1751 in an attempt to limit Acadia – which
had been ceded to the British – to peninsular Nova Scotia, Beauséjour
was captured by an Anglo-American force in 1755. The fort was renamed
Cumberland and maintained by the British until 1835. As an operational
fort, therefore, it was Beauséjour for four years and Cumberland for
eighty years.[3] It was during the much longer British period that the fort
was besieged a second time by another New England force. These two
military events were quite different in nature. The siege of Fort Beauséjour in 1755 was part of a war between two nations, France and Great
Britain, while the siege of Fort Cumberland in 1776 was part of a civil
conflict, an incident of the American Revolution. New Englanders were

engaged in both sieges; they were the clear victors in the first, but in the second, in the rebellious spirit of 1776, they appeared on both sides, among the patriot attackers and the loyalist defenders. Attackers and defenders were intimately acquainted: some were neighbours living close to the fort; others belonged to the same society of Congregationalists; a few were veterans of the siege of 1755. The capture of Fort Beauséjour helped clear the way for the settlement of Nova Scotia by New Englanders, who soon formed the majority of the population. The siege of Fort Cumberland twenty-one years later revealed the loyalty of that planter majority and measured the extent of local rebellion at the beginning of the American Revolution.

In 1776 Fort Cumberland was encircled by the important planter community around present-day Amherst and Sackville, and was well placed geopolitically to influence the Acadians and the Micmac and Maliseet nations. Its strategic importance derived from its commanding presence on the narrow Isthmus of Chignecto at the head of the Bay of Fundy. Throughout the American Revolution the fort was recognized militarily as "the key to the whole province."[4]

Seventeen seventy-six was a crucial year for Nova Scotia. On the Isthmus of Chignecto periods of political agitation were interspersed with violent rebellion. Local patriots such as Jonathan Eddy, John Allan, Samuel Rogers, and Josiah Throop encouraged a network of radicals in several districts of the province and communicated with the American military, the Massachusetts Legislature, and the Continental Congress. In the Nova Scotia capital of Halifax four months of government crisis ended when the king removed the governor. The town was thrust into the limelight as a result of the fall of Boston to the patriots in March and the consequent British retreat to Halifax. News of political unrest in the outsettlements and of open rebellion at Cumberland drew the uncharacteristic notice of an administration accustomed to ignoring anything beyond the limits of the capital. In that eventful year both Halifax and Cumberland attracted attention from London to Philadelphia and from George Washington and George III.

These factors – location, timing, and circumstance – make the siege of Fort Cumberland an appropriate centre-piece for a study that explores Nova Scotia's role in the early years of the American Revolution. The attention paid to the colony and the isthmus by all parties in the conflict provides a rare opportunity for historians. The siege itself is a unique focal point from which to glimpse overall events; it is a tiny prism that sheds light on the larger context of the Revolution and on the varied spectrum of Nova Scotia society in the 1770s.

Studies of the Cumberland region have evolved steadily from Pierce Hamilton's initial 1880 essay to James Snowdon's thesis of 1974.[5] On the

larger question of Nova Scotia's position in the American Revolution historical thinking was dominated for a long time by John Brebner's thesis of
neutrality as set out in his 1937 classic, *The Neutral Yankees of Nova Scotia*.
Geographically remote and politically stillborn, most Nova Scotians, argues Brebner, remained neutral, although patriots "were distinctly more
numerous" than loyalists.[6] Having devised a geographical explanation for
the Acadian neutrality of the 1750s during a war between two separate nations, he extended the same rationale to the 1770s and applied it to another community in different circumstances. That the New England
planters of Nova Scotia had no tradition of neutrality and were involved in
a civil war failed to sway Brebner. Only in the 1970s, through the work of
George Rawlyk, was the Brebnerian thesis of neutrality challenged author-
itatively. Rawlyk's *Nova Scotia's Massachusetts* presents an alternative overview of the colony's position in the American Revolution. The perplexity
of the planters and the introspection that resulted in an explosion of indigenous innovation, particularly in religion, are explored by Rawlyk; he
reconstructs a context on the basis of which local studies such as this one
can proceed.[7]

Any examination of Nova Scotia in the revolutionary period must also
contend with Brebner's failure to recognize provincial loyalists.[8] Even
from within his neutrality straight-jacket Brebner was able to refer (however briefly and disparagingly) to local patriots and their movement, but
about the loyalists opposing them he was notably silent. If, as Mary Beth
Norton and others have shown, loyalty was the norm in America perhaps
as late as 1774, it should not be surprising that loyalty continued as the
norm in Nova Scotia throughout the revolution.[9] That there were local
loyalists is well recorded: those who resisted the rebellion were referred
to as loyalists by their contemporaries, many Nova Scotians were granted
land for loyal service, and a few who sustained losses in the Cumberland
siege were actually compensated by the Loyalist Claims Commission.[10]
Soon after the arrival of the more numerous American loyalists, distinc-
tions were drawn that narrowed the term loyalist to include only American refugees. Excluded by changing standards and obscured by new
terms such as pre-loyalists, resident loyalists have generally been lost to
Canadian historiography. J.M. Bumsted has noted that Brebner perpetu-
ates the distinction that emerged after 1783 between residents and
American refugees.[11] Resident loyalists merit literary discovery; the
planters, in particular, need to be viewed in their capacity as loyalists.
Nowhere is this more apparent than in a study of the Cumberland rebellion, a conflict in which loyalists prevailed.

Since the Cumberland siege was part of a much larger civil war between loyalists and patriots, it is necessary to review some of the different
theories on the origins of the revolution. In the early twentieth century,

as a result of work by American historians such as Arthur Schlesinger Sr and Charles Andrews, economic determinism came to be widely regarded as the motivating force of the revolution and still influences the thinking of many historians.[12] These progressive-era historians maintained that the revolution effectively originated in the British Treasury and the search for new sources of revenue. An elite merchant class in Boston and elsewhere, acting out of self-interest, resisted a new tax policy and proceeded to rouse the masses. Once aroused, the mob refused to disperse and grew out of control. The merchants tried to draw back politically but it was too late; they found themselves in a revolution.

By the mid-twentieth century a new generation of American historians had rejected the Schlesinger-Andrews emphasis on self-interest and asserted the importance of politics as the driving force behind the revolution. Strands of political ideology reaching back to the Glorious Revolution of 1688 in England inspired American colonists to resist the perceived suppression of liberty, argue these neo-Whig historians. They believe ideas and not economics led the colonies to revolt. Inevitability played an even stronger role than in the earlier thesis of economic determinism. Not only was patriot ideology logical, coherent, and compelling, it was also thought by neo-Whig historians to have prevailed inevitably. The patriot ideal as presented by the consensus school of historians eventually became so prevalent that it was unclear how any sensible, informed person could have opposed the revolution.[13]

Not surprisingly, neo-Whiggism was challenged. Two studies have considerably expanded the challenge. John Tyler's *Smugglers and Patriots* breathes new life into the earlier thesis of economic determinism. Using extensive data on the Boston merchant class of the 1760s and 1770s, Tyler identifies which merchants became loyalists and which became patriots, then reinterprets their activities in this critical period. His analysis confirms that "economic concerns appear to have played a far larger role in shaping the revolution than proponents of an exclusively ideological interpretation profess."[14] Tyler's work achieves a vital balance between the two main theses by concluding that economic self-interest and political ideology were inextricably linked.

The consensus approach, particularly the inevitability of patriot ideology, is balanced brilliantly by the landmark study of Janice Potter, *The Liberty We Seek*, in which a common loyalist ideology emerges from analyses of the public writings of leading loyalists in the 1760s and early 1770s. This ideology provided a logical, coherent alternative to republicanism and a reasoned interpretation of the origins and nature of the Revolution. While it defended the imperial status quo, it was neither reactionary nor static – it advocated renovation of the imperial system and reform of American institutions. The patriot ideal, emphasizes Potter, "was not inevitable."[15] Potter points out that loyalist ideology was apparent not only in New York and Massachusetts, the focus of her work, but in the middle and southern colonies as well. The extent to which Nova Scotians shared this common ideology was not considered by Potter, but Nova Scotia may well have been the colony most receptive to loyalist ideology. Indeed, the different political reality in Nova Scotia permitted the ideas advocated to be tested in the field and played out in practical ways that by the 1760s and early 1770s were no longer available to leading loyalist thinkers in New England. Unwittingly, by emigrating to Nova Scotia New England planters gained a decade and a half of grace not only to weigh ideological alternatives but to innovate politically. That loyalist ideas were relevant to eighteenth-century American society is clear from Potter. What is also probable is that such ideas influenced the development of non-republican North America from as early as the 1760s.

The thousands of New England planters who moved to Nova Scotia in the early 1760s avoided the political upheaval that preceded the military events of 1775–76. This period was "the real Revolution," believed John Adams, when there was "an important alteration in the religious, moral, political and social character of the people."[16] No such alteration occurred among the planters and other residents of Nova Scotia. This is not to say that the political development of planters ceased when they waded ashore in Nova Scotia; rather, new realities imposed new priorities, causing planter politics to diverge from the New England mainstream. Besides the trauma of emigration to an unfamiliar land and the substitution of a near wilderness for a highly structured landscape, planters faced the stress of establishing farms and businesses in an infant, cash- starved economy; proximity to suspicious Native people; and political interaction with an often inept, over-militarized colonial administration. They also faced the new possibility of becoming economically independent, enjoyed greater religious freedom, and adjusted to a general loosening of traditional structures.

These were factors that conditioned a new political environment. There was also the population itself. As Bernard Bailyn has recognized, Nova Scotia, for its small size, "constituted a society of remarkable ethnic complexity."[17] Acadians, Micmacs, Maliseets, Old and New Englanders, Blacks, foreign Protestants, Yorkshire folk, and Scots-Irish were found in linguistic amalgams, cultural enclaves, and distinct nations in the social strata and sub-strata of the multi-ethnic Nova Scotia of the 1760s and 1770s. After a decade and a half of political advance and disappointment, religious crises, land speculation, agricultural growth, and economic depression, the Nova Scotian reality differed from that of New England.[18] Planter heritage remained strong through economic and familial ties, but still the planter majority in Nova Scotia viewed the world with an altered perspective from those who had stayed put. During the revolution this often caused confusion.

The unique development of Nova Scotia stamped its patriot and loyalist movements with indigenous qualities that were reflected in the special nature of the rebellion at the head of the Bay of Fundy. The ethnic composition and economy of this region was typical of the colony. Every ethnic group in Nova Scotia was represented in the siege of Fort Cumberland, most on both sides. Regarding the economic background of the region, no one has described the period leading up to the rebellion more succinctly than Josiah Throop, a resident patriot. The planters left New England and "went down poor" to Nova Scotia. When the depression struck in 1770 some "returned discouraged" to New England "and gave the Country a bad name." Those who stayed "did not understand the Improving of Marsh," but struggled on anyway. Slowly, the economy improved and agricultural proficiency increased, until Throop could report that Cumberlanders "have dyked large Quantities" of marsh and by 1776 had "raised a Competency of bread for the Country." Optimism returned with self-sufficiency and "great preparations" were made to raise wheat for export "in vast Quantities."[19] This plan for prosperity was dashed in 1776 when their joy in the future, as poet Charles G.D. Roberts explained, "had fall'n in the shadow of pain" – the pain of civil war.[20]

Revisiting the Tantramar to examine the rebellion and siege provides a regional study with contextual value. Paradoxically, the history that is almost palpable amid the ruins on the weathered brow of Cumberland Ridge has long since, from a literary standpoint, faded into the background, or in Roberts's words, "all but died from remembrance." The rebellion has not been examined in depth since W.B. Kerr's 1941 *Maritime Provinces and the American Revolution,* and regional studies have relied on Brebner's 1937 overview rather than more recent scholarship.[21] A new examination is warranted not only by the lapse of time and new perspectives, but also because of extensive primary sources newly uncovered in Great Britain, Ireland, Canada, and the United States.

To David Bell who encouraged me to undertake the project and George Rawlyk who drove me to complete it, and to both of them for professional advice and criticism at each phase, I acknowledge my debt. Their own work and scholarship provided my inspiration. A creature of primary research, this work in its initial phases required numerous visits and persistent enquiries to dozens of institutions in four countries. What stands out in my recollection of this otherwise arduous task is the co-operation, service, and sheer courtesy of the staff in these institutions; my thanks to this multitude. I acknowledge Barbara Schmeisser, an expert on Fort Beauséjour-Cumberland, who read an early draft, and I thank Darlene Moore for technical assistance on the final manuscript. My appreciation goes to Alberta, my wife, for her assistance and to our children, Aaron and Naomi, for their support throughout.

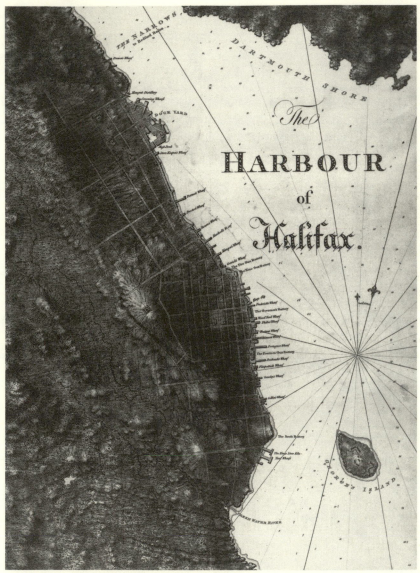

"The Harbour of Halifax," showing the waterfront, Royal Dockyard, Citadel Hill, and the grid pattern of the town. J.F.W. DesBarres, 1777. (National Archives of Canada [NA] NMC 28, 063)

The town and harbour of Halifax, looking toward Governor's Wharf, St Paul's, and the horizon of Citadel Hill. Detail of a painting by Serres from a drawing by R. Short, 1759. (Art Gallery of Nova Scotia)

"The Governor's House, Halifax." Detail of a painting by Serres from a drawing by R. Short, 1759. This site was later occupied by the provincial legislature. (Art Gallery of Nova Scotia)

"View of Fort Cumberland in Nova Scotia taken from the French 1755, from a View taken on the Spot by Capt. J. Hamilton of his Majesty's 40th Reg't." (NA C-2707)

View of Fort Cumberland, April 1803. Painting by Benjamin Gerrish Gray in a manuscript catalogue by Gray of books in King's College Library. (King's College Library)

"The Church of Saint Paul's." Detail of a painting by Serres from a drawing by R. Short, 1759. (Killam Library, Dalhousie University)

Soldiers drilling on the Grand Parade. Detail of a painting by Serres from a drawing by R. Short, 1759. (Killam Library, Dalhousie University)

Commodore Sir George Collier. Another likeness of Collier, made when he was older, was published in the *Naval Chronicle* 32 (1814), but this earlier painting should be a better likeness of the thirty-six year old Collier in Nova Scotia. (National Maritime Museum, Greenwich, England, AS807)

Commodore Marriot Arbuthnot, dockyard commissioner and lieutenant-governor of Nova Scotia. Painting by Charles H. Hodges after John Rising, 1792. (National Maritime Museum, Greenwich, England)

Major-General Eyre Massey. Engraving by J.J. Van Den Berghe from an original miniature painted by R. Bull. (National Library of Ireland)

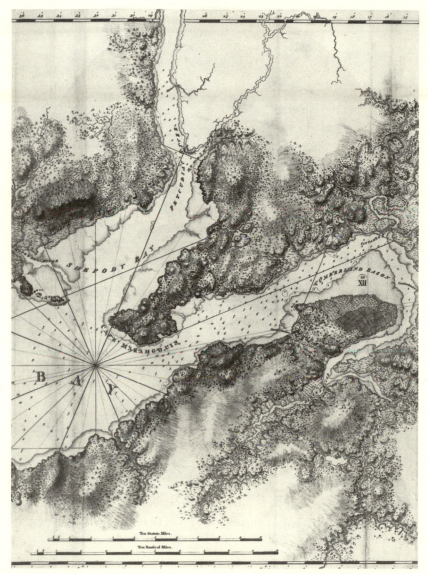

Shepody Bay and Cumberland Basin at the Head of the Bay of Fundy. Colonel Goreham's Shepody Outpost was at the junction of the Petitcodiac and Memramcook rivers that flow into Shepody Bay. J.F.W. DesBarres, 1777. (NA NMC 27,978)

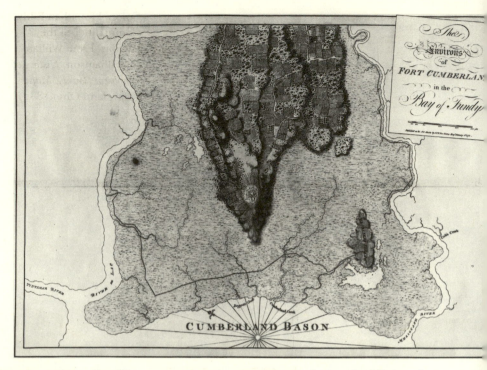

"The Environs of Fort Cumberland in the Bay of Fundy." Note the Missiguash River, the Aulac River, and Cumberland Creek. J.F.W. DesBarres, 1777. (NA NMC 27,983)

Christopher Harper's home in relation to Fort Cumberland. Surveyor's plan in the land papers of the Public Archives of New Brunswick.

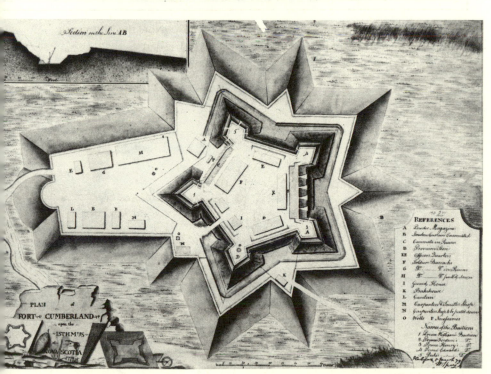

Colonel Jonathan Eddy, Commander of the Patriots. From William D. Williamson, *History of Penobscot County, Maine* (Cleveland Ohio 1882).

"Plan of Fort Cumberland upon the Isthmus of Nova Scotia 1778" by William Spry. (NA C-34708)

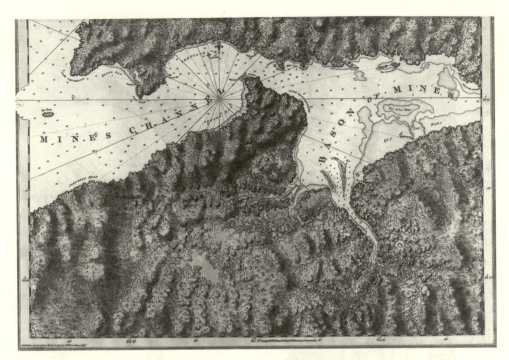

Minas Channel and Minas Basin in the Bay of Fundy. J.F.W. DesBarres, 1777.
(NA NMC 28,352)

"Cape Blowmedown [Blomidon] open with Cape Split." J.F.W. DesBarres,
1777. Detail. (Killam Library, Dalhousie University)

"The Entrance of Minas Basin." J.F.W. DesBarres, 1777. Detail. (Killam Library, Dalhousie University)

"Found we could not weather Cape Chignecto," exclaimed Captain James Feattus of HMS *Vulture*. Detail of a view of Cape Chignecto by J.F.W. DesBarres, 1777. (Killam Library, Dalhousie University)

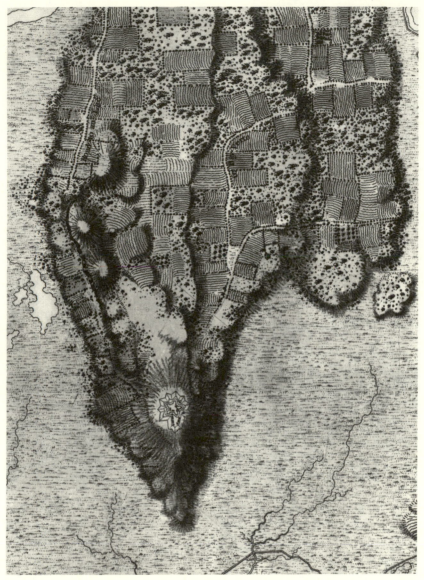

Fort Cumberland, the Baie Verte Road, and Camphill. J.F.W. DesBarres, 1777. Detail. (NA NMC 27,983)

The Siege of Fort Cumberland

Summers and summers have come, and gone with the
    flight of the swallow;
Sunshine and thunder have been, storm, and winter,
    and frost;
Many and many a sorrow has all but died from
    remembrance,
Many a dream of joy fall'n in the shadow of pain ...

From Tantramar Revisited by Charles G.D. Roberts

Introduction

There is an appearance of Great Britain being under a Necessity of
coming to blows with the whole Continent, Halifax and Quebec excepted.
Many parts indeed of Nova Scotia begin to grow refractory.
British official, Boston, November 1774[1]

A pessimistic official view of British North America circulated on the
eve of the American Revolution. Rebellion was so advanced that negoti-
ating a political solution seemed out of the question. War was inevitable
and necessary if Britain were to maintain control of the colonies. This
view held that when war came it would have to be waged everywhere on
the continent, Nova Scotia and Quebec excepted, Quebec's loyalty was
not questioned, but rebellious tendencies were discerned in Nova
Scotia. War with either colony was unlikely, but the future of Nova
Scotia appeared uncertain.

Evidence of a refractory Nova Scotia was at hand. To British officials
the New England majority guaranteed a republican spirit in the population and the potential for rebellion. The astute observer could point to
suspicious political activity in 1774. "Meetings and Assemblies of the
People at different times in several of the townships have been called
and held for various purposes contrary to the Publick good," observed
Governor Francis Legge in September. This activity became so common
that Legge decreed people must "refrain from all such Meetings and
Assemblies."[2]

One such meeting was called by Halifax merchants John Fillis and
William Smith (former New Englanders) prior to Legge's decree. They
wished to protest the local distribution of a shipment of East India tea,
but the meeting was declared illegal. The two merchants quietly acquiesced and never held the meeting, and they were promptly dismissed
from their government offices.[3] Other meetings carried on unchecked
by the decree, especially in the outsettlements. Political dissent thrived,

particularly when it came to local issues such as the contentious glebe dispute in Cumberland on the Isthmus of Chignecto, and the growing discontent with Legge's administration. The glebe dispute pitted the established church against the Congregationalists and a planter township against the central government in Halifax. Local radicals tried to exploit the situation and link the dissent to the broader issues of the continental rebellion. Nova Scotians were aware of republican politics and some (like Smith and Fillis) had embraced certain aspects, but there was little popular support for rebellion. Issues that provoked New Englanders to rebel, such as the Coercive Acts recently passed in the British Parliament, did not excite Nova Scotians in the same way, as witnessed by the ease with which the Smith-Fillis meeting was checked.

Through the winter of 1774–75 politics in Nova Scotia were sufficiently noisy to attract the attention of external observers, and the continental rebellion lurched inexorably towards war. The British parliament declared Massachusetts to be in rebellion and from Philadelphia the proceedings of Congress were circulated to British colonies in North America for consideration. Several colonies adopted them, but on reaching Nova Scotia in March they were ignored officially and caused no discernible public reaction.[4] Other than a few meetings held after the decree there was no direct challenge to the government in Halifax, all aspects of which functioned normally. By comparison Massachusetts was in a state of anarchy with "neither Form nor Order Amongst us," a situation one Bostonian (a former resident of Cumberland) accurately predicted "we cannot long continue."[5]

The war that some regarded as necessary broke out with the warm weather of spring, the first shots being fired at Lexington and Concord on Wednesday, 19 April 1775. The patriots besieged Boston, the headquarters of the British army under General Thomas Gage and where the fleet was concentrated under Admiral Samuel Graves. News of these events spread quickly, reaching Halifax in just three days.[6] While other colonies, such as New Hampshire and Rhode Island, rallied to help Massachusetts, and while riots broke out in New York, Nova Scotia remained calm.

Steps were taken to maintain the calm and tighten provincial security. Local patriots detected government efforts to "use every means and method to prevent giving uneasiness to the people" so as "to preserve the peace."[7] At the request of Lieutenant-Governor Michael Francklin, the Halifax committee of the Society for the Propagation of the Gospel (SPG) warned missionaries in the province to avoid "all Controversy with the Inhabitants of different persuasions, and provoking them to disgust and Animosities."[8] Fresh in everyone's mind was the glebe dispute at Cumberland which had embroiled dissenters and church people in a court battle, drawn in the government, and caused township rights – a political issue of concern to ethnic New Englanders – to resurface at an awkward time.

The second means adopted to preserve peace was dear to the heart of the central government – the extension of Halifax rule more effectively across the province. Two reviews of the justice system proposed the abolition of the inferior courts located in the counties, a move intended as much to curb political activity as to introduce a measure of judicial reform. From a legal standpoint the inferior courts were "full of absurdity and Defect," but in the government's view were worse still. They were political forums – "places of Entertainment and pernicious pastime" – attracting those better kept out of "popular meetings."9 In the end Halifax did not adopt this legal proposal, nor were the SPG's missionaries entirely muzzled, but local patriots, by their own admission, suffered a setback due to the partial measures taken by the government.

It soon appeared that the events of 19 April in New England would not cause Nova Scotians to revolt and that the government could maintain order. It was evident that the New Englanders besieging Boston had different motivations from those who were settled in Nova Scotia. It was not that New England was taking action and Nova Scotia was doing nothing, but that each was responding to a specific political reality. Local patriots needed an issue to link their province to the continental cause. One did emerge which held the promise of doing this perfectly, one that by its very nature touched nearly everyone in the province and offered the means by which patriots could gain support.

SUPPLY OF THE BRITISH GARRISON AT BOSTON

Barricaded in Boston, cut off from the hinterland, with only a trickle of goods coming in from England, General Gage and Admiral Graves desperately needed a source of supplies for the British army and navy and the many loyalists trapped in the town.10 Nova Scotia was an obvious choice and the British were not disappointed. Barely two weeks after hearing the news of hostilities, over twenty vessels had either sailed or were about to sail from Halifax, Lunenburg, and the Bay of Fundy with "all sorts of provisions" for Boston.11 The response was spontaneous, and if those Nova Scotians who proclaimed it "very wonderful" were merely relishing their "very considerable profit," this was acceptable to the British.12 The reaction of Nova Scotians to the news of Lexington and Concord was the opposite to those in New England. Whereas Americans converged in arms on the British garrison at Boston, Nova Scotians, both in Halifax and the outsettlements, rushed supplies to that same garrison.

Nova Scotia's reaction was deemed a hostile act by the Americans and retaliation came quickly. Exports to the province were banned and privateers were outfitted and sent to harass Nova Scotia.[13] "They have marked us out as objects of their resentment," complained Legge of the Americans.[14] Some transport ships were captured and many were delayed in Halifax, on the South Shore, and in the Fundy ports.[15] Privateers captured a schooner on the St John River with supplies for Boston and chased a schooner into Liverpool Harbour in August. A ship "fully laden with livestock" from the Bay of Fundy was captured just outside Boston Harbour.[16] Admiral Graves ordered warships to sink the "pirates" and "lay Waste and destroy every Town" where they were outfitted. This escalation of the rebellion culminated in the burning of Falmouth (now Portland), Maine, in October 1775.[17]

The delays in supplying Boston lasted only until Graves sent other ships north for escort duty.[18] Then the traffic resumed with Nova Scotians in all coastal villages selling livestock and goods that were transported in dozens of ships to Boston until the town was evacuated the following year.[19] In Cumberland, trade was brisk. Of the livestock on the isthmus, a resident reported "many will be fatted, both Oxen and Cows, for the use of the Army." Forage followed the same course: "most of the Marsh ... that grows about Cumberland, is and will be sold to the troops at Boston." All summer and autumn transports shuttled in and out of Cumberland Basin. "The Marsh," exclaimed an inhabitant with glee, "it is more valuable than I supposed."[20]

The supply of Boston that "enraged the Americans" was a "pain and Grief" to local patriots.[21] They campaigned earnestly against the trade, appealing to planters not to lend "the least assistance to the army which has been endeavouring to enslave their friends and relations." This appeal was futile; friends and relations were already at each others' throats. Consanguinity, after all, is the stuff of civil strife. The patriots turned to threatening and then harassing the shipping agents.[22] Nothing worked. The campaign honed their political skills but failed to generate a revolt out of a very promising issue. In defeat they blamed the Halifax government. "Since the Concord Battle," exaggerated one patriot, "we have Experienced Tyranny in as great perfection as it is Capable of arriving to in a Christian land."[23] Unlike American patriots, they were unable to seize the political initiative, disrupt the government through terrorist acts, or undertake military action.

Revolutionary America made extraordinary strides in the same period, particularly in the military field. The force besieging Boston grew to 15,000 soldiers from several states. Congress formed the Continental Army, appointed George Washington as its commander-in-chief, and approved the conquest of Quebec. The new army was strong enough by June 1775 to absorb a major defeat in the set piece battle at Bunker Hill. Patriot bands seized arsenals of weapons at New York, Baltimore, and in Georgia, and the British armed schooner *Margaritta* was captured at Machias, Maine.

In nearby Nova Scotia there was almost no collective action by patriots. They were blamed for two failed attempts to burn the dockyard in Halifax and for a fire that actually consumed a stack of hay intended for Boston, but nothing was proved.[24] More was expected from a refractory population; more was required of an effective patriot movement. No time was more favourable than the summer of 1775, no prize greater than Halifax with the only royal dockyard in America, and no motivation stronger than a revolutionary victory in Boston which must have followed a revolt in the colony on which the British depended for supplies. Only thirty-six troops were posted in the province and no ships were assigned to the naval station.[25] None of the frontier posts was garrisoned and, as for Halifax, "there is not the least kind of defence about the town," reported Legge.[26] Nothing protected Nova Scotia except its loyal populace, its mere presence intimidating the patriots, as they admitted, blinding them to "the least glimpse of success" and preventing them from being "active in the glorious struggle." They rejoiced not in their own deeds, but in the American rebellion and in the rumour "that an invasion was intended."[27]

The startling growth of the rebellion after Lexington seemed to overwhelm British colonial officials. In Halifax in July Governor Legge worried because "our inhabitants of Passamaquoddy and St John's River are wholly from New England, as are the greatest part of the inhabitants of Annapolis River and those of the townships of Cornwallis, Horton, Falmouth, and Newport, some of which are not forty miles from this town." Because of their "connections with the people of New England little or no dependence can be placed on the militia" in the event of an invasion.[28] The mere proximity of ex-New Englanders to the capital was enough to worry the paranoid Legge who had been in Nova Scotia for nearly two years but was still perplexed by the province. Unsuitable as governor, Legge had neither political acumen nor political experience, only political connections. Already a cabal had organized against him. Legge confused this opposition with disloyalty to the king and misrepresented it as evidence of republican sentiment lurking all around him. Yet it is clear that three months after the outbreak of war he feared invasion more than internal rebellion. Even at his most pessimistic he did not believe that Halifax would become another Boston, surrounded by Nova Scotians in revolt.[29]

Legge had exaggerated concerns about the planters, but his fear of invasion was well-founded. Already there were raids: "Rebels from New

England in Armed Vessels had made descents at Passama-quoddy and upon the River St John" where, at the end of August, Fort Frederick, an ungarrisoned post at the mouth of the river, was burned by privateers from Machias.[30] "Other Armed Vessels from the same Country insulted the Southern and Eastern Shore of the Province," harassed the Canso fishery, "proceeded to the Island of St. John" (now Prince Edward Island) in November, and captured that colony's attorney-general.[31] Later two schooners landed near Cape Sable and "surprised and took several officers" of the loyal militia.[32] Patriots underplayed these raids, claiming weakly that hostilities had not really commenced. The burning of Fort Frederick was explained euphemistically as an "act of inconsideration."[33] However, their making light of the raids publicly while secretly appealing for an American invasion was complicated by the forewarning in the summer of 1775 of a larger plan of American conquest.

A new policy of conquest was adopted by American revolutionary governments in the summer of 1775. Massachusetts proposed an attack on Nova Scotia, but Congress decided to attack Quebec first. On 17 June Congress resolved to mount an expedition from Fort Ticonderoga, New York, which had been captured by a small band of patriots the month before.[34] A second, "secret expedition" against Quebec, to be led by Benedict Arnold, was planned via Maine up the Kennebec River to Montreal with forces diverted from Boston. It was left to Washington to explain the reasons for putting off Massachusetts. He was less than forthright in his reply: "I apprehend such an Enterprise inconsistent with the General principle upon which the Colonies have proceeded." To attack Nova Scotia "is a Measure of Conquest rather than Defence," he declared, while at the same time helping to plan the conquest of Quebec.[35]

There was knowledge of the Massachusetts plan in Nova Scotia and rumours of attack were heard late into the autumn, rumours that multiplied when Americans mobilized at the mouth of the Kennebec River prior to marching overland to Quebec. It was concluded wrongly that this force was intended for Nova Scotia. Both Graves and Gage supported that conclusion and certain travellers between Nova Scotia and New England spread the rumour of attack.[36] Despite these rumours, the local patriot party did not grow significantly in this period. Whether loyalty increased cannot be ascertained. Since quiescence continued to be the norm in Nova Scotia after 1774, there was no specific group of loyalists comparable with the patriot party. Society in general bore the stamp of loyalty, although at times the imprint was barely visible because of factional disputes. The Reverend John Breynton of Halifax believed the province should reap benefits from the uprising in America but was losing out because of "Domestic and political wranglings" which were nearly as confusing as the rebellion.[37] The fact that patriots could not exploit these internecine disputes was as much a measure of underlying loyalty in the general population as of disorganization in the patriot party. Passive loyalty was also evidenced by the absence of collective violence at a time when New England was engaged in aggressive rebellion.

Loyalty in Nova Scotia in 1775 need not, however, be proved by negative means alone; overt expressions appeared in the darkest hours, when the colony was virtually defenceless. In November, when the worst was expected in Quebec and the province lay open to attack, upwards of 700 of "the principal inhabitants" of Halifax, Kings, and Annapolis Counties signed the oath of allegiance and entered into an association "acknowledging their duty and fidelity to His Majesty."[38] Personal testimonies offset the impression that Legge gave in his letters to London of widespread disloyalty. In England, Joshua Mauger was "an advocate for the Inhabitants [of] that unhappy and ill-governed Province" and told the King that Legge was "very wrong" in his opinion. He praised Nova Scotians "whose Loyalty has been so conspicuous in the Present Crisis."[39] Writing from Nova Scotia, Michael Francklin asserted to an official in London that Legge's opinions "are totally untrue and without foundation." Legge had "lost the confidence and affection of the King's best subjects," and if the ranks of the disaffected had grown, it was due to his "Arbitrary and impolitic Conduct."[40] Francklin was Legge's political opponent, but even a Legge ally, the Reverend William Ellis of Windsor, testified to local loyalty: "The opinion conceived at home, of this Province being on the point of joining the Rebellion, is ill-founded." He added an important postscript: "notwithstanding we have great numbers of New England people among us who may be reasonably enough suspected of dissatisfaction."[41]

Instances of loyalty surfaced throughout the summer and autumn of 1775. Two provincial regiments, the Royal Highland Emigrants and Royal Fencible Americans recruited locally "and many of the men have been enlisted."[42] Nova Scotians fought in the siege of Boston and in the defence of Quebec.[43] In August thirty-six carpenters and mariners were hired to assist the garrison at Quebec.[44] As fractious as society was, loyal forces were at work and, although weak, they were regarded as implacable by the patriots. One patriot advised Washington of "my inability of performing anything in this great struggle and the danger I expose myself and family to" by pursuing radical politics at Cumberland. Patriots would be active if they could, but it was "impossible."[45] With no troops in Cumberland and only a handful in Halifax, any check to patriot progress was of a political nature and erected by loyal elements in the population.

The political affairs of continental patriots, on the other hand, advanced with breath-taking speed after Lexington. Congress convened again at Philadelphia and chose John Hancock as president. A revolutionary council assumed control in New York, a similar body in New Jersey supported the Congress, and another in South Carolina expressed solidarity with the patriot cause. The royal governors of North Carolina and Virginia were forced from office. Meanwhile, without a single sentry to guard his residence, Governor Legge emerged to convene the summer session of the House of Assembly, an elected body comprising several overlapping factions.[46] There were members who supported Legge's administration on every issue; members who opposed it for various reasons and on different issues; others who were suspected of supporting the American cause (who supported or opposed Legge depending on the issue); and those who were outright patriots. That patriots still operated in the system after the outbreak of war was significant in itself. Their performance was weak in their own judgment. Feeling "under so many embarrassments" and ineffectual, "they could not make their good will manifest," much less disrupt government business.[47] Nor could they prevent the adoption of an address to the king that was remarkable for its innovative proposals for resolving the revolution in North America, and for political, administrative, and fiscal reform of the colony.[48] Still, the summer session, which lasted until July, was difficult enough for Legge; the dissension centred on local issues, primarily the Governor's leadership style.

The patriot movement in Nova Scotia was small and uncoordinated at the time of the legislative sessions of 1775. There was no forum of radicals until after Lexington, and as late as the beginning of 1776 patriots admitted that "the great contest between Britain and America has hitherto been only treated with speculation amongst us."[49] This speculative movement was scattered in the outsettlements, with a concentration at Cumberland. Communication was assisted by the "interwoven Connection" between magistrates who had a reputation for radicalism.[50] Political inspiration came from New England and, being derivative, sounded stilted. By autumn 1775, patriots were better organized and began making formal contacts with New England. One of the first was a meeting held before October between the Maugerville group and the Massachusetts Council.[51] Committees-of-Safety were formed at Passamaquoddy, Maugerville, Cumberland, and Cobequid. In October the Passamaquoddy committee petitioned the Congress to join the revolutionary association.[52]

The pre-eminent group of patriots was centred on the Isthmus of Chignecto. What made the isthmus a friendly place for radicals was an accumulation of grievances – resulting from a series of incidents in its brief planter history – which by 1775 had formed a tradition of political dissent. The chief political zealots on the isthmus were Jonathan Eddy and John Allan. Eddy was a slave owner, farmer, and minor official of Fort Lawrence where he owned large land tracts. He represented Cumberland township in the Assembly until 1775, but was too single-minded to be an effective politician. His rhetorical talents were locked to a military mind. A retired army officer in his late fifties, he had leadership qualities and tactical ingenuity equal to his rank of captain. As a soldier he was tough but erratic, revealing his blind determination through gratuitous optimism. Eager and impatient, he saw little chance for indigenous rebellion without the stimulus of an American invasion.[53]

John Allan of Bloody Bridge (now Point de Bute) was over twenty years Eddy's junior. Allan spent part of his youth in Boston where he was exposed to radical politics. In Nova Scotia he felt constrained by his influential father, a business person in Halifax. The elected member for Cumberland in 1775, Allan was shrewd with the skills of a politician or, more precisely, a diplomat, but not of a soldier. He was a farmer, but it was as a trader that he travelled the province, was absent from his family for long periods, and became known in Native settlements through "frequent interviews" with the inhabitants.[54]

Eddy and Allan were the leaders of the patriot party, the military experience of the former ostensibly complementing the political prowess of the latter. There were other leaders. Samuel Rogers, an outspoken member of the Assembly for Sackville, was seafaring and hard working, but a failure as a farmer. A neighbour confessed: "I would not trust Samuel Rogers with three Coppers"![55] Josiah Throop, a former member of the Assembly, was a business person, surveyor, school teacher, and clerk of the inferior court. Between April and October of 1775 these and other local patriots struggled for the people's attention without any notable success. Nova Scotians regarded the rebellion with horror, envy, or fascination, but they were primarily spectators, not participants. Their initial task – supplying the British in Boston – was decidedly unpatriot-like. The best route to creating local rebellion now seemed to entail exploiting the strife between political factions, or taking advantage of the governor's ineptitude. Gaining allies among the Acadians and Native nations was also beginning to dawn on Eddy and Allan. Time appeared still to favour the patriots. New England was making military gains and provincial defences remained extremely weak.

The war was going against the British and criticism was aimed at those in charge, at General Gage for allowing the army to be trapped in Boston, at Admiral Graves for failing to protect the supply lines, and at both for a lack of initiative. Gage was cited by the king for neglecting the defence of Nova Scotia though "directions have been repeatedly given to the Commander-in-Chief to attend to it."[56] Both were relieved of their command. General Sir William Howe replaced Gage in October but Graves's successor, Admiral Molyneux Shuldham, would not arrive in North America until the new year. Changes in the North American command also brought changes in local defence. The security of Nova Scotia had been an object of the king's "care and Solicitude" from the beginning of the crisis, but improvements failed to match royal concern.[57] No warship was assigned to the Nova Scotia station and while the garrison was strengthened in early October by the arrival from Boston of the Royal Fencible Americans, a new provincial corps under Colonel Joseph Goreham, the garrison still had no more than 200 effective troops. Other improvements were gradual. On 31 October Commodore Marriot Arbuthnot arrived from England to be commissioner of the royal dockyard.[58] Also, "His Majesty's apprehensions for the Safety of Halifax" led to a small reinforcement from Ireland under General Eyre Massey that arrived on the last day of November.[59] Finally, Sir William Howe, acting with more vision than his predecessor, ordered a review of the province's defence works. He intended to re-garrison frontier posts, including Fort Cumberland.[60] Although these measures and the new arrivals – Goreham, Arbuthnot, and Massey – changed the complexion of local defence, Nova Scotia was still inadequately protected.

The new arrivals formed a remarkable trio of veterans. Joseph Goreham, at fifty the youngest of the three, was familiar with the province having acquired large land interests, as well as large debts. He was appointed to Council where he opposed the governor, a political stance complicated by the fact that he was also a rival of Michael Francklin, who spearheaded the opposition. Goreham's experience in dealing with Native nations (he was a former Indian agent) would be an asset in the present crisis.[61]

For General Eyre Massey, six years older than Goreham, this was the "fourth or fifth war in which [he] has been an active Officer." A soldier's soldier who held the respect of those he commanded, Massey lacked political sense. Perhaps the trauma of several war wounds contributed to his unpredictable manner that undermined any efforts he made to co-operate with his peers in the navy and the administration. Since local officers found that "Legge has washed his hands out of us," it was left to Massey to take charge of the army, clear up insubordination, and restore authority.[62] Then there was Marriot Arbuthnot. He was sixty-four and had retired after an undistinguished forty-year naval career; one might have presumed that his best years were behind him. A look beneath the affable exterior, however, revealed a keen political sense, an instinct for personal advantage, and a readiness to confess to superiors the errors of others. The leading local business person was quick to refer to Arbuthnot as "the good Commodore."[63] These new arrivals – individualists all – put a better face on the military, but they also added to the already complex circle of power and influence in Halifax and were apt to complicate local politics as well.

The autumn session of the Nova Scotia House of Assembly opened on 20 October in an atmosphere of tension and against a backdrop of calamity in Quebec. The Atlantic province was isolated: "almost the whole Continent is in open Rebellion."[64] The chief item of business was how to deal with the threat of invasion, but the solution arrived at re-awakened the spirit of dissent in Cumberland and inflamed the province. By this time two more royal governors had fled their official residences in South Carolina (Legge's predecessor in Nova Scotia) and New York.[65] Yet Government House in Halifax was still unguarded and the only complaint heard from dissident members concerned the inopportune timing of the session due to a small pox scare in the capital.[66] In the end all factions attended the House, even patriot members. For Cumberland, John Allan "took the usual Oaths and his seat."[67] How startling it was in late 1775 for the province's leading radical to accept a seat in His Majesty's legislature! Anyone doing so in North Carolina, by contrast, would have been declared an enemy of the state. This illustrates how different Nova Scotia was from the rest of North America and how weak its patriot party.

THE MILITIA ACTS

Coastal raids, privateering, and invasion threats kept the province "in continued Alarm." There were too few troops with "little or no hope" of reinforcement.[68] The British army might as well be out on Sable Island as "cooped up in the Town of Boston," commented one critic.[69] Self-help seemed the only answer so "under these critical Circumstances the Legislature … was called together."[70] Legge and his Council had already agreed to increase the militia and initial results were promising with companies mustering in many areas, including Acadian communities. Then, in the autumn session, "a more general plan was proposed" to the Assembly. Legge wanted a portion of the militia "collected to add to the strength of this place" – Halifax.[71] His plan implied that the capital was more important than the outsettlements which were equally at risk in the crisis. Two acts were passed, one to select militiamen by ballot and bring a fifth of them to Halifax, the second to levy taxes to cover expenses. Legge saw the acts as the only "possible means" of defending the province.[72] Politically, they were a disaster.

The debate over the militia legislation was one of the most acrimonious ever held in the Assembly. At one stage the members refused to attend a meeting requested by the governor and Council to discuss the acts. Two members, Samuel Rogers of Sackville and Samuel Archibald of Truro, stood in the House to declare "that the People would rise in Arms" to oppose the acts. "We must entreat your Excellency," pleaded other members, "to feel for the Poverty of this Province."[73] Increasing in intensity, the debate spilled into the streets and beyond. "Many Persons, who both within and without the House endeavoured to prevent the passing of the Acts," when they failed, took their case outside the Assembly "to be spread in the country."[74] Scarcely able to believe their good fortune, the patriots exploited the debate for their own ends. Legge considered the legislation a defensive measure, but they portrayed it as holding "the greatest implication of a declaration of war" against New England.[75] Employing "many untrue Suggestions," they encouraged opposition to the acts.[76] At Cumberland and elsewhere these "enemies to His Majesty's government," complained Legge, "propagated a report that my intention was to draw them to Halifax and thence to transport them to New England and make soldiers of them." By this tactic the patriots "inflamed the whole country" against the acts.[77] At last they had "roused a spirit among the people."[78]

It was a heady time for Nova Scotia patriots who were assisted by agents from New England.[79] Declarations were made "which before were not heard." The most radical wanted to apply immediately for continental help. Public meetings proliferated despite the official ban, especially in Cumberland: there was "Nothing to be heard but war, this County in particular"! When the commander of the militia called an assembly to draw an enlistment, the men "complied with the order" then defied the officers "on their peril" to draw one man.[80] The isthmus was in a "universal uproar"![81] Here, at last, was rebellion.

Dissent spread in the militia. "Many companies refused to assemble," not just in Cumberland, but in Kings and Annapolis.[82] The tax to support the militia "is opposed in all the settlements."[83] The opposition included loyalists. "The Act is hardly calculated for this Quarter," protested Charles Dixon, Yorkshire immigrant and Legge ally on the Isthmus of Chignecto. He explained how the most loyal family could not comply with its terms and how it would not be "possible for the Civil power to enforce it."[84] Having never visited the townships, Legge was insensitive to their inability to pay the tax in the cash-starved countryside and to the damage that must result if fathers and sons were drawn from farms in the current labour shortage to join the militia in Halifax or elsewhere. On these points there was near unanimity, yet a Legge associate charged that "the alleged indigence and fewness of the

People are altogether groundless and insidious."[85] This rebuff derided patriots and loyalists alike, including Dixon who pleaded through an intermediary for the Governor to withdraw the bill: "For God's sake use your interest and wisdom in this matter"![86]

The patriots held the momentum and debated tactics. The radical wing led by Jonathan Eddy advocated invasion, and a plan for inviting the Americans into the province was promoted publicly. The moderate faction, under John Allan, argued that this tactic was untimely. With more political foresight than Eddy, Allan saw a chance to foment rebellion by widening the opposition to the militia bill. The moderates succeeded in having the invasion plan set aside temporarily and Eddy's hard-liners "were obliged to publicly discourage it till all Lawful means was tried" to persuade the Governor and Council "to Suspend the present Act."[87] At this stage, sharply-worded remonstrances and petitions were sent to the Governor. Typically, "one of the fullest" and most "explicit" came from Cumberland.[88] An unusual amalgam of legitimate protest and veiled sedition, its blunt comment on the militia legislation – "we cannot comply with it" – was supported by New Englanders, Acadians, and Yorkshire folk, by church people and dissenters alike, producing a rare instance of consensus in the district. For loyalists the remonstrance was a reasoned explanation of how the bill would wreak havoc on their families who "must inevitably perish" under the effects. Patriots were pleased with the passage implying that the militia bill (hence government) was more dangerous than an American invasion. John Allan was elated by the provocative call in the remonstrance for dissolution of the House of Assembly and an election.[89]

Several Yorkshire immigrants were among the 246 signatories to the Cumberland remonstrance. Some of the signatories probably felt like Dixon when he signed, "obliged to become all things for Quietness Sake." Another factor behind the protest was the tradition of dissent in the district and the inclination of the people to oppose central government.[90] The protest was a compromise: patriots resented the declaration of loyalty while loyalists disliked the implied support of rebellion. John Allan would not have signed a second remonstrance so mild nor Charles Dixon one so strong.

The militia crisis coincided with American success on the battlefield. The situation was so grave that Legge declared martial law on 5 December, the same day he learned of the surrender of Montreal to the Americans.[91] These events encouraged patriots and concerned loyalists. Both groups were hopeful as Josiah Throop folded the remonstrance and commenced the long trek to Government House in Halifax. Remonstrances were also sent from Truro and Onslow, as were petitions from Hopewell and Yarmouth.[92] The former cannot be classified strictly as documents of rebellion as they were signed by known loyalists and because opposition to the Legge administration was not in itself a sign of disloyalty. After all, Legge's loyal opponents were at the same time preparing petitions and remonstrances to send to England complaining of the governor's conduct. The Hopewell and Yarmouth petitions were even further removed from qualifying as documents of rebellion. Both vividly capture the vulnerability of Nova Scotia at the outbreak of war and eloquently plea for government protection. Both reveal that petitioners did not identify with the continental cause, and both contain explicit expressions of loyalty. The community's exposure to privateering raids caused the Yarmouth petitioners to ask if they might be excused from militia duty, but their desire "to be Neuter" should not be construed "that we are in any measure disaffected to our King or his Government"; their only motivation was "self preservation."[93] Unlike in Cumberland, the Yarmouth militia had actually mustered (with disastrous results) and one Halifax official, the newly-arrived Marriot Arbuthnot, perceived "the absurdity" of Legge ordering people to muster whom he did not trust enough to supply with arms.[94] One community complied with the militia legislation. Liverpool, otherwise a typical New England planter community, went to some length to certify its loyalty during the autumn session of the House. Unlike Cumberland's tax assessors who refused to act, those of Liverpool finished their assessment for the militia.[95] Yet opposition to the Militia Acts was nearly unanimous and in its wake came rebellion in Cumberland. How much the situation had changed between April and November 1775!

At the outbreak of war in America few Nova Scotians saw reason to revolt and most were disinclined to join their rebellious neighbours. This initial stance was taken without encouragement from the British military. The planter majority observed political upheaval in their former homeland and followed the public debates in America and Great Britain with an objectivity unavailable to the protagonists. They understood the general spirit of discontent, the institutional disarray, and such basic concerns as the consequences of a deeply religious people challenging a divinely-appointed king. The established order was threatened by forces no one claimed to understand. Certain Nova Scotian realities were also undergoing structural alteration. The Congregational Church, for example, was in decline and facing an uncertain future.[96] This toppling of old orders ushered in a period of confusion which had an equal chance of being followed by religious reformation as by the apocalypse. The crisis of civil war could result in windfall profits or the agony of invasion. The province had been stable since April, but the Militia Acts adopted in October changed the picture dramatically. Now to the threat of American invasion could be added the danger of internal rebellion, that is, of "insurrection apprehended in the heart of the province."[97] The uproar at Cumberland was spreading across the province. Ironically, the cause of discontent resulted from action taken at the very centre of government in far-off Halifax.

The tiny capital of 5,000 people in 1775 spread itself with military precision on the east-facing slope of Halifax Harbour, its straight east-west streets intersecting equally straight north-south streets regularly at right angles to form blocks of exactly the same size in happy defiance of topography from the shoreline to Citadel Hill. In the centre of this tilted grid a double block served as the Grand Parade where a meagre garrison drilled daily, overlooked on the south side by St Paul's Church. In other blocks neat rows of shops and houses were laid out. Large and small, nearly all were wood-framed, even the Governor's residence. Beyond the grid, in the town's north suburb, was the Royal Dockyard with its careening jetty for heaving down ships and stone walls protecting it to landward. Because of its importance, Arbuthnot was erecting a scaffold "round the Walls for Men to stand upon to fire over."[98] Any works to defend the town would have to wait until spring.

Another Halifax thrived at the water's edge. An assortment of dozens of establishments for drinking and entertainment crowded chaotically between the piers, catwalks, and storage sheds north and south of Governor's Wharf in sharpest contrast to the deliberate arrangement inside the grid. This was a temporary-looking but memorable part of Halifax. To the grid pattern belonged the respectability of orderliness, but it was the untidy waterfront that gained Halifax international notoriety as "the gin-shop of America."[99] Life thrived there, especially in times of crisis. In the previous crisis of 1758 an officer wrote satirically of the town, probably from a vantage point on the waterfront:

Oh Halifax! the worst of God's creation.
Possest of the worst scoundrels of Each nation;
Whores, rogues and thieves, the dregs and skum of vice
bred up to villany, theft, Rags and Lice.[100]

In late 1775 another crisis was bringing Halifax to life. While the population was growing, business was recovering, the night-life was expanding, and politics was becoming more heated. Two blocks south of St Paul's the Assembly wrapped up its stormy fall session and members assembled in the Council Chamber for the closing formality.[101] Thanking them for their "zeal" and promising to "exert my utmost" for the protection of the province, the governor ended his address: "As the Severity of the Season is approaching, and your private Affairs require a Recess, I shall detain you no longer."[102]

The session prorogued, assembly members and councillors emerged into the failing light of the short november day.[103] The politicians enjoyed the feeling of release that comes at the end of a legislative session, before dispersing in the direction of the Pontac Inn or in search of a waterfront tavern, braced against the harbour chill. For one politician, turning his back on the seat of government that afternoon was symbolic; Samuel Rogers was walking through "the horrid gloom of Halifax's shade" for the last time as the member for Sackville on the Isthmus of Chignecto.[104] Frustrated in the Assembly, he was "convinced of the Improbability of doing anything there towards a Consideration with the United States."[105] He was disappointed but undaunted. After months of trying in vain to stir up the people, the Militia Acts had aligned them solidly against the government. More determined now than ever, he was going home to help foment an indigenous revolution.

1 Revolution Indigenous
January to May 1776

As I had long been weary of this Tyrannical Government, I came to a full resolution to leave it in order to form a Revolution.

Samuel Rogers, MHA for Sackville[1]

Good horses, neat sleighs, and a frozen Tantramar comprised the formula for winter fun in eighteenth-century Cumberland, where the cold season was a pleasant time of year. During all other seasons the marsh mud restricted traffic to a narrow cart track and reduced travel to drudgery. But winter was magical. It was a sublime, mosquito- less interlude when new avenues of travel opened in all directions. Far from huddling in cramped houses in sub-zero weather, Cumberlanders were enticed outside by a Tantramar marvellously transformed. "We can run over undyked marshes and rivers to any place we want," wrote a settler about the thrill of his first winter on the snowy speedway. "If we ride to a neighbour's House at Fort Lawrence or Cumberland, you will meet perhaps four, five or more Slays driving away with all ... fury!" One could gallop anywhere, and smoothly! "Our Horses are very useful in winter [and] the Slays are very neat ... They are a very comfortable carriage in the Winter season, when we go to Church, or any other place, Especially [for] Women."[2]

The ease and comfort of winter transport improved communication and increased social and political activity. Ice in Cumberland Basin cut off the outside world, but on the isthmus meetings of all kinds flourished. When the snows descended in December 1775, the topic of debate was the militia bill. This legislation agitated all factions of the community, energized the group favouring rebellion, and put loyal residents on the defensive. At last patriots had an issue, courtesy of Governor Legge, and at an auspicious season of the year. It stimulated the debate that caused Cumberlanders to remonstrate against the government. If the coalition against the militia bill that embraced planters, Acadians, and Yorkshire immigrants could be converted to disaffection against Halifax, serious attention would be given to forming a republican government. The patriot movement would, members imagined, spread beyond the borders of Cumberland, sweep through the sympathetic regions of Sunbury, Cobequid, and Pictou, attract the Maliseet and Micmac nations as well as the Acadians, and finally encompass the whole province. Political dissent would become open rebellion, then revolution. The process could be accelerated by another topic of debate: a New England invasion. Since Cumberland held the greatest potential for indigenous rebellion, the region played a critical part in deciding Nova Scotia's role in the continental crisis. In 1776 the future of Nova Scotia was determined on the snowy plains of the isthmus at the head of the Bay of Fundy.

"BUSINESS WAS ENTIRELY STAGNATED"

January 1776. When the Nova Scotia Assembly prorogued in late November 1775, Samuel Rogers walked home to Sackville. He arrived on 2 January after a dangerous journey, weary, cold, and with feet severely frost-bitten. His injury prevented him from attending the many meetings of the Committee-of-Safety held during January.[3] Little else was accomplished on the isthmus: "business was entirely stagnated!"[4] The issue was the militia bill and never had "the Temper and Spirit of the people" run so high.[5] After Josiah Throop returned to Cumberland (also in early January) with no response from Legge to their remonstrance, the debate intensified. "Rebellious Meetings" followed in which the patriots "are joined by the Acadians and the Majority of the Country people in general thereabout, for what they call the preservation of Liberty."[6] Boisterous events, they "had the appearance of approaching Riot and Disorder." The patriots "rather terrified" the people who had not signed the remonstrance and these "conspicuous friends of Government were apprehensive of Insults to themselves or Damage to their Property."[7] One such conspicuous friend was John Eagleson, local SPG missionary, who noted in January that "we had nothing but Committees upon Committees every day and night ... Nothing but an open Rebellion," he believed, "will satisfy them."[8]

The committee met at Amherst, Sackville, Fort Lawrence, Cumberland, and along the Baie Verte Road, travelling from house to house by sleigh and taking advantage of a month when chores were less burdensome than usual. Similar meetings were held in the Cobequid district with both committees "considering how to proceed in joining with the continent." The two committees "began to consult for immediate safety."9 January had always been a month of political action and religious revival.10 January 1776 was a natural time for patriots to be active. These "Incendiary Villains," as loyalists termed them, spread false rumours "tending to the disadvantage of our King's Troops."11 One rumour – that Bunker Hill had been recaptured by the Americans – resulted in patriots achieving a publicity coup on the smooth snows of the Tantramar. "A Triumphal Sleigh drawn by Six Horses with postilions and Flagg of Liberty went through different parts of the County" trumpeting the false Bunker Hill rumour. With banners streaming and enveloped in the freezing mists rising from six galloping horses, this unlikely apparition appeared and disappeared on the flat horizon, racing from hamlet to hamlet, postilion outriders struggling to rein-in the powerful beasts on entering Westcock, Cumberland, and Amherst. Under a bright but low-angled sun, the ice-spangled caravan would draw up before the gathered spectators to serve as a platform from which "an Oration [was] spoke in praise of Liberty."12 This event underscored local interest in the larger crisis and was a high point of the Nova Scotia rebellion. For northern patriots continental unrest was proceeding like a triumphal sleigh. Allan posed a timely question with inspired symbolism: would Nova Scotia, like a postilion, ride the winds of political change on the beast of revolution?

Another of January's rumours was that Quebec had fallen to the Americans. This rumour was cheered by patriots in Cumberland and viewed seriously in Halifax where an army officer exclaimed: "All America is now in the hands of the Rebels, Except this pitiful province." Council conceded that defeat was "probable."13 The true situation – Colonel MacLean's New Year's Eve victory over the Americans at Quebec City – could not be confirmed for another month. Based on the false rumour, it seemed plausible to patriots and loyalists alike that the Americans would soon invade Nova Scotia. "The Rebels will most surely attempt us in the spring," prophesied Legge, and the attempt he determined would be made near Cumberland, a prospect which "has thrown the people of that County into great confusion."14 Several patriot meetings were devoted to how best to help the invaders. The patriots determined that the invasion would come not from New England, but from Quebec via the Gulf of St Lawrence to the Northumberland Strait. The Americans, using ships trapped in the ice at Quebec, would sail for Nova Scotia by the first of May and land on the north shore between Baie Verte and Pictou. Halifax officials developed strategies to stop such an invasion: "a considerable Naval Force" in Northumberland Strait "would effectively prevent it."15 The patriots wondered how to effectively assist it. Two by the names of Earle and Dawson began an inventory of cattle, hay, and other goods purchased for use by the King's army.

Their plan was to confiscate everything, kill the cattle, and salt the meat for the Americans. The committee purchased empty casks for storage. News of this plan soon reached the Governor's desk in Halifax.[16]

"THIS IGNORANT TYRANT, OUR GOVERNOR"

Winter in Halifax was never as exhilarating as winter in Cumberland. In 1776 it had a gloomy aspect. January was the dark hour for Haligonians weighed down by uncertainty over Quebec, afraid their own province would be invaded, troubled by rebellion in Cumberland, and saddled with a governor many believed was the wrong one for the times. The future was risky: "If you can Insure your Property in this Town," a merchant advised his friend, "it ought to be done."[17] Fearing catastrophe, the residents welcomed distractions. An "excellent Band of Music" belonging to the 27th Regiment (part of the recent British reinforcement) and conducted by the popular Mr Morgan, performed a public concert "to add to the Diversion of the Town." That winter Morgan taught music and dance three times weekly at Pontac House.[18]

Woman and men danced and sang while at Government House Francis Legge, with no time for diversion, struggled to hang on to the reins of power. He learned that certain members of Council had sent "a memorial of complaint" about him to London; factions in the business elite were conspiring against him; and everywhere he perceived "secret and dark attempts" to undermine his authority.[19] Now the outsettlers had turned against him. Their remonstrances opposing his militia bill had landed on his desk, first from Cumberland, then from Truro and Onslow. Militia members had defied his mobilization orders at Cumberland, Cobequid, Kings County, and Annapolis Royal.[20]

Legge was "going on in the same obstinate way" in January although complaints about his "Tyrannical Proceedings" had reached a crescendo that would soon be heard in London. "Numberless letters are going home against him from all quarters," noted council member John Butler. Winkworth Tonge of Windsor was off to England "loaded with Complaints," and Joseph Goreham of the Royal Fencibles "has wrote strongly against the Governor."[21] The new dockyard commissioner, Marriot Arbuthnot, also soon understood local politics. His naval friend explained that Legge had "quarrelled with everybody in this Province and rendered himself so very obnoxious to the People by indiscriminately calling them all Rebels."[22] Arbuthnot, whose broad pennant flew from HMS *Savage* in the harbour in January, was already referring to Legge's "bad policy," a comment the king would soon be quoting.[23]

In John Butler's opinion, a man "so full of Resentment" as Francis Legge "cannot Remain ... without Ruin to the Province!"[24] New England refugees were Legge's latest target. Many wanted a new life in Nova Scotia, but they were "personally abused" by the Governor, it was alleged, and "prevented from carrying on any Trade or making any Settlement in this Province."[25] If true, Legge was not fulfilling the king's intent. "This ignorant Tyrant, our Governor," was the cry in Halifax, "if he is not moved, we shall all be in Flames!"[26] Two petitions addressed the king in January: one by several members of Council and the other by "the Principal Gentlemen and Inhabitants." Twenty-three Haligonians signed these petitions. "At a time like this," they began, "it is with the utmost reluctance and regret that we prevail upon ourselves to disturb the Royal Ear with Complaints." What followed was a royal earful of invective against Legge. "Unless this Gentlemen be speedily removed," they concluded, "this valuable Province may be lost."[27] That these complaints were against the governor and not the government and were addressed to London and not Philadelphia was a reflection of the maturity of provincial politics that entertained dissent without revolt even in rebellious times.

Not even an "Ignorant Tyrant" could ignore the "universal uproar" over the militia bill. By January Legge was questioning the practicality of transferring the militia to Halifax in the winter. Even if the move could be made, it would weaken the rest of the province and cause "great expense" without being of "any real benefit." Given the "temper and disposition of the people," he mused, it would add little to Halifax's security. The measure was now superfluous. "The arrival of the 27th Regiment with detachments of the other Regiments has given such an addition of strength as not to require the Militia from the out-settlements,"[28] Legge determined. As the protest mounted Legge could afford to compromise with Cumberland's winter-time politicians.

There was a boldness about the Cumberland rebellion in January. Plainly, for all to see, the patriots "came into their measures determining to oppose Government whose Authority they made a slight of, hinting that it would soon be chang'd for one more eligible."[29] They operated openly and intimidated the populace. "There are many timorous and weak persons among us," explained John Eagleson, "who aw'd by fear, are drove to do what they would avoid, if they durst."[30] Magistrate Samuel Wethered, an active patriot, declared there would be no more court sessions and no couriers would cross the isthmus to and from Halifax. The committee inspected all letters posted to Halifax to prevent intelligence of its proceedings from reaching the capital.[31]

Censorship failed and news of the Cumberland disturbance drew the usual reaction from Halifax. From the safety of the capital and comfort of their offices, government officials called on loyalists to "shew themselves firm on this occasion and ... not suffer themselves to

be terrified by the insolence and the threats of these people."[32] Had
they resided in well-armed Cumberland where the rule of law had
lapsed into anarchy, they too might have remained quiet. Misunder-
standing was endemic to the capital. When Michael Francklin, the lieutenant governor, pointed out that Cumberlanders were "generally well
affected to government … and that this ferment has been occasioned
by a few Active, Disaffected men, perhaps half a dozen," Legge replied
with sarcasm. If it were only "six or seven bad minded Persons … I
shou'd think the Securing of them wou'd be easily effected by the well
dispos'd of the County themselves" and there would be no need to appoint a special commission (as recommended by Francklin), "much
less [send] a Force into that part of the Province."[33] In his haste to attack Francklin, Legge failed to realize that loyalists were helpless in the
furore over his militia bill. Neither armchair advice nor sarcasm was
useful to Cumberlanders in January; what they craved was an enlight-
ened response to their remonstrance which had been their only point
of consensus during the winter's agitation.

Halifax's answer to the remonstrance, given by the Executive Council on 11 January, reached Cumberland quickly despite the weather
and censorship. The compromise reply was a rare display of political
acumen by Francis Legge. The militia and tax acts were suspended. Militia officers were ordered to cease mobilization. Legge assured the
people "they shall not be removed from their habitations" and promised to "exert myself to give them every aid and protection in my
power." Tax collection would be "deferred for the present."[34] Martial
law remained in force (not uncommon in wartime) and the Assembly
was not dissolved as demanded. By standing firm on these last points
Legge faced squarely the patriot challenge to the structure of government. By yielding on the two chief objections – removal of men from
their farms and imposition of an onerous tax – he admitted merely to
errors of detail. The answer satisfied the majority in Cumberland and
elsewhere, but was the worst possible response for the patriots. For Allan only two possible responses were acceptable: all or nothing. Had
Legge granted all demands, Allan's political position would have been
enhanced. Outright rejection, on the other hand, would have given
him the best chance of transforming political dissent into open revolt.
The governor's compromise diffused the political issue. The Committee-of-Safety reeled with the shock.

Halifax officials calculated correctly that while the protests had carried many signatures, the number of Nova Scotians actually favouring rebellion comprised a short list indeed. At first John Allan adopted a brave
front. Threats were made, more meetings held, and a "General Congress" scheduled for month's end. There was talk of a second remon-

strance, but it was empty rhetoric; the patriots lacked the necessary support and enthusiasm as political dissent was waning. At a meeting on 27 January at Eliphalet Read's farm the committee wrestled with the new political reality and tried to deal with loyalists emboldened by Legge's response. On motions by Allan two loyalists, Charles Dixon and Mrs Cossins, were voted enemies of the "Common Cause," he for retracting his signature from the remonstrance and she for leaking secrets.[35] But the extra meetings and the belligerence of the committee could not widen the patriot base. People were no longer prepared to climb aboard Allan's "Triumphal Sleigh." The political option was dead.

The climax of the January meetings was the "General Congress" held on 29 January.[36] It was to have been the coming out, so to speak, of the Cumberland rebellion. Instead, it was one of the last open meetings ever held by the committee, now on the verge of going under-ground. The success of Legge's response and the failure of Allan's initiative reduced the agenda to one item: an American invasion. The more militant patriots, led by Jonathan Eddy, were back in the forefront of proceedings and their argument was simple: it was fruitless to negotiate with government. It would be better to invite an invasion before Halifax could send troops to Cumberland. Most were aware of the government's plan to reopen Fort Cumberland. Military personnel from Halifax had recently surveyed the fort for repairs and James Law of Cumberland, brother-in-law of Samuel Wethered, was employed to prepare estimates for renovating the barracks.[37]

Even moderate patriots realized the futility of the political option. Without American help, the future was bleak and dangerous; it was believed that loyalists were plotting against them. Allan acquiesced to Eddy's plan and the "General Congress" appointed a special committee to draft a petition to Philadelphia "on the subject of becoming worthy [of] their Notice and Consideration." It pleaded for "Redress and reinforcement." Since time was of the essence "as the Enemy were daily expected," it was felt that George Washington would respond quicker than Congress, so the petition was addressed to him.[38] Shortly after this final meeting, John Allan fell ill with smallpox and Samuel Rogers was still laid up with frostbite. Thus, at the end of January the patriot leadership was ailing, but it was Governor Legge who undermined the group's base.

"THEY MIGHT HAVE NIP'T THESE DISTURBANCES IN THE BUDD"

While the patriots were deciding to write to George Washington, Nova Scotia Native representatives were meeting him face to face. Three men from the Maliseet and Passamaquoddy nations, with Native people from Montreal, "honoured me with a Talk today" Washington later reported to Congress (30 January). "God is on the side of our [American] brothers," the visitors proclaimed. "Next Spring many of our Nation will come and help the New England people," they added vaguely, then more emphatically, "We are in much want of powder to hunt with; the old English will not let us have any, unless we will fight against our brothers and countrymen." They did not mention that Governor Legge had already given them "Ammunition, Supplies and Clothing" for the winter at a conference in Halifax in exchange for the same assurances of friendship now professed to Washington. But their gratitude was genuine on receiving from the Americans "Ammunition and Provisions" for the winter.[39] To be supplied doubly after years of neglect must have gratified the Native peoples, but they were not so naive as to believe that the largess stemmed from an underlying concern for their welfare. Rather, it was the seriousness of the war that compelled both sides to court the Natives. This need for "Cultivating the Savages" was emphasized by loyalists like John Cort, while patriots like John Allan identified Native people as "a most dangerous set of neighbours and liable to do great damage if there is not some step taken with them."[40] Both sides were planning more overtures for the spring. Washington intended to write to the eastern Native nations "in the strongest terms" to set them against the Nova Scotians, and Legge followed up his conference by having agents contact the Natives in their winter settlements.

February 1776. Cumberland's petition to Washington was dated Thursday, 8 February, and was supplemented by a letter of the same date.[41] Their pleas were similarly abject. "We have not had it in our power to do anything in conjunction with the other Colonies," they wrote. Anxiously they waited for America to "cast an eye of pity towards this forlorn part." They were helpless: "We have been harassed much ... Threatened are we." Conditions were so bad that "we agreed in our Committees that nothing should be done publicly." They could not seize power; rather, they were forced underground. Not only must they operate in secret, Washington was asked to keep their correspondence secret so fearful were they of loyalist reprisals. The reasons for their fear were apparent in this second week of February: Legge's response had dramatized the weakness of their political position; the American defeat at Quebec was now confirmed; and the reopening of Fort Cumberland appeared imminent.[42] So insidious appeared government and so pervasive its agents that even Washington's headquarters might be vulnerable to a discovery of their illegal correspondence. The future of Nova Scotian republicanism was at stake. "It all depends on your bounty ... please relieve us"![43]

The document was an open invitation to invade Nova Scotia and, for its thirteen signatories, an act of treason. They intended to carry it to New England as a delegation, but by the time it was complete the situation appeared more critical and they feared for the safety of their families should they leave. Instead, Jonathan Eddy volunteered to "immediately set off by land" with the letters. "We found the means to send off Mr. Eddy," a patriot explained, "he will, no doubt, fully prove that he is capable for the undertaking." An Acadian, Isaiah Boudreau, joined Eddy, as did Samuel Rogers, at last recovered from the frost bite.[44] Eddy vowed "they would soon return and with force Sufficient to destroy what Persons or property they may chuse in these parts!"[45] The three set off on foot on 9 February, disappearing into the snowy forests west of Sackville in the general direction of Boston. "With longing Eyes and ardent wishes," John Allan watched them go and would "wait the Expected Relief."[46] Of the three sectors of Nova Scotian society whose loyalty was questioned by Halifax officials, the Native peoples had already visited Washington, and spokespeople for the Acadians and the New England planters were on their way to meet him. Disloyalty appeared widespread.

On the day the patriot trio left for New England, a recruiting officer arrived from Halifax. Thomas Procter of the Nova Scotia Volunteers (Legge's regiment) was under orders to recruit his company at Cobequid, Cumberland, and St John's Island.[47] Given the folly of the Militia Acts it was no surprise that people were wary of enlisting in anything, or that Procter failed to recruit a single soldier at Cobequid or Cumberland. Bad weather prevented him from visiting the island. Such failure mattered little to officers of the Nova Scotia Volunteers as their full salaries were paid even though the regiment had no more than fifty soldiers. With time on his hands and interests in Cumberland, Procter remained there for a month and scrutinized local rebellion.[48]

With Eddy gone and the committee underground, the community appeared quiet, but Procter "found the people very much dissatisfied and turbulent" after the commotions of December and January. The leaders "of these Commotions" were named and the "encouragers of Rebellion" pointed out; John Allan was "particularly accused." Procter's first view of the local situation was a pessimistic one. People believed that Eddy would soon return with American troops, but "by what I can learn, there is not above ten persons in the County but would joyn 'em on their first appearance" Procter observed. Gradually, after hearing how they had suffered, he realized they were more frightened than rebellious. At first mistaking inaction for disloyalty, he soon discovered that the rule of law had lapsed. Death threats and "accusations against individuals" had paralysed the system. Justice could not be obtained. "Many of 'em" asked

Procter to set up an enquiry. "I have no power to take such a step," he told them "it is the Duty of the Magistrates." To this the people replied that the magistrates had refused to perform their duties, nor would they give "redress and fair tryall." Procter's strongest criticism was levelled at these officials: "I firmly Believe had some of the people in power here exerted a little Spirit they might have Nip't these disturbances in the Budd." A little initiative might "have prevented what now seems to threaten Rebellion and the Effusion of Blood."[49]

Paralysis in civil matters created a power vacuum. The first party to strengthen itself politically could grab civil power in Cumberland and the first party to attract outside military support could dictate the future of the region, perhaps the province. The longer Procter stayed the more he was convinced of the need for troops. Charles Dixon and others pleaded for troops. John Eagleson believed a garrison was needed "to Secure our Lives and property." In Procter's view a detachment of troops would reassure the people and terminate the rebellion. "I believe several who are now deterr'd by fear from acknowledging themselves on Government's side would then throw off the disguise."[50] His concerns were sent by courier to Halifax and in mid-February Council pondered the problem of Cumberland, seeking "the best method ... for restraining the Licentious and Rebellious disposition which by late Information appears to run so high in those parts of the Country." They decided, with "Unanimous opinion," to send 300 troops to the fort "as soon as the Season will possibly permit" and passed the request onto Eyre Massey. That officer interpreted his mandate narrowly and thought "he could not comply ... as it would be greatly lessening the defence of the Naval Yard." Pressure would mount on Massey, who was stubborn as well as narrow minded, to change his thinking as the winter dragged on, week after stormy week.[51]

A peculiar stalemate settled over Cumberland in late February. Both sides felt powerless to act. Loyalists feared for their lives and property; patriots were "liable ... to be cut in pieces." That each side was helpless yet capable of destroying the other was a contradiction. Patriots could not assist the Americans because, as they put it, "the Iron Rod of Despotism [was] keeping them from having a Share in the Glorious Revolution."[52] At the same time, loyalists criticised the government for not protecting them. Empty threats and rumours enabled contradictory positions to be held simultaneously. The two positions were used interchangeably: the appearance of strength was adopted when threatening the other side, or of weakness when appealing for external help. Perception was reality in Cumberland and the stalemate was rooted in perception. Procter remained until March and was only one of several Haligonians who travelled there early in 1776 on official business.[53]

Each witnessed the vivid contrast of heated political debate against the stark Tantramar plain that in the winter extended across ice-bound Cumberland Basin.

Ice was common in Cumberland Basin, not in Halifax Harbour, but this was a hard winter. From drafty wood-framed Government House, Francis Legge confirmed that "we have had a very severe season; this harbour was shut up for a day or two."[54] On 10 February it "was totally froze up," with ice floes four feet thick. On a warship frozen in the harbour, "the meat which was served to the ship's company was always sawed in pieces with a cross-cut saw as no other instrument could penetrate it."[55] At least the capital was safe from invasion. The severe season, however, was no guard against internal rebellion. Couriers maintained communication even in winter and the news they conveyed from the outsettlements in February prevented any relaxation in Halifax. From Cumberland came first-hand accounts of the rebellious meetings and disaffection. "It becomes a Serious consideration," Arbuthnot observed, "how this Province is to be preserved."[56] The problem of the governor was also evident to the new dockyard commissioner who had already joined the anti-Legge camp. He reported the fiasco over the Militia Acts and Legge's failure to recruit his regiment to England, along with his opinion that Legge had deliberately misled Sir William Howe, the commander-in-chief. Legge suffered from "overheated zeal," charged Arbuthnot.[57] Via Lord Sandwich, his patron in London, these opinions soon gained the king's attention.[58]

King George was fed up with his representative in Nova Scotia. Legge had alienated the military, "the old servants of Government," the church, "the principal inhabitants," the business elite, the outsettlers, and the dockyard commissioner. Orders were issued on 24 February recalling Legge to London to answer to the charges against him. Government administration was devolved to Marriot Arbuthnot who assumed the lieutenant-governorship.[59] This meant that Michael Francklin lost his post, a move that checked those opposed to Legge. A clever balance was evident in the king's decision and the choice of Arbuthnot was a calculated one. His naval background, the king believed, should go over well in Halifax and his conciliatory style would be useful in uniting the factions. He could be counted on not only to overlook the sharp business practices of the merchant elite, but to join in heartily and do them one better. Whether he could preserve the province in the present crisis was uncertain. But nothing in the Halifax government changed for nearly two months, the time it took for the king's orders to reach Halifax.

March 1776. "Thick weather" was reported in Windsor on 9 March. There was snow and sleet all day. It looked as if Michael Francklin had picked the wrong day to call a meeting. Who would come out in such weather? Notices went out only three days before, but to his surprise the meeting house was filled. Everyone there "had come several miles in as bad a Day as we have had for some time past." It was only an exploratory meeting, an opportunity for Francklin to present his plan for recruiting a volunteer militia.[60] His plan was an adaptation of one found in a New England newspaper. It did not have Halifax's blessing, yet he hoped it would replace the suspended act. "The late Militia Act might be a proper model to proceed from ... but unfortunately that act had exceedingly alarmed the whole Country." The alarm, however, "does not appear to be founded on a General reluctance to Defend the Colony but from the apprehension of being called forth and detained from their habitations to the ruin of their families."[61] He believed that the people of Windsor, Newport, Falmouth, Horton, and Cornwallis were "well disposed for taking up arms for the Defence of the Province; all they request is to be under the Command of such officers as are agreeable to themselves, and that they be not called from their own families but in case of actual invasion."[62] What was needed was an enrolment "adapted to the Sentiments and wishes of the People."[63] With more acceptable terms the volunteer militia could also thrive in Cobequid and Cumberland. Francklin came across an enrolment form used in Virginia in the newspaper. This was what he had in mind. He clipped it out and sent it to Halifax for Legge's approval, along with his proposal and request for blank officers' commissions. Francklin was so excited about his discovery that he called the meeting before hearing back from Legge.

"There appeared great zeal and forwardness" among the people in the Windsor meeting house. "I was desirous to know who would turn out Volunteers upon Conditions similar to those I Communicated to them." The response exceeded Francklin's hopes. Seventy-seven men declared a willingness to volunteer, officers were recommended, and "the few who hesitated declared they had no objection to signing." Francklin was certain "of being able to Compleat here two Companys of Fifty men Each."[64] These results were immediately reported to Halifax and Francklin renewed his earlier request. Having been rebuffed by Legge in February for suggesting a commission of enquiry or small military force be sent to Cumberland, he now asked to go there and to Cobequid himself. He would take his enrolment form and use his influence to recruit the militia in those districts.

The governor and Council approved Francklin's enrolment form the day before the Windsor meeting and a week later, after hearing the results, voted to "entirely approve of your plan for raising volunteers." This time Francklin's request to go to Cumberland was accepted. Massey, who earlier could not see his way clear to spare troops, now agreed to provide a captain's party of fifty soldiers to go with him.[65] "I am happy," sighed Francklin at Martock House, his home outside Windsor, when he heard the news. Only the ice in Minas Basin could delay him now, but not for long: "the Season advances fast ... I expect in about a fortnight the Navigation will be free for Cobequid and Cumberland." He busied himself in the meantime in his own region and shortly recruited a militia of 384 men.[66]

The work of Michael Francklin in March proved that loyalty existed in Nova Scotia even among the New England planters. Indeed, a transformation in the stance of this majority was beginning in the townships on the south shore of the Minas Basin. By stepping forward in the Windsor meeting house that stormy Saturday to answer the militia call, and by volunteering in large numbers immediately afterwards, they were shunning the revolution, the great cause of their continental cousins. In the past year they had seen the face of chaos and drew back. Revolution held a compelling fascination and might even be cheered from afar, but not indulged. Americans were seeking independence from Britain; Nova Scotians were seeking freedom from radicalism. That they chose freely is not in doubt. The Windsor crowd was not coerced to loyalty by the British army or navy, which were insignificantly represented in the province, nor by the royal governor who had lost control of the government. The new confidence of loyalists in Windsor and the helplessness felt by patriots in Cumberland contrasted with their counterparts in Boston where patriots swarmed the gates of the town and loyalists were panic-stricken. A large British garrison was in retreat.

"HALIFAX ... A CURSED, COLD, WINTRY PLACE EVEN YET"

March 1776. The siege of Boston entered its terminal phase when the Continental Army occupied Dorchester Heights unexpectedly on Sunday night, 3 March. It was plain the next morning that "Boston was no longer tenable" for the British.[67] There was no choice but to retreat to the safety of Nova Scotia. Within the week, General Howe announced publicly his intention to evacuate the town and began indirect negotiations with General Washington. A date of departure was fixed and in the interest of saving the town from destruction, it was agreed the British would retreat unmolested. Families began to board the ships as early as 10 March.[68] For a week thereafter Long Wharf was "a scene of confusion ... women, children, troops and merchandise, indiscriminately thrown into boats, to be conveyed to the transports."[69] The inability of refugees to take more than bare necessities added greatly to their distress. The Reverend Henry Caner had only a few hours to prepare for the evacuation. Having abandoned nearly everything, even his books, he carried aboard bedding, a few clothes and "a little provision" for himself, his daughter, and his servant.[70] Refugee Edward Winslow managed to snatch the royal coat of arms from the Council chamber and stow it with his few belongings.

The last parade of British troops along Boston's King (now State) Street formed up at three o'clock Sunday morning, 17 March, the day of the evacuation. Mines were exploded on Boston neck to keep the Americans at bay and "an immense cloud of smoke balls" covered the embarkation.[71] There was no panic among the 11,000 soldiers and 1,100 loyalists who represented a thorough cross-section of society: "women, children, soldiers, sailors, governors, councillors, flatterers, statesmen, and pimps."[72] Free of the siege at last, they were anxious to get under way, but the weather would not co-operate. For ten more days they languished in Boston Harbour crowded on nearly 200 ships. Spring arrived before the fleet hoisted sail for Halifax on 27 March. By then the first refugees to embark had already been afloat seventeen days. The voyage could take another week. There was trepidation about their destination. We "sail tomorrow for Halifax," wrote one refugee, "a cursed, cold, wintry place even yet. Nothing to eat, less to drink. Bad times, my dear friend!"[73]

Washington's army camped at Cambridge during the siege of Boston and commandeered buildings of Harvard College for military use (temporarily uprooting to Concord the comfortable academic world of Caleb Gannett, former missionary to Cumberland). It was at Harvard that the Nova Scotia Native representatives met Washington in January and where Jonathan Eddy, Isaiah Boudreau, and Samuel Rogers found him in March.[74] Washington was preoccupied with the consolidation of Boston and had no idea where the British were sailing to. In fact, he had "no doubt" then that they were going to New York and not Halifax.[75] Nevertheless, he took time out to convene "several conferences" with the three Nova Scotians. Congress had asked him in February to investigate the conquest of Nova Scotia, thus he was willing to listen to any information on the subject.[76] It was also possible, he believed, that his idea for using the eastern Native nations could be developed by discussions with these Nova Scotian patriots.

The meetings were not very productive. Washington learned that local patriots were in "a Distressed situation," unable to manage their own rebellion or join the revolution. Without an invasion of 500 to 600 men, they would be compelled to take up arms on the side of the loyalists. Eddy pointed out the "valuable consequences" of an invasion of Nova Scotia: local patriots could then assist the Americans; the Native peoples of the region (of whom, Washington agreed, "there are a good many") would become their allies; and the British would be deprived of an important supply base. All were "good purposes," agreed Washington, but whether they could be met "is impossible to determine in the present uncertain state of things." Should Howe be en route to Halifax as rumoured, "a much more considerable force [than the 500–600 requested] would be of no avail." If not, and if Nova Scotia "possessed the friendly disposition to our cause suggested in the petition and declared by Mr. Eddy," an invasion might work. If Washington was not entirely convinced of the merits of Eddy's plan, his obligation to investigate the conquest of Nova Scotia was fulfilled by his consideration of it and he therefore "judged it prudent to lay it before Congress for their consideration."[77] The Nova Scotian letters were enclosed in one of his own and posted to Philadelphia on 27 March, the day the British sailed away from Boston. Eddy, Boudreau, and Rogers stayed at Harvard until the end of the month. They likely went into Boston the next day (as did their friend Caleb Gannett) to join the victory celebration led by Washington. During the warm spring days that followed the three men met several more times with the general and gained his agreement to sponsor Eddy to go to Congress and plead their case personally.

Spring had arrived in Boston, but was only tentatively approaching northern Nova Scotia. The hard mantle of snow on the Tantramar was just beginning to break up and the Baie Verte Road was only briefly muddy in the noonday sun. Along that road at *Inveraray* farm the Allan household was joyous. A baby boy was born on 13 March, their fifth child, and his twenty-nine year old mother Mary was well. The family also rejoiced over John Allan's recovery from the smallpox which had debilitated him through much of February. With many relatives in Cumberland, including the Pattons, McGowans, and Campbells, the Allans celebrated new life, good health, and the American rebellion. The new baby was christened George Washington Allan.[78]

The political stalemate in Cumberland continued as spring approached. Certain loyalists tested the political climate with discouraging results. At Shepody, Moses Delesdernier, "making a game affair of it," drew up a petition to the governor, "assuring him of our Loyalty and went to every house at Hopewell, Petitcodiac and Memramcook to have the petition signed by the inhabitants." Whether timing doomed his effort or just "his ostentatious way" of doing things, Delesdernier felt able to report only the negative results: "About seventy-five ... Refused it."[79] The deputy-sheriff and his assistants, with orders to "exert themselves to apprehend all such persons ... favouring the designs of Rebellion,"[80] went to William How's home at Fort Lawrence. How, who was county coroner, treasurer of the Congregational society, and a patriot, took out his gun and threatened to kill them, an "outrage" that drove him into hiding.[81] Tensions were sometimes unbearable. Not knowing when troops would arrive or if they would hail from Boston or Halifax was unnerving to all Cumberlanders, particularly for those like How and Allan who had committed themselves so publicly to rebellion. Perhaps it was during his illness and while searching for a strategy to break the stalemate that Allan became convinced of the need to make allies of the Native peoples. He had been too sick to investigate rumours that Legge's agents were among the Native peoples in February trying to turn them against the patriots. Instead, his Acadian friends made enquiries and brought back "such satisfactory answers that I had no reason to expect any difficulty." Restored health permitted Allan to renew his Native diplomacy and "early in the Spring to pay them a visit at Cocagne."[82]

"Satisfactory answers" to Legge and Washington, and now to Allan's Acadian friends, were just what the Native people intended to give until they understood the true nature of the revolution. At first glance, satisfactory answers to all parties seemed to be a confusing, even incoherent policy; certainly, Boston and Halifax were confounded by it. Viewed from the Native perspective, however, it was the reasoned response of a strategically located, yet scattered and vulnerable people. It was a policy dictated by the need for immediate subsistence support. A long-term strategy would be needed eventually, but Native political consensus entailed a series of conferences with a dozen or more chiefs, lesser chiefs, and elders. To that end "a general meeting" of Native communities from Bay Chaleur to Cape Sable – the entire Micmac nation – was convened in March, "for what end we could not learn," worried Allan, who was "again alarmed" at the prospect. Cumberlanders were concerned by this Native activity which they considered a threat. Also in March, Allan heard that a Micmac delegation would come to Cumberland "in order to do something." This news, together with the birth of his son, caused him to cancel his planned spring visit to Cocagne.[83]

Another spring visit to the Native communities was being prepared for in Halifax. Joseph Bennett drew up a list of items – presents, provisions, small schooner, interpreter, pilot – required to itinerate among the Micmacs as a missionary of the Society for the Propagation of the Gospel. This time, however, he would go to the mission-field "in a dubble capacity both as a Clergyman and with a power from Governor Legge." This presented no conflict to Bennett, who advocated such initiatives to bring people "to a just sense of Religion and a due Subordination to Government."[84] The race for the hearts and minds of the Native peoples was on. By the end of March, General Washington was leading the race.

April 1776. "This letter will be delivered you by Jonathan Eddy," wrote Washington on 1 April. Having encouraged the Nova Scotians to appear at Congress, he penned a letter of introduction. "They seem," he continued on that April Fool's Day, "to be solid, judicious men," and he gave Eddy fifty dollars "to defray his expenses."[85] He was in a generous mood after driving the British from Boston, but he was also anxious to leave for New York which he still considered to be the destination of the British fleet. His Cambridge camp was therefore breaking up and the academics – from Harvard president to Caleb Gannett – were so delighted with the prospect of retrieving their campus from the military that they conferred an honorary degree on the General.[86]

Washington and the Nova Scotians probably departed from Harvard on the same day, he for New York and they for Philadelphia.[87] At the same time loyalist Bostonians and the British military were sailing to Nova Scotia in "the most disagreeable" voyage one officer had ever had. "In bad plight we go to Halifax," accorded the refugees.[88] The first ships reached Halifax on 2 April. The town had never seen such a sight: "Upwards of 200 Sail" filled the waterfront. They anchored in clusters north of George's Island or, beginning at the docks, tied up rail to rail in lines stretching out into the harbour. To reach dockside, passengers had to climb from ship to ship across decks, through a grove of masts and tangles of ropes, avoiding those vessels thought to carry smallpox.

"OF ALL THE MISERABLE PLACES I EVER SAW, HALIFAX IS THE WORST"

Boston had rejected them, and Halifax was unprepared for them. "They have little or no provisions" with them, "nor can this place supply them with any" the *Nova Scotia Gazette* reported.[89] The town could not cope with so many people.[90] "There is no describing the Hurry, Confusion and Expense that attended the arrival of the Fleet ... Army and ... Loyalists from Boston," explained the Reverend John Breynton, who aided several refugee ministers, put up five refugees in his own home, and sheltered others in St Paul's Church.[91] The influx more than doubled Halifax's population and caused a housing crisis in which rents increased five-fold.[92] Uprooted by the revolution and having abandoned their possessions in Boston only to be fleeced of their remaining means in over-crowded Halifax, loyalists bewailed their misfortune. "By this cursed rebellion," wrote one refugee, "I am drove to this wretched place"![93] Conditions were worse for the military. No more than a third of the troops could leave the ships at a time to be "Quartered on the Inhabitants" in barns and sheds, and they could stay on shore only a week at a time, being replaced in turn by other troops from the ships "to keep in health as they were very much crowded."[94] As shipboard odours increased, officers were ordered to "air their Men when the

Weather permits on Georges Island or on the Dartmouth side of the Harbour."[95] After the first week some relief was gained by sending three divisions of dragoons (the Light Horse) to Windsor to encamp at Fort Edward for the summer. Although its barracks were "not fit for hoggs," repairs were under way.[96] Construction of barracks began in Halifax, but even if completed quickly they would not be large enough for all the troops. "Our situation at present is very far from comfortable," understated an officer in April, "of all the miserable places I ever saw, Halifax is the Worst!"[97]

"All things are violently dear in Halifax," so dear that price controls were introduced.[98] Food was in such short supply that by the end of April military rations were reduced "to two thirds allowance."[99] The weather was "unaccountably severe" even by Halifax standards; as late as mid-April the ground was covered in snow. The streets were frozen in the morning, slick and slippery on the down-slopes in the afternoon leaving people "over shoes in mud from the rains," and filled all day with the homeless of Boston.[100] At night, where the grid pattern merged with the waterfront, refugees joined soldiers and sailors, and the places of entertainment overflowed. An eyewitness to that first chaotic week of April in Halifax wondered "that the Earth does not sink under the Sinful Inhabitants thereof."[101]

Even with the problems, the retreat to Halifax in the spring of 1776 benefited loyalist Nova Scotia by bringing new immigrants and the temporary presence of a military headquarters to the city. Boston loyalists strengthened the government's hand and influenced the population. Indigenous loyalty was generally untested, not so refugee loyalty which had survived months in the revolutionary crucible that was Boston under siege. Moreover, these loyalists were New Englanders to whom the majority of the population easily related. As well as reversing an eight-year population decline, these new residents, already inured to war, broadened the base of military recruitment, not just for the regular army but for provincial regiments as well, including the Royal Fencible Americans.

This first large-scale influx of loyalists, so early in the war, gradually influenced political attitudes across the province, although the transformation had already begun as witnessed by the militia recruitment in Windsor in March. Other forces that would hasten the process were also active. Another event unfolded in April 1776, without notice and ridiculously modest in comparison with the loyalist influx, that would also influence Nova Scotia's response to the revolution. Thursday 18 April was a day of fasting and religious meetings. The weather was still cold in Windsor. Hail storms the day before were followed by rain in the night and Thursday was "cloudy and threatening." At one of the meetings, in the nearby village of Falmouth, a young farmer named

Henry Alline, after an inner struggle regarding lack of formal education, stood and for the first time "came out and spoke by way of exhortation." It was a painfully tentative beginning to a public ministry. His
short speech was no literary match for the discourses Anglican missionary William Ellis delivered to the British dragoons just settled in at Fort
Edward. He "had some liberty" with his few hearers but he felt horribly
inadequate, suffering "under great trials" and afterwards "The devil was
all night against me." Yet barely a month later it was reported throughout that district "that Henry Alline was turned New-Light preacher."
The religious reformation of Nova Scotia had begun.[102]

The presence of the British headquarters in Halifax focused attention on the strategic importance of Nova Scotia. General Howe and his
staff were able to inspect provincial defences firsthand and, although
they stayed barely two months, more attention was paid to local military needs as a result. Reinforcements from Britain were expected in
May when Howe and Shuldham planned to return to New England,
but in the meantime, they became familiar with local affairs. One military decision was reversed immediately. The meagre captain's party offered by Eyre Massey to escort Michael Francklin to Cumberland was
cancelled in favour of a proper garrisoning of the fort, a key part of
Howe's strategy. A few weeks on the local scene enabled Howe to de-
vise a comprehensive defence plan, and thus Francklin's visit to Cumberland was delayed a second time.

The arrival of Howe and Shuldham further undermined Governor
Legge's authority, but the axe finally fell on 20 April when the *Harriet*
brought the king's orders to recall him to London.[103] The news was received rapturously by his many political opponents, especially Marriot
Arbuthnot whose promotion was on the same ship. Legge's sycophants
reeled with the shock and Government House was in confusion. The
news spread to the outsettlements where minor officials indebted to the
administration feared for their future, and political opportunists such as
John Allan anticipated a crisis, but there was none. While the *Harriet*
waited at dockside for the several weeks it took the governor to pack his
bags, the change-over went smoothly. While Howe and Shuldham remained, the province was protected even as the government changed.
Government pressure on local patriots actually increased and the British
retreat from Boston complicated the task of the Cumberland delegation
which was nearing Philadelphia at the end of April.

When Congress received Washington's letter endorsing Eddy's plan
for invading Nova Scotia, "some time [was] spent therein" and later,
when Eddy and Boudreau reached Philadelphia and presented the
appeal in person, more time was spent by a Congress preoccupied
with General Howe's intentions and busily drafting an independence

document. Because of the crisis facing Americans in the spring of 1776, and possibly because of the apparent lack of local commitment to the project, the appeal was turned down after due consideration. An immediate invasion of Nova Scotia was rejected, although the plight of patriots there evoked the sympathy of Congress members who granted $250 to Eddy and $100 to Boudreau.[104]

"When Capt. Eddy gave me a narrative of what he ask'd for and what was Concluded on by the Honourable Congress, I found it much short of my expectations," complained Samuel Rogers when Eddy and Boudreau rejoined him in Providence. "If put on a good footing," Rogers was convinced "that the Inhabitants of Nova Scotia might be as serviceable in the Glorious Cause of Liberty as any in America."[105] It was clear that American help was unavailable, so the three men set out to return home to Nova Scotia.[106] Eddy's hopes were dashed, but at home the threats of internal unrest and privateering were still real, so real that the Supreme Court circuit was cancelled on the last day of April. A visit that spring to Cumberland would be "attended with great danger to themselves," feared the judges.[107] Halifax was safe, at least for the moment, but the time had come to secure the rest of the province.

May 1776. In early May General Howe revealed the defence plan he had drafted for Nova Scotia. The plan focused on Fort Cumberland and depended on naval support, particularly in the Bay of Fundy which was the expected entry point of an attack. Fort Edward in Windsor would retain a garrison and a small outpost would be opened at the head of Bedford Basin.[108] Fort Cumberland would receive 200 Royal Fencible Americans, and 100 Royal Highland Emigrants would replace the Dragoons at Fort Edward, who were going south with Howe. On 8 May the Fencibles were ordered "to hold themselves in Readiness, on the Shortest Warning, to march to Windsor there to embark for Fort Cumberland." It was a welcome order to soldiers whose most important service to date was catching fish in Halifax Harbour to feed Howe's hungry army.[109]

Also ready to leave Halifax were General Howe and Admiral Shuldham. All month they prepared to sail to New York for the summer campaign. Marines and regular troops to be left behind were chosen and ships with transport vessels in convoy were sent to Windsor to meet the Fencibles and take them to Cumberland, a manoeuvre that was part of a sweep of the Fundy coast to buy supplies for the army going to New York. All the while the commanders waited for the fleet of reinforcements from England. When preparations were complete, it was intended that the two fleets would sail south together.

For Francis Legge the waiting was over. On 12 May, he boarded the *Harriet* for the voyage to London to face the enquiry into his conduct. A collective sigh of relief arose from nearly everyone as the ship "came to sail."[110] Legge was gone, and Howe and Shuldham were preparing to go, as were the Fencibles and Royal Highland Emigrants. One official who was happy to stay behind was Marriot Arbuthnot. In just five months he had been promoted to the top administrative post in the province and had moved from the dockyard compound in the north end to the governor's residence on Hollis Street in the centre of town, a location better suited to his outgoing personality. Arbuthnot was a veteran naval officer, but the role of chief executive was a new challenge for the sixty-five year old.

It was cloudy with "fresh Breezes" when HMS *Tamer* rounded Cape Blomidon to entered Minas Basin on Monday 20 May. "At 2 pm anchor'd in Windsor River … Anchor'd here 12 Sail of the Convoy."[111] Later, the armed schooner *Neptune* joined *Tamer* and the transports. These ships were now ready to rendezvous with the Fencibles. In the meantime at Halifax on Wednesday, General Howe announced that "Lieutenant-Colonel Goreham, Royal Fencible Americans, is appointed to the Command of Fort Cumberland" and that the regiment would march to Windsor on Friday 24 May to meet the ships. Goreham was delighted with the appointment, hoping it would be a stepping stone to the position of army commander in Nova Scotia on Massey's departure. The highlight for the soldiers was the order just before the march "to apply to the Quartermaster for their proportion of Tobacco": 300 pounds to the Fencibles. It was still cloudy on Friday when the march began. The Fencibles were joined by a detachment of Highland Emigrants who were off to replace the dragoons at Fort Edward. With their women and children beside them, these troops marched into Windsor on Sunday.[112]

The provincial troops thronging Windsor at the end of May added to the district's prosperity, which began with the arrival of the British dragoons in April. With labourers and tradespeople repairing the fort or fortifying the countryside, unemployment had disappeared.[113] Farmers could sell all they grew either at the fort or to Howe's agents who were sweeping the Bay of Fundy for supplies. Farmers needed their sons at home but the opportunity for other pursuits attracted many youths. At Falmouth Henry Alline considered the offer of a commission in the militia and only refused because of a stronger calling to the gospel ministry.[114] There was something in the tumultuous times that spawned zealots and this factor also added to the agricultural drain. "It has come to the turn of all sorts of men to be zealous," noticed William Ellis in Windsor. Although his own congregations were growing he was nervous of the trend. "Zeal may be without knowledge," he propounded, "in which case it must be hurtful to the cause of religion and may be dangerous to civil society." Uneducated "Labourers and Mechanics turn

Preachers, and are much encouraged."[115] Henry Alline was not the
only aspiring preacher in Falmouth that spring whose parents were reluctant at first to see him leave the farm. But his followers "would come
from other towns, even whole boat-loads," to hear the untutored but in-
spirational Nova Scotia planter.[116] Ellis would not have considered that
the response to Alline might have represented as loyal an impulse as
the response to Francklin's militia proposal or to the deployment of
provincial troops to outsettlement forts.

By the beginning of the last week in May, the Emigrants were sharing Fort Edward with the dragoons, and the Fencibles were on the
transport ships in the Avon River. Michael Francklin was also on board,
at last on his way to Cumberland to observe rebellion and recruit the
militia as he had offered in January and planned in April. On Tuesday
morning, 28 May, with rain drizzling down, *Tamer*, *Neptune*, and the
twelve transports set sail for Cumberland.[117] With Fort Edward defending the Minas Basin and Fort Cumberland soon to be on guard again
at the head of the Bay of Fundy, the only district where rebellion went
unchecked was the St John River valley.

"WE HAVE UNANIMOUSLY SIGNED A PAPER TO JOIN NEW ENGLAND"

Jonathan Eddy, Isaiah Boudreau, and Samuel Rogers were also en route
to Cumberland at the end of May. At Machias they learned of the reward
offered for their capture "dead or alive," so they "proceeded along the
shore in as private a manner as possible and arrived at the Mouth of the
River St. John." Because of the reward, "we were obliged to proceed with
great precaution."[118] However, Sunbury was friendly territory for patriots and in May rebellion there was at its peak. Religious revival in the
winter in Sunbury was followed by political unrest in the spring that culminated in a series of meetings during the first three weeks of May. As a
result, Eddy found an active Committee-of-safety in control of civil and
military affairs. Inhabitants needed passes from Chairperson Jacob
Barker to travel outside the valley, and they might be called upon at any
time to make "a plain Declaration" of their politics. Some loyalists were
actually held as prisoners.[119] Eddy, whose visit to Boston and Philadelphia had been a failure on a practical level, must have had his spirits
lifted by what he saw in Sunbury.

Under the ministry of Seth Noble, Maugerville had experienced religious revival in January, when several people "happily put on Christ
which is life eternal."[120] Noble also supported the revolution and
"manifested a great zeal to have a hand in it." With evangelical fervour,
he "imprest upon the minds of the people that it was their duty to be

ingaged in the cause."[121] Bad weather prevented news of the end of the militia bill from reaching the valley as quickly as it reached Cumberland. "It seems to be still as to political affairs,"[122] confirmed Noble in February, but when the news did arrive it caused the same sensation as it had on the isthmus.

Political meetings followed the revival meetings and continued to the end of April as those who favoured the American cause became agitated. "Our governor hath thought proper," they fulminated, "to prevent our being supplied with arms and ammunition ... At the same time [he] requires us to assemble in Martial array and by force of arms to Repell all Invaders."[123] Such conflicting measures seemed absurd to the most neutral settler, and there was more: "Martial law is published throughout the Province," they cried, "and Civil authority made subordinate. Exorbitant taxes are required of us to support the war. Under these circumstances," they argued, "it is impracticable for us to Continue as Neuters, and to Subsist without Commerce."[124] In May when the ice flowed out of the river, two privateers appeared at Maugerville with the message that Nova Scotia would be invaded, that "privateers were thick on the Coast, and would stop all manner of Commerce with us unless we joined them." Should the Americans "be put to the expense" of conquering the St John River valley, "they must be paid for their trouble; consequently, our Estates must be forfeited."[125]

"About the same time," it was learned that the Maliseets had received a letter from George Washington which "set them on fire" against Nova Scotians. They "threatened some of the people to kill them if they would not join the Boston men" and displayed a "spirit of insolence by interrupting the trade on the St John River, and taking away a few cattle from the settlers."[126] Not only loyalists were pillaged but Sunbury residents in general. The settlers felt pressed between rebellious Massachusetts set to invade on one side and a Native nation inflamed to violence on the other. Caught between Machias and Maliseet Aukpaque with no help from Halifax, Sunbury "appeared neglected by government." We are "a Defenceless People," they cried and their dilemma gave patriots the issue needed to mount a rebellion: "We had a general meeting and unanimously agreed to submit ourselves to the government of Massachusetts."[127]

A crowd assembled in the Maugerville meeting house in the morning of 14 May and appointed a committee, with Jacob Barker as chairperson, "to prepare a draft paper for the proceedings of the Assembly." By mid-afternoon the committee was ready to report and clerk Israel Perley read out a list of eight resolutions to the assembly. After each was read out, a vote was taken. All the resolutions "passed in the affirmative unanimously." These resolutions form a remarkable revolutionary document.[128] The first three were ritual declarations about justice in the revolution. "We can see no shadow of justice" in British actions; on the other hand, the Americans "are just in their proceedings." Given their analysis, the Sunbury patriots predictably chose the American side, being "ready with our lives and fortunes to share with them." Having fallen in with the "just," concern turned to home rule. Resolutions four and five established an interim government. A committee was appointed that "shall conduct all matters, civil and military, in this County, till further regulations be made." The committee was supreme, obliging the people to "most strictly adhere" to measures adopted "for our conduct." Its first action was to apply to Massachusetts "for relief" on behalf of the county. A fledgling government is by nature insecure, so the final three resolutions concerned security. Measures were adopted to "put ourselves in the best posture of defence," Taxes were levied to support the committee and fund the rebellion. How these compared with the "Exorbitant taxes" proposed by Governor Legge was apparently not calculated. With an eye to internal security, the people were bound to report all instances of political opposition which in a small community amounted to spying on one's neighbours. More important, people would be linked in punitive solidarity that would "bind and obligate ourselves firmly each to the other, on penalty of being esteemed enemies and traitors."[129]

"The whole Assembly subscribed to the foregoing Resolutions," but this was not enough. Everyone on the river had to subscribe, there could be "no dealings or connexions with any person ... that shall refuse."[130] The twelve draughtspeople were voted in as a standing committee to take control of the county and petition the Americans. To lend credence to the resolutions which were to be presented in Boston, they were first circulated for signing up and down the river. In total 125 names were collected which, if not a majority of inhabitants, was an impressive minority. In view of how the signatures were collected, the list was not a true indicator of support either for the resolutions or the rebellion. While coaxing people to sign, Jacob Barker and his men, borrowing a tactic from George Washington, "had Canoes full of Indians ready to put their threats into Execution."[131] As a result, more people signed than would have otherwise been the case; even the loyalist Charles Jadis felt compelled to sign.

More meetings followed the Sunbury assembly and the committee began exercising its authority with the support of Maliseets and Americans. Their support was difficult to manage but there was no denying its usefulness. The Native allies burned the home of Charles Jadis and "he and his family hardly escaped with their lives." Jadis was detained by Barker who intended to send him to Machias.[132] John Anderson's stores were "plundered and carried off ... by the Rebells and Indians" and in May he and his family were turned over to Machias patriots and "forcibly carried to New England where he was detained."[133] Other loyalists were intimidated but the committee also had concerns. The Maliseets "are plundering all people they think are Tories," which the committee wanted, but "when that is done, perhaps the others may share the same fate.[134] While getting used to their power, the committee wrote the petition to join Massachusetts. "Esteem the River St John as a part of your Province," it begged, "We ... Humbly ask your Protection."[135] This document was finished on 21 May, one week after the assembly. Committee members Asa Perley and Asa Kimball were chosen to carry the petition, resolutions, and list of signatures to Boston. During the religious revival, Asa Kimball and his wife were "brought out into marvellous light."[136] Now in May Kimball was reborn in politics as well and about to present himself spotless, as it were, to the republican council at Boston.

Sunbury loyalists lacked a united leadership to counteract the patriot committee. Leading loyalists such as James Simonds, John Anderson, and Charles Jadis were prominent primarily for their business interests and they were fiercely competitive in trade. Typically regarding each other as "sworn enemies," they were slow to unite against the patriots while most inhabitants watched from the sidelines and "affected a neutrality" to avoid trouble.[137] The field of action was left to the patriots who, enthused Seth Noble in May, "are making all possible preparations for war." Near the end of the month the residents assembled "in a Military manner and Body and chose Majors, Captains and Subaltern Officers, and form'd Companys to join the Rebellion."[138] It was hoped that Perley and Kimball would obtain military supplies at Boston.

It was at this stage – patriots wielding power and loyalists intimidated into silence – that Jonathan Eddy and his party paused at Maugerville on their way home to Cumberland. Some of the events of May must have been witnessed by them. "After a few days stay" in the valley, the journey home was resumed. The trio divided for reasons of safety with Isaiah Boudreau travelling overland by the Kennebecasis River while Eddy and Rogers went by boat up the Bay Fundy.[139] Their concern for safety indicated that all was not well at Cumberland. Unlike Maugerville, their own committee was ineffective, their congregational society had lost its visibility, and they had no dissenting minister, patriot or otherwise.

By the end of May, not even the most sanguine patriot believed that Nova Scotia would revolt. The radicals were too weak "to form a Revolution" as Samuel Rogers had hoped at the beginning of the year. The only visible group was at Maugerville; those at Cobequid and Cumberland were underground. On the other hand, loyalty was in the ascendency –

the signs were unmistakable even in some planter outsettlements. Disillusion with the revolution had set in early and was causing a change of attitude. It was not so much that the planters were turning away in revulsion (they remained fascinated and involved for the duration); rather, they were beginning to view the conflict from an indigenous perspective and their children, now grown, found inspiration in their own reality.

The view that Nova Scotia was more than an outpost of New England went beyond the vision of local patriots who saw potential in Nova Scotia but only as "an invaluable Prize" for New England exploitation. Planters, on the other hand, were beginning to envisage the province as a milieu for religious reformation, alternative political development, and social progress. The new trend of looking inward produced a rash of indigenous thought and action. In Kings County this trend served equally to swell Michael Francklin's volunteer militia and to create a following for the charismatic Henry Alline. At the end of May the transformation from New England planter to Nova Scotian had only just begun. The war raged on and it was still uncertain in which direction the province would go or if it would go in any direction at all. Perhaps it would remain stationary, its people merely confused by events. What seemed most unlikely in the summer of 1776 was that Nova Scotia planters would revolt. The small patriot party would need outside help to repeat the siege of Boston in Nova Scotia. To conquer Halifax, local republicans would need the support of the Native nations, but most importantly, they needed an American invasion.

2 Revolution Imported
June to October 1776

Those rabble Rebels have had the audacity to crawl up the Bay of Fundy
and land at Cumberland ... Those fellows have been invited there by three
or four profligate fellows of Cumberland.
Richard Bulkeley, provincial secretary[1]

The southern brow of Cumberland Ridge – a rain-soaked, windswept
knoll cleared of trees since the mid-eighteenth century – is wonderfully
bleak. The fort ruins compound the feeling of desolation. Weather is
dramatized on the ridge and has always been at war with the fort. In
spring the barracks, built without proper foundations, heave and lurch
as frost leaves the ground from a depth of four feet. Walls tilt, sheathing
rips, and roof boards separate before this seasonal dance ends. Then the
summer sun curls the shingles and weeds grow tall in front of the grey
walls and out into the parade square, untrampled by military drill. From
1768 when the British garrison withdrew until 1776, Fort Cumberland
Ridge was a forlorn place.

In the summer of 1776 the adjacent village was also a quiet place. The
political action of winter had subsided and farmers were on the land,
making hay on the saltmarsh, cultivating upland, tending orchards, and
fighting mosquitoes for, if winter was dangerously cold, summer had its
own peril. "One is tormented all summer with mosquitoes and almost
frozen to death in the winter." Farmers suffered especially: "The mos-
quito will bite them very often so that they will throw down their scythes
and run home, almost bitten to death." Even clothing styles and women's
fashions were modified to combat the nuisance. "Everyone in this country wears trousers, and some of the women wear them, for the mosquitoes fly up their petticoats and bite them terribly!"[2]

There were really only two places of refuge from the insect that inspired sartorial regionalism in Cumberland: the deck of a ship (the
centre of the basin exceeding the flight range of even that superior

insect) and the ramparts of the fort on the windy ridge. Sailors and soldiers on watch fared better than farmers at work, but Cumberland had seen neither sailor nor soldier for eight years. That changed in the summer of 1776 when the Royal Fencible Americans waded ashore at Cumberland Creek. Occupation of the fort, the political situation, and the summer doldrums mitigated against the patriot party and indigenous revolution seemed more remote than ever. If revolution could not be home-grown in the icy cold of January, it was even less likely to take root in the sultry heat of July. To succeed in Nova Scotia, revolution would have to be imported.

"SURROUNDED WITH AS DAMNED YANKEY REBELLS AS ANY IN AMERICA"

"At one pm fired 21 Guns it being the Anniversary of his Majesty's Birth Day ... Moored at Fort Cumberland ... Fresh Breezes and Cloudy ... *4 June 1776.*"[3] The ceremonial cannonade marking King George's birthday that Tuesday was heard by loyalist and patriot alike. June was also the anniversary month of the siege of Fort Beauséjour twenty-one years earlier. A generation had grown up since and veterans were past middle age. Thomas Dixson, for example, was forty-three; Jonathan Eddy was fifty; Benoni Danks was sixty. They were a volatile lot. Some heartily cheered the royal birthday; others declined just as heartily. As a local exclaimed, "what a pity it is Old England should be oppressed by supporting such a company of halfpay Rebbels!"[4]

Seldom had so many ships filled the basin. *Tamer,* from whose guns the royal salute boomed over the Tantramar, *Neptune* and twelve transports had arrived four days earlier, with 200 fencibles and all the gear needed to sustain them for the summer, right down to their 300-pound allotment of tobacco. The two-day voyage from Windsor was uneventful except that *Tamer* struck a rock in the basin "and lay a-Ground" for three hours before the crew was able "to haul her off" with the tide.[5] Now the ships lay anchored in that long narrow body of water which is framed on east and west by lines of low hills, with the marsh rolling away expansively to the north. Only in the very centre of this green panorama was the soft contour broken by the constructed edge of the fort. "The Country has a very pleasant appearance from where we lye," noticed one of the hundreds of sailors who spent their time bartering with the locals who rowed out to the ships with their sheep, fowl, pork, potatoes, and rum. The sailors ate well off this floating market; one "made the best meal that I had made for about six months past."[6]

Even from the deck of a ship Joseph Goreham could see that the fort was run down.[7] Remembering the defence works from the 1750s when they were new – the crisp angularity of its French design, the steady line of the parapet, the smooth contour of the glacis – he was unprepared for the rain-eroded shambles that he viewed in the distance as he sailed up the basin. The fort's silhouette was unevenly rounded and the oddly-shaped spur, appended to the south side by the British after its capture, was a slum of neglected buildings. A site inspection after disembarkation confirmed Goreham's worst fears. The parapet was undermined, the ditch filled with debris, the barracks uninhabitable, and most of the palisade lay rotting on the ground. The troops were put to work on the clean up and were augmented with local labour. Despite the resentment of patriots who knew the troops had come "to accumulate their Trouble," the return of the garrison was welcomed by the people for economic reasons if not for security, and the ships were welcomed for the same reason.[8] To John Allan's chagrin some patriots did business with the shipping agent. "They will sell the Troops anything they have," pointed out one local, "necessity obliges them to it."[9] Captain Mason's task was to protect the transports while they loaded hay and other goods purchased from the farmers on the Fundy coast and then to convoy the fleet to New York where the supplies would sustain the British army engaged in the American Revolution. Disembarking the garrison and overseeing the loading of the transports would take three weeks.

After months of planning and several false starts, Fort Cumberland was occupied in answer to loyalist pleas and as part of a government plan to secure Nova Scotia. The new garrison and the arrival of Michael Francklin signalled an end to Halifax neglect. Even those in the outer townships who felt insecure now had the option of moving closer to Cumberland, and this is what Moses Delesdernier of Shepody did. News of "the unfriendly Proceedings of the Indians at the river St John forced me to remove under the protection of Fort Cumberland."[10] He was there to greet Francklin (his chief creditor) and probably to assist in his tour of the district. Delesdernier's sloop was also requisitioned by the government and put to work with the *Tamer* and the transports in Cumberland Basin.

Another part of the security plan was the improvement of Native relations and this initiative also began in June with Goreham playing a key role. Reopening of the fort was as much an occasion for Native inhabitants as it was for European settlers; both groups had benefitted from its presence in the past, the Micmacs since its construction by the French in 1750. The significance of having the king's military commander present in the region was not lost on them; the officers' barrack was hardly swept clean before five Micmac chiefs from Cocagne appeared before Joseph Goreham with greetings. As a former Indian agent, Goreham was qualified to negotiate with Native nations. The chiefs were given assurances of royal protection and "returned [home] loaded with provisions and ammunition."[11]

John Allan was caught off guard by this meeting. When he heard about it he hurried to Baie Verte to intercept the chiefs on their way home. "I only found one of the chiefs just setting off" for Cocagne and although Allan tried very hard, he could not find out what the chief's "business was with Goreham." The chief was extremely cool, even "cross" at times, surprising Allan because he had always regarded this chief as his friend. The uncertainty about Native intentions unsettled Allan who until now had considered relations between Native and settlers at Cumberland to be his sole domain. As if the garrison was not enough cause for alarm, government efforts to form an alliance with the Micmacs "occasioned great fear" among local patriots who felt that Goreham might set the Native people against them.[12]

Colonel Goreham had his own problems in June. In the midst of setting up camp and organizing work crews, he staged the diplomatic welcome for Micmac chiefs and assisted Michael Francklin with the militia. He arbitrated local disputes as loyalists sought revenge for the insults suffered during the winter and was called upon by local magistrates, who were attempting to untangle legal affairs, to search for fugitives like William How. The colonel also realized that repairing the fort was a bigger job than he had anticipated; a proper renovation was impractical and James Law, who had been charged with restoring the barracks, had done next to nothing since April.[13] But his biggest headache was the desertion rate. During June, Goreham's first month in Cumberland, fifteen fencibles deserted the fort.[14] In April he lost ten men in Halifax but only two left in May at which time he was able to supply the troops with adequate provisions and march them away from the distractions of the capital. Now in Cumberland they performed hard labour and lived in temporary quarters. These hardships were enough to cause some soldiers to bolt, but a bigger reason was the influence of the community. As one officer put it, they were "surrounded with as damned Yankey rebells as any in America" and desertion was the natural result of "permitting the soldiers to Work with every Rebel in the Country." Patriots assisted deserters to flee down the Bay of Fundy to Machias.[15] Goreham recognized that it was essential to adopt measures which would curb desertion and control local patriots.

"DISARMING THE SUSPICIOUS AND CONFINING THE NOTORIOUS"

Although the patriot party made no visible gains that summer, they wielded influence behind the scenes by inciting fencibles to desert and in local politics. John Allan renewed his patriot efforts, but with a lower profile than formerly. Plans to overthrow the government were also kept alive. The news of Jonathan Eddy's failure to attract American help may have reached Cumberland before Eddy's return, but Allan proceeded to advance his "plan for reducing the province" by sending a letter by courier to Massachusetts. A feature of his proposal which was absent from Eddy's was his plan to recruit a regiment of Nova Scotia Micmacs for which he required American approval because of the officers' advance commissions that would be required for such an undertaking. A reply from Boston was eagerly awaited.[16] Allan's chief political challenge in June was the one presented by Michael Francklin. He was determined to blunt Francklin's influence in the district and he was at least partially successful. Compared with Francklin's expectations and his results in Windsor and Kings Counties, his June visit to Cumberland was a failure.

Francklin set out through the townships as soon as he arrived to recruit the militia, but he found the going nearly as difficult in June as Thomas Procter had in February. Accepting the new garrison as the fulfillment of Governor Legge's promise to defend them, Cumberlanders saw little need for a militia. At the same time John Allan threw his weight against the effort by exposing Francklin's private motives. Allan had been trying to discredit the new government and its friends since May. Just before Legge left the province, Allan held a general meeting in Cumberland ostensibly to thank the governor "for your just Administration" and "the Attention you had paid to their Memorial." His motive was certainly not to praise Legge but to discredit his opponents who now formed the government. Allan was willing to portray Legge as a champion of the people and to describe his administration as "just" if by so doing he might alienate the people from Legge's opponents, of whom Francklin was chief. His motive was so obvious that the general meeting was "deem'd an unlawful Assembly."[17]

There was no denying that Francklin was a power to be reckoned with in Cumberland; he had land interests there, influence with the Yorkshire settlers whom he attracted to the region, and impressive diplomatic skills (Allan conceded that Francklin was "remarkable" for his "art and finesse"). So Allan aimed his political blows at Francklin's most vulnerable side, his financial well being. As a result of losing the lieutenant-governorship, Francklin was more financially strapped in June than usual, if not quite "reduced to a state of beggary," as claimed by Allan. The real purpose of his recruiting drive, according to Allan, was to "show his popularity," regain the king's attention, and "get himself established ... on the Government."[18] The combination of local indifference to the militia and Allan's hardball politics defeated Francklin's recruiting drive. No more than thirty volunteered and 100 took "the

Oath of Obedience." This result was no better than what Moses Delesdernier had achieved in the spring.[19]

Francklin was also in Cumberland to investigate the rebellion. He was
instructed by the government to "make a strict enquiry into the
behaviour ... of the Inhabitants." He was to inform himself "of any riots
or disturbances which may have happened there," encourage the "wa-
vering, fearful and irresolute," and, more importantly, "intimidate the
ill-disposed," and "apprehend all persons ... guilty of any rebellion."
With Goreham, he should "call in the Military to his assistance in disarming the Suspicious and confining the Notorious."[20] In this task
Francklin fared better. His presence lent official status to the pattern of
retribution already under way and supported the restructuring of the local administration along loyalist lines. Rewards were offered for the arrest of Jonathan Eddy and other patriots who were known to be out of
the province, and evidence was collected for the expulsion of Samuel
Rogers and John Allan from the House of Assembly. Francklin returned
to Windsor exhausted and disappointed but content that his efforts had
"weakened the influence of the rebels very essentially."[21]

The British army and navy sailed from Halifax for New York in early
June leaving Nova Scotia, and thus Cumberland, on its own. Howe's defence plan was in place and the militia had been recruited in strategic
areas, with the notable exception of Cumberland. Cumberland was considered the defence key to the province and this was not the result
Francklin and Arbuthnot hoped for or expected.[22] In a sense the stalemate in Cumberland continued, broken by neither Francklin nor Allan.
The patriot leader attracted support when he criticized legislation, alleged corruption, or discredited an individual, but he could not close
the political gap between discontent and revolution. However, his limited victory over Francklin left the door open for future rebellious action, and more freedom of action was expected to be available generally
now that the British fleet was gone.

Howe and Shuldham had hoped to leave Halifax in May with the
spring reinforcement from Britain in a bid to end the war in America.
When June arrived and no sails appeared, they agreed to act unilaterally,
before the campaign season advanced any further, and sail southward
with the forces at their disposal to occupy New York, there to confront
Washington. The British reinforcement could follow later. The weather
on Sunday 9 June was so foggy that Shuldham thought it unsafe "to
break the fleet loose today."[23] The next day was clear and by that
evening Halifax Harbour was empty.[24] Accommodating the army and
navy had strained every facility of Nova Scotia and "drained the Province
of Provisions, and even the Farmers' breeding stocks."[25] Landowners
and merchants made handsome profits and business people built a net-

work for purchasing supplies for the army and navy that lasted throughout the war.[26] The economy improved and the impact was felt in other
ways: "A considerable number of women and children amounting to
2030 persons were to be left at Halifax on Embarkation of the Army."[27]

Marriot Arbuthnot was pleased to see the army and navy leave. He
could now conduct affairs in his sole as the lieutenant-governor without
interference and would no longer have to share with superior officers
the prize money from enemy ships condemned in Vice-Admiralty Court.
Now he could issue licences for the rum and molasses trade which
promised rich remuneration to the assiduous chief executive. He would
organize to his benefit the procurement business which had grown so
much over the last two months. Arbuthnot excelled in that eighteenth-
century tradition of combining public and private interests, overlooking
nothing in his public duty that might add to his private wealth.[28] With
Howe gone, he could also confront his political opponents – Legge's sycophants – without fear of them appealing to the general. These people
had been under pressure since Legge's removal; some reported to
Legge that they "felt the effects before you were many leagues on your
Voyage." The main charge against them was their padding of Legge's
regiment, the Nova Scotia Volunteers, an over-expended, under-re-
cruited shell of a corps. With a full slate of officers, all on full pay and all
Legge's friends, but fewer than fifty recruits, it reeked of patronage. Arbuthnot froze regimental funds, ejected many of the officers, reorganized the Volunteers, and attended to all three provincial regiments,
glad to be free of interference from Howe.[29]

"Tis strange to see the Doings here since your departure!" In letters
to Legge in London his Halifax friends revealed the pain of a fall from
power. Slights were felt at social events. "At the Levy on the King's Birthday the coolness with which we were received by the Lieutenant-Governor" contrasted with "the particular Attention, Warmth and Respect
paid" to Arbuthnot's party. "This damned Party" was now the "reigning
Party" and "the Power of their Malice" was dreaded. Legge's friends
knew how the political game was played; they had enjoyed power and if
they now feared the worst, it was because of the excesses of their own regime. Revenge was familiar to them; it had been a hallmark of Legge's
administration. As the new government began "driving out" Legge appointees, they cried "we shall all be ruined" and beseeched Legge in
London to "put a stop to those Leeches!"[30] They longed for his return
which alone could restore their privilege. In Windsor William Ellis, who
had lost ground to John Breynton of St Paul's in the political shuffle,
asked for divine assistance: "I pray God to restore your Excellency to us,
or to remove me out of this Country, my prospect is so dismal!"[31] There
was no disloyalty in these murmurings, only the pain of patronage lost.

If anything, the crisis demonstrated political strength in Nova Scotia. When John Allan tried to promote rebellion by driving a wedge between Legge's friends and opponents at the general meeting in Cumberland he met with little success. Halifax survived the removal of an incompetent governor at the height of the revolution without political upheaval, and installed in Province House in June a conciliator whose challenge it was to harmonize the factions.

With the fleet gone and the capital returned to normal, Arbuthnot was able to concentrate on government. His first priority was to call a session of the House of Assembly which he did on 15 June, the first since Legge's departure. It was soon evident that the style of the new chief executive was more accommodating than that of the governor. In short order, members moved to end the vendetta carried on by Legge against certain members, to repeal the militia acts, and to take advantage of the improved economy (the result of burgeoning wartime trade) by raising taxes and duties. The seats of some members were declared vacant, including those of John Allan and Samuel Rogers, and by-elections were set for August. Because in June there was still the possibility that Legge would be restored to his post, the session featured a joint address by the Assembly and Council which thanked the king for removing him.[32] This measure was "carried through in a great hurry," according to one of Legge's friends who concluded correctly that it was "to prevent your return" – a "last vindictive act" against the governor.[33] Opposition grumbling aside, the June session was free of acrimony and was a turning point in relations between the Assembly and Council, both fractious bodies under Legge. The harmony in the House was due in large measure to the new lieutenant-governor.

Perhaps the most thankful one of all for the June session was Arbuthnot himself who had benefited immensely from Legge's removal. Only months before he was an obscure half-pay officer with nothing but a dockyard commission. Now he was the chief executive of one of the few remaining loyal colonies in North America and commodore in charge of the important Nova Scotia naval station. Choosing the side of Legge's opponents so soon after arriving in Halifax was a shrewd political judgment. His choice had paid off handsomely and in June he rode a wave of popularity.

"WE HAVE NOW GOT A GOVERNOR OF OUR OWN"

Marriot Arbuthnot stood out in the minds of local politicians as one "whose Affable Deportment affords a pleasing Prospect" and they anticipated the "greatest satisfaction" in working with him.[34] No one who knew him in Halifax considered him a pushover and he certainly was not gullible. Unlike Legge, he was no ideologue; according to one Haligonian, one could "hardly tell what principles he is of, besides those of a blustering Tar."[35] Of his many faults, perhaps the greatest was his forgetfulness. When the reinforcement fleet finally appeared off the harbour on 23 June and enquired after Howe and Shuldham, Arbuthnot forgot that he had been given secret written instructions for the rendezvous at New York. This error, which might have been disasterous for the British, was made while the Assembly was in session, during Arbuthnot's first month as Nova Scotia's chief executive.[36]

The House of Assembly prorogued on 29 June after "a very short session." Arbuthnot continued to set the tone of the new government by marking the closing with "a public dinner" for politicians, officials, and friends at Pontac Tavern. Massey and Francklin came, with many assembly people and councillors. On one of the hottest days of summer, the dimly lit tavern overflowed with people in a jovial mood as "they proceeded to feasting and joy." Toasts were followed by speeches, with the ruddy-faced commodore at the centre of a celebration that would have been inconceivable during Legge's tenure. Arbuthnot was proclaimed a man of the people by William Nesbitt, Speaker of the House, that day in the tavern: "We have now got a Governor of our own," he was heard to exclaim above the noise. It was agreed by friend and foe alike that Arbuthnot had changed the style of government dramatically. After a prolonged party, "I took my leave of them," declared the happy chief executive, "and we parted in much good humour!"[37]

The Sunday service at St Paul's Church the next day was well attended with the Reverend John Breynton officiating. Deeply involved in the intrigue against Legge, Breynton was relieved by Arbuthnot's victory. Paranoid in their defeat, Legge's friends derived a sinister meaning from every public utterance, even Breynton's sermon. The text that Sunday was: "Let us pray for the peace of Jerusalem" in which "Jerusalem" might have referred to Halifax and "peace" to the period following Legge's removal. But Legge's friends detected more and paraphrased Breynton's text as: "Let us pray for a clear and uninterrupted Road to the Loaves and Fishes."[38] In other words, the new administration now had a clear path to provincial patronage, which was perfectly true, but the opposition imagined Breynton to be gloating over a political reality in the very selection of his Sunday text.

Exception was also taken to a comment in Breynton's sermon that sounded like "the most fulsome praise to the Lieutenant-Governor that was perhaps ever heard." Being mildly vain, Arbuthnot was vulnerable to flattery and opponents were quick to note that Breynton's praise "would have made any other man blush, but he swallowed it all." The support for Arbuthnot during the first month of his tenure was galling to Legge's friends. They took umbrage with "the Quibbles, Subterfuges and Cunning" used to "justify" his actions in the June session of the Assembly, in the "public dinner" on Saturday, and in Breynton's Sunday service at St Paul's.[39] Gradually, Arbuthnot's popularity enabled him to ignore the petty viciousness. He was too busy to pay it much attention anyway because of unfinished business, such as the overture to the Micmacs undertaken by Joseph Bennett. When that missionary went out in the spring it was Legge who sent him, but he returned to find Arbuthnot ensconced in Government House.

"I am just returned from a visit to the Indians," related Bennett in Halifax in late June. The visit had taken him to Native settlements along the Eastern Shore for the purpose of securing Micmac allegiance in religion and politics. "I have been successful in both respects," he concluded. Three chiefs accompanied him back to Halifax and Arbuthnot plunged at once into the intricate field of Native diplomacy by assuring them "that their interest shou'd be always duly attended to," and adding that Bennett would return to their villages for a second visitation. They seemed "very happy" and while in Halifax were "very well treated by the Lieutenant-Governor and General Massey and sent away perfectly satisfied." Arbuthnot was left "fully convinced of the attachment of the Indians to the English Constitution."[40]

The alliance of Native nations became an issue in Nova Scotia in 1776 as it always did in wartime, and bore on the strategic considerations of both sides in the revolution. Patriot plans required the military use of Native peoples. The alliance of Native militants and patriot politicians was already evident in Sunbury County. But it was Washington's attitude which had the greatest effect on public opinion. His persistent interest in the Native peoples of Nova Scotia was seen as a hostile act even to apolitical Nova Scotians, and drew a demand for government action. After a slow beginning, followed by the delay of administrative change, Arbuthnot continued Legge's effort to secure the loyalty, or at least the neutrality, of Native nations.

Joseph Bennett's second visit to the Micmacs became a major foray into the wilderness while at Fort Cumberland Joseph Goreham merely awaited their arrival for his second meeting. The first meeting was little more than a formal welcome and Goreham had been quick to invite them to a substantive conference later in June. This time five Micmac chiefs of the Miramichi region, who had been "persuaded to go to Colonel Goreham" joined the others.[41] Travelling down the Baie Verte Road on their way to the meeting, three of the chiefs called early in the morning at John Allan's farm to discuss politics and show him a letter they had received from George Washington. Allan read that the Micmacs should attack his neighbours at Cumberland and recognized that the American general, like himself, had visions of using the Micmacs in the current conflict. The chiefs also explained the purpose of their journey: "that Goreham had invited them to come and see him."[42] Hoping to distract them, Allan offered drinks which the chiefs refused until after their meeting with Goreham. He then suggested they go at once but return afterwards and review the proceedings with him. Cleverly, to ensure their return, he offered to hold the Washington letter until after their meeting. This was agreed to and the chiefs went on to Fort Cumberland.

It was one of the first truly warm days of early summer with an excellent breeze blowing off the basin to the brow of Cumberland Ridge. Crews of soldiers and civilians were repairing the fort as the chiefs made their way to the officers' barrack where Goreham awaited them in full military dress. The parade square was untidy, the colonel's quarters shabby, and the sounds of construction were pervasive, but somehow the proceedings achieved the appropriate solemnity. The welfare of Native people from Cocagne to Restigouche was discussed, as was the general situation of the war. Goreham "told them they should have everything they wanted" as allies, "But if they would not take up arms in favour of the King, he expected they would not take up arms against him." Professing loyalty, the chiefs remained non-committal on action, yet received on leaving "ammunition and provisions," being "everything they wanted."[43]

"In the Evening they returned very sober" and briefed Allan on the meeting as requested. With official business over the chiefs relaxed and presumably accepted Allan's invitation for drinks. They camped overnight at the farm and, according to Allan, the "next morning we conversed pretty largely on matters." Perhaps while admiring John and Mary's baby, they proclaimed admiration for his namesake, George Washington, and said that two of their young men, John Baptiste and Matua, had been sent to answer his letter personally and "tell their good wishes towards their Brothers, the Boston Men." In fact the chiefs sent the two emissaries to find out what the Americans had to offer the Micmacs. Allan undertook "to instruct them" regarding the revolution and revealed "my plan for reducing the province," including the role he envisioned for the Native peoples. Their situation was "particularly mentioned" in his recent letter to Boston in which he proposed a Native army and asked for supplies to be sent to the Native peoples, a request which he now (perhaps while eyeing Goreham's generous gifts to the chiefs) turned into a virtual promise. Promising also to go soon to Cocagne to instruct their whole tribe on these matters, Allan bid farewell to the Micmac chiefs.[44]

The chiefs asked repeatedly, "how comes it that Old England and new should quarrel and come to blows?" Their old allies France, Quebec, and Acadia had never done so. As for the Micmacs, "we cannot think of fighting ourselves till we know who is right and who is wrong."[45] They were waiting not so much to find out who was right as who was stronger, on the basis of which they could draw their own conclusions. They would not have been impressed by the Royal Fencibles – soldiers without uniforms who deserted regularly. On the other hand, the Fencibles' commissary was full and accessible even to neutral parties, whereas American generosity was a question mark and John Allan, although an avid orator, had no commissary at all. First Nations elders were seeking an independent position in the Native interest. That position was developing even as the chiefs walked the Baie Verte Road in June. For the moment their main interest was a well-stocked commissary; their strongest impression was of the generosity of Joseph Goreham, and their most vivid memory was of Cumberland Basin filled with British warships and supply ships.

Cumberland Basin was devoid of the king's navy at the end of June (*Tamer, Neptune,* and the convoy sailed 25 June) when Jonathan Eddy and Samuel Rogers beached their small craft on the Tantramar after an eventful journey up the Bay of Fundy.[46] They returned from their long American visit, not to a triumphal welcome but as fugitives in the night, their families setting up watches to warn of fencible patrols. To hard-pressed patriots on the isthmus, Eddy's quest for American help was a bitter failure and his return went almost unnoticed. "To their Great affliction," Allan "heard only that Captain Eddy was come but without succour for them."[47] Having been away four months, Eddy and Rogers found the situation in Cumberland had changed drastically. Eddy had to meet surreptitiously with the Committee-of-Safety to explain his New England mission and to make future plans. He expounded on Washington's interest in using Native support which until then was known only by the letter to the Micmacs. It was discovered that Washington's ideas, as related by Eddy, coincided with Allan's plan for using Native recruits to help capture Nova Scotia, and this discovery raised hopes for a new initiative. In view of Eddy's failure, the only plan on the table was the one Allan had mailed to Boston and to which he "was in daily expectation" of receiving a "satisfactory answer."[48]

Allan's plan, his letter to Boston, and the effort to encourage fencibles to desert the garrison seemed like reasonable measures to Eddy as far as they went, but as a man of action he wanted more. How to implement the plan and promote an invasion were questions he wanted answered. It was at this point that the idea of building a road to New England was raised. The suggestion seemed outlandish. Even the simplest trail would be an ambitious undertaking, but remembering their own winter trek to Cambridge, Eddy understood the benefits of improved land communication. Such a road would forge stronger links with their Maugerville colleagues, assist deserting soldiers, be an invasion route, and provide a ready war-path for the Maliseets. "I was sensible of the great Utility of a Road through the Wilderness between Cumberland and ... Massachusetts," recorded Samuel Rogers. Rogers might have suggested the idea and was "prevailed on to stay and reconnoitre it in order to find proper ways through for Roads."[49] Allan's plan was revised to incorporate the road as patriots continued to discuss an invasion. Important details such as the strength of the fort were also checked out by Eddy. The veteran British officer might have felt some nostalgia on seeing the fort in which he had once served filled once more with soldiers. "To ascertain the true condition" was no problem. "We got Intelligence from our friends of the Strength of the Garrison." Zebulon Roe succeeded in getting inside the fort and "thoroughly examined it without exciting suspicion." But the most important "business" of the patriot party during those difficult days of summer was left to Samuel Rogers: "I went to making the Road, as was agreed on."[50]

July 1776. A political watershed for thirteen of Britain's North American colonies was reached during the first week of July 1776.[51] For Britain's colony around the Bay of Fundy a turning point of sorts was also in the works. A new regime of a distinctly loyalist hue was inaugurated in Cumberland on Monday 1 July, with the commissioning of two Yorkshire settlers, William Black Sr and Christopher Harper, as justices of the peace.[52] It was hoped in Halifax that these appointments in conjunction with the new garrison would strengthen the government's administrative grip beyond the capital, improve law and order, pacify the people, and restore the "precarious" real estate market.[53] Civic calm and political stability were the qualities esteemed by the Nova Scotia government, not the political radicalism of the Continental Congress. While the remarkable event of independence occurred in America, Black and Harper began to help Goreham restore order to Cumberland. It became clear that the garrison, no matter how slovenly clothed and desertion-prone, impressed "luke warm" loyalists, a point conceded by John Allan who found the people no longer interested in political argument. The population was determined to remain quiet "on any terms." If the new regime had a calming effect on the general populace, it appeared to sanction a backlash against patriots. "The Friends to America became new objects of Vengeance,"[54] explained Allan, himself being one such object.

The Declaration of Independence was announced in Philadelphia on Thursday 4 July. This unilateral action by the united colonies cut final ties with England and excluded Nova Scotia. While political dissent was triumphant in America, it was cause for persecution in Nova Scotia.

Seen through patriot eyes, Nova Scotia had a military government and an arbitrary one at that. Magistrates came in for scurrilous criticism. To Josiah Throop they were "chiefly old broken subalterns, sergeants or drum[mer]s used to condemning, Kicking, caning and flogging, and never easy!" The enthusiasm with which the recent appointees tackled their jobs led some to suppose that Arbuthnot "gave unlimited discretionary Commissions" to his magistrates. Black, Harper, and other appointees were seen as tools of the government sent among the people to spy on them. There were instances, it was said, of settlers being arrested "by these Creatures" on suspicion alone, "never examined," and confined at the fort "to be abused and insulted by the Soldiers." They were arrested simply for "being Suspected to be friendly to the United States." By the "Arbitrary Order" of a magistrate one settler was sent on board a warship in Cumberland Basin; others were put in gaol in irons at the magistrate's pleasure, "without even the Ceremony of an Accusation!" Asked Throop rhetorically: "did the States Ever Serve Torys so?"[55]

Of course "Torys" in the new United States suffered more than "Rebels" in Nova Scotia; it was in America that the civil war raged and the military crisis mounted even as independence was declared. Considering the emergency and acting on a plan proposed by George Washington on 4 July, Congress agreed to incite the Native nations against Nova Scotia. The decision was taken for tactical reasons and Washington could not have been aware of the plan John Allan had recently sent to Massachusetts, a plan that also proposed to employ Native people. "At a crisis like the present," rationalized Washington, when Britain was waging war "with unexampled severity" and in the course of which "have excited Slaves and Savages to Arms against us," he felt that Americans were "impelled by Necessity ... to call to our Aid so many of the St. Johns [Maliseet], Nova Scotia [Micmac] and Penobscot Indians as I might judge necessary." From the information he had, the prospect for recruiting a regiment of Nova Scotia Natives seemed bright; "it ought to be done," urged George Washington on that first Independence Day.[56]

"TRIFLING PRESENTS AND FAIR WORDS"

Washington's scheme was to raise a regiment of Native people from the Penobscot, Passamaquoddy, Maliseet, and Micmac nations to serve "for two or three years," be provisioned by Congress, and put on continental army pay although, added the parsimonious general, "Having professed a strong Inclination to take part with us ... It is probable they may be engaged for less pay." The Native regiment would be of "infinite service in annoying and harassing" the enemy, thought Washington. It was widely presumed that they favoured America and Washington likely read the newspapers which had reported recently that the Maliseets were "highly incensed against the ministerial party and are determined at all Hazards to join the Americans." He foresaw full recruitment. "I have been told ... perhaps five or six hundred or more," would join up he informed Congress and Massachusetts, the state to which Congress deferred "in this business," and asked to negotiate the international treaty that would set the eastern Native nations on the warpath.[57] Washington was not alone in supposing that the Native peoples could be bought cheaply. Nova Scotians also assumed that Native allegiance was an easy bargain. John Cort, the Miramichi merchant, expressed the general view when he said of the Native people that "with a few trifling presents and fair words, they might be made very serviceable subjects."[58] Chronic indifference to Native rights and studious neglect of their needs were interrupted by the revolution and in the summer of 1776 both sides courted the Native peoples with words that were as frivolous as their presents were trifling.

Less than a week after declaring itself independent the United States hosted an international conference and authorized the signing of one of its first treaties. Negotiations with the Micmac and Maliseet nations were held in the Watertown meeting house by the Massachusetts State Council at the request of Washington and with the approval of Congress. Having been conveyed from Machias to Salem in Francis Shaw's sloop, the ten Native delegates "rode hither in Carriages" to Boston and were already there when Washington's final instructions arrived.[59] It was cloudy on 10 July but the mood was festive because news of the Independence Declaration had just reached town. At one o'clock a crowd gathered on the Town House steps to hear the Declaration read and "an Huzza ensued." Toasts were given by President James Bowdoin in the Council Chamber where wine, crackers, and cheese were "set for all the Company."[60] After the ceremony, Bowdoin chaired the preliminary meeting with the ten delegates in the Council Chamber, while outside in the street the celebration continued with a raging bonfire fuelled by the king's arms from Faneuil Hall, the crown and mitre from King's Chapel, and any other combustible royal symbols that could be found. The royal coat of arms was nowhere to be seen as Edward Winslow had rescued it in March.[61] The meeting adjourned after formal introductions and more toasts were made before the Native delegates retired for "refreshments" with Francis Shaw who had "ordered good Lodgings and entertainment" for his international guests.[62]

The delegation had not come to Boston to sign a treaty and lacked the authority to do so. The most senior of the ten was Ambroise St Aubin of Aukpaque on the St John River, a secondary chief of the Maliseets. The Micmacs of Cocagne were represented only by two "Young men," John Baptiste and Matua, in New England to seek supplies and

bring good wishes to Washington.[63] But the Americans were not dis-
suaded by St Aubin admission that "it's not in our power to answer now
for the whole of our Tribes," and formal negotiations began two days
later at Watertown. The State Board and House of Representatives sat in
joint session across the table from St Aubin's delegation. French was the
official language of the sessions.

Native demands were simply stated: "We want a truckhouse and a
Priest." The priest had to be French because "we shall not hear any
prayers that come from England." As for trade, they expected "proper
Goods for our Furs and Skins and we want them up the St. John River."
The Americans were not sure they could find a French priest and could
hardly operate a trading post in Nova Scotia. Machias would have to do
for the time being and they could only pay "for your skins and furs the
same price they will fetch in Boston." The Americans pursued Washington's request to make military allies of the Native peoples. "It was strongly
urged upon them to join with us in the war." The sessions lasted a week.
Hospitality was lavish and Congress paid the bill. Eventually, St Aubin
agreed Native people would "join in the War on your side. You may depend upon it ... We will not break our Words. We will not Lie!" He was
also heard to say: "we will engage in the War ... We love Boston!"[64]

"Would your Warriors form a Body in conjunction with a number of
our people?" asked the Americans, getting down to specifics. "Yes," was
St Aubin's reply. In an effort to strenghten the commitment the chief
was asked in a later session if "you are hearty to enter into the War with
us?" He replied, "yes we are" and he shook hands with Bowdoin. It was
only after tallying the numbers of those capable of bearing arms in the
widely scattered Native villages that it became evident only a fraction of
the force envisaged by Washington might be available and only at a fraction of the speed. St Aubin admitted "it is not in our power to tell how
many Men we can raise; we will git as many as we can."[65] Even using
Bowdoin's generous estimate, the Native nations "could furnish about
120 men" only, and they "could not engage to come till next Spring."
Under pressure St Aubin "promised to return early in the Fall with
about 30 of their Tribe" and four delegates actually offered to go at once
to join Washington. By any measure, these results fell far short of Washington's request "to engage ... five or Six hundred Men ... and have
them marched with all possible expedition to join the Army here." The
Americans were just as equivocal in meeting Native demands. When
pressed on the trade issue, for example, they responded in generalities,
promising to supply the Penobscot truckmaster with "a further Quantity" of goods to meet the "Necessaries and Conveniences of Life."[66]

The document signed on 19 July was "a Treaty of Alliance and Friendship." In Bowdoin's mind it satisfied Washington's request. He had

urged the Native peoples to join the war, "and accordingly they have engaged to do it, and have signed a Treaty for that purpose." The delegation supposed their people would enjoy enhanced trade with the United
States. Both sides portrayed the treaty as a great achievement but it remained that the Americans struck a deal with an unauthorized delegation which, like the American team, offered up considerably less than
hoped for by the opposite side. Also, the Penobscots, the nearest Native
nation to Boston, were not included in the treaty; Bowdoin intended to
meet with them shortly to bind them to the same terms. Perhaps in recognition of the treaty's weakness, "the Council thought it best" to send
agents home with the delegates "to procure" with "utmost expedition"
the number of Native soldiers Washington wanted. If these agents were
effective, the treaty might yet serve to generate a Native uprising in Nova
Scotia as desired by George Washington and John Allan.[67]

The Native peoples also intended to advance their interests under the
treaty. At Machias, the truckmaster was already under pressure, being
forced to pay a higher-than-Boston rate for beaver pelts "to hinder them
from trading with Nova Scotia." Some Native people refused to pay their
bills and subjected the truckmaster to "many insults." Their position was
clear: either the Americans would supply them or they would "rely on
the assistance of Nova Scotia."[68] It was a position they used in reverse
with the Nova Scotians and which doubled their supplies.

Second Chief Ambroise St Aubin returned to the mid-summer heat of
Aukpaque a few miles upriver from Maugerville on the St John River
with a treaty he believed gave the Maliseets favoured trading status with
the Americans. This nation appeared to be drifting into the American
camp and Nova Scotia was doing nothing about it. The overture made to
the Micmacs spearheaded by Goreham and Bennett may have been late,
but it was more forward-looking than the disregard of the Maliseets.
This was a serious lapse. In some respects they were strategically more
important than the Micmacs: they were less dependent on Halifax, generally more belligerent and closer to the war-path, and their territory lay
closer to Massachusetts. It seemed likely in the summer of 1776 that this
nation, bound now by treaty to New England, would join forces with
Barker's patriots who had applied to join Massachusetts.

Barker's patriots, who had already sent one loyalist family to gaol in
New England, were ready in July to transport a second one. Charles
Jadis had been "a prisoner" in Maugerville since May, his wife and five
children were "proscribed" and a penalty was placed on anyone giving
them supplies. The family suffered many hardships and Charles was
presseured to join the rebellion. When he resisted, the patriots sent
for their Machias friends to come and "take him and a few others" to
New England. Faced with the real prospect of following John Anderson

into American captivity, Jadis decided to make a pretence of co-operating with the patriots in an attempt to escape their grasp. A note was "sent to the Committee to inform them he was ready to join in any Enterprise or Service they would appoint him to," using his military skills on the side of the patriots, as the Committee-of-Safety wanted. A delighted Barker informed the Americans of his committee's success in recruiting a veteran army officer (who also had naval experience) to the cause. Captain Jadis was welcomed by the patriots and, by gaining their confidence, he was able to observe their organizational structure and become privy to their plans for the overthrow of the government.[69]

The local patriot organization was a loose structure centred in Cumberland, Cobequid, and Maugerville, with minor centres in Pictou and Passamaquoddy. The centres were linked with Machias but agents of the Maugerville group generally maintained contact beyond there to Boston and to Washington's headquarters. Militant Native groups were linked in Maugerville and Cumberland. Various plans for adding the Nova Scotia stripe to the American flag were advanced that summer with most conceived in Cumberland, the political centre of the network, where John Allan and others operated in the shadow of the fort, having now to "meet in a private manner." Results of these meetings, including plans and rumours of plans, were circulated through the network and to Machias by patriot agents.[70]

The many plans for the reduction of Nova Scotia differed only in detail. Invariably they relied on American invasion, a Native uprising, and the commissioning of local officers to lead a patriot army that was expected to grow considerably in Nova Scotia. The plan to which Jadis became privy foresaw an army of 6,000 Americans and Nova Scotians with an auxiliary force of 300 Native people. The plans never varied in strategy: Fort Cumberland was the first objective ("which must have fallen an easy conquest," admitted Jadis) after which the army would advance on the capital. The Native members would have already infiltrated Halifax under the guise of having deserted the Americans. The capital would fall and then the whole province would fall. Jacob Barker and the Maugerville committee explained this fantastic plan to Charles Jadis. In command of the army with the rank of major-general would be none other than Jadis himself.

"As soon as he was in possession of these Facts," Jadis devised "the means of his escape." Anyone leaving the St John River valley needed Barker's permission and a plausible excuse was demanded. Jadis found one: "the ill-state of health he was then in (owing to his late hard treatment) proved a very plausible ... pretext." He asked to go to New England "for the recovery of his health" and "gave out" that he intended to join George Washington. This story was believed and, "As soon as he had obtained the Pass" and after "some delay and great distress," the Jadis family "escap'd in the night time."[71] Making his way to the river mouth, Jadis "committed himself and family, then six in number, to the mercies of Providence and the Dangers of the Sea in a small Birch Bark Canoe and crossed the Bay of Fundy." To brave these waters in a canoe took courage and faith. On the far side the family "was providentially taken up at the Mouth of the Gut of Annapolis by the *Viper* Sloop-of-War" and delivered safely to Annapolis Royal.[72]

The plight of Anderson and Jadis demonstrated the power of the Maugerville committee, but it did not have absolute power. Sunbury's member of the Assembly, James Simonds, and others of the trading cartel of Simonds, Hazen, and White remained at large in the valley and neutral in politics. To be publicly neutral in Sunbury that summer was an act of defiance, but even when pressed these loyalists avoided being drawn out. Chairperson Barker singled out James Simonds, his partner James White, and Jarvis Saye who had "not thought proper to fall in with" Committee of Safety mandates; "neither have you declared against them," pointed out the committee clerk, Israel Perley, hopefully. "This conduct of yours gives uneasiness to many of the Inhabitants" and, he might have added, reflected poorly on the authority of the committee. In June Perley had requested that the three make "an explicit Declaration of your sentiments." He foresaw a preference for neutrality "but this will not be a satisfactory answer." Simonds, White, and Saye did not respond. In July, when Simonds "was up River," he was questioned closely by the committee. Still he refused to co-operate. Fumbling for compromise, committee members suggested Simonds "leave something privately with the Committee expressing his Sentiments"; even this "he declined," adding obliquely "that he could be of more service to the People, not to Do it."[73]

Retreating still further from their initial position, the Committee-of-Safety asked Simonds to guarantee that he would not inform Halifax of their treasonous act of "Entering into an alliance with the People of New England." This also "he refused," causing some members to complain "that they could not Esteem such a man their friend, nor a friend to the Cause," nor could they have dealings with him. Simonds dared to clarify that "if he Did Do Such a thing" as they requested, he would have to write "that he was compelled to do it which," he added cleverly, "would be Rather against the People."[74] By standing up to the committee, Simonds, White, and Saye revealed its weakness. As strong as local patriots were in July they dared not deal with all loyalists as decisively as they had with the unfortunate Charles Jadis. Sunbury loyalists were weak and lived under the double shadow of Machias and Aukpaque.

By July the centre of patriot activity in Nova Scotia had shifted from Cumberland to Sunbury County. Although Barker was not in total control and St Aubin had still not won over Chief Tomah, these patriot leaders enjoyed far more freedom of action than their counterparts in Cumberland. The events that signalled this shift were the Maugerville declaration of rebellion in May, the arrival of the Royal Fencibles in Cumberland in June, and the return of St Aubin to Aukpaque in July. Another sign was the return of Perley and Kimball from Boston with arms and ammunition "for the use of their constituents." They delivered a barrel of gunpowder, 250 weight of lead, and a stand of small arms.[75] Political inspiration still issued from the Cumberland zealots, but the avenue for action and the fountainhead of rumour was the St John River valley.

The most persistent rumour in Halifax that July was of an attack by Maliseets and New England patriots along the lines of the plan known to Charles Jadis. "It has often been reported," wrote an officer of this rumour; "we are daily alarmed," wrote another. The number of patriots was estimated as high as 2,000 and Goreham heard they "are within three days march of his Post."[76] Even more extreme versions of this rumour circulated. The alarm was due in part to news of the formal contacts between the Maliseets and the Americans that reached Halifax in July. That news pointed to an alliance of Native peoples, Americans, and local patriots. Arbuthnot heard that Eddy was back in Nova Scotia "with power" from New England "to try to corrupt the St. John's Indians."[77] In the end, Council concluded that the rumour of an attack was false. It was false (or at least premature), but it was not groundless. The rumour supported Jadis's contention that a plan existed, and the march from the St John River to the Petitcodiac, the direction of the attack, would be made easier by the road Samuel Rogers was in fact cutting through the woods. The rumour mistook a plan of attack for an actual attack; the plan was real as Jadis well knew and tentative steps were under way to implement it, but there was no current danger.

Jonathan Eddy was in the province as Arbuthnot had heard, but his freedom was circumscribed by Goreham's patrols and restricted by the warrant for his arrest. The situation was intolerable in Cumberland for patriots; they dared not assemble except on the most urgent business and only in secret. Many ceased political activity. The new magistrates were so diligent that it seemed a matter of time before accused patriots must surrender or flee the isthmus. "We were drove to our wits end," explained one patriot. William How had already fled because of his altercation with the deputy sheriff in March and Eddy decided to leave in July, no more than a month after his return. He was forced into exile but he went also on official business: he set out to make a final bid to obtain American help for local rebellion. "Eddy was to return to the Honourable Congress," announced Samuel Rogers and "we found means to send off Mr. Eddy," added Josiah Throop, a member of the committee.[78]

Eddy's second mission to America was prompted by the news that Allan's letter had not reached Boston. It was "thrown overboard" in St John Harbour when a warship challenged the vessel carrying it.[79] Lost was the invasion plan with its idea of using Natives (so much like the plan of George Washington); it was now up to Eddy to carry the message directly to Congress. He and his family left near the end of the month with some optimism that the Native peoples, Acadians, and New Englanders in Nova Scotia were ready for action if only he could bring back American help. Left behind were Allan and Rogers, the former carrying on in closely watched Cumberland and the latter beyond the Petitcodiac, chopping a line through a vast forest alive with black flies and stifling in the July heat. They laboured under difficulties that were purely local. The focus of irritation had shifted away from Halifax where a more adroit administration managed affairs. Unlike the antagonistic Legge, the new chief executive avoided issues that might promote dissent in the outsettlements. Arbuthnot was not one to stay out of sight; he was planning a public relations offensive that would carry his loyalist message directly to the people.

With the fleet gone and the Assembly prorogued, Arbuthnot felt freer than he had in months. Now in a more relaxed mood, he decided on a remarkable initiative – a tour of Nova Scotia outsettlements. The idea was pure Arbuthnot, a genuine effort to meet the people by one who genuinely enjoyed pressing the flesh. Nothing less characteristic of Governor Legge could be imagined. Arbuthnot's affability, however, was edged in cleverness, even cunning, and the tour would be no idle walkabout but a calculated scheme for the encouragement of loyalty pursuant to his official instructions. These were similar to Legge's instructions but light years separated the former governor's methods from those of the jovial commodore. Arbuthnot would stress informality and visit districts never seen by a governor. Justice Isaac Deschamps would go with him and also Michael Francklin who was for most Haligonians the acknowledged outsettlement expert.

Into the wilderness behind Citadel Hill and across the centre of the Nova Scotia peninsula rode the Halifax delegation led by the chief executive himself. To a sailor like Arbuthnot the forested, hilly interior was an exotic place, sultry in the mid-July heat and lacking the salt air he was used to. His interest in North American fauna was indulged. The wildcats that roamed those woods especially took his fancy; a live one would make a perfect Christmas present for his London patron, the Earl of Sandwich.[80] Arbuthnot and Deschamps were joined by Francklin in Windsor and together they circulated through the townships of

Horton and Cornwallis. Arbuthnot reviewed the militia in each community by meeting the volunteers and conversing with their officers. He
got to know the magistrates and "bettermost people by dining together." The commodore was a memorable host. Robustly overweight,
with a prodigious appetite, sturdy drinking habits, and a string of stories (of the crude, nautical variety), the red-faced, cheery, "blustering
tar" regaled his guests nightly through the Annapolis Valley. "It seemed
to have a good effect," Arbuthnot observed as when officers were asked
for their opinions "they unanimously expressed much loyalty, zeal and
satisfaction." Not a little of the good effect resulted from the contagious
optimism and nightly good humour of their chief executive.[81]

All that dining did not have a good effect on Michael Francklin whose
health was never robust. On the delegation's return to Windsor he fell ill
and went home to his bed at Martock House. His wife's illness had kept
Francklin at home in the spring and now he was out of action for the
rest of the summer. This was bad luck for Arbuthnot who on 26 July
boarded with Isaac Deschamps the naval sloop *Gage* in the Avon River
for the most ambitious leg of his tour: a visit to the Cobequid district
across Minas Basin.[82]

"LEFT TO BE THE PARENT OF THEIR OWN WORKS"

The three townships of Cobequid, which comprised some 200 families, were situated on the north coast of Minas Basin: Truro, the inner-
most, at the head of tiny Cobequid Bay; Onslow, near the centre point
of the coast; and Londonderry, down the coast towards the trail that
leads across the watershed to Cumberland. Judged by their remonstrances against the militia acts, Onslow was the most rebellious, but
patriots from all three townships conspired during the past winter to
revolutionize the district and failed. One of their number, Thomas
Faulkner, was in the Halifax gaol charged with treason.[83] The 100 or
so families of Londonderry, the most populous of the three townships,
lived on the edge of a lowland that supported their prosperous farms.
One of these was *Little Dyke* farm, home of John Morrison, Assembly-
member and revolutionary of the previous winter. *Little Dyke* farm af-
forded a full view of Minas Basin, including the wide foreshore where
the marsh was a rich green in late July, and Cape Blomidon and Cape
Split high on the far shore. It was a fine setting for an auspicious event
on that clear Friday evening of 26 July when at seven o'clock the *Gage*
anchored in the creek. While shadows lengthened on the mud flats,
the generous bulk of Marriot Arbuthnot was seen to disembark, the
first chief executive ever to step ashore in Cobequid.[84]

From Friday until Monday, with that congenial style that was his forte, Marriot Arbuthnot met the people of Londonderry: David Smith, Presbyterian minister; John Morrison in the guise of a loyal Assembly member; and John Morrison's constituents, most of whom were recent immigrants from Ireland and had less in common with New England republicanism than those living in the neighbouring townships. *Gage* sailed the chief executive next to Onslow where another thirty to fifty families lived, mostly New Englanders. Some of the district's most vociferous patriots were from Onslow. There was Joshua Lamb who drafted Onslow's toughly-worded remonstrance and who was evicted from the Assembly in June. There was Charles Dickson, a patriot sympathizer who was running for Lamb's vacant seat. There were Carpenter Bradford and John Polly who "are much disaffected at least in their conversation," and John and William Cutting who "have frequently Endeavoured to convince the people that the Rebells' cause was just."[85] Not even Onslow's reputation of at least talking a good rebellion was in evidence during Arbuthnot's visit; the facade of local loyalty was maintained.

In Truro there were another fifty families and a political mix somewhere between that of Londonderry and Onslow.[86] The Scots-Irish majority, which made its way to Nova Scotia via New Hampshire, had the anti-British reflex of Irish Londonderry and the republican sensibility of the New Englanders of Onslow. Those who greeted Arbuthnot in Truro could have ranged from Daniel Cock, the loyal Presbyterian minister, to John Fulton of *Liberty Hall* farm, a patriot leader. Arbuthnot's strongest impression in all three townships was of the prosperity of the people, who were "the finest men in the province, settled on the best land, and the most flourishing because they are the most industrious." He was welcomed everywhere; there were no protests, only polite responses from the people and assurances from officials.[87] Rebellion was invisible because the patriots were as demoralized in July as their Cumberland counterparts. Without a garrison in their midst, they should have enjoyed more freedom of action, yet their circumstances appeared unfavourable. They lacked the political leadership of Cumberland and had no close allies like the Committee-of-Safety at Maugerville. Independent and instinctively anti- Halifax, they nevertheless had weaker ties to New England than either Cumberland or Maugerville. Moreover their ministers, Smith and Cock, were no friends of the New England cause. So down-hearted were Cobequid patriots that just before Arbuthnot's visit they wrote a letter to Massachusetts pleading for help. As part of their ongoing dialogue with Cumberland, this letter was given to Eddy to carry to Boston on their behalf.

Arbuthnot was astonished that no governor had ever visited Cobequid. They were "a strong, robust, industrious people," he repeated; "bigoted

Dissenters, and of course great levellers." How could it be otherwise, he asked rhetorically? "They have been left to be the parent of their own works." With 500 men capable of bearing arms (Arbuthnot's own estimate), neglect could be folly so in the pleasant warmth of July he accepted their expressions of affection and encouraged loyalty.[88] He could have gained no more than a superficial view of Cobequid during his brief visit. Without the advice of the knowledgeable Francklin, who had intended to be his guide, undercurrents of dissent were easily overlooked. He knew of the political agitation earlier in the year and Judge Deschamps might have advised him of the treason charge against Thomas Faulkner (as well as the weakness of the Crown's case). Patriots were unlikely to identify themselves and there was little time for more than social chit-chat with loyalists. In any event, it was not Arbuthnot's purpose to seek out dissent; rather, he was there to set a tone, to arouse by his very presence a positive feeling towards government, and to forge relationships with local leaders such as David Smith. Allowing for the fierce independence of the district, its paranoia of central government, and its isolation, Arbuthnot's weekend visit was a relative success.

The official Halifax entourage departed on Monday, 29 July. *Gage* delivered Deschamps and Arbuthnot to Windsor and the latter rode back to the capital convinced he had gained useful insights into the enigma that was Cobequid. That the district was a provincial asset was not in doubt, but he believed it also to be peopled by a loyal majority. It was true that settlers had a record of causing trouble for Halifax but to Arbuthnot they seemed more obstreperous than revolutionary. That was Francklin's opinion; now, with minor reservations, it was also Arbuthnot's, but the important point was that firsthand knowledge played a part in his opinion. Exposure to life outside Halifax was the real benefit of the summer junket for the pleased but weary lieutenant-governor.

August 1776. A month-long rest was accepted by Marriot Arbuthnot as his due and the capital relaxed with him. No such luxury was enjoyed by the plotters of rebellion. On the first day of August Jonathan Eddy was in Boston in "fair and very hot" weather to promote the cause.[89] This time he did not have a Cumberland petition with him, instead he presented the Onslow letter to the Council the next day. That body had just been informed that the Penobscot nation "conclude not to engage in the Continental Army at present." This discouraging news, the first formal response of the eastern Native peoples to Washington's call for their recruitment, might have established the mood in which Eddy was received. Outlining the "distressed situation" in Nova Scotia, Eddy prayed for American relief by sending an invasion force or at least by helping patriots to flee. The Council professed to "be glad to afford them assistance were it in their power but as the General Court is not sitting ... we are not authorised to do anything." They recommended that Eddy try the Congress in Philadelphia and referred the matter to Congress representatives: "We leave it with you Gentlemen to take such steps in the affair as you may judge best."[90]

While Eddy was shuffled from Council to Congress in pursuit of a real invasion, rumoured invasion was again the talk of Halifax. The August rumours were more extreme than July's. From Hillsborough in the Shepody region, Charles Baker warned "that New England Troops have finished the Road from St. John River to Shepody" and that 800 Native people were waiting for them to "demolish the Fort Cumberland," after which they planned "to Proceed to Halifax to destroy the King's Yard." Arbuthnot agreed to order HMS *Scarborough*, then in Halifax harbour, to sail to the St John River and on to Cumberland "to ascertain the degree of credit to be given to this intelligence." That no ships were stationed in the Bay of Fundy did not accord with Howe's defence plan but the naval aspects of that plan had also been mislaid by the forgetful Arbuthnot with the result that naval affairs were neglected that summer. Massey gave no credence to Baker's story: "I think the Rebels dare not attempt to invade this Province while General Howe is in motion with so large an Army." He was right. The Americans were occupied with Howe in New York.[91] As in July, no invasion of Nova Scotia was under way. Only invasion plans circulated through the patriot network with the inevitable – perhaps planned – leaks to the general population. Halifax was just settling back into the quiet routine of summer when the Jadis family arrived from Annapolis Royal to warn of an American attack.

"Immediately on his arrival at Halifax," Charles Jadis "waited on Governor Arbuthnot and General Massey and informed them of the intended expedition against Halifax." He ended his description of the patriot plan dramatically with "the rebels intention of burning Halifax." Arbuthnot and Massey paid little attention to this escaped prisoner who risked his family to warn them. When he urged "in the most pressing terms" that an expedition be sent to Sunbury, they remained apathetic. "If they would give him an armed schooner and an hundred Men," Jadis would "go back and take the Committee and all the leaders in that part and bring them Prisoners to Halifax or lose his life in the attempt!" He would lead the expedition himself "without Fee ... but this was rejected." The town's leading citizens listened sympathetically when Jadis turned to them for support but they could only advise him to make a legal claim against the patriots for his losses. So persistent was Jadis that rumours began to circulate of a loyalist expedition to the St John River and even of a foray into New England. Rumour and counter-rumour, and accounts of expeditions both to and from Nova Scotia appeared in the newspapers.[92]

That no action was taken on Jadis' warning was not unusual given the unfounded rumours of August. Jadis' credibility was also undermined by his reputation for attracting trouble to himself. Even if he had been taken seriously, there might still have been no response – Halifax had slipped into the doldrums of August. As was clear to Jadis, there prevailed "a Supineness, which at this time was but too apparent."[93] The government was complacent. The outposts were garrisoned, the counties were quiet with the apparent exception of remote Sunbury, and news of decisive victories by General Howe in New York were daily expected. Departure of the British army and navy had returned the capital to sleepy quietude.

But all was not calm. The Royal Marines were chafing at having been left behind in Halifax and feared that the war might be over before they could participate.[94] Massey, who had not yet organized the fall supply of the frontier outposts, found inactivity to border on incompetence. Arbuthnot, although blithely unaware, was causing a furore in New York by having forgotten the secret orders for the British reinforcement. The rumours of August were so many and so inaccurate that they were ignored like the plight of the Jadis family, and this permitted the Maugerville rebellion to build unchecked.

The negligence, forgetfulness, and inertia that insulated the administration from alarms in August did not forestall changes in the Assembly already set in motion during the June session. Elections held during the third week of August refilled vacant seats to create a more solidly loyal House. An exception was Robert Foster, elected in Sackville Township. He was a member of the patriot committee and his election at a time when loyalists were being returned *en masse* to the House established Sackville as the seat of rebellion in the province.[95] While Foster could now oppose the government from within the Assembly, other patriots continued to oppose from outside and some, such as Eddy, opposed in exile.

The reception for Eddy at Philadelphia was no more rewarding in August than it had been in April. Crises had multiplied since the earlier visit and Congress was engrossed in the military campaign. There was sympathy but no agreement to invade Nova Scotia. Instead, that the colony's Native nations had not heeded the Congressional call to arms attracted plenty of concern. Hard-pressed by the British, Washington wondered where the Native peoples were: "I have heard nothing from them." They must supply a regiment of Native soldiers according to the treaty; "it is a Matter of the greatest consequence," pleaded Washington to Massachusetts in early August.[96] Congress might also have wondered why it was that Nova Scotia's patriot movement was so weak. All that Eddy achieved was an agreement to go along with any assistance Massachusetts might choose to provide. The matter was referred back to Boston. Facing failure again, Eddy was forced to modify his demands and try again before the Massachusetts Council. If he reduced the scale of his appeal, perhaps he might obtain token support. With this in mind he journeyed back to Boston where two other patriot exiles, William How and Zebulon Roe, joined him. Together they devised a fresh strategy to use in a last attempt to obtain American sponsorship for their rebellion.

Eddy, How, and Roe petitioned the Massachusetts Council on 28 August. Wisely, they did not dwell on the weakness of indigenous rebellion, emphasizing instead that Nova Scotia could be captured by local patriots with only a little American help. Cleverly, they described the danger to New England posed by the newly repaired forts in Cumberland and Windsor and suggested they could be used as bases by the British to mount attacks on America. No army of American soldiers was asked for, just "a Small number" to join "our Brethren there" and if only they "Could be Supply'd with Some Necessarys as Provisions and Ammunition," they could "Easily destroy those Forts and Relieve our Brethren and Friends by permission From Your Honours for so doing."[97] A few soldiers, some supplies, and American permission to attack was all Eddy needed, or at least all he felt the state would grant.

On the day the petition was presented it was supported from Machias by a letter from Francis Shaw to the State Council. Because it bolstered one of Eddy's main arguments, its favourable timing might not have been coincidental. Shaw had heard that the Native people seemed eager to help capture Fort Cumberland. Those visiting Machias (probably Maliseets) were "very desirous of going to Cumberland," and some had offered to kidnap officers of the Royal Fencibles. "Conquest of that Fort may be easily effected by our Friends there and a few Indians," went on Shaw in a paraphrase of Eddy's petition. His opinion, he explained, was "lately received" from friends in Cumberland.[98] With Shaw's support, Eddy did all he could to convince the Americans and by the end of August had exhausted every means to bring about an American invasion of Nova Scotia. Visiting New England twice in 1776 and shuttling between Boston and Philadelphia ended in a final plea for modest help. While Eddy implied in his petition that Cumberland was ready to take strong action, the district appeared quiet to Halifax and safe enough to risk renewal of the Supreme Court circuit there.

"CULTIVATING THE TREE OF LIBERTY IN A NOW BARBAROUS SOIL"

September 1776. A schooner from Windsor moored in Cumberland Basin on 1 September after conveying her passengers to the tiny estuary of Cumberland Creek. Two judges of the Supreme Court, Justice Isaac Deschamps and newly-appointed Chief Justice Charles Morris Sr, filed ashore with all the dignity permitted by the steep mudbanks. The rebellion, which had caused their court circuit to be cancelled in the spring, was nowhere to be seen. Instead they found a village at peace, a garrison in good order, and a people "well dispos'd." It was not that the loyal party was triumphant or that rebellion was quelled; rather, the balance of petty viciousness had shifted to the loyalists and political dissenters found wisdom in silence.[99]

Patriots had been driven into the background of local society by the "accumulated vengeance" of aggrieved loyalists. Some were driven into exile. The "publick as well as private prejudices" of local officials were keenly felt. Josiah Throop found it impossible to promote republicanism, likening the task to "cultivating the Tree of Liberty in a now Barbarous soil." Other fruits cultivated in the rich Cumberland soil were procured at fair market value for Goreham's commissariat, from patriots as well as loyalists. To John Allan's despair, at least two committee members joined the bonanza and "engaged to Deliver for His Majesty's use" their farm produce.[100] Allan was isolated, a fugitive on the isthmus, discouraged by the duplicity of associates and the loss of his letter in St John Harbour. By that misfortune, he related, "I was not only frustrated in my plan for reducing the province, but at a loss what to say to the Indians," or how to keep the promise he had made in June. He delayed his visit to Cocagne, not wishing to go empty-handed. "We were also during this period attacked on every side by various false reports" intended "to keep peaceable" the residents and encourage them to comply "with the mandates of government." Allan had become "rather detrimental to the Peace of the community as several express orders had come to apprehend me." Other patriot leaders had fled and by the beginning of September John Allan also found his "situation too precarious to continue in the county."[101]

These complex undercurrents were not easily discerned and Judges Deschamps and Morris saw only the public facade of loyalty. Clothed in the robes of their office (but without education in their profession), they opened court the day after they arrived and heard the grand jury declare allegiance "openly in Court." An incident occurred that hinted at the tensions underlying the community. A delegation appeared on behalf of a settler who was under arrest on suspicion of being "friendly to the United States," and appealed for his release. According to Josiah Throop the judges professed "no power to do anything, even to order an Examination." At the end of the session Chief Justice Morris remembered only the good decorum in his court, finding "the Common people of the same Sentiment" as the grand jury, and "in that Temper of mind we left them" five days later.[102] But appearances were deceptive in Cumberland: the appearance of rebellion in January was replaced by an appearance of loyalty in September. The judges left a people who although quiet on the surface had local agents of disquiet in New England seeking American support.

The case before the Massachusetts Council appeared an easy one to deal with, several points being in its favour. No large-scale invasion was demanded, only permission to attack Fort Cumberland and a request for supplies, but no more than had already been granted to the Sunbury patriots in June. The petition also accorded with the latest intelligence from Machias. Only five days later, on 2 September, Council complied, instructing Eddy to attack Fort Cumberland and permitting him to recruit as many men as he could in the eastern part of the State. He was granted "two hundred pounds weight of Gunpowder, five hundred weight of Musket Ball, three hundred Gun flints, and twenty barrels of Pork."[103] When these were issued three days later, only ten of the twenty barrels of pork were drawn because Eddy judged that "a quantity of Bread would be much more useful." The whole was loaded onto a boat for the one-day voyage up the coast to Newburyport. There, "a small Vessel" was chartered and by the second week of September Eddy, How, and Roe were sailing north to Machias "at which Place we arrived (after Many Unfortunate Accidents) in about three weeks from the time of our setting out." Jonathan Eddy was finally on the move; he had a plan, he had American backing, and he was determined to succeed.[104]

His determination was unshakable but Eddy's plan, in so far as it relied on Native support, was showing signs of unravelling. Native assistance was presumed to be secured by treaty, yet in late July the Penobscot nation declined to go to war and now the Micmacs were drawing back. Their delegates, John Baptiste and Matua, returned to Cocagne in mid-September with a copy of the treaty and dropped this "great Packet" like a hot potato into the laps of their chiefs. The chiefs were perplexed as they had sent the two to America to acknowledge Washington's letter and to plea for aid, not to sign a treaty. "An alarm was spread among us," since their reasonable interpretation of the document was "to require us to take up the hatchet." For a nation whose councils were strongly advising neutrality as the policy best meeting national interests, the treaty was a setback; according to the chiefs, it was definitely "contrary to our desire." The chiefs were "very angry and uneasy" with John Baptiste and Matua, how could they have done this? "They were imposed on," replied the two, "and had signed things that were not read to them." Pleaded Baptiste, "I believe we did not understand one another." It was concluded that Ambroise St Aubin had coerced them into appearing "in the character of Chiefs and made a Treaty to go to War."[105]

"We never authorised those Persons to do such a thing," cried the chiefs. They were "very much displeased" and were "determined to return" the treaty. At the same time as they hoped America would take "no offence," they hastened to explain their position to Halifax. Any chance the Americans had of gaining Micmac allies was squandered by their management of the treaty negotiations. John Allan, at last in Cocagne to explain the patriot cause to the whole tribe as promised in June, found them in turmoil, and the chiefs disclaimed the treaty when he met them on 19 September. He realized at once that the case for Native allies was closed and the policy of Native neutrality entrenched. All future bargaining would be over the price of neutrality – the price to keep them from assisting Nova Scotia – and that price would probably be as high as it would have been to recruit them into the Continental Army.

The Micmacs were realists. Living on the seacoast in a settlement pattern similar to that of the non-Natives, they were accessible, vulnerable, and economically dependent. "Indigent" was the term used in Halifax and the Natives admitted it candidly: "we receive our present support from Old England." This reality shaped their national policy in this British civil war. "We don't want to Quarrel" – they could not afford to and if they did their families would feel the pressure. Recalling the ships in Cumberland in June, they would not provoke Halifax "for fear they will send their big Vessels in our Rivers and prevent us from fowling and Fishing."[106]

Although Allan criticized Baptiste and Matua and defended his New England friends "who made the treaty," he could not refute their logic and in the end was forced to denounce the treaty in front of them: "You do right to be at peace in your situation." Would they at least assist any Nova Scotia patriots who joined the United States in the war? They were non-committal: "When we see a sufficient Power in this country, we will tell you what we will do." Micmacs knew they "must submit to the strongest Power." When asked if they would "screen" any patriots fleeing for safety, they would only agree not to "hurt them." There was a tightrope to be walked in this civil war: the chiefs must neither be "destroy'd by the Old Englishmen, nor be thought Enemies by the New England Men!"

If the Micmacs were alarmed by their obligations under the treaty, they were contemptuous of American obligations. Allan could tell the New Englanders that a trading post at Machias "is no service to us, Even should we have things for nothing, the distance is so great"! Frustrated by the botched treaty and the reaction of the obdurate Micmacs, Allan could extract only ritual expressions of friendship which he knew were merely their open door to American aid. He accused the Micmacs (not to their faces) of deception, criticizing them hypocritically for using "every Art to gain their Ends" and unwittingly praising them by adding, "where they perceive an opportunity to get something, they will exert every faculty to obtain it." Micmacs were as clever, and as devious, as their non-Native neighbours, but in concluding there was "no Government among them," Allan was dead wrong.[107] Not only did they possess government – a decentralized exercise in consensus perhaps unrecognizable as such to Allan – it was fully functional and capable of steering an independent course in the midst of major conflict while at the same time manipulating protagonists in the national interest.

The chiefs used Allan to carry the treaty and their letter of denunciation to New England which he expected he would visit in the near future. On the way home he learned that Goreham had established an outpost on Shepody Point at the mouth of the Memramcook River and with "certain advice that every step will be taken to seize me," he "went out of the way" to avoid Fencible patrols.[108] During Allan's expedition to Cocagne, Samuel Rogers was forced to flee; it was impossible to carry on with the Shepody Outpost located at the terminus of the road he was building. "Being hard drove by the Enemy and much fatigued by the business, I thought proper to leave that dangerous Imployment," Rogers explained. He escaped in a canoe with a Fencible deserter, intending to go to Machias and rendezvous with Eddy and other patriots.[109] Allan could wait no longer and also escaped in a small boat at night. Like Eddy, he carried with him a plan for American invasion, but it was a long-term plan that required Native support and included himself in the pivotal role of American Indian agent. A long report on the Micmacs, written after his Cocagne visit, would form Allan's application to Congress for that job.

The denunciation of the treaty and the flights of Rogers and Allan were good news for Halifax, which received another much needed boost in September. His Majesty's frigate *Rainbow* with Commodore Sir George Collier aboard sailed from New York on an important mission to Nova Scotia. The Nova Scotia command had been shared by two people: General Massey in charge of the army and Commodore Arbuthnot in charge of the navy, the latter also being dockyard commissioner and lieutenant-governor. Burdened with three responsibilities, Arbuthnot needed relief; this was dictated at any rate by his serious error in mislaying the naval order for the security of the British reinforcement. Collier was therefore sent to relieve Arbuthnot of the duties of commodore.

HMS *Rainbow* arrived "in the middle of a fine moonlight night," accompanied by the sloop *Hope*.[110] The two ships "at 5 am, anchored in Halifax Harbour with the best bower in 13 fathom water. Veer'd half-a-Cable, Georges Island south- southeast. Unbent the sails and got the longboat out."[111] Towns-people were surprised at the sight of the forty-four gun, two-decker flying Collier's broad pennant on Saturday morning 21 September, as was Marriot Arbuthnot. With due regard for his reputation as a blustering tar, Collier first "sent one of [his] Officers to the Lieutenant-Governor" to deliver the news of the change of command. Arbuthnot was taken aback. Collier, a much younger officer, had come "to dispossess Him of the Command of the Ships, which of His three Employments was the one that he most valued." So it was with trepidation that Collier, after waiting for two hours, rowed ashore to meet Arbuthnot face to face. "It seemed rather doubtful whether the Commodore wou'd resign his Command," but it had to be done. Stepping ashore at Governors Wharf, Collier entered the town in which he expected "to remain a considerable Time." The surroundings were pleasant and he was pleased with his destination: "the Governor's House is a handsome and very convenient structure ... in the Centre of the Town, and has a pleasant view of the Harbour, Shipping, and opposite Shores." His meeting was unpleasant.[112]

"I visited the old Gentleman soon after, who received me with Civility but with apparent concern." The change of command was explained and Arbuthnot was assured that the only difference "he shou'd find was having the troublesome part of the Duty taken off his Hands." A heavy silence followed. "After appearing a short Time like a sulky ... Child, He laid down the Truncheon with as good a Grace as He cou'd." Arbuthnot was polite but his peevishness was not easily masked and, "notwithstanding these Civil professions," Collier would be convinced that "my superseding Him ever rankled in this Man's Heart, and He never forgave me for it!" Collier was also quick to size up General Massey and he saw trouble ahead. Although Massey was also polite, Collier guessed that "it was not the Nature of the Animal to be upon good Terms with anybody long and He did not seem inclin'd to except me out of his general Rule."[113]

The change in the Nova Scotia command was in place the next day, the anniversary of King George's coronation which Arbuthnot, Massey, and Collier marked with a twenty-one gun salute fired from the *Rainbow.* The trio was not a united team. The personalities of its members clashed fundamentally and co-operation in future crises was unlikely to spring from natural friendship. None the less Collier began his naval command smoothly. Captains were issued fresh orders and ships deployed around the coast and at the entrance to the Bay of Fundy. His ships had also to protect coastal traffic from privateers and for this he was fortunate in having the crack privateer hunter, Captain James Dawson. The captain's speedy, black-hulled sloop *Hope* "loos'd Sails" and slipped out of harbour on the night of 23 September with HMS *Diligent* to cruise the Eastern Shore past Marie Joseph to Canso which had been harrassed by privateers. The vital supply link with the British army in New York had to be maintained and cartels arranged for the exchange of prisoners with New England. Since the Quebec victories, captured Americans had been shipped to Halifax in large numbers and more were expected from the summer campaign. It was left to Collier to arrange exchanges through negotiations with American agents, usually out of Newburyport.[114]

Collier carried out his initial deployment during the last full week of September and the first results came in before the end of the month. Enemy shipping was captured all around the coast: at Annapolis Royal, the *Viper* (which in July had rescued the Jadis family in the same waters) brought in three prizes; on the South Shore, another ship took "several prizes"; and *Juno*'s and *Milford*'s prizes yielded over 100 prisoners. While protecting the Canso fishery on 27 September, *Hope* chased a privateer on shore in Petit de Grat Harbour. "The crew made their Escape by swimming ashore," and the next morning Captain Dawson sent "in Persute of the Rebels" a landing party which returned with thirty-four prisoners although the ship's captain, William Carleton, escaped into the woods with a few of his men. By the end of September Collier felt "settled in the command" and satisfied all around: his ships were stationed and achieving results, Halifax society had welcomed him immediately, and his London play was doing well. *Selima and Azor,* a "dramatic romance," which he had adapted for the stage, was being "favourably received" that summer on Drury Lane.[115]

October 1776. On land and sea, in Cumberland and around the coast patriots felt the pressure. Privateers adjusted to Collier's revitalized naval station while exiled patriots converged on Machias. Samuel Rogers "arrived in Machias about the first of October and in a few Days Capt. Eddy arrived." These two were pleased to be reunited after pursuing their cause separately all summer. Eddy's zeal, after visiting Philadelphia and Boston, was evident to Rogers, as was his determination to capture Fort Cumberland and join the province with the United States.[116]

Recruitment of an invasion force took longer than expected because the patriot leadership at Machias was in disarray in October. The Committee-of-Safety was "much dispersed": two members were prisoners of the British, another was away on business. "Indeed, we are all in a poor broken situation," confirmed James Lyon, another member, who was on hand and lent Eddy all the support he could. Lyon resembled Eddy in his rash, direct manner. The fact that he was a Presbyterian minister in no way conflicted with his political activity. Rebellion had compelled Lyon "to step aside from the peaceful and salutary paths in which my profession leads me." Like Eddy, he considered "the reduction of Nova Scotia to be a matter of great importance." Having once lived there, he "knew the country well," claiming acquaintance "with almost all the principal men." In his opinion, "that Province is invaluable" and he was anxious "to bestow upon them the same glorious privileges which we enjoy." Only a month ago Lyon himself pleaded with Boston "for a small army to subdue Nova Scotia," but was refused. Now he was delighted with Eddy's success.[117] "I highly approve of the noble spirit and resolution of Capt. Eddy, and heartily wish him success and all the honour of reducing Nova Scotia!"

"I believe men enough might be found in this country"[118] to attack Nova Scotia, said Lyon in support of Eddy's recruiting drive at Machias. Francis Shaw was also active in the search for volunteers and the call went up and down the Machias River and through the district. The right to plunder was a common condition of recruitment, one that Eddy readily complied with since he had no means of offering regular pay. And the volunteers appeared: from Chandlers River came John Mitchell, from Mount Desert Richard Parsons, and there were others. Under Shaw's influence Eddy "obtained Capt. [Jabez] West and several other good Men, to the amount of about Twenty, to join me in the Expedition against Fort Cumberland." As an invasion force it was woefully small but if Eddy thought it insufficient, or that the "small number" asked for at Boston was more than the "about Twenty" actually obtained at Machias, he never complained nor wavered. The deficiency was noticeable to Samuel Rogers who "thought his Force inadequate to the Undertaking," although he saw that Eddy was "determin'd on the enterprise." Neither did the remnants of the Machias Committee-of-Safety (Lyon excepted) "altogether approve of Captain Eddy's going there [Nova Scotia] in so loose a manner and with so small a party."[119]

Any shortfall in the invasion force would be made up by recruitment in Nova Scotia. Lyon agreed that Eddy would be "relying much upon the readiness of the inhabitants of Nova Scotia to favour his bold enterprise," just as his own plan relied on indigenous support, but he had asked for blank officers' commissions to use in recruiting a regiment on continental army pay.[120] Eddy had neither asked for nor received blank commissions and without that incentive he would have to rely on the potential for local rebellion and his own power of persuasion to attract Nova Scotian recruits. One advantage of the small invasion force was that everyone fit easily into Captain Elijah Ayer's schooner that was engaged to carry the men as far as the St John River. Ayer, a resident of Sackville, was a member of the patriot committee there but carried on a coastal trade with both sides. On Sunday morning 13 October Zebulon Roe, William How, Jonathan Eddy, and the twenty "good men" of Machias boarded Ayer's schooner at the falls in Machias River. Samuel Rogers joined the force despite misgivings and "tho' not recovered of the Fatigue of my summer's work." Sails were hoisted and with James

Lyon's blessing – he believed it was divine will that Eddy succeed – the vessel slipped downriver to the ocean and Captain Ayer steered for Passamaquoddy Bay and Nova Scotia.[121]

"HE WAS BOUND FOR CUMBERLAND TO REDUCE THAT FORT"

That same morning a small boat embarked from Campobello Island and set a southerly course for Machias. In it were John Allan and a few others who had escaped from Cumberland more than a week earlier and were about to go into exile in the United States. Allan stayed at Robert Wilson's place on Campobello where he learned from Ross Curry that Eddy was in Machias. At "about sunset," after sailing most of the day, "we saw a schooner and a boat" and recognizing William How in the boat, a reunion of Cumberland patriots followed. When Allan learned that Eddy and his men were "on their way to Cumberland," he tried to convince Eddy of the folly of the expedition. The young Scottish revolutionary had often clashed with the veteran British officer but in the gathering darkness, as the tiny invasion force entered Nova Scotian waters, Allan found Eddy in a sanguine mood; moreover, he seemed to have convinced those with him of the feasibility of the expedition. "I acquainted them with the impropriety of their proceeding," Allan recorded, but he had no more recent intelligence on the strength of the fort than Eddy had obtained from Rogers, and he made no headway with that argument. Eddy was reminded of how important Native involvement was, and that the Micmacs had refused to go to war. This was news to Eddy, but Allan had the letter of denunciation as proof. No matter, that still left the Maliseets. Eddy could point to New England newspaper reports that the Maliseets were ready for war. Furthermore, his firsthand knowledge of this tribe was probably more current than Allan's as he had spent the last few days with Francis Shaw who had recently returned from Aukpaque. Reluctant to concede defeat, Allan "took every step and used every argument to dissuade them but all to no effect." No understanding was reached and no reconciliation; all that was agreed was that Elijah Ayer would hold his schooner at Campobello until Allan could write to Eddy from Machias. Allen returned to his boat and his own party, taking with him Nathan Longfellow, a Machias recruit, who would return with the letter.

John Allan sailed on to Machias, arriving there the next morning, 14 October, and met promptly with Francis Shaw and others to discuss "the movements of Eddy." Although they had apparently supported Eddy only a few days before – it had been through Shaw that Eddy obtained the Machias recruits – they now appeared to oppose the expedition. In a complete change of heart Shaw advised Allan to write to Eddy and ask him "to desist." The most likely reason for Shaw's about face was Allan's proof that the Micmacs had renounced the treaty. Later the same day Longfellow began the return journey to Passamaquoddy with letter in hand. Allan did not accompany him. Unlike Samuel Rogers, who joined the expedition despite misgivings, Allan had no intention of following Eddy either to help in the attack or even to protect his own family. The two men could no longer abide each other and Allan was anxious to go on to Boston to seek the job of American Native agent.[122]

Despite Allan's note, the patriots pausing at Campobello remained determined to strike a blow against Nova Scotia. Enthusiasm ran so high that "a few more" men (about nine) were recruited on the island to form a small Passamaquoddy contingent. These were the first Nova Scotians to join the force and they included Robert Wilson who had been Allan's Campobello host. Without further delay Ayer's schooner set sail for the St John valley.[123] Armed schooners patrolled Nova Scotian waters as a part of Commodore Collier's naval defence but Elijah Ayer navigated unnoticed among the islands and into the Bay of Fundy.

The intricate coastline of the province precluded a blanket naval defence, made it difficult to protect coastal communities by naval means alone, and enabled Elijah Ayer and others on both sides to engage in illicit trade. Collier's fresh approach however was bringing results. His strategy was to localize naval defence in much the same way as had been done in land defence. Naval vessels carried troops drawn from the three provincial corps who had been released by Massey for that service. A coast guard was also created: chartered schooners carrying militia forces cruised discrete sections of coastline such as Minas Basin. Other armed vessels small enough to pursue American privateers "into Shoal Water and Creeks" (where warships could not go) were outfitted "to protect the Navigation on this Coast and to prevent any Outrages being Committed on Shore." This effort was combined with an order to send small land detachments of thirty to fifty soldiers to "unhappily situated" communities such as Liverpool and Barrington. Collier, who seemed naturally inclined to offence, felt secure enough in October to take the war to the Americans by sending one of his regular ships to New England to cruise north of Cape Cod and attack commercial shipping. The inshore integration of land and sea forces and the combined defence tactics were innovative, particularly in view of the ruling triumvirate in which affairs between Arbuthnot and Collier were correct but not cordial, and those between Massey and Collier – the army and navy – were actually breaking down.[124]

The ship Collier stationed at the entrance to the Bay of Fundy was to watch for and give warning of a concerted American invasion, something that Ayer's little schooner with thirty men on board categorically was not. Ayer slipped easily through the loose cordon, made Partridge Island without incident, and glided into the safety of St John Harbour. As the schooner passed up the harbour the ruins of Fort Frederick came into view on the port side. Perhaps a cheer went up for "the O'Brien Gang" of Machias for burning it down in a raid the previous year. Inspiration for the task ahead might have been gained from the sight of its charred timbers. No more time was spent at the mouth of the river than was necessary for equalizing the tides in Reversing Falls, nor in Portland Point which bore the most loyal stamp of any community on the river. Eddy proceeded directly to the friendly environs of Maugerville, sixty miles upriver: this posed no challenge for Ayer's little schooner.

The Sunbury patriots were still in control in Maugerville when the visitors were welcomed by Chair Barker and Clerk Perley. Civil authority was backed by a revolutionary militia with an arsenal of American arms and ammunition. Impressed, Eddy supposed the inhabitants "almost universally to be hearty in the Cause." Appearances can be deceptive and matters were not progressing as well as Barker and Perley would have liked. The patriots felt neglected by Boston, having "Received no Direct answer" to the petition they sent in May. They had endeavoured in the meantime "to Regulate our Conduct" along republican lines "as far as we have been able to get Information but our Remote Situation Renders it Difficult."[125]

Another petition was drafted in September and given to Francis Shaw to take to Boston on his way home from a visit to the Maliseets. Barker and the Committee-of-Safety pleaded in this second petition "that if the Inhabitants of the River St Johns are Esteemed as a Part of the free States of America your Honours would be pleased to Signify it to them." They professed to be "ready at all times to Pursue Every measure (in their Power) that you shall propose."[126] No reply of any kind had been received. The remoteness of Sunbury may have been an obstacle to communication with Boston, but it also protected them from speedy retaliation from Halifax. This factor more than any other gave the Sunbury patriots the appearance of being stronger than their counterparts in Cumberland. Despite a clear field of action all summer the committee marked time and failed to attract majority support at the political level or to prepare for independent action. The local leadership was deficient, lacking the broad political comprehension of John Allan and the single-minded drive of Jonathan Eddy. Religious leadership – Sunbury's advantage over Cumberland which had no dissenting minister – seemed also to have failed with Seth Noble (although an avowed patriot) unable to be the political evangelist that James Lyon was in Machias. The Sunbury committee had not advanced

much beyond the state Eddy had found it in during his visit at the end
of May.

Sunbury patriots were content to store their American arms in a safe
cache, to drill their militia occasionally, and to lie comfortably by in an
attitude of defence. It took the fiery Jonathan Eddy to jar them from
their lethargy and turn them to the offensive. It was time to seize the
opportunity and strike a blow for the republican cause. Eddy urged
them to take their New England supplies out of storage, combine them
with his, and go with him to Cumberland. He had American approval
to attack the fort and they had promised to pursue "every measure"
the Americans proposed. Unable to resist his forceful call to arms, they
appointed a committee "for forming the Cumberland party" and ordered Hugh Quinton and Daniel Jewett to muster their militia. Volunteers began to trickle in. Edmund Price and Benjamin Bubar of
Gagetown joined "the Cumberland party," as did Elijah Estabrooks of
Conway. From across the river in Burton came Edward Burpee, "an active rebel." Five-year-old Mary Coye, whose father was "a rebel committee man," watched as her elder brother Amasa took up his gun and left
for Maugerville. William McKeen Jr of Amesbury "joined the rebels"
and John Whitney left his large family "to attack the Fort at Cumberland." Twenty-seven men volunteered to form the St John River contingent. Eddy's call was not a resounding success, but he still had two
other communities from which to seek recruits in the ethnically diverse valley. He proceeded upriver next to Aukpaque, centre of the
Maliseet nation.[127]

The Penobscots and Micmacs had refused to go to war, but the
St John River patriots expected considerable Maliseet involvement.
For New Englanders, they were a legendary nation whose exploits in
war were vivid in living memory. Less than a generation separated the
Maliseet from the warpath – from the last time they returned to their
ancient capital of Meductic with New England prisoners-of-war.[128] Already in 1776 they had pillaged loyalists on the St John River and New
Englanders were fascinated by recent news reports of political upheaval at Aukpaque, of an inclination to join the Americans, and of
Ambroise St Aubin winning out over Grand Chief Pierre Tomah. They
also read "that an Indian (of the St Johns Tribe) was executed for
damning his Excellency General Washington."[129] If one eastern Native
nation could be persuaded to attack the Nova Scotians, New England
would choose the Maliseets and Eddy was optimistic as he approached
Aukpaque (seven miles north of present-day Fredericton) in mid-October.

Eddy's hope of recruiting the Maliseet army was dashed, but he did
not leave Aukpaque empty-handed. Contrary to newspaper reports

Chief Tomah, who favoured the British, had prevailed in tribal councils and a policy of neutrality was adopted. "Half-Boston, half-English and would not take up the hatchet," was how Tomah would enunciate this policy.[130] But a novel approach to neutrality had resulted from there being both strong pro-British and pro-American factions on council. It was a policy of active neutrality that was broad enough to permit a variety of tactics to the point of occasional violence if properly circumscribed and sufficiently remunerative. If Eddy agreed to compensation equal to that provided traditionally by the French and if only a token contingent was supplied from the pro-American faction, Maliseet involvement in the Cumberland adventure might not be inconsistent with national policy. Ambroise St Aubin was all for it, Eddy argued strongly for his cause through his interpreter, and Native policy could encompass it.

Compensation was a problem. Under the treaty Native soldiers were eligible for Continental Army pay, a point Francis Shaw had reaffirmed when he visited Aukpaque in September. Eddy had no funds and no blank officers' commissions and the Maliseets would not put one foot on the warpath without compensation for themselves and their families. So he made them the same offer that he made the Machias contingent: a share of the plunder which he projected as having great potential. It had been argued that an invasion of Cumberland could be financed totally with plunder. Although attractive to the Maliseets (who had done some plundering of their own that spring) the breakthrough came when the Sunbury Committee-of-Safety agreed to supply provisions to Native wives "while their husbands was absent." This was a big undertaking that would vary depending on the number of soldiers involved and time of service.[131] Finally a deal was struck with Ambroise St Aubin and fifteen armed warriors: "Cap't Eddy persuaded them to go with him."[132] It was a small contingent and while it would not have been released without Chief Tomah's consent, he was too clever to include himself in the venture. For Tomah the agreement meant that the needs of a large number of dependents would now be fully looked after by Maugerville.[133]

Eddy also hoped to recruit the Acadians of Sunbury. The French-speaking settlers of the St John River were scattered in the upper valley from St Ann's Point (Fredericton) to Meductic, with clusters of homes at Lower French Settlement (Kingsclear) and Upper French Settlement (Mazzerole Settlement). Besides Acadians there were French Canadian families from Quebec. These settlers were closely associated in their daily lives with the Maliseet nation in whose territory they lived and Aukpaque was a convenient buffer between them and the New England settlements of the lower valley. In July Ambroise St Aubin declared to Bostonians that these settlers "are all for you." Nothing was further from the truth.[134] Not a single French-speaking settler of the St John Valley

joined Eddy and the reasons are evident. These settlers were more isolated than the Acadians of Cumberland and therefore not as subject to
patriot influence. Their frequent communication with Quebec contributed to their loyalty; at least their direct knowledge of American defeats
in Quebec would have left them cool to Eddy's proposal. They lacked
clear title to their land and were vulnerable to pressures from both sides,
but at least they were not tenants like the Acadian farmers on John Allan's estate. Known locally as "an inoffensive people," they were unlikely
recruits and it is not surprising that they refused Eddy's offer.

Eddy came back downriver to Maugerville to collect his forces for the
push to Cumberland. With forty-three recruits in the valley he now had
a total of seventy-two soldiers. During the brief spell of mild weather
known locally as Indian Summer, Eddy was ready to proceed when Captain Elijah Ayer left the valley with his schooner on other business, leaving the patriots stranded. Three whaleboats were pressed into service
and the Maliseets used at least five of their own canoes. Small sails were
mounted on the whaleboats and the canoes could be towed when necessary. This modest armada departed Maugerville near the end of the
last full week of October.[135] In Jemseg, once the leaves have fallen,
Grand Lake can be glimpsed through the bare trees which from a line
where the valley widens dramatically. Here the boats and canoes slipped
by on the gentle tide of the lower river and passed the long delta to the
coast. Like the reprieve of Indian Summer, the sail down the St John
River was a pleasant but brief interlude; like harsh winter the hazardous
part of the voyage lay just ahead in the ceaseless plunge and roll of the
mighty Bay of Fundy.

In the frail craft of the tiny flotilla rested the full hopes of Nova
Scotian patriots, the totality of American support, and the men and material of the entire invasion force. Success would depend on the coinci-
dence of a fort weak to the point of dereliction and a community with
enough republican zeal to multiply Eddy's force several times over.
Both factors were in play that October. Instead of trained soldiers behind strong defences, ragtag fencibles deserted a military ruins. Instead
of a loyal community with an active militia, a passive populace awaited
events. The government was relaxed, believing the season of invasion
was past, and the country-side was quiet. The expedition was ambitious
but not impossible and not unprecedented, nor was it inconsequential
considering the strategic importance of Nova Scotia and that the initial
objective was the key to the province. The year before, Ethan Allen of
New Hampshire captured Fort Ticonderoga, the gateway to Canada,
with a force of the same size and irregularity as Eddy's. Allen had used
boldness and determination to achieve success, the same qualities now
displayed by Jonathan Eddy of Cumberland.

The calm of the river was left behind suddenly as Eddy and his men rounded the headland to be caught in the draw of the world's highest tides and hit by icy gales rushing the full length of the Bay of Fundy. For the next two days they followed the north coast in their small boats. Seldom have men of such diversity been crowded so uncomfortably into such dangerous space: young men and veterans, fathers of large families and bachelors without responsibility, weak men and strong, fugatives and pillars of the church, republican zealots and apolitical adventurers. Opposing qualities sometimes appeared in the same person. Nothing was shared in common except the courage to sit rigidly all day astride the rolling Fundy swell, enduring the constant lift and dip of the horizon with nothing but the thickness of a board separating them from the dark, freezing waters (or worse, a layer of birch bark) and nothing to ward off the chill of wind and spray. Presiding over the tightly packed band was Jonathan Eddy, his grim determination evident to Samuel Rogers crouched in the same whaleboat: "He was bound for Cumberland to reduce that Fort and endeavour to bring about a Union of that Country with the United States"![136] If all went well they would make Shepody Point by Tuesday, 29 October.

3 The Shepody Outpost
Tuesday 29 October to Monday
4 November

Heard that Cap't. Walker with some men had been taken lately by the
Rebells from Shepodie.

Sampson Moore, Cobequid resident[1]

There is nothing so lonely as serving at the outpost of a frontier fort,
but occasionally disparate forces combine to create a busy crossroad
even beyond the verge. Fifteen miles past the already remote village of
Sackville, the Shepody Outpost of Fort Cumberland stood at the border
of a vast wilderness northwest of the Nova Scotia peninsula. Wolves,
bears, and panthers prowled the region causing residents to lament to
"see our cattle exposed to the ravages of Wild Beasts."[2] The tiny post
had been there only since September but already had proved its worth
to Joseph Goreham.[3] It was only "an Out party" of fourteen Fencibles
and a lieutenant but "tho' small" he believed it was "of the greatest Service at this juncture in putting an entire stop to Desertion and preventing any intercourse with this Country thro' their Rivers by the Machias
people."[4] Hard labour and the enticement of patriots caused frequent
desertions during the first months in Cumberland.[5] Now the Shepody
Outpost barred the way of deserters fleeing the isthmus and had
curbed the activities of at least two leading patriots: politician John Allan and road builder Samuel Rogers.

Lieutenant John Walker, who was in charge of the outpost, was one
of Goreham's long time friends. They were together at the second
siege of Louisbourg in 1758 and in other battles. In 1775 Walker had
for over a decade been retired and living on a half-pay pension on his
farm at Worcester, Massachusetts. So much had happened since then
to test his loyalty to King George. He was stopped by patriots that
spring while trying to reach Boston to join the British. On refusing an
officer's commission in the patriot army, he was sent back home where

his house "was broken open by a mob and robbed." Leaving his wife, Christian, at Worcester, he fled again towards Boston, finally arriving there via Rhode Island. For veterans like Walker, loyalty to the king was often indivisible from loyalty to one's old commanding officer. Thus on reaching Boston it was natural for him to seek out Colonel Goreham who was raising the Royal Fencible Americans and it followed that he should enlist in that new provincial corps. And so it was that Walker "proceeded to the Province of Nova Scotia" with the regiment and "after having performed several services for the Garrison" in Cumberland, he found himself in charge of the Shepody Outpost, far from his home in Worcester and far from his wife, to whom the patriots left only a corner of the farm and their pew in the meeting house.[6]

Walker had been in Cumberland nearly twenty years before when, as a ranger in the French War, he joined in at least one raid on an Acadian village.[7] Considering his exploits then, he may have been bored but probably not unhappy with life in the same region in 1776. Camped in tents and a small hut overlooking Shepody Bay, he and the fourteen soldiers of his command lived in splendid isolation on a point of land between the mouths of two rivers: the Petitcodiac on the west and the Memramcook on the east. Their tour of duty, which by the end of October had stretched to several weeks, resembled a leisurely camping expedition more than a military patrol. Compared to Fort Cumberland, life at Shepody proceeded at a greatly reduced rate. They cut firewood, patrolled the footpath that meandered into the wilderness in the direction of the St John River, kept in touch with local residents, and watched the bay for boats. Life could not be easier. They enjoyed the crisp autumn air, record high tides, and clear nights under a harvest moon, and were pleased enough to be away from the garrison with no superior officers and no extra duty patching up a hopelessly run-down fort. Food was plentiful and regularly supplied; another shipment was expected in a few days.

The valleys of both rivers bordering the outpost were settled and other settlers lived on the shores of the bay and in hamlets near Shepody Hill. These were the people of the outer townships: Hopewell, Moncton, and Hillsborough. They were passably loyal; a few of their young men had joined the Fencibles. They were good neighbours, as were the Acadians of Memramcook. Yorkshire settlers and several New Englanders of the district had expressed "our Attachment to His Majesty," their alarm at recent events, and an awareness of their vulnerability. "Separated as we are from the most settled part of this Country," they were in a "deplorable situation" that caused "distress." In the struggle to survive in a remote area in wartime, "Wild Beasts" were but one fear of settlers who were as "likely to become a prey to famine or the

pillage of any Enemy."[8] Their great fear was that American revolution-
aries would incite the Micmacs to attack them. To the north at Cocagne
and Miramichi lived the mainland Micmacs who appeared more warlike than their peninsular cousins. The Maliseets to the west, a nation
inhabiting the upper valley of the St John River, seemed more hostile
still. Via Grand Lake, the extensive watershed of this river nearly
reached the headwaters of the Petitcodiac, affording an age-old route
directly to Shepody. Stories of Maliseet raids on Cumberland ten and
twenty years ago were remembered by residents of the district. "Unfriendly Proceedings this spring at the River St John's" by the Maliseets
restored those memories to daily conversation and so alarmed the settlers that a few, such as Moses Delesdernier, moved "under the protection of Fort Cumberland."[9] But most, including Charles Baker of
Hillsborough, decided to "stand [their] Ground."[10] So far the district
had been quiet and the rumours of an American invasion seemed false.
There had been very little work for the Fencibles. The Shepody Outpost was a backwater; John Walker and his men could afford to relax.

"PROCEEDED TO SHEPODY HILL IN THE NIGHT TIME"

Tuesday, *29 October*, was a typical autumn day of variable weather in Nova
Scotia: moderate and fair in the morning, cloudy by mid-day, winds picking up from the north-west with squalls criss-crossing the Bay of Fundy in
the afternoon. HMS *Juno*, a thirty-two gun frigate with the loaded provision sloop *Polly* in tow was making a wide sweep around the southern tip
of the province before entering the Bay of Fundy, so wide that at two
o'clock the lookout "saw Mount Desert [Maine] from the masthead" fifteen leagues to the north-west. Not until late afternoon was Grand
Manan spotted and it was later still when Captain Hugh Dalrymple set a
northerly course up the Bay with Long Island off Digby Neck visible to
starboard. Considering the damage suffered by the sails and rigging already on this voyage and staring into the squalls ahead, Dalrymple may
have been thinking of the uncertainty of navigation in the Bay of Fundy
at this time of year and of the previous warship in these waters which
had turned back in the face of foul weather and abandoned the delivery
of winter supplies to Fort Cumberland.[11]

Cumberland depended on Halifax for supplies not available locally,
but lines were tenuous and naval visits infrequent. A vessel under naval
escort should already have delivered the vital winter supply of heavy
clothing and food items. For the past two months sentries scanned the
Minas Basin in vain, and it was supposed the fort was forgotten by Halifax, which appears to have been the case. General Massey failed to or-

ganize a timely supply of the frontier forts at Windsor, Annapolis Royal, and, most critically, Cumberland. As Commodore Collier explained, those outposts were such a long distance from headquarters, "and not possible in the Winter to supply them with Provisions by land, it was therefore always usual to compleat them in July or at latest in August."[12] When he came to his senses, Massey applied to Collier "for a Man of War to convoy a Vessel loaden with Provisions for Fort Cumberland (which by some strange Neglect had scarce any remaining)!"[13] Collier blamed "Massey's Neglect and forgetfulness," but although "it was a bad and dangerous Service at that advanced Time of Year from the intense Cold Weather, continual Storms, And Tides so rapid," he agreed to send a ship to Cumberland. However, "She was blown back and Massey was raving at the distress his Neglect had reduced the outpost to!" The General was beside himself: "he swore, He curs'd and behav'd like a Frantick Mad Man, blaming the Captain of the Man-of-War for not arriving at the Port!" A clash between the heads of the army and navy was avoided only because of the urgency of the situation. "I took care, however, his neglect shou'd be remedied and his Garrison supply'd," disclosed Collier, who smoothed over the "personal rudeness" of Massey to his captain.[14] On the 19 October, Collier ordered another ship, the *Juno* frigate, to sea with a provision sloop.

Already in the Bay of Fundy on Tuesday afternoon of 29 October, well up near the head of the Bay, was the birch bark armada of Jonathan Eddy. Each canoe and whaleboat had unfurled a sail so as to be driven on the squally weather towards Shepody Bay.[15] Standing in the lead whaleboat, Jabez West navigated through the choppy waters ahead. Having followed the shore for several days – past Quaco Head, Cape Enrage, and Hopewell Rocks – and camping on the isolated gravelly beaches of that rugged coastline, the patriots steered their boats around Grindstone Island and landed on the Hopewell shore early Tuesday evening. The sun had already dropped behind Shepody Hill and darkness was gathering on that cold October evening when the canoes and whaleboats hit the muddy shore. Eddy had returned to Cumberland County after months of exile but the occasion went unheralded. No fanfare awaited him. No delegation of grateful Nova Scotians greeted the liberator as he waded ashore. Winds had dropped to a moderate breeze and the sky cleared as the seventy-two invaders scrambled up the banks in the dark. Candlelight flickered from a single farmhouse where Ruth and Abiel Peck lived with their eleven children. It would be hard to imagine a less auspicious landing place than the one chosen by the patriots.[16]

Yet it was not a chance landing at Shepody; the Pecks were known to Eddy, How, and Rogers. The political sympathies of this planter family were ambiguous. In the spring they had claimed to be "dutiful and loyal subjects" while stressing their vulnerability. Perhaps they concluded that the government could not protect them at Shepody.[17] Probably they were surprised tonight by the sudden appearance of so many armed men. The mud flats were crawling with strangers as groups of patriots appeared and reappeared in front of their home. In the darkness and general confusion it was difficult to estimate numbers and easy to imagine one saw more men than there really were. Ruth Peck thought she saw at least 150 men coming and going on the beach. The appearance of armed Maliseets might have alarmed her at first; eventually though, familiar faces appeared at the door: "Rogers, Eddy, and How had the direction and command of the party." Their purpose was soon revealed. They wanted information about the Shepody Outpost five miles further up the coast, and also about Fort Cumberland. And they wanted Abiel to be their guide. However reluctant he might have been to leave his family and assist Eddy, he had no choice and the patriots were leaving immediately. Ruth Peck gathered her children about her as Abiel went down to the boats. She overheard Eddy's plan for attacking Shepody Outpost and watched as the patriots "proceeded with her Husband in Boats up the River Petitcodiac and Memramcook, designed for River Cocken [Cocagne] to collect Indians." She also heard that "others were sent to take possession of the Pass to Partridge Island."[18] But the main party – "a competent number of them" – set off in canoes, crossed Shepody Bay, and followed the opposite shore in the direction of Shepody Point.[19] In the darkness they passed the point of land on the port side where the outpost was located. The glow of its campfire could be seen through the trees that grew down to the shore. When they reached the Memramcook they "went over the River,"[20] beached their canoes above the post, and quietly entered the woods to surround the camp.

Another fresh autumn evening was being enjoyed around the campfire by Johnny Walker and his soldiers. This bucolic backwater bred lethargy and blunted reflexes and these Fencibles, including the lone sentry, were in an advanced state of relaxation. Undetected, the patriots fanned out through the bush under bright moonlight. Except for the Maliseets, Eddy's force was unskilled in the standard military manoeuvre of encircling an enemy. Ineptitude eventually made contact with inattention on that lonely tree-covered point of land.

The outpost was indefensible but Walker was a "brave officer" and willing to resist overwhelming odds.[21] A sudden alarm, abrupt orders, a dash for cover, and a hale of musketry ruined the quiet October evening. In the sharp exchange, Fencible Solomon King was struck by a musket ball and fell to the ground dead. Only when Walker himself was wounded was the position conceded.[22] The acrid smell of gunsmoke had already dissipated on the crisp air when the surrender was completed. Fourteen prisoners – an officer and thirteen privates[23] – were in patriot hands and the action had been "without loss" to the patriots.[24] The invasion of Nova Scotia had begun with triumph and Eddy now expected a warm welcome from his countrypeople. On the following day he would move decisively to expand his force and secure the countryside.

"WE SHALL WORSHIP ... JESUS CHRIST AND GENERAL WASHINGTON"

The patriot army awoke under clear skies on Wednesday morning, *30 October*, excited by the previous night's victory. Eddy wished to deploy his men and recruit the extra troops needed to attack Fort Cumberland. In planning an Ethan Allen style of attack, surprise was the key element. Allen had actually caught the commander of Fort Ticonderoga asleep. Only after capturing the fort had Allen and his Green Mountain Boys gone on to subdue Crown Point. By first subduing Shepody – his Crown Point – Eddy imposed a deadline on himself with respect to the element of surprise. News of the event could not be kept from the garrison for long. Speedy action was crucial. "Dividing themselves into three divisions"[25] the patriots moved out, leaving only a prisoners' guard at Shepody. One party went to Maccan on the far side of the Tantramar to block communication to Windsor and to spy out the fort. This action indicates Eddy's resolve to follow up his success at Shepody with an early attempt to surprise the fort, but not until he had more troops. The second party, including Maliseet emissaries and Abiel Peck, started north towards Cocagne to recruit Micmacs. Leading the main detachment, Eddy "proceeded to Memramcook" to hold "a Conference with the French." The Acadians listened attentively to his long harangue that afternoon but "they saw the Weakness of our Party," admitted Eddy who realized he would need more time to convince them to join his force.[26] The Acadians of Bloody Bridge were enthusiastic patriots and Eddy had high hopes for strong support from the entire Acadian community. The conference would have to continue tomorrow.

Wednesday's conference left Eddy uncertain about the Acadians and he had no reason to expect success with the Micmacs. He was apprised of their renunciation of the American treaty but public opinion in New England, where Eddy spent the past summer, was that the eastern Native peoples were all for America. Like many others, Eddy held high expectations for a nation that declared: "All that we shall worship or obey is Jesus Christ and General Washington"![27] Despite the treaty he hoped to augment his Native contingent. It would take several days, however, for his delegation to return from Cocagne to Cumberland with a Micmac war party.

The "party of Rebells and Indians" on guard duty at Shepody spent the night in the vacant home of Moses Delesdernier who described how they "made use of and destroyed the ... Remainder of my Stock and other property to a considerable Amount."[28] Their fourteen prisoners would be shipped to New England in a few days to be exchanged for patriots held by the British or recruited into the Continental Army since many of them, indifferent to politics, would as soon fight on one side as the other. An exception of course was John Walker as Eddy well knew. "Take particular care of cap't Walker," he warned, who "wou'd be very glad of an opportunity of Joining the Regulars again."[29] But on this Wednesday night there was no need to worry. The old officer was in considerable pain as he bunked down for the night, "labouring under the wound he received when taken prisoner."[30]

As the wounded Walker tried to sleep, Fort Cumberland's winter supply was near at hand. Having had excellent sailing all Wednesday in favourable winds, and having cracked open in passage cask number 926 filled with 320 pieces of salt pork (two pieces short) for the 220 sailors as the vessel passed Cape Enrage in Chignecto Channel, Captain Dalrymple tacked *Juno* into Cumberland Basin after dark. At eleven o'clock he cut *Polly* loose to make its own way up to the fort the following morning. The weather was already deteriorating with clouds sweeping in from the southwest, so Dalrymple dropped the best bower eleven fathoms to the muddy bottom. *Juno* rode at single anchor, veering first a half cable, then a whole cable an hour later.[31]

When daylight emerged through the cloud and rain on Thursday morning, *31 October*, the garrison was gratified to see two ships: *Juno* and *Polly*, exclaimed Goreham, "appeared off the mouth of the Harbour ... and anchored."[32] While the frigate lay well down Cumberland Basin, the other vessel – "no more than a small unarmed Sloop hir'd to transport Provisions, and Navigated with three Men" – made its way to Cumberland Creek.[33] *Polly* entered the flooded estuary of this tiny creek where at low tide it would rest unceremoniously on the mud and "began unloading as soon as possible." This task would take several days so Goreham arranged with the captain to put on "a night Guard ... for her protection," but as he climbed back up rain-soaked garrison hill he must have lamented that Halifax failed to send his Fencibles any uniforms.[34] Attention was naturally focused on the supply sloop; Goreham was ignorant of the vital importance of the frigate, appearing as it did only two days after Eddy's invasion. Its yard and top gallant mast were lowered and the topmast rigging was removed for repairs that would take the crew all Thursday to finish.[35] In the meantime, Captain Dalrymple shifted anchorage to the head of the basin where *Juno*'s presence ensured the fort's safety, for no matter how successful was Eddy's recruiting drive, he would never dare to attack with thirty-two guns ranged just off-shore.

The Acadians reconvened in Memramcook on Thursday to hear Eddy resume his call to arms. After another long session and while claiming his listeners "Readily joined us," he recruited about two dozen soldiers, but only after promising to establish an Acadian contingent payable as Massachusetts militia.[36] The result was not outstanding. Although the recruits were considered reliable, they hardly represented a majority of the Acadian community and their support was purchased with a commitment Eddy was not authorized to make. While in Memramcook disturbing news was delivered by one of the reconnoitring party. "As they were lying in ambush near the fort," the party member explained, "they discovered a frigate and a sloop, both of which went up as far as the fort."[37] They had identified *Juno* and *Polly* and Eddy was quick to realize that his plan for taking the fort might be ruined. No matter how firm his resolve to surprise Goreham, nothing could be done with a warship in the Cumberland Basin. All he could do was hope that *Juno* sailed quickly and in the meantime redouble efforts to conceal his presence. Strong measures were issued to confine the inhabitants to their homes and secure the countryside. With the Acadian conference over and the new problem heavy on his mind, Eddy embarked in the rain on the next stage of his recruiting drive which was to march his detachment "12 Miles through the woods to Sackville,"[38] there to consult Committee-of-Safety members and enlist soldiers among the planters. Recruitment was still the priority, but of equal concern was the need to maintain a veil of silence around the garrison.

How was it that patriots were able to seal the isthmus so quickly and thoroughly and what was the reaction of loyalists to this feat? "It was a great grief to us," they declared, but they explained why they could not rally to the garrison or even get a message to Goreham. "The sudden appearance of the Enemy" was the reason they had been cut off so easily. "Our situation in the Country so scattered, occupying a space of Fifty miles, intersected by rivers and Disaffected neighbours," enabled the patriots "to disarm us ... and to cut off our communication with his Majesty's Garrison."[39] William Black Jr, whose family was one of those cut off, concurred they "disarmed all who were friends of the Government."[40] To secure the region and avoid counter-attack, Eddy prevented loyalists from assembling by issuing strong threats. "We were forbid on pain of Death to stir from our several Habitations," and by this means "We were deprived of assisting, consulting, or even condoling with each other."[41]

Disarmed, confined to their homes, and isolated from neighbours, loyal Cumberlanders were unable to organize a resistance. They could only "lament [their] Condition and with silent patience and Christian Fortitude, to submit to every insult, and Act of Lawless power and Depredation they [the patriots] thought proper to exercise."[42] They were under a reign of terror: "Now here was a time," thought the pious Methodist William Black Jr when referring to this period, "that called for repentance and preparation for death!"[43] The intimidation was evidently real but the fact that not one resident succeeded in warning Goreham during the first days of the invasion was due as much to the ambivalent attitude towards the garrison as to Eddy's terrorism. Although the secret of Eddy's presence could not be kept for long, Goreham was still in the dark on Thursday, two days after the Shepody landing.

"DEPENDING UPON HIS AUTHORITY FROM THE STATES"

On Friday, *1 November*, Eddy convened a meeting in Sackville to confirm support for his expedition. A select group attended, Eddy having "sent for some of the Inhabitants,"[44] these being "The Friends to Liberty in the County."[45] He launched his speech with revolutionary rhetoric which, being imported, sounded stilted and strangely out of place. His hearers were complimented for avowing their sentiments openly "during this unnatural and cruel War," for having "Declared the Zeal and attachment for the Cause of America."[46] Before going very far, Eddy established his credibility and purpose, "acquainting them that he had come by an authority from Massachusetts State in order to Assist them in throwing off the Yoke of Britain and unite them with the new States." Resistance was encountered from the outset, the weakness of Eddy's party being obvious to the most unquestioning friends of America who murmured with "uneasiness at so few of us." Others who observed "that he was unprovided with Artillery" were fearful about the "consequence of attacking the Fort."[47]

"Upon a serious reflection, Examining minutely into the situation of the Country," Eddy's audience concluded there was no hope of taking the fort and asserted "there could be no probability of success, but liable to every Evil and fatal consequence to the inhabitants!" Angry at this rebuff Eddy exhorted his hearers "to rouse and assert their rights," and sharpened his rhetoric with accusation. Remembering how the inhabitants had traded with the British during the siege of Boston, he lashed out at what he regarded as their duplicity. Emphasizing that he spoke officially – "in the name of the United States" – he charged that "they had supplied the Enemies of America which had much displeased the States." Seemingly propelled by his own opinion, he blurted out "that the Congress doubted their Integrity," and racing on, unable to stop, he reduced his harangue to threats. "If they would not Rouse themselves and oppose the British power in [Nova Scotia] they would be looked upon as Enemies!" He painted a bleak picture of what would happen if they did not to follow him. "Should the Country be reduced by the States they would be treated as a conquered people." Building to a climax as the morning wore on, and stressing his official status, he warned the people that "if they did not incline to do something he would report them to the States!"[48]

Eddy worked the crowd in Sackville and stood his ground before a sceptical audience. It was raining heavily in the afternoon when, having reached the extremity of his arguments and still sensing a residue of reluctance, he strove desperately for that final point that would convict everyone of the certainty of his mission. "If they would now assert their Rights publicly against the King's Government, he was then come to help them and in Fifteen days [he] Expected a Reinforcement of a large Body of men!" Tired from the strain of speaking and pressed by the crowd, Eddy sought to counteract the effect of his army's weakness by stretching the truth. Reinforcement from New England, as Eddy was aware, was unlikely, certainly not in two weeks. He claimed that Francis Shaw would lead the reinforcement from Machias but, according to John Allan, Shaw was now opposed to Eddy's expedition and at this moment was travelling with Allan to Boston, in the opposite direction from Nova Scotia.

Eddy's promise of a reinforcement convinced most of the crowd and his threats swayed the rest. "On a second consideration, choosing rather to meet any Difficulty than to be thought Enemical to America," they acquiesced and "depending upon his authority from the States, they Readily submitted to his Command." But it was the promise that left his hearers "encouraged by the Hopes of soon having a Large Reinforcement."[49] One reason for their reticence had been *Juno* in Cumberland harbour. The menacing outline of this large warship could be seen clearly from Sackville. The sailors on board it faced a menace of quite different proportions which they were constrained to deal with even as Eddy was speaking. A sailor's life in 1776 was a hard life: quarters on the frigate were confined, not particularly clean, and required frequent fumigation to keep at bay the various pests with which it was infested. Before leaving Halifax two weeks ago, Dalrymple smoked the ship thoroughly between decks but they were back again, so this Friday the crew "Continued Smoking the Ship with Powder and Vinegar."[50]

The return on Saturday, *2 November*, of the Cocagne delegation, sent out Wednesday to recruit Micmacs, brought bitter disappointment to

Jonathan Eddy, although he had been warned by John Allan. Only four of that nation volunteered to join the attack on Fort Cumberland. None of the eight chiefs returned and nor did Jean Baptiste or Matua, the discredited treaty negotiators.[51] Micmac neutrality had hardened since Allan's visit in September and the delegates simply ran into a brick wall in their recruiting attempts. The Micmacs were not surprised by Eddy's men appearing in Cocagne nor by the nature of their request. In September "an alarm was spread among us" that New England would attempt "to require us to take up the hatchet," so they were ready with their refusal which was concealed in expert dissembling and softened by ritual professions of friendship. Native objections were plentiful: it would be out of character to go to war, "our natural inclination being Peace." They professed no military aptitude, being "only accustomed to hunt for the subsistence of our family." Their lamest excuse was "our numbers being not sufficient."[52] The delegates must have been incredulous as they listened to the chiefs of the Micmac nation which by all estimates had 500 men capable of bearing arms. What about the treaty they and the Maliseets signed with the United States? The treaty had been renounced, answered the Micmacs; they wished to be friendly with both sides. The advantages of neutrality were already apparent in Allan's promise of American supplies and in the open commissary at Fort Cumberland. With wise diplomacy and a friendly attitude, neutrality could be marketed to Old and New England alike and for a high price. Alone among the communities of Nova Scotia, the Micmacs had developed a policy on the revolution. No such unanimity of purpose was apparent among the passive Acadians, certainly not in the fractious planter population, and loyalists were split by party strife. Eddy fell victim to Micmac policy and his delegates were no match for Native diplomacy.

Eddy was more successful in policing the isthmus, intimidating loyalists to stay at home, and preventing news of his presence from reaching Goreham than in expanding his army with local recruits. In Cocagne, in Memramcook, and even in Sackville, the seat of Nova Scotia's rebellion, he had worked harder than expected for results that could only be regarded as disappointing. Insufficient ardour for republicanism, the obvious weakness of his invasion force, a well thought out Native strategy, the warship in Cumberland Basin all contributed to the delays and rebuffs. For the time being the delays were not critical since Eddy's timetable for attacking the fort had been altered by *Juno*. Not often was Cumberland Basin graced by a ship of the royal navy. With winter supplies finally delivered another naval visit could not be expected until spring. With an eye to the shallow waters and tricky tides of the basin, his ship now repaired (and fumigated), and his orders "to look in at Annapolis Royal" after delivering *Polly* still unfilled, Dalrymple was anxious to sail southward. Goreham gave no indication that he needed *Juno*'s protection and obligingly assured the captain that he "was free of apprehension from the rebels."[53] Perhaps he felt that winter was too close for an attack and indeed the sleet and snow swirling around Cumberland this Saturday afternoon as *Juno* began unmooring procedures reminded everyone of the lateness of the year.

To seaward Commodore Collier's ships were hunting American privateers. This Saturday evening off the South Shore HMS *Lizard* (Captain Thomas MacKenzie) "saw a sail, got up the top gallant yards and gave chase." Fortunately for MacKenzie the weather was clear because the chase lasted all night. Once near midnight he sailed close enough to fire "four 3-pounders and one 9-pounder but she still kept her course." Not until early Sunday morning, *3 November*, was he able to fire *Lizard*'s cannon again "which made her bring to." It was found to be a privateer with five guns and twenty-three men. "Brought the rebels aboard," explained MacKenzie, "and sent an officer and nine men on board the prize."[54]

All day and night and on Sunday, the pursuit of American privateers continued to general approval. The reaction against privateering was strong and Collier's efforts were heartily cheered. In 1776 Nova Scotia was a thoroughly sea-going province; farmers, tradespeople, merchants, as well as fishers were skilled mariners, knowledgeable in every nuance of the politics and details of privateering. Religious leaders reflected the public mood in their condemnation of privateering. "Methinks a privateer may be called a floating hell," Henry Alline, the young charismatic preacher would remark. "Let them that wish well to their souls flee from privateers as they would from the jaws of hell," he warned.[55] At the same time as privateering was denounced, there was a clamour to join the activity. In November, just as Collier was beginning to achieve success, a councillor declared that "had this Government been empowered to Commission Privateers for our own defence, we should have been able to defend our property."[56] Predictably, when Great Britain began to issue letters of marque later in the revolution, Nova Scotians excelled at privateering although the debate over its propriety persisted.

"SHOULD I BE A SUFFERER ...
I TRUST I WILL BE RESIGNED"

With the exception of the early morning violence off the South Shore between the *Lizard* and the American privateer, it was a peaceful Sunday in Nova Scotia. Divine service in Cumberland was conducted in the fort by John Eagleson in line with his custom "to hold Church here

regularly every Sunday."[57] Until the rebellion, this Anglican missionary, the only settled minister in the county and now chaplain to the
garrison, circulated widely in his parish, preaching "for the most part
in Cumberland" but also in Amherst, Fort Lawrence, Sackville, and
Tantramar "as often as the roads and Season will admit." Occasionally
he reached Baie Verte, Shepody, Hillsborough, and Moncton. There
were visitations to St Johns Island and sermons at St Paul's in Halifax,
and Cumberlanders were grateful for his work in obtaining their first
school.[58] "The quick increase of sedition and tyranny" since December
1775, however, narrowed Eagleson's focus and blunted his perennial
optimism.[59]

Conspicuously loyal, Eagleson was a target of abuse by local radicals.
Political upheaval threatened his vision for the mission – "to form a re-
spectable Society at Cumberland as in any part of the Province, the
Capital excepted."[60] Plans in 1776 to build "a Parsonage House all of
Stone" and to reclaim his marsh lot were cancelled.[61] He struggled to
prepare himself mentally for the trials he saw ahead. "Should I be a
sufferer," he wondered, "I trust I will be resigned."[62] Resignation however was an unfamiliar state of mind to Eagleson, so after his life and
property were threatened, he kept a case of pistols in his home along
with his bible.[63] He also curtailed his travels so that Sunday services on
3 November were confined to the garrison.

In a barracks room rendered "decent and comfortable" for chapel,
Eagleson officiated from behind a reading desk built for him by his parishioners.[64] Preaching without notes in a style both authoritative and
articulate, "his sermon [was] a well-connected, sensible, Catholic discourse delivered extempore without hesitation or repetition."[65] Fewer
residents than usual joined the soldiers in the service and no naval officers swelled the congregation. The *Juno* had weighed anchor at seven
o'clock that morning.[66] The minister and his hearers were oblivious to
the threat around them, unaware that Eddy's band, armed with weapons
from Massachusetts, ringed the marsh from Sackville to Maccan even as
they worshipped. Unaware even that the Shepody Outpost had fallen,
Joseph Goreham was planning to resupply it when the service was over.

The patriots were not in church, although some Baptists with Eddy
might have worshipped in private homes. Nonetheless, they experienced something like a miracle when their sentries, while shivering on
the marsh and staring into snow flurries driven on a raw wind, saw *Juno*
unfurl its sails and manoeuvre down the narrow Cumberland Basin
against the wind. By ten o'clock, to Eddy's immense relief, it could
barely be seen on the grey horizon. In a wave of optimism he wrote
that morning to his New England masters that "we are all in high spirits, and our party increases daily."[67] He had feared since Thursday that

word of the invasion might have leaked into the fort and that the *Juno* was staying on to protect the garrison, in which case the whole expedition would have been in vain.

Religious services were held around the province on this Sunday. In Horton two sermons were preached with "much effect" by Henry Alline. He was twenty-eight years old, unordained, and had been preaching publicly for less than a year. "The people seemed to have hearing ears," for the young itinerant who was there by invitation. The meetings were held only a few miles from his home in Falmouth and Alline had yet to venture in his ministry beyond the five townships on the south shore of the Minas Basin. Nevertheless, large crowds gathered to hear him and this Sunday already revealed certain attributes – attraction of the curious and appeal to youth – of a ministry that would soon convulse Nova Scotia in religious reformation. No stranger to Horton, Alline had been there on less serious occasions, and for some in the congregation "it was a strange thing to see a young man who had often been there a-frolicking now preaching the everlasting gospel." Yet his morning sermon "gained the attention of the people," while the evening one "left a solemn sense on some youths."[68]

In a district "where Fanatical Preachers are starting up every day," there was nothing very unusual about Alline at this early stage, and nor was his decision to enter the gospel ministry untutored remarkable in the local context. His decision was made in a district in which labourers were encouraged to become preachers and indigenous learning was held in high esteem by a people who, according to William Ellis of the Established Church in Windsor, "are offended that men should be sent on purpose to instruct them, who are all wise and learned in their own opinion." Even certain beliefs espoused by Alline, such as the unimportance of the sacraments, were common currency in Windsor and Cornwallis.[69] Aspects of his preaching style – the absence of political rhetoric and an assertion that Nova Scotians were a distinctive people – if not overtly loyalist, lent his message an indigenous quality, but it would be wrong to conclude that Alline was even unintentionally responsible for the loyal tenor of his district. In November 1776 his ministry had barely begun while loyal sentiments had been evident locally for nearly a year. Alline was a benefactor, not the determinant, of prevailing conditions in Windsor and Kings County.

Although by Sunday Jonathan Eddy had been in Cumberland nearly a week, Colonel Goreham knew nothing of it. Even as he thanked Eagleson for his usual stellar preaching and walked back to the officers' barracks, he was planning changes to the Shepody party to enable that outpost "to continue till the frost set in." He wanted a sergeant and six men to stay there "about twenty days longer." For this purpose the

garrison command boat was ordered to sail that same Sunday for Shepody. Provisions would be left for a sergeant's guard and the boat would return with Lieutenant Walker and the remaining men. Two civilians at the
fort joined a corporal's boat crew for the short voyage to the outpost.[70]

On Monday morning, *4 November*, the command boat suddenly reappeared in a calm Cumberland Basin. The surprised Goreham did not
expect it so soon but he was in for a much bigger surprise when the
crew ascended the hill to the fort. They explained how they had sailed
to Shepody on Sunday and landed at Hopewell. Ruth Peck and the
children came down to the boat apparently upset and told them what
had happened. "A party of Machias people and others from the Westward with a number of Indians … came there on Tuesday the 29th
[October], some in Boats, and others by land, prest her Husband,
went over the River and took Captain Walker and the party"! How
many were there, Goreham wanted to know? Ruth Peck thought "in all
150 or 200," at least that was what she told the boat crew and they corroborated her story: "by the tracks of the Feet in the Mud, they think
there must be near two hundred men." They also agreed with Ruth, after checking with other settlers in the area, that some patriots had arrived by land; they concluded a "great part of them came by land as
they could not learn that they had more than three large Sail Boats."[71]
The estimate of 200 patriots was readily accepted in the garrison;
surely an invasion force would not be smaller! Goreham never considered that Ruth Peck, startled at night by the sudden influx of strangers
on the beach and overwrought by the abduction of her husband, had
not been in the best frame of mind to make an accurate estimate. That
no patriots had been seen arriving overland was not discussed, nor was
the likelihood of Walker's detachment discovering a landward party of
patriots. Ruth's reliability was not questioned and the possibility that
the Pecks had helped Eddy was not considered. Thus the impression
left was that the invading army was more than twice its actual size, but
even that exaggeration was far less than the 5,000 men reported by
Charles Baker back in August.

Strong winds and cloud followed the bad news into Cumberland on
Monday evening, replacing the morning calm. Inside the garrison, the
invasion was the topic of conversation, a full week after the fact. Because of their inability, unwillingness, or ambivalence, the local populace (including the Yorkshire settlers) had failed to warn the fort. Local
loyalty appeared circumscribed by realism and ambiguity, and nowhere
was this attitude of qualified loyalty more evident than in the large New
England community. The Pecks were typical of the majority. They were
ready to be loyal, even to defend the province against invasion, or so
they said, and in the next instant they appeared to assist the enemy,

only to co-operate later with authorities when it was expedient to do so. The vulnerability of a politically malleable people enabled the patriots to move at will in the region. Eddy's whereabouts concerned the garrison and the lack of fresh information was disconcerting. The week-old story told by Ruth Peck was the most up-to-date intelligence anyone had. According to her, Eddy was recruiting Micmacs in Cocagne, Acadians in Memramcook, and intended to isolate the district by blocking the road at Maccan. The news was alarming. It appeared likely to Goreham that Eddy had already expanded his 200-member invasion force and would move against Fort Cumberland in a few days.

4 Cumberland Creek Raid
Tuesday 5 November to Saturday 9 November

I have been a great Sufferer Within this Three Years by the Americans, Especially by ... Col. Eddy and his party at Cumberland ... for their proceedings was infemous and Scandelus to the highest Degree.
John Hall, Ship commander and Member of the House of Assembly[1]

The head of Cumberland Basin resembles a gigantic amphitheatre in which the central and best view is from the fort. All attributes of the region are on display from this favoured location: the extensive agriculture, transportation patterns, and even the pace of daily life are discernible. The basin itself – the main entrance to the county in the eighteenth century – can be seen in its entirety from garrison hill, as can the estuaries of the many creeks and rivers that flow into it. All this lies beneath an enormous horizon encompassing the hills behind Amherst to the southeast and those rising beyond Sackville in the opposite direction. A New England visitor in 1771 was enthralled by the sweeping view from the "lofty eminence" of Fort Cumberland. He had just arrived by schooner from Baltimore, checked into Martin's tavern and after "refreshing myself, I took a walk around the town to view the situation, the beauty of which can not well be described."[2] On the promontory in front of the fort (then vacant three years and "much out of repair") was an incredible panorama. Looking southwest he saw the whole length of Cumberland Basin: a corridor-like vista, "a league broad and running straight till it opens into the Great Bay of Fundy," with Shepody Hill a distant mound of blue haze. To his left towards Amherst he saw "interspersed with woods and plains ... a large tract of marsh, clear and level for many miles, in the middle of which upon high ground ... formerly stood Fort Lawrence, which has been demolished."

Turning around to the northwest towards Sackville the visitor saw "still a much larger tract of marsh, clear and level for several leagues, at length gradually rising into broken ridges, interspersed with woodland upon which appeared many farms and some villages." The central feature of this magnificent vista is still the marsh which he described as "clear and covered with grass and herds of cattle." Tilting imperceptibly towards the basin, the marsh is cut by tidal creeks and rivers that rise and fall and flow with the tides, meandering and muddy, in either direction. In the foreground Aulac River flows serpentinely past the village of Jolycure to the basin, while further off but still visible are the great ogee curves of the Tantramar and Sackville Rivers. All were navigable in the eighteenth century, even the smaller creeks, by the vessels on which the communication and trade of the district depended. From his vantage point, the visitor appreciated the utility of these "several small navigable rivers ... whereby the crops ... may be conveyed [to] the farmers' doors."[3]

In its central elevated location Fort Cumberland was the focus of the narrow Chignecto Isthmus, functionally as well as visually, especially after its reactivation in June 1776. All roads passed by or terminated at the fort: the Sackville-Amherst road connected the peninsula with the mainland and, at right angles, the upper and lower roads crossed the isthmus to Baie Verte on Northumberland Strait. Near the fort the lower road ended in the trail leading down to Cumberland Creek. Flowing from the face of the ridge and insignificant in size, the muddy estuary of this creek provided convenient shelter to the supply ships, work boats, and command craft that linked the garrison to the outside world. The provision sloop *Polly* was anchored there in early November, its masts projecting above the flat horizon and its fat ungainly hull filled with supplies. The diligent observer could watch the trickle of goods which were being carried from its hold at intervals of low tide. The activities of the garrison were highly visible; those of Eddy's patriots scattered in small detachments were far less so. Visibility was one thing, communication was quite another. Eddy had prevented news of the invasion from being communicated to the fort for nearly a week. Would he be as effective in preventing that news from spreading beyond the isthmus to Halifax?

"PROCEED IMMEDIATELY TO SEA"

Still stung by the loss of his Shepody Outpost and wary of the potential for expansion of what he understood to be a 200-member invasion force, Joseph Goreham proceeded cautiously on Tuesday, *5 November* – Guy Fawkes day – to gather intelligence from the countryside. Commemorating foiled intrigue, namely the gunpowder plot of 1605 when an attempt was made to assassinate the king and blow up both houses of the British parliament, 5 November was a day of celebration in Nova

Scotia as elsewhere in the British empire. On that morning Goreham sent out two spies: Private David Dobson, a soldier "in disguise to re-connoitre at Memramcook" and James Darthwait "an inhabitant to Major Barron's at River Hebert for the same purpose."[4] Goreham needed to learn more about the movements of the invasion force. He wanted to know whether the Acadians had really joined Eddy, what had happened to the Shepody settlers, what the Yorkshire settlers were thinking, and the mood of the Native peoples. A measure of public opinion was essential and he knew the countryside would be full of rumour and intrigue. The two agents departed in opposite directions and were not expected back until the following day.

In the meantime, Goreham desperately wanted to alert the outside world to his plight. "An express to Windsor" was prepared but there was a question about which way to send it.[5] The usual route was the overland trail to Maccan, up River Hebert to its headwaters, along "a narrow ridge called the Boars Back running for eight miles," then down through a series of hills to Minas Basin and the Partridge Island ferry which travelled to Windsor. This route was forty miles from fort to ferry and travellers could be refreshed twice en route in taverns at River Hebert and on the Minas shore.[6] If this route was blocked at Maccan by the patriots as suspected, the more roundabout water route – down Cumberland Basin, around Joggins Point to Minas Basin, and up the Avon River to Windsor – was the only alternative. Goreham would have to await Darthwait's return before choosing the proper course. Nothing further could be done on this Guy Fawkes day except to continue repairing the fort in "moderate and cloudy weather." This same weather extended over much of the province including that other centre of rumour, intrigue, and false alarm: the capital.

The five ships of the Royal Navy anchored in Halifax Harbour on Guy Fawkes day, took bearings off Georges Island and the flag staff on Citadel Hill and at one o'clock, at a signal from George Collier, *Rainbow, Scarborough, Hunter, Albany,* and *Diligent,* fired thirteen guns "to Solemnize the day, being the ... anniversary of the Gunpowder Plot."[7] Amid the bonfires and celebration there was talk in the streets of an invasion but, ironically, not of Eddy's invasion of which there was no knowledge in the capital. Marriot Arbuthnot had picked up a rumour and passed it to the council. "I have received information from pretty good authority as far as concerns the informant," he explained, "that the rebels are meditating an invasion on this province from the eastern part of Massachusetts and have cut a road from Casco to the St. John River."[8] Having discounted Charles Baker's August rumour of a road extending all the way to Shepody, credence was now given to the first stage of such a road. According to the source, provisions had been cached along the road to assist an invasion force "now assembling in New England." Councillors were impressed by this account and decided to send the navy to the mouths of the Kennebec and Penobscot Rivers and to patrol Passamaquoddy Bay, all points the Americans must pass to invade Nova Scotia.

In a manner reminiscent of Goreham's decision that morning to send spies into the countryside to gather intelligence, council agreed that afternoon to send two ships to New England "in order to get such intelligence as may be had." Perhaps it was the spirit of Guy Fawkes day that inspired such action. Council continued in the same conspiratorial vein with concern expressed "for the security of the town" and the safety of council. "A nightly Patrol" was instituted "for enquiring into the characters and employment of all strangers coming into town" in growing numbers, attracted as much by the varied night life as the strong economy.[9] Joining the mariners in the waterfront taverns, the patrol's presence added to the rumours that were common fare in this important wartime post in North America.

Commodore Collier translated council's request into naval orders on Wednesday, *6 November.* Captain Michael Hyndman of the sloop *Albany* was ordered "to proceed immediately to sea" and take with him the brigantine *Diligent* under Captain Edmund Dodd. When they reached the Maine coast they should check for invasion preparations "and in case of receiving any authentic information" Hyndman was "to lose no time to communicate it by ... proceeding ... into Annapolis [Royal] and dispatching an express immediately" to Halifax.[10] With *Juno, Albany,* and *Diligent* covering the entrance to the Bay of Fundy as far down the coast as Kennebec, the province should be safe from invasion, Collier believed.

On the opposite coast a small trading schooner from Annapolis Royal sailed up Cumberland Basin and anchored in Aulac River. After reporting to a local magistrate and hearing about Eddy's invasion, ship captain John Hall went back on board with the apparent intention "to bring her into Cumberland Creek where the Provision Sloop had for some time been unloading for the Garrison."[11] He delayed doing this and instead remained anchored in Aulac River all day. Some claimed Hall was a patriot sympathizer. This would explain how he sailed the Bay of Fundy without interference from privateers, and why this Wednesday he was in no hurry to go around to Cumberland Creek where he would be under the protection of the fort's guns.

While two warships prepared to sail from Halifax in pursuit of rumoured invasion, actual invasion was a week old and Colonel Eddy was pondering his next move. When recruitment slowed it seemed that Goreham would learn of the invasion before Eddy was ready to attack.

Miraculously, this did not happen as proved by *Juno*'s departure on Sunday. Eddy must have been elated to learn that he still retained the element of surprise and his failure to attack then is inexplicable. By missing the favourable moment to seize the prize he squandered the element of surprise and endangered the expedition. With the garrison now on alert and recruitment still not up to expectations, the invasion could falter badly. There was cause now for hesitancy and a need for some interim action, a lesser prize to boost recruitment and raise morale. In seeking a military diversion, Eddy's attention was readily drawn to the *Polly* "which lay on the flats below the Fort, loaden with provisions and other necessaries for the Garrison."[12] The ship's unloading had been going on at a leisurely pace, the work being carried out only at low tide when the ship was high and dry on the mud. The most critical cargo, the cannon, along with some food, had been removed to the fort, but after a full week most of the cargo was still in the hold. Perhaps *Polly*'s proximity to the fort and the guards on board at night lulled Goreham into thinking there was no hurry to empty the hold. Possibly he viewed the ship as a convenient temporary storehouse while repairs continued on storage rooms in the fort. Eddy viewed *Polly* as an attractive, heaven-sent prize.

Work on the provision sloop was only one of several matters concerning Goreham who had to supervise repairs on the fort, train the Fencibles, instill a sense of urgency in complacent civilians, and gather intelligence on the movements of the enemy. At least desertion was no longer a problem and the soldiers for the most part seemed loyal. Private Johnson dutifully reported on 6 November that a man from Westcock, who he had once seen at Machias, tried to bribe Johnson to reveal when he would be on sentry duty and to let a party of 500 patriots into the fort. These men were supposed to be near Westcock, about five or six miles away, and "intended to attack the Garrison that Evening by Surprise."[13] Eddy was less concerned with traffic in and out of the fort now that his presence was no longer secret; indeed, it could be used to convey inflated estimates of patriot strength. At the same time, patriot patrols ranged closer to the fort and announced themselves to nearby residents.

"THE LAWS ARRESTED ... AND PLACED IN THE HANDS OF USURPERS"

In the central room of his home on the glebe a morose John Eagleson sat by the fireplace in the most comfortable of his ten chairs. It was a large fireplace with tea kettle hanging from a newly-installed crane over a flame that lit the entire room and its contents: paintings hung above the wainscotting, a large clock, and the minister's special pride, his library. A chest was filled with items appropriate to his profession: six fine shirts with stock collars, as many handkerchiefs, and six pairs of stockings. This member of the clergy was ready for winter with potatoes picked, oats and barley stacked, thirty pounds of candles made up, and a full larder containing 140 pounds of butter and cheese and plenty of loaf sugar.[14] His farm had prospered since he won it in open court from the Congregationalists and in his victory he was generous, reserving nothing for himself. The ministerial right, which normally would have accrued to him personally, he annexed to the glebe and deeded to the Society. Most of the land was leased to an English farmer.[15] Bachelor Eagleson's needs were modest: thirty sheep, a sow and litter of pigs, and "one fat cow" were kept with a riding horse, the latter being essential to a minister with a large parish.[16]

Generosity and bachelorhood aside, he had made improvements to the glebe and more were planned before the political turmoil of recent months discouraged him. The 3,000-board feet of clear pine drying in his shed for the next building project attested to his faith in the future, a faith finally shattered this Wednesday by the surprise visit of a squad of Eddy's men. They invaded his home abruptly and, one imagines, with a special glee reserved for this outspoken man of the church who had been a thorn in the patriot's side. Now the patriots were the law and Eagleson could forget his privileged position. He would also be without recourse to a magistrate in the republican New Jerusalem. The insults and threats they issued on departing shocked Eagleson into rare silence, put him "in bodily fear" and brought him to the agonizing decision to go immediately to the fort for protection.[17] As he reclined briefly by the fireside before leaving, Eagleson was evidently deeply troubled. All his efforts to prevent rebellion had failed and now, with this raid on his home, "he had the mortification to see the laws arrested from the legal magistrates and placed in the hands of Usurpers!"[18] The prospect of leaving his comfortable home threw the normally gregarious Eagleson into a fit of melancholia. The room was so familiar, the hearth so warm, and his beloved books – it was enough to drive one to drink!

On this same Wednesday an armed patrol also visited the farm of Elizabeth and Christopher Harper located "within Gun Shott of the Fort."[19] The presence of patriots so close to the fort in broad daylight may demonstrate equally Eddy's boldness or his inability to control his troops. Harper's was a model farm with "a considerable quantity of fine cleared land" on which they grew extensive crops, grazed over twenty head of cattle, operated a store and lived in "a very pleasantly situated ... manor house with all the household furniture ... utensils of Husbandry, gardin orchard etc." Their farm improvements since moving to Nova Scotia from Yorkshire in 1775 were the envy of Cumberlanders and had been accomplished with an industry quite in contrast to that of their easy-going (some said "lazy and indolent")[20] planter neighbours. For patriots the envy ran much deeper. Harper's recent appointment as magistrate and his officious manner in carrying out his duties made him a target.[21] The visit of the patriots left Christopher "frightened,"[22] and their threats "greatly disturbed him ... and his Family."[23] No doubt they would return, but whereas Eagleson's reaction was to flee at once to the fort, Harper determined to collect as many members of the militia as possible and go into the fort the following day.

When the agitated John Eagleson reached the fort on Wednesday evening he was surprised by the attitude of complacency there. Discounted in all quarters was the patriot threat. Private Johnson's report of an attack that evening was "but little noticed or believed by the Gentlemen of the Garrison."[24] Only Goreham treated the matter seriously by ordering "an Officers' Picquett in the Spur and a number of non-Commissioned [officers] and privates to lodge in the ... Guard room, and the whole Garrison to lay on their arms." However, no new measures were taken to secure the provision sloop. Edward Barron Jr suggested they send an express to Windsor by the overland route but Goreham declined because Barron appeared anxious only for the safety of his father who lived at River Hebert. Whether to use the land route or water route was still a question that could not be clarified until the spies returned. Their whereabouts was already a topic of dinner conversation and their delay "rather alarmed us."[25]

A mood of unreality settled over the garrison on Wednesday night like a fog that had rolled in from Cumberland Basin. It was as if the inhabitants of that artificial, concentrated little world were intent on snatching a few moments of enjoyment before some vaguely perceived catastrophe. The arrival of the loquacious Eagleson, the phoney war atmosphere of the crisis, and Goreham's call to arms combined to induce a peculiar party spirit in the officers' rooms with people drinking more than usual and lingering at the dinner table late into the night. Doctor Walter Cullen, the garrison surgeon, was there with Edward Barron Jr who was much recovered from the wound he received while serving with the British in Boston. As a consequence of the wound, Barron had "obtained General Howe's leave to pass the winter with his Father" in River Hebert and when the fort reopened in June he became acting engineer and stayed in Cumberland.[26] The special camaraderie of the military suffused the ill-lit, smoky, but by no means uncomfortable, barracks room. Eagleson, who could be counted on to enliven any gathering, fitted easily into this crowd.

"THE POOR DEVILS ... SURRENDERED WITHOUT FIRING A SHOT"

Wednesday night was cold with a damp fog draped over a wet Tantramar. From Sackville Colonel Eddy "sent off a small Detachment which marched about 12 Miles through very bad Roads to Westcock" on the Aulac River. There a large stack of wood was found – "40 cord on the marsh" – with James Law's boat nearby. Realizing barrock-master Law had been contracted to supply the wood to the fort for fuel, it was heaved into the river, all forty cords, and Law's boat was seized. Other boats were seized further down the river and near the mouth they "took a Schooner in Aulack River loaded with Apple Cyder, English Goods, etc. to the Amount of about 300 lbs."[27] This was John Hall's schooner which had moored there earlier that day. Hall was perplexed: "Col. Eddy and his party ... tuke a Schooner of mine with a Cargo of 300 lbs.," he complained. But Hall's vessel should have been safe. He knew Eddy when both were members of the Assembly and he was sympathetic to the patriot cause. "I never Did any of my American Brethren any hurt," he protested, "but have helped and Gave the American Prisoners [in Halifax] so much in thare Captivity." Like many planters, Hall still had family in New England, including a brother, sister "and Aged Honoured Mother."[28] Eddy knew Hall as "a good Friend to the Cause of Liberty" and declared his intention to release the schooner.[29] Eddy's real target was a much bigger prize: the provision sloop *Polly* anchored in Cumberland Creek, about a mile along the basin shore.

The boats seized in Aulac River had to be guarded on the spot until the incoming tide floated them down to the basin, so before embarking on the raid in Cumberland Creek, Eddy called for another party "as a Reinforcement to the first Party, making together about 30 Men, in Order to take the Sloop." Zebulon Roe was put in charge of the combined party that marched along the shore, invisible in the foggy darkness. At the mouth of the creek they turned inland towards the objective and "after a Difficult March arrived opposite the Sloop."[30] *Polly* loomed abruptly out of the thick mist, appearing strangely out of scale and, with the tide out, resting awkwardly in the mud. The silence was eerie and no one could be seen on the hulk although, as Goreham later decried, "the sloop had a sergeant and twelve men on board at night as guard."[31] No guards could be seen tonight. "Had they fired at our people," concluded the patriots, they "must have alarmed the Garrison in such a Manner as to have brought them on [our] Backs."[32] Considering the party going on in the officers' quarters, Zebulon Roe need not have worried about that threat, and the guards were dozing.

He seized the opportunity. "Our men rushed Resolutely towards the Sloop, up to their Knees in Mud, which made such a Noise as to alarm the Centry who hailed them and immediately called the Sergeant of the Guard!" The critical moment in the Cumberland Creek raid had arrived, thick with tension and causing both sides to pause breathlessly. The armed patriots stood motionless in the mud, staring up at the armed guard likewise motionless on the spectral hulk of the sloop.

Roe and his little band of thirty men stood with upraised muskets. The sentry, finally alert, called his sergeant and the rest of the guard on deck to meet the foe. "The Sergeant on coming up Ordered his Men to fire but was immediately told by Mr. Roe that if they fired one Gun Every Man of them should be put to Death, which so frightened the poor Devils that they surrendered without firing a Shot!" Surprise and bluff won the prize for Roe: surprise because he had appeared suddenly out of the fog and bluff because, as he explained, "our People Could not board her without the Assistance of the Conquered, who let down Ropes to our Men to get up by."[33]

The provision sloop, "loaded with the King's stores," was in patriot hands but it was of little value while sitting high and dry in Cumberland Creek within gunshot of the fort.[34] The night was nearly gone and dawn would break before the tide was high enough to float the ship. At this point Roe could retreat to safety, stay with the sloop in hopes of getting it off in time, or exploit his victory by boldly attacking the fort. He chose the middle course: to stand fast in the mud while sending most of his men with the prisoners back down the creek to the boats with orders to sail east to Fort Lawrence as soon as possible. Roe stayed on *Polly* with a small crew and waited for the tide under the cover of darkness. Why had he not retained his men and continued his surprise and bluff by marching up garrison hill, storming the gates of the fort, and demanding Goreham's surrender? Why had Eddy not planned for such a contingency by having reinforcements standing by? These questions bear on Eddy's ability as a strategist and on his officers' ability to think on their feet – a crucial attribute in a loose unstructured force.

It might also be concluded that Roe and his men were immobilized by cowardice. This was the charge levelled by Sir George Collier when he heard of the raid: "Nothing but the Cowardice of the Rebels prevented the Fort from being surprised in the same Manner [with the guards asleep as on *Polly*]."[35] But Collier was venting his antagonism on the Fencibles as much as impugning patriot bravery. It is more likely that Roe, knowing that Eddy had already squandered the tactic of surprise, believed that the fort was now too well guarded to attempt in this manner. Eddy might have been at fault for not developing plans for exploiting a successful raid, but Roe displayed daring in capturing the sloop and courage in remaining under the fort's cannon. Fortunately for the patriots, the cover of darkness was replaced by the cover of fog at dawn on Thursday morning, 7 *November.*

Captain Barron, Doctor Cullen, and Parson Eagleson were up early – perhaps they never went to bed – and with lingering concern for his father's safety, Barron once again pleaded with Goreham to let him go to Halifax by the overland route, thereby passing the family home in River Hebert. The spies, Dobson and Darthwait, were still missing and presumed to have deserted or been captured. Goreham relented: "Captain Barron prevailed on me to let the Command Boat go off at daylight this morning with my letters for the General [Massey]."[36] Barron readied himself to leave amid work parties which were forming on the parade square before going to the creek to unload supplies from *Polly* in the hour or so before the tide ran high. The tall bastions surrounding this milling crowd disappeared into heavy fog, preventing sentries from seeing beyond the parapet let alone detecting anything amiss in Cumberland Creek.

Enveloped in fog, Zebulon Roe waited impatiently for the incoming tide to save him and his prize when he heard voices in the direction of the fort. A work party was descending the hill to the provision sloop. Roe stationed men in the tall grass by the pathway and there "came down Several Parties of Soldiers from the Fort, not Knowing the Sloop was taken, who as fast as they came were made prisoners by our men and ordered on board."[37] Among those taken was Edward Barron on his way to Maccan to carry the express to Halifax. Possibly for no better reason than to bid farewell to a friend, Eagleson and Cullen accompanied him down to the creek and were also surprised in the fog and captured. In Eagleson's case an additional reason was his hangover from the previous night's party. "Mr. Eagleson ... by his unseasonable drunkenness the evening before, prevented his own escape and occasioned his being taken in arms."[38] The prisoners numbered "above thirty."[39] but this windfall did nothing to calm Roe's nerves. The fog was lifting, a faint outline of the fort was emerging, and the sloop was still stuck in the mud, "laying under the command of their cannon."[40]

"The thick fog and haze cleared away about 7 o'clock in the morning," according to Goreham, when "I discovered several boats full of men coming along shore from Westcock and the merchant schooner under way just ahead of them." These were the boats seized in Aulac River. Smaller than *Polly* and lying in a larger stream, they floated sooner and were under sail to Fort Lawrence as Roe had ordered. Goreham swung into action: "ordered [the garrison] to beat to arms; detached Captain [James] Grant and fifty men to cover the provision sloop; hauled one of the cannon on the parapet, there being no embrasure cut, [and] fired about twenty shot which fell rather short of the enemy's boats and the schooner."[41] The cannon fire was a welcome diversion for Zebulon Roe as he anxiously watched the creek rise. The tide was running well in and, relieved to feel "the Sloop now beginning to float," he loosened its sails. On seeing the sails Goreham, still unaware of *Polly*'s fate, became suspicious. As Eddy explained: "the Garrison, who observing our Sails loose, thought at first it was done only with an Intent to dry them."[42] Goreham was not long deceived: "Captain Grant returned and confirmed our suspicion that they had also taken the Provision Sloop which they soon got under sail and out of reach of his musketry." In exasperation he "ordered a 9-pounder drawn down to the dyke to fire on the Vessel and the Boats."[43] Dragging a cannon down garrison hill, across the marsh, and up the dyke was back-breaking work and slow – slower, as it turned out, than sailing out of Cumberland Creek with barely enough tide to weigh the vessel. Eventually, Roe was out of danger: "Perceiving that we were under Way, [the garrison] fired several Cannon shot at us and marched down a Party of 60 Men to attack us but we were at such distance that all their Shot was of no Consequence."[44] From the fort Goreham watched as "the vessel … sailed further up the Harbour into the River Leplanche," disappearing behind Fort Lawrence ridge. Dejected he "brought the guns up again to the Fort."[45] The Cumberland Creek raid was over and *Polly* was lost. The loss of the stores still on board the sloop would cause hardship for the depleted garrison.

Fort Cumberland had been severely depleted since the invasion started over a week ago. Thirteen Fencibles were captured and one killed at Shepody and today's tally ran much higher. The guard on *Polly* was lost, so were the work party and "spies and others taken and decoyed." The list added up to a captain, lieutenant, chaplain, surgeon, three sergeants and forty-two privates – forty-nine in all – which, when added to earlier losses, amounted to sixty-three men, a quarter of the garrison![46] An inventory of supplies also caused alarm with deficiencies in water, food, and fuel. The fort's water supply was notoriously unreliable and located in the spur, the weakest part of the fort. "There being little or no water in the front well," Goreham "got 13 hogsheads filled for extra use."

"We got but between three and four months flour from the provision Sloop and a few pease," noted Goreham, "the rebels having taken every other store and supply." Only ten days' supply of other rations remained. The shortage of some goods was due to lackadaisical work habits in unloading the sloop which lay in the creek for a whole week before its capture. Meat was scarce, "there being no Pork got from the Sloop," until Goreham "purchased a number of Cattle to serve the Garrison."

Fortunately the Cumberland harvest was in. "Under these circumstances all the horned cattle, hogs, sheep, salt, spirits, potatoes, fuel and other commodities that lay contiguous to, and which might be of use to the Garrison or that could be of service to the rebels was seized."[47] Some loyalists avoided Eddy's patrols and brought produce into the fort. Moses Delesdernier "made an offer to Colonel Goreham of 20 fall oxen and 40 barrels of salt which he accepted with great many thanks."[48] The donations and Goreham's seizures reduced shortages to selected items only; meat and flour seemed adequate for a long siege.

Of all the shortages, the most critical was the lack of fuel. Goreham discovered that "the Contractor for the fuel had not lain in a Fortnight's Wood."[49] This was barrack-master James Law, known locally to be "a worthy man" but General Massey had noted that Law was "married into the family of the worst rebels in this province." Law had earlier applied to Massey for money "to lay in fuel for the Garrison" and was awarded the contract, but Massey would charge that he "never laid in a stick of wood although he got 230 [pounds] for that service ... and the poor officers and men suffer severely for such neglect."[50] Actually, Law's contract required him "only to supply weekly" and in the siege "he cou'd not make sufficient provision of fuel for the Garrison,"[51] his stockpile having been thrown into the Aulac River by the patriots. Although his brother-in-law, Samuel Wethered, was notorious in Halifax for leading the rebellion in January, Law demonstrated constant loyalty.

The fort was adequately armed with the three 9-pounders and three 6-pounders taken from *Polly* before the raid, but only three gun platforms were finished and their embrasures were not yet cut in the parapet. Ammunition amounted to "about twenty Barrels powder and a proportion of cannon ball," and for the troops, "eight or ten thousand musket Cartridges." A review of the defence works only confirmed the worst; Fort Cumberland was a military slum. "Many parts of the parapet incomplete. The face of the bastions, curtains, etc., by being so long exposed by the heavy rains and frost were beaten down to such a slope that one might with ease ascend any part of the Fort." A short, hastily-built palisade surrounded most of the main fort and the spur, "only such as we could provide in course of the summer and placed about three feet from the glacis, but was passable either in or out without much difficulty." There was no time to rehabilitate the run down fort. With an attack imminent, defenses would have to be improvised using scrap materials and ingenuity. In this realization Goreham saw an opportunity to use his skills as a former ranger.[52]

Finally, inventory was taken of the reduced garrison. Goreham counted the Fencibles – "his own Corps" – to find one field officer, two captains, eight junior officers, thirteen sergeants, six drummers, and

142 rank and file: 172 troops. The Royal Artillery added one bombardier and three gunners for a total of 176 officers and soldiers.[53] Several civilians capable of bearing arms were also in the fort but the commander wanted to call in the militia before assessing the total strength of his garrison. The patriots demonstrated in the raid a mobility and command of the countryside that might prevent an effective call-up of the militia. Nevertheless, Goreham issued a proclamation calling on the inhabitants to join the garrison.

Given the shortages in supply, repair, and personnel, what plan could be devised to combat the rebellion which all available information confirmed was engulfing the district? How should Goreham respond to Eddy's challenge? Should he move out boldly in a search-and-destroy mission or stay inside the crumbling fort? Could he keep the garrison on alert and avoid the ignominy of the commander of Fort Ticonderoga, or would he succumb to Eddy's bluff and surprise? Goreham was no strategist and his administrative skills were limited. He had some tactical skills and could respond to daily events in an ad hoc, sometimes creative fashion. He understood his enemy, and was no stranger to terrorism.[54]

In assessing his situation two things stood out. First of all, there was no question of exposing his Fencibles by attacking the patriots in the countryside. To Goreham this would be outright folly. The fort was run down but it was the only prepared defence work in the region and it would be foolish to wander outside it where Eddy's guerrilla fighters might cut them up. His troops were not even adequately clothed, "the Regimental Clothing not yet arrived."[55] No, a better approach in Goreham's opinion was to stay inside the fort where the troops' limited military skills could be effectively employed. Moreover, the fort was Eddy's main objective and to stay in it and accept a siege would be the best way to deny him. Secondly, Goreham believed that a reinforcement was required for ultimate victory. Because circumstances dictated that he should stay on the defensive inside the fort, only a reinforcement would permit him to go on the offensive. Accept a siege and obtain reinforcements; to Goreham these were self-evident truths measured in the light of hard reality rather than pieces of an abstract plan. They became core elements in the strategy for defending Fort Cumberland.

"A MOST DARING REBELLION HAS FOR SOMETIME PREVAILED"

Zebulon Roe relaxed at the Eddy's farm on the east bank of the Leplanche River in Fort Lawrence. He deserved the rest after escaping from Cumberland Creek and outdistancing both Captain Grant's musketry and the garrison artillery. From Eddy's farm he could view a full sweep of the eastern Tantramar with the autumn marsh a rich golden colour in the late afternoon sun. *Polly* and the other boats, including Hall's schooner, with their hulls skewed oddly in the mud, took up the foreground while the low contours of Fort Lawrence ridge cut off the view of Fort Cumberland. On the riverbank, the patriots took inventory and were ecstatic with the cornucopia of supplies in *Polly*'s hold. "A great quantity of stores," shouted Jonathan Eddy![56] "And all intended for the Garrison," exulted his son Isbrook who tallied the stock at 600 barrels of pork and beef, a ton of candles, fifty firkins of butter, 700 new blankets and two hogsheads of rum![57] The gratuitous influx of prisoners seemed like a miracle to Josiah Throop. "As an omen of our success and to encourage our hearts, Divine providence sent ... the soldiers into their hands in ways truly remarkable"![58]

What about Hall's schooner? Eddy, on finding out the previous night "that she was the Property of Mr. Hall of Annapolis ... discharged her."[59] It was surprising then, and frustrating for Hall, to find his schooner still detained this Thursday afternoon. And what about his valuable cargo? It had been unloaded and inextricably mixed with that of the provision sloop; it was impossible to identify it now. "Imbaseled [embezzled] the Cargue," was the indelicate phrase Hall used, "amongst the party at Cumberland"! Nor could he retrieve his ship. Roe would not permit it. Vainly, Hall argued his case. The damages would be greater than the value of the cargo should his ship be detained longer: "500 [pounds] more Damage to me," he fumed, "as I had another Cargue Ready for another Voige a-parrishing." His arguments were drowned out in the patriots' victory celebration. Like the provision sloop, Hall's vessel was a prize of war. It could not be returned so easily; it would take time. Patriots, including the Maliseets, would see their share of the booty diminish if the schooner was returned. Eddy might have wanted to discharge it, as he said, but his control over his men was far from absolute. John Hall went away empty-handed. "Detained the Vessel and [crew] abought a month," he would claim incredulously.[60]

The jubilation by the Leplanche River continued in the almost warm November afternoon. By low tide Jonathan Eddy was ready to lead a pilgrimage across that river and marsh, over Fort Lawrence Ridge, across the Missiguash River and through the large central marsh to Fort Cumberland ridge where he would set up camp within a mile of the fort. The excitement at Eddy's farm had attracted the curious who watched as the exotic little army of Maliseets, Micmacs, Acadians, and New Englanders strung out in a thin line leading westward over the marsh. Eddy's destination was a place called Camphill, a small community on the Baie Verte Road at the top of a small wooded rise. Scattered along either side of this road leading out from the fort were farmhouses as far as the village of Bloody Bridge where the family of John Allan lived with several Acadian tenant farmers. A mile further on was the village of Jolicure, and ten miles past there, on the other side of the isthmus, was Baie Verte on Nothumberland Strait. If from Camphill one looked southwest along the road, Cumberland Basin could be glimpsed through the trees. A short walk in that direction, down the hill and around a curve to the right, brought one to the edge of the woods and to a clear view of Fort Cumberland. Another short walk, past a cluster of buildings and up a steep rise brought one to the front gate of the fort.

The command post of the patriot army was set up on the farm of Eliphalet Read who had opened his home to the patriots during the January rebellion. The nearby farm of Ebenezer Gardiner became the political centre for committee meetings. Barns were turned into barracks for out-of-county soldiers and into storehouses. In a wooded area near Read's the Maliseets and Micmacs erected a circle of wigwams. A commissary and field kitchen were set up, trees were felled to begin a fuel depot, and ox teams hauled supplies from Fort Lawrence. Livestock were donated or requisitioned. Samuel Wethered provided a horse. Although several days would be required to complete it, the army camp was partially operational by nightfall.

Not only had the raid been a material victory for Eddy, weakening the garrison and gaining valuable supplies for his men, it was a promotional victory as well. Camphill attracted wide interest and the patriots were "there joined by a Number of the Inhabitants so that," by Eddy's calculation, "our whole Force was now about 180 Men."[61] Campfires were lit and the feasting began with the topic of conversation being the Cumberland Creek raid. Zebulon Roe, the hero of the day, led the celebration, underpinned by the two hogsheads of rum from *Polly*'s hold.

The Baie Verte Road in Camphill was uncommonly busy with country folk at dusk but fewer people were entering Fort Cumberland partly because of Eddy's patrols. The garrison had just reverted to its night-time schedule; the flag had been lowered, the guard changed, and cattle were herded from the king's common to the safety of the palisade. At night the massive defence walls and looming ramparts imposed a sombre atmosphere on the darkened interior. The closely-spaced buildings in the spur and fort created narrow alleys fitfully illuminated by orange light shining through tiny windows. Vistas were cut short in the cramped spaces by towering bastions that circumscribed the huge starlit Tantramar sky. The alleyways and central square, the crowded buildings and angular defence walls lent an urban, European feeling to the garrison in stark contrast to rural Cumberland. In his quarters Goreham was receiving the local militia. These he described as "the virtuous few who have offered their Lives and Fortunes to stay the progress of Rebellion in this part of the province."[62] Moses Delesdernier had already come in with his "offer of all the Fat Cattle and other articles I Had."[63] Christopher Harper arrived, having "collected 12 Men who together with his family ... entered the Garrison ... and took up Arms for its Preservation."[64] From Sackville came Charles Dixon[65] and from River Hebert in the opposite direction came Edward Barron Sr, a militia officer. Leaving his wife Anne at home, he managed the journey in "a Large Wooden Canoe [with] a number of guns [and] a barrel of gunpowder,"[66] and arrived under the cover of darkness only to learn of his son's capture in the Cumberland Creek raid. Other members of the militia tried to reach the garrison but without success. Thomas Robinson of Fort Lawrence and William Black Sr of Amherst "were going to the fort" but were stopped at a roadblock operated by Samuel Rogers "who forbid them" to pass. Rogers threatened Black with dire consequences "if he stirred off his premises."[67]

When it became apparent late Thursday that no more loyalists were likely to reach the fort, Goreham made a final calculation of the number of defenders. These included his Fencibles, the militia, and the civilian workers capable of bearing arms, "the whole amounting to about two hundred including the sick."[68] With wives and children, the total population within the defence perimeter was perhaps as high as 400 people. It was unlikely that the garrison would be further augmented due to the difficulty in getting past Eddy's patrols and the desire of many loyalists to remain at home to protect their property. However, the garrison was now approximately equal to that of Eddy's opposing force in Camphill.

The information brought in by the militia was unsettling. "Most of the inhabitants of Westcock, Amherst and Jolicure have joined the rebels, who are between four or five hundred." It was heard that "two hundred took the provision Sloop," and that the patriots expected reinforcements. "They expect a number more from St. John [River] and Machias, etc. with frigates and cannon." If credence could be given to these reports, the patriots were gaining support at an alarming rate and Goreham felt constrained to write a manifesto "warning the inhabitants against giving them the least assistance and commanding them to act with the King's Troops in ... driving them out of the province."[69] The manifesto began by referring to Eddy's men who "have lately entered this province," taken prisoners, seized a vessel belonging to the garrison, and were inducing the inhabitants to rebel. Bluntly, he warned that "those in rebellion" who were caught would "subject themselves to an immediate military execution."[70]

The day had been tiring and the hour was late but Goreham had more to do. A message to the outside world was as important as the manifesto to the inhabitants. Since the key to his defence strategy was timely reinforcement, that message had to get out as soon as possible. The loss of engineer Barron forced Goreham to seek other volunteers to attempt a break-out. An old birch-bark canoe was found and three men who knew how to use it – Fencible Ambrose Sherman and two civilians, Mr Shelton of Halifax and Thomas Farrel of Cornwallis – agreed to paddle out of the basin. The frail craft was launched in the creek and the men disappeared into the darkness, but the canoe was leaky and presently they returned. Nothing more could be done until the following night.[71]

Skies were cloudy in Nova Scotia on Friday, *8 November.* The drill-square cadence so familiar on the Tantramar since June was offset this morning by the noise of construction as Goreham improved the defences of the fort. Loss of the provision sloop with its vital supplies and the capture of over sixty men of the garrison convinced him that an early attack was certain. Normal renovations to barracks and other buildings, although not nearly complete, were abandoned in favour of emergency repairs to the walls and other defensive works. Crews were climbing over squared logs on the ramparts, the highest elevation of the fort, when private John Curry slipped and plunged to his death on the parade square below. This tragedy occurred in full view of children and their parents. Later in the morning the news broke that two Fencibles, Michael Griffin and Alexander Jones, who were outside the fort on an errand, had been captured by Maliseets.[72] This second shock rippled through the garrison, but while some might have feared for the soldiers' lives, especially since their captors were Maliseets, the veteran Goreham would have known better; his chief concern was the number of captors, not their treatment of prisoners.

The gloom of the garrison after the death of one Fencible and capture of two others this Friday contrasted with the euphoria in Camphill where news of the success at Cumberland Creek was having a good effect. "On the news spreading," enthused Josiah Throop, "the inhabitants repaired to Eddy and his party to the number of about 200."[73] Supporters from beyond the isthmus began also to appear. From the Northumberland coast came several Pictonians, including members of the large Earle family.[74] Over the Boars Back came a contingent from Cobequid led by Thomas Faulkner, called "Devil Tom," who had recently been released from the Halifax gaol when a charge of treason against him was dropped.[75] The lack of military order and absence of artillery were embarrassing to some patriots. The construction activity at the garrison they were to target could easily be heard. But this was not a day for discouraging words and the aura of victory obscured the dilemma that Eddy himself had created by attempting to bluff enemies and allies alike. He had bluffed Goreham into believing that a reinforcement with artillery was on the way. This suited Eddy's purpose, but he had promised the same reinforcement to his own people in Sackville and claimed it would arrive in two weeks although he knew that none was planned and he had never asked for one. More inclined to savour current success than plan future strategy, he simply believed that Goreham would be forced to surrender before then. Eddy's view this Friday was of a growing rebellion overwhelming a shrinking garrison.

Patriot detachments fanned out across the isthmus that Friday blocking roads, gathering supplies, and always keeping an eye out for recruits. One party went to Fort Lawrence to requisition a derelict blockhouse called Number One, possibly to use as a storage depot. Number One happened to be near the home of Eleanor and Moses Delesdernier so the patriots paid a visit. Perhaps because their son-in-law Richard Uniacke and nephew Lewis Delesdernier were already in Eddy's army, they thought that Moses could be pressured to join as well. They were displeased when Eleanor explained he was not at home, and "exasperated" at his "Keeping in the Fort." She watched aghast as "they took everything valuable out of my House," and was horrified as they "threatened to Burn it and to deliver my family to the Indians." They left her home carrying away their plunder and leaving a promise to return and make good on their threats if Moses did not quickly come to his senses and join the patriots. Poor Eleanor and the children "had nothing to subsist on," for after what Moses had given "for the use of the Fort, they took the Rest".[76] She needed to get word of their predicament to her husband at the fort.

Around the coast of Nova Scotia the search for privateers continued unabated this Friday in blissful ignorance of the rebellion that was spreading across the isthmus and threatened every household as well as the garrison. On the South Shore the *Lizard* looked in at Roseway Harbour but "returned without finding any American vessels."[77] In Minas Basin "a pirate sloop of eight carriage guns" caused alarm on the Cobequid coast, having seized the Partridge Island ferry that ran to Windsor. This vessel had slipped easily past Collier's lone warship guarding the mouth of the Bay of Fundy and it fell to militia commander Michael Francklin in Windsor to investigate. Muttering about how "this Bay has been strangely neglected by the Navy," he chartered a schooner, gathered up "a party of 30 men," and embarked for Cobequid. With Fort Edward on the hill to starboard, this coastal patrol of militia members slipped down the muddy Avon on the late afternoon tide. The weather was clear – frost was anticipated – and a courier was already on the road to Halifax with Francklin's note about the alarm in Minas Basin.[78]

Amidst the many alarms and patrols nothing was said about Cumberland. Goreham had been unsuccessful in getting a message past Eddy's guards. He tried again this Friday night. The wooden boat used by Major Barron had been hauled up to the garrison for repairs. Down to the creek went more volunteers with this boat after dark but on detecting an enemy patrol nearby they were forced to abandon the effort. The frustration of the siege was beginning to show in the garrison cut off from the outside world and locked in each night like inmates in a prison. Being a military objective, they were also objects of target practice, especially at night. The tension always increased after dark when Eddy's patrols moved in close to the fort. The gunfire sounded loud in the crisp night air surrounding the garrison, and louder still in the spurr which had no earthworks to muffle the noise. Women in temporary shelters comforted their children as the musket balls struck the palisade walls. Having been on constant alert since the Cumberland Creek raid, the fencibles fired return volleys into the darkness but no attack came. Eddy was just harassing a nervous garrison and the shooting gradually subsided.[79]

Suddenly out of the night and from amid the danger of random musket fire, there appeared a young girl at the gate of the fort. She explained to amazed sentries that she had walked across the marsh from the direction of Fort Lawrence with a message for Moses Delesdernier from his wife Eleanor. Moses was brought to the girl who had come "in the night to acquaint [him] of her Distress." The girl related the patriots' visit and how his "house was Rifled of Everything," told him about their threats to his property, and to set "the Indians loose on [his] family" if he did not join Eddy.[80] Should he join the rebellion and risk a charge of treason, or remain loyal as he evidently preferred and risk the destruction of his home and family? It was a terrible dilemma and Moses decided on an ambiguous course. The next morning he would seek Goreham's permission to leave the fort and return home. The dilemma faced by Moses and others in the siege was explained by a New Englander: "the inhabitants of that unhappy Country, upon the appearance of Captain Eddy, were reduced to the shocking dilemma of either being plundered and butchered by their friends, or incurring the highest displeasure of their own Government."[81] The Blacks and Robinsons coped by staying at home, by no means an act of indifference nor indication of neutrality; they were under house arrest. What future awaited those who had entered the fort?

"FLYING REPORTS THAT THE REBELS WERE AT CUMBERLAND"

Daybreak on Saturday, *9 November*, found Michael Francklin and his part-time sailors on the deck of a chartered schooner in Minas Basin, "a little below the mouth of this River [Avon]." Their course was set for Partridge Island across the basin where they would investigate the capture of the ferry by an American privateer. As the sky brightened, Cape Blomidon filled the port view and an icy vapour rose from the cold basin into the even colder atmosphere, chilling each sailor with a damp penetrating cold that could, it was said, scar a man's health for a lifetime.[82] The distant Cobequid coast was beginning to emerge from the mist when "an attempt was made to surprise me," recalled Francklin, "by a boat belonging to a privateer which lay below at Spencer's Island."

"This boat had taken the Partridge Island ferry," concluded the militia commander who prepared his own surprise by ordering the men to crouch down below the ship's rail and remain hidden with muskets primed. Not suspecting that the schooner was an armed militia vessel, the privateers manoeuvred in close, anticipating an easy prize. The volunteer militia waited a bit too impatiently to spring their trap. "Fortunate for them," growled Francklin, "our men made too early a show so that they made off instantly on being fired upon." The incident was over quickly and they resumed the voyage across the basin to find the Partridge Island ferry, "which we retook."[83]

"This opened to us a discovery," exclaimed Francklin on retaking the ferry "that a body of rebels had gone to Cumberland, as it was said, to the number of 500 with some Indians under the command of Jonathan Eddy." Despite the blockade which had prevented Goreham from sending out an alarm, the first news of the siege finally reached the outside world with Francklin's arrival in Minas Basin eleven days after the patriot invasion. There was no reason to question the exaggerated estimate of the invasion force, but Francklin's knowledge of the Native peoples left him with the realistic opinion that "the Indians are all from St. John River, Passamaquoddy and Penobscot and, I believe, do not exceed 25 or 30."[84]

With the ferry in safe hands and before returning to Windsor, Francklin interviewed the locals to learn more about the startling news that Fort Cumberland was besieged. James Yuall, a Scottish settler and magistrate from Truro, told him that "there had been flying reports that the rebels were at Cumberland." Mary and Robert Morrison, an elderly couple who "live in an out-of-the-way place and don't hear much news," heard that "about 300 rebels were coming from Cumberland to Cobequid." A surprising aspect of their news was its source. Robert heard it "from two disaffected Cumberland people who had been from thence to Halifax and were at this time on their return back by land." The Morrisons' story, if true, indicated that Eddy had sent spies as far afield as Halifax.

Even details of the siege were gleaned from the settlers. Sampson Moore, an Irish inhabitant of Truro, heard of the Shepody Bay incident from Elicomb Tupper who had been in Cobequid about ten days earlier and had told Moore "that Captain Walker with some men had been taken lately from Shepody by the rebels." And what about support for Eddy in Cobequid, wondered Francklin. Moore did not think it would amount to much. "There cannot exceed ten or twelve men in the townships of Truro and Onslow who will join the rebellion in Cumberland if any," he declared. "And those people," he went on, "are not people of weight or consequence and the people are very indifferent in arms." The people may have been poorly armed, but James Yuall was not so sure about the numbers; "two or three people went from Onslow to join them," Yuall supposed. He felt "the people of Truro will not join the rebels but is afraid many of Onslow will and is doubtful of some of Londonderry." Yuall knew that "about ten days ago one MacGowan and one Sharp, inhabitants of Amherst, came from thence with a letter to John Morrison of Londonderry and Morrison proceeded with them to Major Archibald's." The purpose of their errand and the letter, according to Yuall, was to encourage the people of Cobequid to rebel, but Major Archibald told him "he had greatly discountenanced them," and they had returned with only a few people to join Eddy.[85]

There is no indication that the capture of the Partridge Island ferry formed any part of Eddy's plans or that he even knew about the American privateer in Minas Basin. He had posted guards at Maccan and they had prevented loyalists from using the overland route to Partridge Island. But he had sent his own emissaries down that route to recruit in Cobequid and perhaps to spy out Halifax. It was from the emissaries that news of the siege was heard by those living near the ferry landing. Fearing that a general invasion might be under way, Francklin sent notice of the siege back to Windsor immediately and ordered the carrier to relay the news from there to the capital and through Kings and Annapolis Counties.

Reports of another incident in Cobequid caught Francklin's attention. In mid-October "a number of seafaring-looking men" appeared in Onslow, and began "fitting up an old Boat" on the mud flats in front of Charles Dickson's tavern. There were two groups of American privateers: Captain William Carleton and six sailors of the *General Gates* which had been driven on shore near Canso by James Dawson in September, and several sailors of the *Washington* who had escaped gaol at Halifax. These men combined forces in Onslow, repaired the boat and escaped to New England. The boat had been purchased in Onslow, and the materials needed to make it seaworthy and to meet the men's needs while there could only have been supplied locally. Yet when questioned by Francklin the residents who lived in full view of the mud flats admitted to very little contact with these enemies of the government.[86] The people of Cobequid were the first outsiders to learn of Eddy's invasion but their magistrates failed to warn Halifax, some locals were already in Eddy's camp, and American privateers had found temporary sanctuary in the district. This news was guaranteed to enrage Marriot Arbuthnot, who had gained quite a different image of Cobequid during his July tour.

While Francklin continued his interviews, his message to Arbuthnot about the privateer in Minas Basin reached Halifax. Since this was a naval matter Arbuthnot consulted Collier on the *Rainbow.* "Our coasts have been infested with piratical rebels," lamented the lieutenant-governor, they "have entered our defenceless harbours and done much mischief to destroy the fishery and shipping."

"Infinite mischief," agreed Collier. "The communication between Windsor and Fort Cumberland was cut off by the rebels and the Ferry Boat together with Partridge Island were taken by a pirate sloop of eight carriage guns and full of men." Francklin's news infuriated the commodore who claimed to have responded "instantly."[87] Orders were issued to Captain James Feattus of the sloop *Vulture* anchored nearby. "Proceed to sea at daylight" on Sunday, ordered Collier; "make the best of your way into Minas Basin and so on to Windsor ... Follow the best intelligence you can procure for pursuing the pirate vessel or any other that may infest that coast." Feattus was to make contact with Winkeworth Tonge and Isaac Deschamps, two friends of the government in Windsor. "In going along the coast of Nova Scotia," he was to keep an eye out for other ships. "Should you meet with the *Gage* or *Loyal Nova Scotia* armed schooners," ordered Collier, "take them under your command." Their small size permitted them to manoeuvre in the shallow reaches of Cobequid Bay near Truro. Concern about Fort Cumberland was also apparent in Collier's instructions: "should you not receive any material information at Windsor ... proceed to Cumberland," and confer with Goreham. Only if he found "no apprehension of an invasion from the rebels," was *Vulture* to return to Halifax.[88]

Collier's senior naval captain had been chosen to navigate the the Bay of Fundy at this late season of the year. The experienced Feattus was as familiar with North American waters as he was with naval regulations (and how to circumvent them) and local politics (and how to benefit from them). With a large family to support he kept a son "upon my Book (as my Clerk)" in breach of navy rules. Executive Councillors counted him a friend; "most of them had known [him] many years," and would certify him "a Brave, Diligent and Gallant Officer."[89] Now with Collier's order to in all cases "act as circumstances may require" ringing in his ears, Feattus rowed back to *Vulture* in the cold grey waters of Halifax harbour on this cloudy Saturday, and prepared to ship out the next morning.[90]

"A GOOD HOUSE ...
ELEGANTLY FURNISHED"

Halifax was taking action to combat privateering in Minas Basin, but was still in the dark about affairs in Cumberland. The cordon surrounding the fort was relaxed during the day and this Saturday people came and went with realtive ease. A nearby resident arrived with a letter from the prisoners held in Camphill. Amid noisy repair work, Gorehem read that they were being treated with "humanity and gentility,"[91] but were expecting to be transported to New England. Other loyalists were confined to their homes, the most recent being Moses Delesdernier who had left the protection of the fort that morning. "You Approved of My Returning Home," he would remind Goreham; in fact, "[you] thought proper to send me to my Family in order to Preserve [them from] utter destruction." The result of the colonel's magnanimity was predictable. "Of course, I fell in the Hands of the Enemy,"[92] and by evening he was under house arrest. It remained to be seen if he would have to compromise his loyalty to protect his family. Some leading loyalists, such as magistrate William Black Sr, remained unmolested in their homes, but by answering the proclamation and entering the fort Moses became a target of the patriots. His having a son-in-law and nephew in Eddy's army might explain why he was thought to be susceptible to recruitment, but this may also have provided protection for the Delesderniers. To those loyalists for whom the names Delesdernier and Uniacke were synonymous with rebellion, Moses's motives for leaving the fort were suspect.

Moses Delesdernier's reputation in Halifax in November was that of a loyal Nova Scotian; only in Cumberland under the pressure of the siege was his loyalty brought into question. By contrast, Samuel Wethered had a notorious reputation in Halifax yet he was taking steps to redeem himself locally. It was as co-leader with John Allan of the January rebellion that Wethered gained notoriety. His dropping from view in February could have meant that he was satisfied when Halifax backed down on the militia acts. A stronger indication of his political moderation was the fact that he remained a magistrate throughout 1776, surviving the change of government in April and the administrative change in July. Instead of joining Eddy he continued to operate the family tavern during the siege although it was within cannon-shot of the fort. Business at the Wethered tavern increased tremendously after the Fencibles arrived in

June and hardly diminished with the siege. The Wethereds' Black slave also worked in the tavern during the busy month of November although she was several months pregnant. Eddy's men dared not venture so close to the fort in the daytime but they filled the establishment after dark. This late night clientele did not go undetected by the garrison, some members of which occupied the same tavern chairs by day. The discovery interested Goreham, who was a long-time acquaintance of Wethered, and the two struck a bargain. Wethered would signal the garrison this Saturday night when the patriots were patronizing his place. A candle placed in a certain window would be the signal and Wethered would have enough time to vacate the premises before Goreham bombarded the tavern. He was not to worry about property damage; that would be paid for by the garrison. In the afternoon the bombardier prepared the cannon at his leisure: he calculated the distance to the nearby tavern, intersected it perfectly with the anticipated trajectory, and casually loaded the properly angled gun. The trap was set.

As Saturday night descended on Cumberland, Edward Barron's boat was prepared for another attempt to escape to Windsor. Being unaware that news of the siege had reached Michael Francklin that morning, Goreham was desperate to get out a call for help. But just as the party left for Cumberland Creek, "a number of the enemy" was heard approaching the fort and he was frustrated again.[93] Fearing an assault, the troops were called to the defences but no attack came. Several cannon were loaded with grape-shot and fired blindly into the darkness in the general direction of the noise; the planned barrage of that evening was yet to come. Just how well planned was the bargain struck between Wethered and Goreham? Their signal was hardly fool proof. Had Wethered thought about it, he might have agreed that a musket flash or a lantern appearing in that measureless range of darkness in front of the cannon could confuse the bombardier. Could the light of a candle be seen from that distance? The musketry of the patriots and the grape-shot cannonade kept the defenders on edge. A light of some kind was spotted in the right location so the fuse was lit. The cannon strained its moorings and belched a fiery projectile in the direction of Cumberland's favourite drinking spot which at that moment was filled with Eddy's men according to the signal.

A direct hit was scored on Samuel Wethered's tavern. The cannon-shot punched a hole in the outside wall without noticeably altering its trajectory, then curved in a smoking arc between gaping patrons, many of whom were indeed patriots (at least that part of the plan worked), and passed right through the bar where Wethered stood. The seven-pound ball of hot cast iron caught the unsuspecting publican in the rear, below the waistline, before carrying on to bury itself in the foundations, having traced a path of destruction in splintered wood, rum, and blood. Patrons scrambled out of the damaged building and fled while Samuel Wethered lay in the rubble grievously wounded. His pregnant Black slave collapsed in shock and went into premature labour. Only minutes before, she lit a candle in the exact window that Wethered planned to use later for the same purpose but with quite different intent, and unwittingly brought down the premature bombardment.[94]

The nightly gun battles became a feature of the late autumn evenings. "Scarce a night passed," observed Goreham, "but they disturbed the Garrison by firing their Musquetry."[95] The fort's exposed location on a ridge in the centre of the Tantramar enabled the fireworks to be viewed from a broad area. The roar and flash of guns created a spectacle that attracted the curious to farmhouse windows. Such was the experience of the Blacks: "We could easily see the garrison from my father's house," said William Jr. "In the night they [the patriots] would frequently fire upon the garrison, and the garrison upon them." When later he became a Methodist minister, Black renounced card playing but in 1776 his family would "sit up whole nights" playing cards. "When we heard the cannons roar or the discharge of the musketry, we have frequently gone awhile from our cards to watch the flashing of the guns, during the hottest of the fire, and as soon as that was over, returned again."[96]

Goreham's random gunfire and planned cannonade this Saturday night was guaranteed to break the concentration of the card-playing Blacks, but they also caused the patriots to disperse from garrison hill. Gradually the commotion subsided and all was quiet at the fort. The silence deepened with the cold as the sentries on the parapet peered into the impenetrable Tantramar night. Presently a small light flickered in the blackness and grew, slowly at first, until its location could be marked as downhill and to the east. It then grew faster, until the night sky in that direction turned red. Soon it was a raging inferno plainly not more than a few hundred yards away. Someone shouted it was Harper's place and everyone, including Christopher and Elizabeth Harper themselves, rushed to the parapet to watch. The Harpers were justifiably proud of their home known as "a good house ... elegantly furnished."[97] Its timber skeleton was now a silhouette against the flames "which consumed it entirely" together with barns and outbuildings.[98] The Harpers were disconsolate, their "House and property destroyed by the Rebels"![99]

The siege had settled into a pattern after the Cumberland Creek raid. By day Eddy's men remained beyond cannon range enabling Goreham to renew contact with the villagers, gather intelligence, and make deals. By night Eddy's men tightened the ring around the fort – it was more effective to execute the blockade and skirmish with the defenders in darkness. The purpose of the nightly attacks was not to capture the fort but merely to fray the nerves of its inmates. There were victims both of the nighttime harassment and the daytime intrigue: witness the tragedies of the Wethered and Harper families this Saturday night.

The academic serenity of Harvard college was far removed from the chaos in Cumberland. While Samuel Wethered lay bleeding in the ruins of his own tavern, his partner in the January rebellion was a guest at Harvard of Cumberland's former missionary. Together John Allan and Caleb Gannett visited the library and "dined in the great Hall of the college." In those quiet halls Gannett was in his element. Others might join the frontline of rebellion on whichever side; Gannett preferred the world of ideas, and if, as in the case of Harvard, that world was not exempt from frontline action, it had been kept recently at a comfortable distance. The occupation of the campus by George Washington, which ended in March, seemed remote to Gannett. Remoter still were the rigours of frontier mission work in Cumberland. In his detached manner, he listened as Allan "communicated the state of [his] affairs to him."

Allan had arrived in Boston from Machias two days before, was staying at the home of Francis Shaw's parents, and had already begun his overtures to the State Council in his quest for the position of Indian agent. He had given the Micmac letter to the council president, James Bowdoin, who must have been chagrined by its denunciation of the treaty for which he had been the chief American negotiator. Allan hoped to go on to New York and gain Washington's support (as Eddy had done in March) to appear before Congress. Gannett offered some helpful advice: avoid New York, he suggested, the war at present was raging so inconveniently in that vicinity. If someone of influence was needed to recommend him to Congress, it would be wiser to seek out Congress representative John Adams in nearby, peaceful Braintree.[100] This meeting was a strange one between the academic in his place and the revolutionary in his exile. Gannett was under pressure at Harvard because of his luke-warm politics, and if he was remembered at all in Cumberland it was as the focus of the glebe dispute with Eagleson which had so alienated that district from the central government in Halifax. Both men had forsaken Cumberland at a point of crisis. The former crisis had faded but its echo could still be heard in the current one which was about to enter its third week and reach a critical phase as the patriot invaders organized an assault on the gates of Fort Cumberland.

5 The Fort Attack

Sunday 10 November to Thursday 14 November

> Collecting his whole force inclusive of nine Indians of the St. John's river, he approached the fort in a cloudy night ... by three parties ... Made a furious assault.
>
> Isbrook Eddy, Cumberland patriot[1]

By the second week of November the patriots appeared to have the advantage in the siege of Fort Cumberland. Unbroken success since entering the region twelve days earlier had bolstered Jonathan Eddy's recruitment drive, secured his grip on the countryside, and placed him in a well-stocked camp only a mile from the main objective. Important decisions affecting the whole district emanated from the command centre at Read's farm. Captain Eddy, or "Colonel"[2] as he now styled himself, was a force to be reckoned with on the Tantramar. His tactics were ideally suited to his irregular band. Mobility and speed, guerrilla-style raids executed at night with surprise and daring, expert use of the countryside with a touch of terrorism to intimidate the populace: all had been used to bring the region into line and its garrison to the brink of surrender. The capture of the Shepody Outpost, the provision vessel, and sixty-two Fencibles and civilians were significant victories that raised patriot morale.

The most favourable season of the year had been chosen for the siege. By arriving in late autumn Eddy avoided the oppressive heat of summer and the clouds of mosquitoes and blackflies which would hover above waist-high marsh grass and infest the softwood forests.[3] The Tantramar winter, when temperatures plunge far below freezing and winds sweep the snow into white-outs, was also avoided. The autumn air was crisp but not cold in the daytime. There was frost at night, but the days were free of flies. The greatest advantage was the autumn harvest, the pride of Cumberland. Barns and granaries were filled, livestock was fat, and forests were full of game. Nowhere was the abundant harvest more evident in 1776 than in the Acadian barns scattered along the Baie Verte Road beyond Camphill. These barns overflowed with produce grown locally and hauled in from other farms to supply Eddy's army during the siege.

Advantage and success masked an undercurrent of concern. Eddy had not yet deceived Goreham into surrendering and it was time Eddy made his final bluff even though success was not certain. After sending rumours into the fort exaggerating the size of the invasion and the resurgence of rebellion, he would demand surrender in a written ultimatum. If that did not work the next step was military assault for which full local support was essential. He had wished to win a surrender through bluffing in the manner of Ethan Allen at Fort Ticonderoga but direct action could not be delayed much longer, no longer than it would take for the glory of recent victories to fade. This meant delaying for only a few days at the most since local support was already levelling off. Tales of an incompetent garrison were believed by Eddy who expected the fencibles to desert rather than defend the fort. At the same time he was aware of disciplinary problems in his own band. Timing was critical as he prepared his final move in the game of bluff.

"THE UNNECESSARY EFFUSION OF CHRISTIAN BLOOD"

The American Revolution was prosecuted on Sundays as on all days of the week but the call to Christian worship was no less urgent for that. Although government officials suspected the dissenting clergy in Nova Scotia of disloyalty, fearing that several Congregational ministers originally from New England supported the revolution even from the pulpit, their suspicions were, with one exception, unfounded. Certainly, none of the dissenting clergy in the province in 1776 was as active in the patriot cause as the reverend James Lyon of Machias, Maine, who was a member of the local Committee-of-Safety. Near Lyon's former parish on the Cobequid coast of Nova Scotia on Sunday, *10 November*, the second Sunday of the siege, David Smith preached to some empty pews in Londondery. Some of his parishioners were on their way to join Eddy in Cumberland. "He preached sensibly," according to one who had heard Smith, "but not an orator."[4] Whatever the quality of his exhortation, Smith was not cut from the same republican cloth as James Lyon and was exasperated with his parishioners. The same was true of Daniel Cock, Smith's colleague in Truro.[5] Neither of these Presbyterian ministers counselled rebellion, but a little of Lyon's political sentiment remained on the Cobequid coast to play a part in the recent activities of the district.

It was a "pleasant day" on Nova Scotia's South Shore but Simeon Perkins, a leading merchant of Liverpool, could not attend the service in the new meeting house, being ill and "having taken a portion of salts." The brief itinerancy of Samuel Sheldon Poole in that town, which Perkins helped to arrange, ended a few days earlier and "we do not expect him anymore." Poole, a Congregationalist and Harvard graduate, returned to his home near Yarmouth and the service in Liverpool was conducted by the deacons. This new place of worship had opened about a month earlier following a religious cleavage in Liverpool that saw Israel Cheever, Congregational minister at the old meeting house, forsaken by many of his parishioners who then set up the new meeting house. Seven pews had already been sold and Simeon Perkins, who led the revolt against Cheever, was gratified to learn, albeit from his sickbed, that attendance was running three-to-one ahead of that which Cheever, also a Harvard graduate, still attracted to the old meeting house.[6] The problem in Liverpool so evident that Sunday in November had no political overtones, being instead a controversy over Cheever's social habits. The dissenting clergy in Liverpool and Cobequid and elsewhere in the province, with the exception of Seth Noble in Maugerville, remained loyal despite opposite claims by Halifax officials. This was certainly true on the South Shore. Samuel Poole was back on his farm working to become an enterprising Nova Scotian. As for Israel Cheever, "having a very numerous Family" and a congregation unable to meet his salary in its reduced state, the cleavage in Liverpool could only aggravate his well-known drinking problem.[7]

A district with no religious leadership this Sunday was Cumberland. With the fort under siege, an armed camp a mile away, and residents under house arrest, there was little scope for organized worship and John Eagleson, the only settled minister on the isthmus, had been taken prisoner by Jonathan Eddy. This meant there was no service held at the garrison where repair work was suspended for the day. Nearby residents reported the results of Saturday night's shooting incidents to Joseph Goreham: "two of the inhabitants living just under the Garrison came early this morning to inform me." Eddy's men had been at their house "most of all night." How many, wondered Goreham? "Between six and seven hundred men in Arms, waiting for a favourable opportunity to attack," was their answer.[8] "They approached in small partys near the Fort," the residents recalled, "but found our Centrys so alert, and firing on them, they retired." The commander was gratified by the latter part of this account but distressed by news of the tavern keeper with whom he had made the deal that went terribly wrong. "Wethered has had about half of his buttocks taken off by a cannon shot from the Fort," it was reported, "when he was in his own house, there being many rebels in it"!9 He had been removed to the home of neighbour Jotham Gay where he was resting very uncomfortably and without medical help since the surgeon, Dr Cullen, was also Eddy's prisoner. The tragedy did not end with Samuel Wethered. His unfortunate slave, who had been frightened by the incident into premature labour, died in childbirth.

No patriot casualties were reported in these incidents but informers felt able to describe Eddy's force. "Among these people, there appeared all the French Acadians of the country," and other inhabitants were recognized from Amherst, Westcock, and Jolicure. The Acadians of Bloody Bridge had "made prize" of a schooner lying at Baie Verte, a trading vessel from Halifax.10 In their agitated state and considering that events occurred "during the night" the informers might have honestly believed that such large numbers of men had been coming and going near the fort the previous evening; they might have been repeating the exaggerated estimates planted by the patriots to impress their enemy; or they deliberately misled Goreham, in which case they were Eddy's agents. Such errors were commonplace. Ruth Peck made a faulty estimate (perhaps by design) of the number of patriots that landed in Shepody on 29 October. Her figures were accepted by Goreham then and there was no indication that he disbelieved his informers now. In rumour-filled Cumberland almost any estimate of patriot strength seemed credible.

War on this November Sunday, at least in Cumberland, was waged chiefly with the pen. Eddy sat down to write an ultimatum demanding Goreham's surrender. With inflated estimates of his army's strength having reached Goreham's ears, he believed a summons would have the desired effect and deliver the fort. This was pure bluff; should it fail he would have to attack, a prospect he did not relish. Very seriously he began to write: "To Joseph Goreham ... of the Royal Fencibles Americans Commanding Fort Cumberland:

"The already too plentiful Effusion of Human Blood in the Unhappy Contest between Great Britain and the Colonies calls on every one Engag'd on either side to use their utmost Efforts to prevent the Unnatural Carnage." Having expressed an abhorrence of war, Eddy went on to explain why he had to wage it. "The Importance of the cause on the side of America has made War necessary, and its Consequences, though in some Cases shocking, are yet unavoidable." He then moved to the real purpose of his letter. "I have to summon you in the Name of the United Colonies to surrender the Fort now under your Command to the Army sent under me by the States of America. I do promise that if you Surrender Yourselves as Prisoners of War you may depend upon being treated with the utmost Civility and Kind

Treatment; if you refuse, I am determined to storme the Fort, and you must abide the consequences." The orders and threats were consigned to paper. It only remained to add a deadline. "Your answer is expected in four Hours after you receive this ... I am Sir, Your most obedient Humble Servant, Jonathan Eddy."[11]

Goreham had advance notice of this ultimatum when the two informers who came to the fort earlier that morning "said they [the patriots] intended to send a summons this day to the Commanding Officer to surrender the Garrison." So when "a letter under colour of a Flag of truce" arrived at the main gate, he was not surprised and fired off a reply within the time limit. "Sir," he addressed Eddy. "From the Commencement of this Contest I have felt for my deluded Brother Subjects and Countrymen of America and for the many Innocent people they have wantonly Involved in the Horrors of an Unnatural Rebellion, and entertain every humane principle as well as an utter aversion to the Unnecessary effusion of Christian Blood." Although also registering his abhorrence of war, Goreham felt under no compulsion to justify his defence of the fort, so he went directly to his counter-summons. "[I] command you in his Majesty's name to disarm yourself ... and Surrender to the King's mercy." The letter closed on a point of honour. "Be assured Sir, I shall never dishonour the Character of a Soldier by Surrendering my command to any Power except to that of my Sovereign from whence it originated ... I am Sir, Your most humble servant, Joseph Goreham."[12]

A copy of the manifesto to Cumberland residents, that Goreham drafted on Saturday, was enclosed with the reply and both were delivered to Camphill. The contrived politeness of their prose reflected the formality of eighteenth-century siege etiquette. As required by the rules, Eddy declared himself before the gates of the fort with military intent and Goreham, with the requisite protestations and much to Eddy's chagrin, accepted the siege. In Eddy's attempt to bluff a surrender through the formal device of a summons and in Goreham's rebuff no room was left for negotiation. With their pens the two commanders had forced the issue to an impasse which could now be broken only by military action.

"WE HAD RATHER DIE LIKE MEN THAN BE HANG'D LIKE DOGS"

Activity resumed in Fort Cumberland on Monday, *11 November*, with renewed vigour in view of Sunday's ultimatum. An attack could come at any moment and whatever measures that could still be taken to strengthen defences had to be completed quickly. Defence of the spurr was a nagging concern. The short palisade around it, erected hastily during the summer, was part of the problem; yet, Goreham wrote, our greatest apprehension [in the spurr] was in the facility of setting fire to those old buildings, either by throwing bundles of hay or other combustibles over them short picketts." If the spurr caught fire the entire fort would be in danger. Steps were taken to reduce the hazard. First "the powder was removed from the magazine [in the spurr] to one of the old casemates in the Fort" where it would be less vulnerable to fire. Secondly "the decayed and most dangerous situated buildings" were "pulled down." Finally "a Traverse [was] erected to the Fort and Spurr Gate and the windows of several well situated houses barricaded in the Spurr." Even these measures did not satisfy Goreham. The spurr still bothered him and spotting some "fence rails of about fifteen feet long which lay near the Garrison," he had them placed around the short palisade with one end stuck in the inside trench and the other end "bearing on the Ribbons of the short palisade and pointing out over the Glacis." The idea was bizarre but effective. Goreham thought the fence rails "not only made the access in or out very difficult but prevented their throwing Combustibles over them." He was pleased with his innovation, thinking it had an architectural appearance rather like a "frieze."[13]

While improvements were made to the fort, a white flag fluttered on a pole being carried at the edge of the woods. Its bearer approached the main gate of the fort. More correspondence! For a moment it was thought Eddy had accepted Goreham's offer of mercy but the note handed to the guard turned out to be a reply to Goreham's manifesto. Purporting grandly to be "at the Desire of the Inhabitants of Cumberland," the letter was unsigned, but Goreham recognized the handwriting of Josiah Throop, a spokesperson for local supporters of the rebellion. Declaring that the inhabitants "have given incontestable Evidence of their Peaceable Dispositions," Throop presented an astounding reason for the rebellion and siege. "If the Garrison came here to defend and protect them, 'tis very Late to be informed of it – four or five days after a Number of People from the Westward in Arms appeared amongst them with an Intention to take the Fort, Attended by hundreds of Savages who threatened to burn our Houses and destroy our Families if we do not join in the Common Cause. Whatever therefore may be done by the Inhabitants is warranted by the Law of self preservation." Because the fort had failed to defend them, argued Throop, the inhabitants were justified in joining the invaders to attack the fort. In setting out his logic he took the opportunity to inflate the number of attackers and enhance his exaggeration by referring to them as savages. The rebellion was a serious movement that enjoyed divine favour; afterall, "we are not so insensible and Stupid as to run mad in a wild affair but cast ourselves on the Providence of God and expect His Blessings and protection." They were in rebellion, admitted Throop, but nothing could be done as they were caught between the savages and Goreham's manifesto. "Since your Manifesto threatens us for what is already done with a Military Execution, we have no Encouragement to retract," he argued (not without logic) and ended the letter on a note of melodramatic defiance. "We had rather die like Men than be Hang'd like Dogs."[14]

This unexpected correspondence changed nothing for Goreham. If anything it demonstrated a hardening of positions. The question was how large would Eddy's force be when he attacked, as he surely would that night or the following day at the latest. Goreham was by no means certain of the outcome but he was pleased by the improved discipline of his fencibles and satisfied that the old fort had been rescued from the disrepair he had found it in. He was convinced that staying inside was the right course; if relief arrived from Halifax his strategy would be vindicated. But timely relief depended, or so it appeared to Goreham, on sending a message through patriot lines to Windsor and Halifax, and on this point he was frustrated. Although tenuous contact was still possible with people living nearby, Goreham was unable to send a message beyond the isthmus. For example, a note about supplies was sent out of the fort that Monday "to a place called *Number One*, to one Mr. Smith."[15] *Number One* was a derelict blockhouse about a mile from the fort, near the Delesderniers' new residence. William Milburn, an inhabitant who resided in the fort, ran this errand. If he aroused no attention Milburn should be back safely in the fort by the following day.

On Monday night attention again turned to the task of getting out a call for help. "Several early attempts" had been made without success so this new attempt was carefully planned. "Lieutenant [Thomas] Dix[s]on, half pay officer, generously offered himself for this piece of difficult service," together with Charles Dixon of Sackville and two soldiers. These volunteers descended garrison hill after dark and, avoiding Eddy's patrols, launched "a small open sail boat" in Cumberland Creek. Floating down the creek and into Cumberland Basin, they disappeared into the darkness.[16] When they did not return that night Goreham was optimistic that the party had made a clean getaway. If everything went well Dixson's party should be in Windsor in three days and help might be expected in about a week.

Dawn broke grey and cold on Tuesday morning, *12 November*, and still there was no attack. The half-frozen guards came down from the ramparts swathed in blankets, puffing or chewing the last of their tobacco. In the cold weather the men's smoking increased; it was not yet midweek but already individual rations were depleted. Fortunately, tobacco was not on the scarcity list so Goreham doubled the weekly ration to half-a-pound per soldier.[17] Tension also increases tobacco use and a tense atmosphere had prevailed since Eddy's deadline expired last night. It kept the garrison on edge and sharpened their claustrophobia. Waiting was also boring for many but for Goreham, the old ranger and author of countless improvisational defences, waiting stimulated creativity. Amid the cloud of tobacco smoke he came up with two more ways to strengthen the fort. He had been concerned about the "line of small Pickets only of about Ten feet in height" around most of the fort. Unlike the palisade around the spur, which was strengthened by the frieze of fence rails, this palisade was unprotected and weak, having been erected hastily in the summer. No pickets at all guarded the protected way. If Eddy should breach these weak outer defences, they could cross the shallow ditch and ascend the eroded slopes all the way to the ramparts. Goreham turned his ingenuity to this problem and again found a solution in the litter on garrison hill and on abandoned farms. He found logs which he dragged into the fort and the "large logs were fixed all round the Parapet on rollers." Poised at the top of the wall, they would be cut loose to roll down on intruders who breached the palisade and attempted to storm the slopes. While gathering logs Goreham noticed a great many thin poles and confiscated them as well. As a final touch, "one hundred spare bayonets [were] fitted on poles of 12 feet long which were place[d] in readiness on the ramparts." These pikes were "in readiness" to use on any intruders who succeeded in avoiding the rolling logs. The log rollers and pikes were Goreham's most bizarre improvements yet and they illustrated his ingenuity and his commitment to rehabilitating the fort as best he could.[18]

Not many miles away Thomas Dixson and his party were making slow progress after successfully breaking away from the siege. Cramped in a small boat and paralysed by the damp cold, they were still far from Windsor and were concentrating on clearing Cumberland Basin in bad weather. They were unaware that their voyage, however heroic, was redundant. News of the siege already circulated in Windsor and would soon reach Halifax as a result of Michael Francklin's discovery the previous Saturday. Responses were under way. In Annapolis Royal this Tuesday "upon the first alarm of Cumberland being invested by the Rebels," a town meeting was held and the militia was called up to defend the county.[19] The extent of the crisis was unknown and a larger invasion was feared with attacks expected in Windsor, Annapolis Royal, and other points on the Fundy coast. Even with the early warning (several days earlier than Dixson was able to provide) much time would elapse before a relief expedition could be mounted. In the meantime Fort Cumberland would have to cope on its own.

Having completed the business with Smith and after sleeping in *Number One* for the night, William Milburn was "about to return to the Garrison" when he was approached by Richard Uniacke, one of Eddy's outguards who lived nearby. Uniacke demanded "that he must goe along with said Smith to the Rebel Camp." Milburn "at first refused." Travel was controlled, explained Uniacke, and Milburn needed permission to return to the fort. He would not be made a prisoner but he needed permission; it was the rule, and the young patriot explained "that Col. Eddy ... of the Rebels would never forgive them if he would not goe to him, and [if he] would Imagine they harboured any person from the Garrison, he would never forgive him." Milburn did not want to go to Camphill but "Uniacke insisted he must go, otherwise the Rebel Centrys would carry him there by force." On hearing this threat Millburn conceded the point and, "choosing rather to goe to the Centry of himself than be carried by violence," he proceeded to Eddy's headquarters.[20]

Camphill, like the garrison, was tense. Pressure was mounting for an attack now that the bluffing game was over. Eddy hesitated but his officers pressed for a decision. All groups wanted an attack, none more than the Machias contingent which coveted the garrison as the supreme prize. It was becoming increasingly difficult to control the unruly troops and their excesses were straining relations with the country people. Eddy wished that he had blank officers' commissions to attract more officers "so that Proper Regulations may be made and many disorderly actions prevented."[21] Inactivity was the chief cause of the restlessness. It had been a week since the *Polly* was captured and nearly two weeks since the Shepody Outpost fell. The aura surrounding those successes had faded. Recruitment – the greatest benefit of these victories – had levelled off and was unlikely to increase again without another dramatic success. Eddy wanted to delay the attack, hoping for outside help to bolster his enterprise. An American privateer in the basin would do fine and the prospect of seeing one was not far-fetched, but he had no reason to expect the reinforcement he had so rashly promised while recruiting in Sackville. That promise now caused embarrassment and undermined his credibility. With the sheen of past victories worn off, revolutionary enthusiasm would dampen quickly. His leadership was at stake, the troops were restless, Camphill was near chaos, and the countryside was turning against him. The garrison had to be captured. He would attack tonight.

Setting aside his problems, Eddy fuelled his natural optimism by dwelling on the many weaknesses of his enemy: the dilapidated fort, the low estimate of garrison strength, the poorly equipped fencibles, the contempt for their fighting spirit. As far as he was concerned, the Fencibles would not fight; Fort Cumberland was theirs. His troops seemed to catch his enthusiasm, especially the Machias men eager for the prize. In this mood the following senior officers gathered for instructions: Jabez West the Machias captain, Lieutenant-Colonel Zebulon Roe lately promoted for his heroics in the Cumberland Creek raid, Major William How of Fort Lawrence, Captain Thomas Faulkner of Cobequid, and Captain Hugh Quinton of Sunbury. Tactics were decided, small arms checked, and special equipment arranged: shovels for trenching, saws and scaling ladders for breaching the palisade. The work went on all day and many tactical and logistical problems were resolved. Mustering troops was a chore as they were scattered widely in the evening in taverns and homes. Frontline troops were particularly hard to find. Despite a professed enthusiasm for the attack, it was amazing how many had other essential duties to perform; others simply could not be found. The search went on into Wednesday morning before the strike force was assembled.

Preparations for the attack were in full swing when William Milburn approached Camphill but he had little trouble entering the encampment and finding the patriot leader. "He told ... Eddy what he came about, and to let him return with Mr. Smith to the Garrison." To improve his chances he added that Smith "had teams with him to bring out some Goods." On hearing that goods might be coming out of the fort, "Col. Eddy said he had no objection." But just as Milburn was about to leave, "some Frenchmen, particularly one John Cassie," protested that Millburn "was a spy sent out from the Garrison," The malleable colonel changed his mind; perhaps Milburn had seen too much of the mobilization for tonight's attack. Permission was withdrawn and Milburn was detained as a prisoner.[22]

Although the attack was to be an all-out effort – the first phase in a campaign to overrun the province – when the hour arrived to move out, Eddy could muster a force of only "about 80 Men."[23] Absenteeism was endemic in the various contingents; for example, only nine of the sixteen Maliseets were ready to go. The reason was not that Eddy underestimated the task ahead, but that he was unable to force his patriots to join the attack. Assaulting prepared defences frontally was dangerous business requiring blind courage, mass discipline, and martial co-ordination: assets in short supply among the irregulars of Camphill. To the most resolute patriot – whether a veteran for whom over fifteen years had passed since the last military order, or a youth with no military experience – the fort, even in its advanced state of decay, looked formidable. To coax volunteers to attack was immensely difficult; forcing them was impossible. Yet a force of only eighty of his more than 200 troops represented Eddy's failure to concentrate maximum strength for the main effort. Military convention dictated that attackers outnumber defenders of a prepared fortification by a ratio of at least three- to-one. Incredibly, the defenders outnumbered the attackers that Tuesday night because Eddy failed to command his total force and, to make matters worse, he acted on faulty intelligence, believing the defenders "were 100 strong in the Fort."[24] Since they in fact exceeded 200, Eddy's error was considerable but he would continue to believe the intelligence even after the siege was over. Ironically Goreham, who overestimated the size of the besieging force, also continued in his error until after the siege.

The composition of Eddy's eighty-man strike force is still a subject of speculation. The twenty Machias men formed its nucleus although some might have returned to Boston with the prisoners. Besides the nine Maliseets, between thirteen and twenty-one Acadians were among the attackers. The Passamaquoddy, Sunbury, and Cobequid contingents, totalling sixty-one men, were represented by perhaps as few as thirty-five men. The remainder of the force (if no Micmacs or Pictonians were involved, but they likely were) was from Cumberland – the vanguard of Nova Scotia's rebellion. No matter how the calculations are made it is unlikely that there were more than a dozen Cumberlanders in the strike force – not a very good showing for the local rebels. A subject equally open to speculation is the number of local defenders. Among those who carried arms in the fort were "Fifteen Carpenters, One half pay Lieut., Three Militia Officers and nine Inhabitants," all of Cumberland, totalling twenty-eight locals. In their "numerous Familys" were additional defenders and some of the Fencibles were from the district. But even if family members and local Fencibles are discounted, the minimum number of local defenders exceeded the maximum number of local attackers. It is a simple fact that the garrison and not Camphill had the edge in terms of local content in the wee hours of Wednesday morning.[25]

"A HEAVY FIRE ON THE FLAGG STAFF BASTION"

Wednesday, "4 o'Clock in the morning," *13 November,* "it being exceeding dark ... their first grand attempt" on Fort Cumberland began.[26] "Collecting his whole force" of eighty soldiers, Eddy divided them into "three parties" for the assault. According to the strategy worked out with his officers, the first party, mostly Acadians, would lead a diversionary attack; the second party carrying ladders and tools would scale the outer palisade; while the third party from "different quarters" would make "a furious assault."[27] To increase the chance of gaining access, Eddy appended a curious element to his plan. A Maliseet would try to sneak into the fort and, during the confusion expected from the diversionary attack, would attempt to unlock the main gate in time for the all-out patriot charge.

The weather was cloudy as Eddy's band marched down the Baie Verte Road and fanned out over the dark hillside to the north of the fort before creeping along the old trenches built by General Moncton in 1755 when Beauséjour was captured by the British. The basis of Eddy's strategy was to send in a feint attack against the flagstaff bastion in hopes of diverting most of the fencibles to that point, then to attack in force "the Curtain opposite the Bakehouse between Prince's and Howe's Bastion which was the weakest part of the Fort."[28] In that way, he hoped to storm the fort, force his way inside and demand Goreham's surrender. Newly-appointed Lieutenant Lewis Delesdernier, who was fluent in French, was "detached with 25 or 30 others as the covering party in the feint attack." Leading his men and "shouldering his musket," Delesdernier went into combat for the first time.[29] They crept into position seeking cover in "the Brick kiln and drains at the foot of the Glacis and other hollow places," and opened up "a heavy fire."[30]

The garrison was not surprised by this "first grand attempt," having been on alert since the expiry of Eddy's ultimatum on Sunday. The intelligence provided by informers and the patriots' own actions indicated an attack was looming. So with the initial burst of musket fire from the Acadian corps at four o'clock in the morning, the fencibles sprang to action. Those in the flagstaff bastion began laying down a heavy fire of their own and for the first time "the whistlers," as Lewis Delesdernier referred to musket balls, flew over his head.[31] The sham attack of the Acadians did not fool the veteran Goreham. Being aware even more than Eddy of the weak spots in the fort, and knowing from long experience how to deploy a force for the best defence, he reacted calmly to the gunfire over at the flagstaff bastion, guessing correctly that Eddy was acting "with a view to draw the principal part of Our Strength to Support that post." He was not very worried about that bastion, a relative strong point; his fencibles could hold off the enemy there. Besides, enemy fire in that quarter did not sound heavy enough for the real attack. Goreham stood pat with his main force at the weakest point of the garrison. "The Main Guard, being kept as a reserve to reinforce occasionally where most required," was stationed in front of the bakehouse. With Prince bastion to the left and Howe bastion to the right, the troops faced the rundown curtain wall in between. He was not persuaded to redeploy this main body of troops or, more importantly, to reangle his cannon to the current hot spot. "Their real attack was intended on the Curtain,"[32] surmised Goreham, and he waited for it. Sure enough, a fusillade soon opened up from Eddy's main force directly in front of the curtain wall, and the bombardier unlimbered the garrison artillery.

While the noise of battle erupted over Cumberland, the Maliseet managed in the darkness to get within the defences of the fort according to Eddy's plan, perhaps at the protected way which had no pickets. Unchallenged amid a chorus of reverberating military orders and unnoticed in the melee of people and terrorized cattle, he stole along the inside of the palisade towards the main gate. Just as he reached the gate and attempted to remove the bar that would permit Eddy's men easy entry, he was spotted by a fencible who drew his sword, dashed forward, and slashed at the man's upraised arm, maiming him but securing the fort at a critical moment.[33] Having so far failed to breach the walls, Eddy pressed his men forward but the fate of his frontal assault was decided the moment the bombardier issued the order to fire the cannon. By staying inside the fort, Goreham added to his numerical superiority the advantage of a prepared defence, either of which could have decided the battle in favour of the loyal Nova Scotians. With the addition of a third advantage, namely the fort's artillery directed against the main body of attackers, Eddy's fate was sealed. The attackers were frightened out of their wits by the concentrated fire of the fort's heavy guns. Eddy's attack plan was useless. "They soon found themselves deceived in their schemes,"[34] exulted Goreham. In the crisp night air, the bombardment was deafening – "a furious Cannonade" above the attackers' heads, "but harmless"! Beneath that cannonade a few of the assailants succeeded in getting close to the walls of the fort. In shock from the fearful roar Private Isbrook Eddy, the Colonel's twenty-two year old son, was close enough to see above him the large log rollers poised ominously at the edge of the parapet ready to be cut loose on anyone ascending the glacis. The impression of those rollers silhouetted against the faint moonlight shining through the cloud cover would never fade from the youth's memory. Fifty years later he would still exclaim about those "logs, stretched along the declivity, which might be rolled down with the utmost ease, and with great violence, upon any assailants."[35]

Decrepit as it was, Fort Cumberland was too formidable a prize for the patriots, crouched in the "hollow places,"[36] and stunned by the loud cannonade. "We thought fit to Relinquish our Design," admitted Eddy about his decision to retreat, "after a heavy firing from their Great Guns and small Arms without intermission for 2 Hours, which we Sustained without any Loss (Except one Indian being wounded), who behaved very gallantly, and Retreated in good Order to our Camp." Eddy vowed "that Never Men behaved better than ours, during the engagement never flinching,"[37] but Goreham noted from his vantage point that they "received such heavy fire that they threw down their Scaling Ladders, Saws, and other implements for cutting down the pickets, [and] quitting some of their arms fell flatt on the ground and scrabbled off." He estimated "they had an Indian and several others wounded."[38] The short casualty list on both sides (the garrison suffered no casualties) was a fortuitous outcome of the main attempt to capture the Nova Scotian fort. Goreham's anticipation of Eddy's plan was nothing less than uncanny to many patriots who attributed it to a spy in their camp. Isbrook Eddy always believed that Goreham "had been apprized of the design."[39] It is more likely that Goreham, who had anticipated his enemy on more than one occasion in his long career, was simply acting with the wisdom of a seasoned commander.

Daylight on Wednesday morning found Camphill in disarray. Soldiers were in shock and exhausted by a sleepless night and disastrous attack. Their officers gathered in Read's house to absorb the pain of defeat and to try and salvage remnants of the siege. Excuses abounded. We found the fort "stronger than we imagined," offered Eddy. They were "over-powered by a superior number of British forces," agreed Elijah Ayer. The fencibles "made a brave defence," conceded Isbrook Eddy. We were stymied, believed Josiah Throop, because "the Fort was Piquetted in and the walls and Ramparts lately repaired." They knew of the early repair work – Zebulon Roe had inspected it – but not the innovative repairs made just before the attack. The lack of artillery was bemoaned; how could they have captured the fort "without cannon or the risk of many lives"?

"Impracticable," answered Josiah Throop. How could they defeat the fort with its "six cannon, about a Hundred men and six hundred Small arms," when Camphill was "without cannon or other Military Articles Save their Small Arms"![40] Other patriots would criticize Eddy's attack as "a hasty and rash operation," and question his leadership. "For some reason," noted John Allan sarcastically when he heard of the attack, "Eddy thought proper to retreat."[41] There is no question that Eddy's star fell after the fort attack. He lost authority in the army camp and revolutionary council and other leaders asserted themselves as Camphill adjusted to the new reality. The Committee-of-Safety was reorganized that Wednesday to co-ordinate defence and assume civil authority which previously had been Eddy's exclusive domain. Patriots "ranged them Selves in Companies" for better military order and, fearing counter-attack, "began Such measures of Self defence as appeared to them best in so Critical a Crisis." Plans to capture of the fort were set aside at least temporarily. Patrols were deployed to maintain the blockade, the one effective tactic remaining. Finally, it was decided to appeal to Boston for help and to beg "that the Counties of Cumberland and Sunbury in Nova Scotia be taken under the Protection of this State till that Province can be Subdued." The appeal would take several forms to ensure it attracted the attention of the Americans. The Committee-of-Safety would petition in writing; a separate letter would be addressed by Eddy; and a personal appeal would also be made by Josiah Throop who was chosen to go immediately to Boston.[42]

The petition began: "Captain Eddy, with a small party, has invaded Cumberland," and enumerated early successes: "taken a guard of twelve men, also a provision vessel with her guard, and a vessel from Annapolis [Hall's schooner]." Only then could Wednesday's disaster be broached. Eddy "has attempted to storm the Garrison but finds it impossible with all the assistance he can raise here." This was an admission that local support was weak and, "as intelligence is already gone to Halifax, we are in the utmost distress"![43] Despite Eddy's boast that "we ... totally cut off their Communications with the Country, keeping them closely blocked up within the Fort,"[44] they knew of Dixson's escape and expected the fort to be relieved. "We ... therefore beg," they went on, "for the preservation of our lives and the lives of our families, for the immediate help of 500 or a regiment of men, if it may be, with 2 mortars, ammunition, and provision."[45] No mention was made of Eddy's promised reinforcement. That promise – a mainstay of his recruiting drive – was assumed to be a sham and their petition was a desperate appeal. "We have ... to Intreat of the Province of Massachusetts for our Selves and for the Inhabitants of Nova Scotia," pleaded Eddy, "Send some Privateers into the Bay and Some Troops and Military Stores." He had "attempted the Garrison but Cannot take it without Some Cannon and Mortars, nor Can we get off what we have taken without Some help as there is a Man-of-War in the Bay."[46] Of course the *Juno* had sailed nearly a week ago, but Eddy was admitting for the first time that he might have to abandon the siege and would need help even to salvage stores already captured.

Suggestions were made as Throop readied himself for what could easily be a two-week journey. With defeat being a real possibility, the cost of the expedition and pay for his men began to weigh on Eddy, so Throop was advised to ask "that our army now in Cumberland be considered as part of the Continental Army and taken into Continental pay." Throop was also asked to beg "that a Colonel's Commission be Sent to Jonathan Eddy Esqr. to command the forces" and render legitimate the rank he already used. With the petition and letter in his pocket, Throop took leave of an army camp "of about three hundred including Accadians."[47] This number was larger than that which Eddy would later concede, but for Throop it was a useful exaggeration to present to the Americans when emphasizing the strength of the local rebellion. Whatever the true size, all professed "a Cheerful dependence on divine Providence." A measure of optimism was restored to Camphill by the plea to Massachusetts, as if the very act of putting to paper the events of the siege and placing their "Safety and Success" in American hands had somehow removed the sting of defeat. Throop was sent off with the esteemed message that "we doubt not but by the Divine Blessing and Your friendly Assistance we Shall Soon add another Stripe to the American flagg and another Colony to the United States!"[48] With God and America on their side the siege might yet be won.

Down the road at Fort Cumberland there was rejoicing over the victory. Crumbling defences and uncertain military skills had proved adequate. Conversation at the main well was more animated, and families were more relaxed than they had been since they came under siege. That the attackers had been driven from the gates was sufficient; Goreham had no intention of risking a counter-attack, being content to deny Eddy the fort while awaiting reinforcement. This defence posture coupled with Camphill's new commitment to the blockade was a prescription for stalemate as the siege entered its third week.

In Boston that Wednesday night John Allan entertained members of the state government, the same group that earlier in the day Josiah Throop had set out from Cumberland to petition on behalf of the patriots besieging Fort Cumberland. These New Englanders "appeared to sympathize very much with the people of Nova Scotia," Allan observed, "but in their present circumstances, they were afraid nothing could be done." They were animated and cheerful, having just "received intelligence that General Howe had retreated," but with heavy fighting around New York "there was such a demand in the States for their own defence" that Nova Scotia was likely to be ignored.

Allan's personal prospects appeared brighter. He was invited to attend a session of the state board on Friday and on Caleb Gannett's advice "had much conversation" with Congress representative John Adams at Braintree. Adams, long in favour of capturing Nova Scotia, promised to use his influence to gain a hearing for Allan in Congress. Earlier that day Allan "Received information by way of Liverpool Nova Scotia that Eddy had occasioned much stir in the Province, that the people in Halifax were much in fear lest the Indians should be immediately upon them."[49] News of the siege had travelled far and fast. To reach Boston so quickly this news could not have come from Michael Francklin but from earlier reports, possibly from the two Cumberland men who travelled to Halifax and who were noticed by the Morrisons as they passed through Cobequid. From Halifax the news could have spread along the South Shore to Liverpool in as little as two days, and then travelled on to Boston.

"EIGHT DOLLARS A MONTH ... AND A SUIT OF CLOTHES"

Another crisis developed in Camphill on Thursday morning, *14 November,* when the Machias contingent decided to go home, "many of them declaring they did not come for such business [a siege] but to seize particular persons with their property."[50] This tiny band of soldiers, the invasion component of Eddy's force, lent credibility to the patriot effort in Cumberland and formed the nucleus of all military action. If they departed, the rebellion would collapse. On the other hand, their continued presence was a source of alarm. They had become a threat to friend and foe alike since their "expectation of much Plunder" was dashed in the fort attack. Some local supporters of the rebellion felt sufficiently threatened by the Machias men to confront Committee-of-Safety members and "were obliged to consult their judgement for Safety." Camphill was in confusion and the Committee-of-Safety temporarily lost control. "Things appeared in a State of anarchy," was how the situation was described, with "no order or Regulation!" A solution had to be found that would induce the Machias men to stay yet eliminate the threat they posed to the community.

Hurried conferences at Gardiner's searched for an end to the crisis. Negotiations continued until the Machias men agreed to a settlement. Under this deal the committee "was obliged to Engage Eight dollars a month for three months and a suit of clothes to Each of Captain Eddy's men, otherwise they were determined to go." Calculated to restore order and hold the force together, this tax on rebellion, which would have to be borne by the populace, might further dampen local zeal for the "cause of liberty." As John Allan understated: "by this time the Inhabitants began to suspect they were Imposed on."[51] But Eddy was optimistic that his leadership would be re-established now that his Machias men were pacified. The blockade might still bring the garrison to its knees, or with reinforcements a second attack could be mounted with results quite different from those of Wednesday's fiasco. The siege would go on.

"Impracticable ... without cannon!"[52] This lament was heard everywhere on Camphill. Nothing of a military nature, it was argued, could be attempted "without some cannon and mortars."[53] A request for heavy guns had been included in the letter to Boston but other sources were also explored. Someone remembered that there were cannon in Charlottetown on the undefended island of St John's. Patriots who had been to Baie Verte recalled hearing Eliphalet Chappell of that place say that "the cannon, when he left Charlottetown, were not mounted but lay in the Sand near the Wharf." Someone, probably Nathaniel Reynolds, wondered whether they could sail there, carry off the cannon, and return to Baie Verte. The schooner seized in Baie Verte by the Acadians might make the voyage. From there the cannon could be hauled down the road to Camphill and used in another attack on the fort. The plan was far-fetched and would require a large crew to sail the schooner and retrieve the guns. But Eddy was desperate to acquire artillery. A detachment departed for Baie Verte to make the schooner seaworthy.[54]

While in detention for the last two days, William Milburn observed military operations in Camphill and identified certain patriots. He knew Thomas Faulkner of Cobequid who conferred often with Eddy; also James Avery who "was their Commissary." Milburn witnessed the return of Eddy's dispirited troops after the fort attack and the attempts to organize them into companies. This Thursday he "saw a Company of men from the River St. Johns" being drilled by Jabez West. Amid his observations, Milburn was visited by Eddy who admitted that "he was Glad they had detained him as a prisoner." Ever the optimist, Eddy explained that "in a few days they expected some Guns from Machias, with Privateers," and he revealed the purpose of his visit. As he knew that Milburn was "more experienced in Guns than any of them, he would make him their Gunner. "As compelling as Eddy's offer was, the prisoner declined. "He would never fire a Gun against the Garrison or his Majesty's troops, but he [Eddy] might do as he pleased!"[55] What pleased Eddy was to keep Milburn a prisoner, but first he had to send him before the Committee-of-Safety at Gardiner's place. There chairperson Robert Foster issued the order that placed Milburn under house arrest in Sackville. The Milburn case demonstrated the growing importance of the committee and Eddy's deference to it.

The struggles in Camphill and in the fort were increasingly internal during this period of impasse. The outcome of the siege now seemed to depend on forces beyond the borders of Cumberland. Problems were managed but seldom resolved. The patriot army had been held intact by placating the Machias men and Eddy was able to continue the siege by sharing power with the Committee-of-Safety. The appeal to Boston and the notion of finding cannon at Charlottetown, if not exactly raising hopes, created a wait-and-see attitude in Camphill. In the garrison, the chief worry was the dwindling commissariat; the chief hope was Thomas Dixson's party, gone now some three days. In fact Dixson was still labouring in the Minas Channel, nowhere near Windsor. Fortunately for the fort this did not matter. The siege was already the talk of Halifax this Thursday and steps were being taken by the navy to lift it.

"Proceed immediately to Sea with His Majesty's Sloop under your Command"! From his headquarters on *Rainbow* in Halifax Harbour, George Collier addressed his crack privateer-hunter, James Dawson, captain of the sloop *Hope*, just returned from South Shore waters off Port Mouton. "Upon the certainty that Fort Cumberland was actually invested by a body of Rebells," he ordered Dawson to sail "in search of His Majesty's Sloops *Albany* and *Diligent*," and send them to Cumberland.[56]

The order resulted from the urgent message sent by Michael Francklin after his mission to Partridge Island. Thus far, in response to Francklin's earlier reports, Collier had dispatched *Albany* and *Diligent* to Passamaquoddy and Penobscot and *Vulture* to patrol Minas Basin. Now he was sending ships directly to Cumberland. *Albany* and *Diligent* were somewhere between Annapolis Royal and Penobscot, or among the Passamaquoddy Islands; when found, explained Collier to Dawson, "you will give Directions to proceed immediately to Fort Cumberland and destroy if possible the Rebel Armament now employed against that Place." If the fort was in danger, Michael Hyndman of *Albany* was "to endeavour throwing as large a Body of Seamen and Officers into it as He can spare from the two Sloops, and to use every Endeavour in His Power to distress and harass the Enemy and assist the King's Troops in those Parts." In all likelihood *Vulture* would be seen in the Bay of Fundy in which event James Feattus as senior captain was to be consulted, given the Commodore's "Directions," and applied to for further orders. It was also explained that Captain Hyndman was "to be attentive to the Basin of Minas and Windsor," and should it turn out that *Diligent* could be spared, "He is to Dispatch Her for the purpose of keeping that Channel clear of the Pirate Boats which have lately infested it." And Collier expected to be kept informed: "the earliest Communication of the State things are in is of the utmost Consequence," with messages to be sent "as often as opportunity serves and any thing of Moment Occurs."[57]

Collier's orders were broadly based because of the fear at this stage of a general American attack in the Bay of Fundy, and because of the possibility that enemy privateers in Minas Basin were acting in concert with Jonathan Eddy. The feeling in Halifax was that Eddy's attack in Cumberland had larger implications and that he intended to "ravage the adjacent Country." By Thursday evening, *Hope* was sailing southward off Chebucto Head. Captain Dawson and all others outside the small siege perimeter in Cumberland were still unaware that the siege had settled into stalemate. For the time being, the focus in Halifax would shift away from the capital to other centres, particularly to seaward as civilian and military officials responded to the news about Cumberland. But Dawson's thoughts were probably elsewhere. The "Pleasant weather" meant speedy progress. If he could find *Albany* and *Diligent* quickly, and should "His Majesty's Service" not require him further in the Bay of Fundy, he would soon be able to revert to his "former Cruizing Orders," a source of consolation for a captain whose first love was hunting privateers.[58]

6 The *Vulture* Reinforcement

Friday 15 November to Wednesday 20 November

A Detachment ... Embark'd Yesterday morning at Windsor and Sailed Immediately under the Command of Major Batt to Reinforce Colonel Goreham.

William Feilding, Royal Marines, Halifax[1]

Windsor in 1776 was an atypical Nova Scotian village. The rural New England character common to many settlements was altered in Windsor by its proximity to Halifax. Of the villages on the Bay of Fundy side of the peninsula, Windsor was closest to the capital and that attribute accounted for the complexity of its social profile. Its "fine clear air" and fertile soil contrasted with the damp bedrock underlying Halifax. Citizens of the capital viewed Windsor as a healthful, spa-like resort – "the Montpelier of Nova Scotia."[2] Business people, judges, and councillors had country estates in and around Windsor; this was apparent to tourists who noted that "gentlemen of Halifax keep their Courts here." To support this elite, Windsor boasted a larger share of artisans and tradespeople than was normal for a village of 600 inhabitants. The town was the market centre for a rural farm district of five townships, and again proximity to Halifax was the key: "Some gentlemen keep stores here to receive butter, cheese or any other produce of the Country which they send to Halifax." The Avon, "a fine navigable river," flows past Windsor "where they can export or import goods to any part of Europe."[3]

Fort Edward added to the complexity of Windsor society. The British dragoons who reopened the fort in April 1776 were replaced by 100 Royal Highland Emigrants at the end of May. These provincial troops mixed easily with the residents and their officers were a welcome addition to the local gentry. The garrison was conveniently supplied overland from headquarters in Halifax or via Minas Basin by small transport ships since "the Avon is navigable as far as Fort Edward for vessels of four hundred Tons."[4]

The region of which Windsor was the "principal township" was noted for its loyalty. When the revolution began, the people there were among the first to enter into an association "to stand by his Majesty with lives and fortunes." Willingly, they took the oath of allegiance: "we do not hear of any who have refused," mused William Ellis, not even the planters. By March 1776 Windsor supported a large loyal militia from all five townships. The south shore of the Minas Basin was thought to be a target of Massachusetts and by autumn an attack was expected, so that "all workmen and all materials [were] at present employ'd in the dismal work of fortifying the country."[5]

Religious life was more varied in Windsor than in most outsettlements. It was one of the few villages beyond the capital where the Established Church exerted a strong presence. Thirty-eight per cent of local families professed Anglicanism in 1770 according to one survey. An equal portion were religious dissenters and a quarter of the families were either Baptists or Quakers, with Baptists forming the largest group in adjacent Newport Township.[6] The only resident minister in 1776 was William Ellis who was supported by the Society for the Propagation of the Gospel. The local church, "or what we call the Church here, was built by general Subscription of the Township," explained Ellis. "It serves for a Church, Dissenting house, Schoolhouse, Court House and occasionally for a tippling house." The church was a multi-purpose centre and the people were religiously experimental. When the previous Anglican missionary could not serve adequately the people of his large parish, they readily "indulged their own whims," and in the first year of the revolution this tendency reached new heights. "Fanaticism has taken strong hold," observed Ellis in September 1776. Tradespeople and labourers presumed to preach the gospel.[7] One was Henry Alline, a farmer and tanner of nearby Falmouth. His influence would eventually exceed that of the others and alter the religious landscape of the province more than Ellis could have imagined. But by November Alline had not yet carried his ministry beyond the religiously volitile district of Windsor.

In the embryonic land transportation system of Nova Scotia, Windsor was a strategic link, being the gateway to the Annapolis Valley and the jumping-off point to Cobequid and Cumberland. The strategic role of this farming district on the Avon River would be maintained at least until a road was cut through the woods to Truro and Cumberland.[8] It was clear in the autumn of 1776 that any task force organized to lift the siege of Fort Cumberland would use the village of Windsor as its staging area.

"THERE IS SOME INVASION IN THIS PROVINCE"

The south Fundy coast from Windsor to Annapolis Royal had been on military alert since Michael Francklin's return from Cobequid with the news that Fort Cumberland was besieged. Steps were taken to prepare a local defence and an expedition to Cumberland. The public sprung into action under the leadership of Winkworth Tonge, Isaac Deschamps, Michael Francklin, and others. "The substantial settlers are all hearty in their Loyalty," asserted Arbuthnot, "especially Windsor whose people turned out, upon the first advice of the Rebels' intention being known, [and] did their duty with great alertness." In Annapolis Royal the militia had been on "constant Guard" since Tuesday, 12 November, the day Francklin's alarm reached there.[9] Halifax had also heeded his alarms: *Vulture* was en route to Windsor, and *Hope* was off in search of *Albany* and *Diligent*. More troops were also "expected up from Halifax."[10] Ships had been requisitioned for the relief expedition. Even the job of outfitting had been started: "measures are already fallen upon to Collect Water Casks for that purpose." News of the Cumberland attack led people to believe that the Minas shore was the next target and Francklin was especially active in preparing for this eventuality. "Every Measure I can think of is taken," he verified on Thursday, 14 November, "to prevent the Enemy from getting into any one of these five Townships undiscovered or unmolested."[11]

It was to the village of Windsor, bustling with the activity of local defence and the relief of Fort Cumberland, that Thomas Dixson and his party sailed their small open boat on Friday, *15 November.* Foul weather had extended their voyage into its fourth day. This morning they tacked up the Avon River at high tide and in a fair wind before beaching on a mud bank in front of Fort Edward. Dixson was soon conferring with Commander Thomas Batt and Michael Francklin only to learn that they already knew of Eddy's invasion. However, his firsthand account was final confirmation "and makes it Certain that Cumberland is invested by the Rebells." They were described by Dixson as "a Party of Rebells, Acadians and Indians, conjectured to be about three or four hundred men, who are daily augmented by the people of the Country." His conjecture was high but it was the lowest yet and gave Francklin a more realistic basis on which to plan the relief expedition. Only a few hours were spent in Windsor before the Dixson party continued by foot on to Halifax. The weather in the afternoon deteriorated to "fresh gales with sleet," making the overland leg of the journey nearly as unpleasant as the sea voyage, but Goreham's dispatch would be in General Massey's hands on the following day.[12]

As in Windsor, plans were being developed in the capital to deal with the invasion. "As there is a probability," wrote George Collier from the *Rainbow*, "that several of the deluded People now in Arms Against their Sovereign may attempt to ravage the Country in the Neighbourhood of Fort Cumberland, or some other part of Nova Scotia, it is extremely necessary that the utmost Vigilance and Attention should be employed to repel and disperse such invaders, by the most vigorous exertion of the Kings Forces by Sea and Land in those parts." Collier's general order to ships in the Bay of Fundy underlined his concern over the invasion of Cumberland and reflected his fear that patriots might be pushing deeper into the countryside. The only naval ship now in the Bay was *Vulture* (tacking hard this Friday in Minas Channel where the crew "saw the Sand" near Cape Split), but by the time Collier's order reached Annapolis Royal he expected several ships to be in those waters. "You are ... Directed," he wrote to his captains, "to cooperate with the Commanding Officer of His Majesty's Troops at Windsor, giving Him all the assistance ... You possibly can, and particularly in the case of a Requisition for transporting troops [to Cumberland], covering a landing, or any other Point which you think can tend to promote the Kings Service."[13]

A public outcry over Eddy's attack had propelled Collier, Arbuthnot, and Massey into action. All three scrambled to avoid criticism: Collier for not stationing ships in the Bay of Fundy, Arbuthnot for assuring everyone that Nova Scotia was safe, and Massey for disclaiming responsibility for defending anything beyond the Halifax dockyard. Collier and Arbuthnot managed to escape public scorn but Massey, the least adept of the three at public relations, was jeered in the streets. The outcry was fuelled by rumours over the size of the attack and the likelihood of its success – rumours that spread quickly to coastal settlements.

In Liverpool the Queen's County Court had been in session for the last three days. Because "there is more business than usual," Simeon Perkins, a member of the court, feared that proceedings would not end until Saturday. Court officials habitually dined at John West's place and this Friday, while eating there, they heard "news from Halifax via Medway that there is some invasion in this province by the New England people and that ... Francklin is taken prisoner."[14] Apart from animating lunchtime conversations in Liverpool, this news confirmed that Haligonians had known of the siege at least since Wednesday (it was now Friday), plenty of time for public opinion to build and exert pressure on Massey, Collier, and Arbuthnot.

"... PROCEED TO WINDSOR WITH THE GREATEST HASTE"

After Dixson's visit, Francklin went back to organizing the Windsor task force with renewed vigour. A note was sent to Annapolis Royal in search of a warship. "We must intreat you," he wrote, "to repair to the Basin of Minas as soon as possible to take the Transports under your Convoy for the Relief of that Garrison [Cumberland]." The Windsor group had also "come to a resolution to send a party tomorrow morning to Cornwallis to fetch round Ratchford's Sloop of 80 or 90 Tons." This vessel and the one obtained earlier, "nearly as large," and two schooners in Windsor would be sufficient to transport the troops. A warship was needed to protect these vessels during the voyage to Cumberland "as Privateers have been and are now in all probability in this neighbourhood."[15] By Friday night Francklin was satisfied with the preparations and shifted his attention to the north shore of Minas Basin. He had heard that a few Onslow residents had gone to join Eddy but his chief concern, which had not been dispelled by Dixson, was the spread of rebellion beyond Cumberland. "This evening I hope to provide two trusty persons to send to Cobequid," he reported to Arbuthnot on Friday, "that we may know how affairs go on there, with orders if any Detachment of the Rebells come that way ... to give ... notice of it."[16]

Outside Windsor on a rainy Saturday morning, *16 November,* teams of oxen could be seen on the Halifax road moving at their usual somniferous pace down the muddy track towards Fort Sackville at the head of Bedford Basin. Their purpose was to fetch arms, ammunition, and flints for the militia of Windsor and nearby townships. News of Eddy's invasion had spread alarm along the Fundy coast and "our people press me with great anxiety," explained Francklin, "to be enabled to defend themselves and their property." The supplies (the ox carts could carry a total of two tons) were requested in a letter sent the previous day to Marriot Arbuthnot and, because of the need for haste, Francklin asked that they be brought out to Fort Sackville where his carts would pick them up. "I shall therefore hope that they will be sent to that post without delay."[17] He need not have worried. Arbuthnot was delighted with the "great alertness" of the Windsor people who "have demanded arms and ammunition, which is sent them."[18]

There was an unusual amount of traffic on the Halifax road this Saturday. In the opposite direction to the ox teams marched two companies of Royal Marines comprising about ninety soldiers in single file in full combat gear. They were coming from Halifax to board the transports collected by Francklin for the relief expedition. With them was Captain

Gilfred Studholme of the Royal Fencibles who would be rejoining his besieged regiment.[19] The marines had been "much hurt at being left behind" in Halifax when General Howe went back to New England, and
after a quiet summer on the Grand Parade they were "exceedingly tired
of Nova Scotia." Only the rumour of an invasion sustained their interest;
"if this is true," wrote a marine, "we shall have something to do this Campaign." Now rumour was reality and the marines had something to do at
last: slog forty miles through the mud to Windsor.[20] They were led by
Captain Huntsbach Branson and the youthful Captain William Pitcairn.

Rain turned to snow in the afternoon over central Nova Scotia. The
weather was no better in Halifax when the bedraggled Dixson party arrived and presented the siege report to army command. One officer
thought it "a very lame account"; Dixson had "no proper information ...
of the Numbers and Force of the Rebels before Fort Cumberland."[21] His
arrival, however, increased public pressure for a strong relief force and
the hard-pressed Massey impulsively ordered another detachment to
Windsor on the shortest notice. "At half an hour's warning,"[22] the Grenadier Company of Highland Emigrants under Captain Murdoch Mac-
Laine was ordered "to march ... as far that night as Fort Sackville and to
proceed to Windsor with the greatest haste."[23] They departed only two
hours after the order was issued.

Communications intensified between Windsor and the capital. Couriers kept Massey and Francklin informed on all aspects of the relief plan:
troop movements, transport assembly, and militia deployment. Naval
matters were Collier's domain and they were not well co-ordinated with
the efforts of Massey and Francklin. A heavy snow squall this Saturday afternoon obscured Minas Basin so that people in Windsor could not see
HMS *Vulture* anchor with its "best Bower" at four o'clock in the mouth of
the Avon River. The weather had been fair during the week-long voyage
around from Halifax. It had been a longer voyage than usual due to the
lack of wind, but it had been uneventful. The ship "veer'd away and
Moor'd a Cable each way; got down [the] top gallant Yards," which were
frozen stiff in the cold sleet. *Vulture's* armed boat was outfitted and ready
to be sent upriver to Fort Edward on Sunday morning.[24] Although Feattus, the captain of *Vulture*, had fulfilled his orders, neither *Gage* nor *Loyal
Nova Scotia* had been sighted, and his was the only warship anchored off
Windsor. Collier had promised a stronger naval presence, and sooner.

"CRUISING FOR THE ANNOYANCE
OF THE ENEMY"

At three o'clock Sunday morning, *17 November*, HMS *Diligent* and *Albany*
were at sea some forty-two leagues off Cape Sable, sailing through the

pitch blackness to Penobscot. After searching Passamaquoddy Bay and the mouth of the St Croix River the two ships were moving to the next phase of Collier's orders of 6 November, to search the coast for signs of an American invasion. At four in the morning Phillip McSavoy, a sailor on *Diligent*, "departed this life" and was buried at sea.[25] Despite the early hour there was also activity at army headquarters in Halifax where at four o'clock Sunday morning Eyre Massey and his associates were mounting horses to ride to Windsor. The general was pleased to be leaving the capital for a few days and had reason to depart before the townspeople were up. His popularity had plummeted since Eddy's attack. He was accused of neglecting Fort Cumberland and "cannot walk in the streets without being insulted."[26] By going to Windsor to supervise the relief force, he could with one stroke escape the insults of Halifax and be seen as boldly defending the province. Massey and his party rode off at a brisk pace on the road to Windsor, skirting the edge of Bedford Basin from which glimmered the only light in the hour before dawn. With the general were his aide-de-camp Captain Wade, Captain Spry, Lieutenant Needham, and two servants: "all well mounted and armed."[27] They were also well bundled up against the penetrating wind and a strong prospect of snow. They should be in Windsor after six hours of hard riding.

Back out to sea, "3 or 4 leagues" from Cape Sable, HMS *Hope* sailed this morning in "fresh gales and squally" weather. Captain Dawson was three days out of Halifax on his way to Maine in search of *Albany* and *Diligent*. He had every intention of fulfilling his orders which instructed him to find the two ships and send them to Cumberland, but Nova Scotian waters offered a rich harvest of privateers and the daring Captain was loath to pass up a prize. When at eight o'clock the lookout "saw a sail to the eastward," Dawson's reaction was predictable. He "tacked and chaced," and a hot pursuit erupted off the South Shore. An hour and a half later the skilful mariner won the deadly race, tacked again, and fired six 4-pounders loaded with grapeshot at his luckless prey. After the blast from *Hope*'s cannon, "the chace brought to" and on closer inspection it "proved to be the ship *Betsy* taken by the rebels."[28] The ship had been captured near Newfoundland on 2 November by the *Washington* privateer and eleven men were put aboard to sail it back to New England. Now two weeks later *Betsy* was back in loyalist hands but the ship's disposal posed a problem for Dawson who had already interrupted his voyage. Not wanting to send *Betsy* alone to Halifax with a few of his men on board for fear the ship would be captured a third time, he decided to escort it personally, and "took charge and made sail to the eastward" bound for Halifax.[29] The search for *Albany* and *Diligent* and perhaps the relief of Fort Cumberland would have to wait.

Dawn on Sunday brought a fair day with fresh breezes. While far to the east *Hope* came about and sailed back to Halifax, *Albany* and *Diligent* held course until noon when "the high land of Penobscot" was visible. About then Captain Hyndman "saw several small sails in shore," *Albany* "made sail and gave chace," and Captain Dodd on *Diligent* lost sight of his companion ship. By three that afternoon, with the weather now cloudy, Dodd spotted a strange sail of his own. He "out reefed topsails and gave chace." In the meantime the boats that *Albany* had been pursuing "got in amongst some small islands" and Hyndman was obliged "to leave off [the] chace." But at four o'clock, on spying a sloop to the east, *Albany* was off again. After chasing this new ship for an hour and a half and "in running past the island of St. Georges," *Albany* struck a rock, "called by the inhabitants the *Old Man*, and is very dangerous being covered at two-thirds flood."[30]

After more than five hours of chasing American vessels off Penobscot, causing havoc and scattering strange sails to port and starboard, the two British warships had accomplished nothing. Instead they fell victim to the very confusion they created. The gravity of the *Albany's* predicament slowly dawned on Captain Hyndman. A veteran mariner who had sailed around the world was caught up on a rock off the Maine coast. Nearby, but not near enough to be of assistance to *Albany*, the frigate *Juno* was also on patrol after supplying Fort Cumberland. Pursuant to orders, Captain Dalrymple was "cruising for the annoyance of the enemy and the protection of the faithful subjects of the Crown,"[31] and with him was the prize sloop *Joseph* (Captain Green), captured the day before near Kennebec. Loaded with lumber and making for Newburyport when brought to by Dalrymple, the sloop was his first prize this month.[32] *Juno*, *Diligent*, *Albany*, and *Hope* had all been guarding Nova Scotia since the beginning of the month, but despite Collier's best intentions *Vulture* was the only ship in the Bay of Fundy and in position to bring relief to Fort Cumberland.

"INFLEXIBLE AS THE DEVIL"

The six riders were covered in wind-driven snow when they rode up to the front gate of Fort Edward later that Sunday morning to be met by Thomas Batt, Michael Francklin, and the naval officer from *Vulture* who had arrived earlier in the armed boat. Eyre Massey gradually warmed up from six frigid hours in the saddle. On learning that *Vulture* was the only warship in Windsor's harbour, he was perplexed. Where were the other ships promised by Collier? Where were the 240 mariners he said would be available and "promised ... should land to cooperate with any detachment"? Had not Collier "put down the numbers that might be spared out of the following ships": *Vulture, Albany, Hope, Gage, Diligent,* and *Loyal Nova Scotia?* Six ships and 240 men – he had scribbled their names at the bottom of Goreham's dispatch. "None came," grumbled Massey, "or has appeared but the *Vulture* while I remained at Windsor!"[33] *Vulture* could spare only fifty mariners using Collier's own figures, but Massey was more concerned with transportation. How would the troops get to Cumberland? Had he made every effort in collecting "as strong a detachment as I could make up to the relief of Fort Cumberland" only to have it languish in Windsor? Here were two companies of Royal Marines in addition to the four garrison companies of Highland Emigrants. And the grenadier company of the Emigrants were at that moment approaching Windsor; he had seen them preparing to march from Fort Sackville that morning. He planned a task force of 420 men and left the impression in Halifax that more troops might be needed. Did not Arbuthnot "highly approve" of this effort and, despite his nocturnal flight from Halifax, had he not remembered "to settle matters with Sir George Collier" before leaving?[34] "With the utmost Expedition," he bragged, "I assembled all the troops I could spare" but the navy was nowhere in sight.[35] It was frustrating for Massey and seemingly unfair. He was under intense personal pressure and daily insulted in the capital while the young upstart Collier in charge of the navy was a virtual hero, lauded by the people as "one of the best of men," and ensconced on his flagship *Rainbow* known as the "one comfort remaining" and the last safe place in Nova Scotia.[36]

Michael Francklin did not think the task force had to be as large as contemplated by Massey. Information gained on retaking the Partridge Island ferry and since then, including the firsthand account of Thomas Dixson, indicated that Eddy's invaders were not well equipped and were fewer than everyone expected. Just as important, Francklin had reason to believe that the people of Cumberland and Cobequid were not rebelling in numbers as large as rumoured in Halifax. His conclusions were supported by Collier who observed "that this body of Banditti are not near so formidable as the first fears of the people represented. They have no cannon and do not exceed 300 or 400 men."[37] Collier never shared his conclusions with Massey. The general knew about the plans for getting the fleet into the Bay of Fundy and the commodore was aware of the troop build-up in Windsor, but their hatred of each other prevented co-ordination of the task force, or even a discussion of its appropriate size. Massey envisaged a large force, Collier a much smaller one. They would not develop a common position nor would Arbuthnot impose one, thinking such matters between officers "too delicate for me to enter upon."[38] It was left to Francklin to distribute the troops in Windsor and make up the navy's shortfall in transportation.

Because Eddy's force was apparently quite small there was fear that attacks were planned for several other locations that would cumulatively account for a much larger force. The privateering in Minas Basin supported this theory. Rather than send all available troops to Cumberland, it was felt that some should be held in Windsor and Halifax, and possibly sent to Annapolis Royal in the event of attacks in those places. The points bearing on the proper size of the relief expedition had to be made tactfully to Massey. Having fulfilled his end of the bargain as he saw it by swelling the garrison at Fort Edward, he would not easily concede that something less was required. Once set on a course of action it was not in his character to make adjustments. A New Englander who had recently been a prisoner in Halifax thought that "Massey ... was as inflexible as the devil himself!"[39] Only a diplomat of Francklin's calibre could steer Massey from his predetermined course by skilfully identifying targets for attaching blame and pointing out avenues for seeking credit.

Tensions ran high in Fort Edward as the size of the task force was debated amid criticism of the navy; the peace of that snowy Sunday was better reflected in the Windsor meeting house where William Ellis preached as was his custom to "a few Gentlemen's Familys well affected to the Church" and to "many of the best" dissenters who gave "me a patient hearing." Service was "performed with considerable decency" despite the secular uses to which the building was regularly put. Of course the "suit[e] of very handsome Church furniture" donated by Governor Legge could not be used "as it would be madness to put anything clean into the place we have at Present." But before a proper church could be built, Ellis realized that "the times must be settled first."[40] The title of his sermon that Sunday is unknown but with the navy calling frequently at Windsor in 1776, Ellis found himself preaching to so many sailors that he composed discourses especially for them. Any of *Vulture*'s sailors in this service might have been reminded that they were "exposed to more dangers than any other men" and hence "run the risque of being called into the immediate presence of God." They would have been warned against the sin of "cursing, swearing and blasphemy" and that they could not hide from a god "equally present in the Tavern and Brothel as in the court of justice."[41]

HMS *Albany* on Old Man rock near the Maine coast illustrated two points in William Ellis' naval discourse: the dangers sailors face at sea, and the sin of cursing and swearing. At six Sunday evening Michael Hyndman fired a distress signal to attract the attention of *Diligent*. "We answered it," asserted Edmund Dodd and, realizing that *Albany* was hard aground, left off his own chase to go to the ship's aid. *Diligent* "endeavoured to work up to her" but with night approaching and being in unfamiliar waters *Diligent* "run under the island of Monhagen" to find safe anchorage. Sunday night felt very long on *Albany*, caught on the treacherous rock, buffeted by the currents, and in danger of breaking up. The sound of the ship's wooden hull grinding on rock menaced the mariners below decks, perhaps encouraging some to repeat the catechism although this might have been as strange to sailors of the Royal Navy as to children of the dissenters of Windsor who at that same time, as they did every Sunday night, were practising the catechism in the meeting house under the tutelage of William Ellis. *Albany*'s "starting water" was emptied to lighten the ship but to no avail, so at dawn Monday morning, *18 November*, Captain Hyndman "manned and armed our boats to go in among the islands to get a vessel to take our guns out." If a ship could be captured and *Albany*'s guns off-loaded, surely it would lighten enough to float free of Old Man rock.

At six in the morning Captain Dodd "got up [the] gallant yards" and sailed *Diligent* out of the lee of Monhagen Island in search of *Albany*. The day being "moderate and fair" he shortly spied the vessel to the northeast still hard aground. The slow process of "working up" to the ship began; by ten o'clock Dodd was still several miles away when he "saw a sloop and two schooners going to *Albany*." These vessels were the lucky catch of the armed boats sent out earlier by an anxious Captain Hyndman. The rest of the day, or until high tide at five o'clock that afternoon, was spent transferring heavy items from *Albany* to these vessels.[42]

With *Albany* aground and *Hope* returning to Halifax, it was not surprising that only *Vulture* had appeared in Minas Basin and that Collier's tardiness was the theme of General Massey's conversation, encouraged presumably by Michael Francklin. While naval delays were a convenient vehicle for Massey to employ in his feud with Collier, they did not actually affect transportation. Sufficient capacity was available in Windsor even for the number of troops contemplated by Massey. Very little of it was Royal Navy capacity, but it was capacity all the same as Francklin had clarified the previous Friday. Referring then to the troops at Fort Edward and those expected from Halifax, he went on to say that "shipping ready and sufficient for their transportation" was present in Windsor. As militia commander he had requisitioned it from the private sector. Ratchford's sloop and Brown's sloop could "commodiously transport 200 troops all the way to Cumberland" and there were the two Windsor schooners that could, "if required, carry another hundred, making in all shipping for 300 men."[43] Considering that *Vulture* could carry at least 150 more, the transport capacity actually exceeded the 420 men Massey wanted. The naval delay was therefore not as serious as he pretended, but his exaggeration permitted him to change his mind about the size of the task force and at the same time fire off a larger salvo at Collier. So after some waffling by Massey and manoeuvring by Francklin to placate him, the idea of a smaller task force was accepted. Instead of 420 men, he agreed that about 200 might be enough to lift the siege. Other worries on this cloudy Monday seemed to make a smaller force more practical. The four private ships proved not to be in first rate condition. Even the best – the *Lavinia* sloop – was poorly maintained, and supplies were not coming in as quickly as expected. Those problems and the dealings with Massey had slowed preparations for the expedition which some people had expected would be under sail today. A smaller task force now seemed essential if Francklin was not to fall dangerously behind schedule.

"OLD MAN ROCK"

The *Albany* crew worked all Monday to free the ship. The larger of the two prize schooners captured that morning was hauled along side and sailors shifted the heavy guns onto its decks. *Diligent* rode in George's Sound ("in 25 fathoms sandy bottom," emphasized Captain Dodd) about a mile away, which was as close to Old Man rock as the captain dared sail, and guarded the disarmed *Albany*. Dodd sent a spare anchor, cable, and some sailors to assist Hyndman. While shifting cargo to the prize ships, Hyndman found baggage belonging to the Fort Cumberland garrison. He transferred this to *Diligent* to ensure that it would reach its destination safely. At five o'clock that afternoon, after lightening *Albany* considerably, Hyndman was ready at high tide to try to free the vessel. Sails were set and with wind and tide combined the hull shifted slightly, but the ship held fast to the rock. "We endeavoured to heave off but could not"! Captain and crew faced another uncertain night at the mercy of Old Man rock. The next high tide was tomorrow morning. The remaining daylight hours of Monday were spent off-loading ballast and the extra anchor supplied by *Diligent* was "laid out astern as well as our own."[44]

After enduring a second night on Old Man rock the crew of *Albany* arose at dawn on Tuesday, *19 November,* to once again try to free the ship. High tide was at five in the morning and sails were set. Hyndman's idea was to work the ship against the anchor cables. "Hove upon both [cables] but the ship did not float" The wind flapped the sails straining the masts alarmingly but the ship was immovable and the tide ebbed. Desperation mounted as it was realized that *Albany* had to be stripped down completely for there to be any chance of freeing the ship. All three captured vessels were brought along side and the crew "hove overboard a great quantity of wood from the prize sloop" to make room for more cargo. They "stove many casks in the hold" in an effort to lighten the ship.[45]

While Old Man rock delayed two of Collier's warships, plans for the relief of Fort Cumberland proceeded in Windsor where Massey and Francklin agreed to include the Royal Marines and two companies of Highland Emigrants in a 200-member task force. An advantage of the smaller force was that only two ships were needed for transport: HMS *Vulture* and *Lavinia*. The headache of procuring supplies was also eased. Only grudgingly was this smaller force accepted by Massey, although he had no qualms about the quality of the troops. His attention was directed to choosing the Highland Emigrant detachment from among the five companies of provincial troops at Fort Edward, and selecting the overall command. Captain Murdoch MacLaine's Grenadiers impressed Massey with their "forced March of upwards of fifty miles," having reached Windsor yesterday "without leaving a Man behind five hours sooner than I expected."[46] So the Grenadiers were chosen as well as the Fourth Company of Light Infantry under Captain Ranald MacKinnon.[47] MacLaine and MacKinnon were put under the command of Gilfred Studholme, senior captain of the Royal Fencible Americans,[48] and Major Thomas Batt, also of the Royal Fencibles and the commander of Fort Edward, was given the overall command of the task force.

Considering all factors, events had moved quickly in Windsor. The troops were ready and shipping and supplies were arranged. All of this should have enabled the expedition to be under sail the next day, only two days behind schedule. No such speed had been demonstrated by the navy. A number of incidents thwarted Collier's plans for getting the fleet into the Bay of Fundy. His problems this Tuesday were best symbolized by Old Man rock in Penobscot Bay.

The weather on the Maine coast turned cloudy in the afternoon and light winds played tricks on the ships holding steady near Old Man rock. The ground tier of water was pumped out of *Albany* and the crew was "getting all other heavy stores out in order to lighten the ship." At five o'clock with the tide running high, Captain Hyndman was ready to gamble everything on a last ditch attempt to free the ship. The wind was allowed to build in the sails to a mighty force causing the two anchor cables to strain and the hull to shudder. An ominous scraping noise reverberated below. *Albany* "hove off the Rock!" A great cheer arose followed by tense moments as the wind shifted suddenly to the southwest. To keep clear the crew slipped the cable and abandoned the anchor loaned by *Diligent*. After two days and two nights grounded on Old Man rock the drama was over. HMS *Albany* was free and afloat. One of its armed boats went ahead to sound the water depth and guide the vessel out of the danger zone. *Albany* and *Diligent* dropped anchor in safe waters at six o'clock and a party of sailors boarded the prize sloop and schooners "to bring them in with our guns and provisions."[49]

The navy was stalled but the army resolved its problems one by one. John Collet, a Fencible captain who had been in New York, replaced Thomas Batt as commander of Fort Edward. "I was ordered to Halifax," he explained, but "at my landing there General Massey Ordered me to repair to Windsor and take the command of Fort Edward."[50] The local militia, the force that retook the Partridge Island ferry, joined the garrison at Fort Edward "with the greatest alacrity."[51] Massey had yielded to Francklin on this point as well; he wanted to send the militia to Cobequid and convincing him not to was as difficult as scaling down the task force. The Cobequid people had incensed Halifax by harbouring privateers, sending a contingent to help Eddy, and raising a liberty pole. Arbuthnot was indignant at being misled by these people whose "rebellious disposition" had been portrayed as self-sufficiency, a characteristic he had praised during his July visit. Had it been merely a matter of gratifying his anger he might well have supported Massey, but for political reasons he backed Francklin. The issue of posting militia outside home districts had been the undoing of Governor Legge and Arbuthnot was not about to make that mistake. He was more adept than Legge (and Massey had no political instincts); for the time being, therefore, Francklin's opinion prevailed.[52]

Having recently interviewed the Cobequid people, Francklin was better informed than either Massey or Arbuthnot. He did not believe that large numbers had joined Eddy, the ferry boat was safe, and the district appeared stable. En route to Cumberland the task force could check Minas Basin for privateers and the two schooners were still available in Windsor for coast guard duty. The two spies he sent to Cobequid on Friday was a better response and a lot less costly than sending in a company of militia which in his opinion was unnecessary and imprudent. This was not the time to order the militia out of home districts. The people of Windsor, Horton, and Cornwallis were genuinely alarmed that New Englanders might invade their coast: "Our people press me with great anxiety," he explained, "to be enabled to defend themselves and their property against this Banditti."[53] Francklin helped them to acquire arms and encouraged them in their desire to defend the district. He could not ask them now to forsake their own endangered district for a fruitless expedition to Cobequid.

Arbuthnot's backing of Francklin in the militia dispute did not prevent him from venting his rage on the people of Cobequid. The angry "Blustering Tar" wrote two letters this Tuesday to David Smith, minister at Londonderry. Expressing astonishment at the conduct of Smith's parishioners, "the particulars of which I have had very minutely related to me," Arbuthnot threatened that unless they showed signs of loyalty "I shall consider them as Rebels and treat them accordingly." He offered a clear choice: "all those who think going to the Rebels is a Milder Government and better than tarrying in this Province, they have my leave to withdraw ... but if they remain ... they shall demean as Loyal Subjects and defend the State or let them look to the Consequence"![54]

While the Cobequid people had permission to leave Nova Scotia, they were no longer free to visit their own capital. As of this Tuesday they could not enter Halifax without a magistrate's pass "signifying their business." As a loyalty test, Arbuthnot ordered the Cobequid militia to mobilize for service anywhere in the province.[55] These measures were meted out to everyone, not just those guilty of rebellious practices, and were not very effective. Arbuthnot came to regret his words and was forced to retract his blanket condemnation of Cobequid. However, passive loyalty was not enough. "More is expected from the whole people than satisfying themselves with not being in Actual Rebellion Personally ... It will be expected at this time of Tumult that the People Associate for their Mutual defence."[56]

Official responses to the patriot threat were gaining momentum: while plans for the task force were complete, it had been difficult to restrain Massey from doing more than circumstances required; and the normally lethargic Arbuthnot was aroused to a pitch of indignation. Only on the naval front did the delays continue to mount. At eight o'clock Wednesday morning, *12 November, Albany* and *Diligent* "hove up with our prizes and run into George's Harbour" where they luxuriated in "7 fathoms water, muddy bottom" while Captain Hyndman rearmed and reloaded his ship. After this all-day task they had to complete their reconnaissance of the Maine coast as ordered. It would be next week before they could return to Nova Scotian waters and leave their captured vessels in the waters of Annapolis Royal where urgent new orders awaited their arrival.[57]

In Halifax Harbour this morning Collier was surprised to see the distinctive black hull of HMS *Hope* which he expected by then to be well into the Bay of Fundy, if not already in Windsor. Annoyance with the daring but unpredictable Captain Dawson lessened only slightly when he saw the prize sloop *Betsy* in convoy. It was only when he considered how the news from Cumberland had changed since he gave his orders to Dawson six days ago that Collier was mollified. Details of the siege had emerged, particularly the loss of the *Polly* provision sloop. "To remedy this Inconvenience," the *Nancy* transport had been loading provisions for a number of days and was ready to embark for Cumberland.[58] The transport ship needed an escort and would it not be convenient to have *Hope* perform this task? The prospect of action would appeal to Dawson and shepherding the drone *Nancy* should prevent him from chasing privateers about the ocean.

The search for *Albany* and *Diligent* – Dawson's earlier task – now appeared redundant as those ships should be reporting soon in Annapolis Royal. Naval orders were changed and Dawson was required to ship out immediately. After every cruise he liked to clean and alter the appearance of his ship to confuse the enemy. No time for that! The commodore insisted he sail with *Nancy* the next morning. Collier would add "ten of his own Seamen" to *Nancy*'s complement, and Massey would provide "an Officer and 20 Marines." Dawson had better be on time and he had much to do! Water had to be taken on along with a couple chaldrons of coal for *Hope*'s stove. A sailmaker had to repair the main top gallant sail, and the prize *Betsy* had to pass through vice-admiralty court, all before leaving port.[59]

"I NEVER SAW A BETTER DETACHMENT MADE UP"

After a concerted effort the *Lavinia* sloop and one of the private schooners were ready to sail down the Avon River on Wednesday evening to join *Vulture* in Minas Basin. Supplies were aboard, the troops had marched down from Fort Edward, and since the weather was fine officials and townspeople could be expected to line the shore for the embarkation. *Lavinia* was bound for Cumberland but the schooner would sail only to the river mouth where the ship's troops would be transferred to *Vulture*. That warship would then get under sail with *Lavinia* in convoy. The 120 Highland Emigrants assigned to *Lavinia* were led up the gangway by officers MacLaine and MacKinnon while the eighty-nine marines filed into the schooner. Joining the marines were Thomas Dixson and Charles Dixon; they had returned from Halifax to accompany the expedition. So pleased were the Royal Marines to be on active service at last that they may have suppressed their low regard for provincial troops, a commonly held sentiment among British regulars and officials. Only recently Lieutenant-Governor Arbuthnot had questioned their value: "As to the Emigrants and Fencibles, God knows our Sovereign has a dear bargain"![60]

"If he succeeds I am happy," sighed Massey as he watched Major Batt, commander of the expedition, go aboard the schooner with Captain Studholme. "But ... you may guess my distress to send so small a detachment when before I left [Halifax] I reckoned on four hundred and twenty." Still stung by the small size of the force he knew where to lay blame: "this was entirely owing to the delay in the naval department"! The 120 Highlanders on *Lavinia* and the eighty-nine marines, two fencible officers, and two local people on the schooner made up a task force of 213 men. "I detest with horror such delays to the King's service," carped Massey, leaving no doubt about his opinion of Collier: "but [I] wish the naval matters left as I found them, carried on by Commodore Arbuthnot." In the end even Massey caught the positive mood of the crowd gathered to bid farewell to the task force. "I must keep in spirits," he agreed, and if small the detachment was of a high standard; it was "admirably well officered," in his opinion. "I doubt not of their success as I never saw a better detachment made up." Afterall, there was credit to be claimed: "Had not I taken this step, in conjunction with the Lieutenant-Governor," and here he excluded any reference to Collier, "this province would be over run."[61]

While Massey warmed slowly to events unfolding in Windsor, Francklin was pleased as they both watched the ships prepare to leave at dusk. Unlike Massey, his concern had never been transport capacity but with protection of the force in transit. That was the reason for his letter to Annapolis Royal on Friday pleading for a warship "to repair to the Basin of Minas as soon as possible to take the Transports under your Convoy."[62] With *Vulture*'s arrival his worries ceased and he was unconcerned with the general naval delay. Arbuthnot shared Francklin's opinion. He would write from Halifax that "*Vulture* Sloop at my request is arrived at Windsor, where General Massey is dispatching 500 men under her convoy to Cumberland."[63] That he supposed the force to be larger only serves to reinforce his agreement with Francklin in the matter.

"O most mighty God, Ruler of Heaven and Earth," prayed William Ellis in Windsor. "Reunite the Divided interests and Distracted minds of our Countrymen. Defend us from seditious rage at home, and from the Designs of all our enemies." The petty politics and strain of the past week dissipated in the failing light at the water's edge as everyone wished success to the troops in lifting the siege and reuniting the divided interests in Cumberland. Ellis prayed as he did whenever a warship visited Windsor: "Bless the Commander, subordinate officers and private Seamen of this his Majesty's Ship of War, and grant that wheresoever their duty shall call them into action, they may approve themselves thy faithful Servants, acquiring advantage to their Country, and Honour to themselves."[64] The sloop, schooner, and armed boat slipped moorings and veered out on the muddy Avon, which in cold November twilight is a river of dark opacity curving into the flat landscape towards distant Minas Basin, and in the autumn of 1776 towards the *Vulture* warship.

Optimism was high in Windsor and among officials in Halifax where Arbuthnot was kept apprised of events. In his own colourful phrasing he pronounced the force "full sufficient to drive those Banditty to their holes!" Accolades were handed out to the militia, to Massey, even to

Collier, but the highest praise and the most warranted was reserved for Francklin "who cannot sufficiently be applauded for his Zeal"![65] The relief expedition had been launched less than two weeks after Francklin's first discovery of the siege on recapturing the Partridge Island ferry, and only five days after the Dixson party confirmed the news to authorities in Halifax. When the ships disappeared in the downriver darkness it must have seemed to Windsor folk that the expedition was well on its way; in fact the ships would have to lay overnight in the mouth of the Avon River and transfer the marines the next morning before *Vulture* could raise anchor and actually set sail for Cumberland. Still, the achievement was remarkable and success came despite logistical shortcomings and in the face of a cranky general and a tardy navy.

An energetic week in Windsor and in the capital was matched by a period of stressful inaction in Cumberland. Loyalists chafed under house arrest. Inhabitants of the crowded garrison took one day at a time as the walls seemingly closed in on them. Patriots watched discipline disintegrate through idleness while they groped for a new strategy for capturing the fort. But time was running out on the siege as the voyage from Windsor to Cumberland is a short one: a day and a half, two days at the most.

7 Battle of Blazing Barns
Thursday 21 November to Tuesday 26 November

During the siege some wanton individuals of the American part ungenerously set fire to a valuable property ... on which your memorialist resided for many years.

John Allan, Cumberland patriot[1]

The siege was lasting longer than anyone had expected and the strain was showing in both camps. Occupation of the countryside was an ordeal for loyalists and a temptation to patriots. Extortion and plunder increased and were not the unplanned acts of an unruly rabble; they were carried out by organized patrols led by Eddy's officers and the garrison seemed powerless to intervene.[2] Loyalists under house arrest had every reason to fear a knock at the door.

Cumberland was ruled by the Committee-of-Safety which was reconstituted after the fort attack. It was backed by Eddy's army and its authority was absolute. It could imprison an offender, sanction a raid on an isolated farmhouse, or confiscate a family's possessions. The former politicians and ex-office holders who comprised the committee convened regular sessions near Camphill at Ebenezer Gardiner's farm which became the Congressional Hall for revolutionary Cumberland. Not surprisingly, the Gardiner farmhouse acquired symbolic importance as the seat of government and became an object of hatred to the loyalists and uncommitted alike, their freedoms being sharply curtailed by the arbitrary power of the committee.

As the importance of the committee increased that of Jonathan Eddy decreased and his weakened leadership had consequences for the future course of the siege. At the outset political direction and military command were combined in Colonel Eddy. He led the invasion at Shepody Point and regenerated the moribund Cumberland rebellion by the force of his oratory in Memramcook and Sackville. But after the failure of the fort attack political direction passed to the Committee-of-Safety which also assumed the control of prisoners. Eddy was still field commander but any military enterprise was now subject to approval by the committee. A result of these changes was a fragmentation of leadership in the management of the siege. Many more individuals than Eddy were involved in day-to-day decisions and this feature in part explained the increase in unorthodox patrols of the countryside. Also a broader range of tactics, unconventional in military terms, could be expected from the expanded leadership than might have been the case had Eddy, the veteran regular army officer, remained solely in charge.

"SOLDIERS PERMITTED TO WEAR THE BARRACK RUGGS"

Benumbed by the raw Cumberland night and a chilling northerly breeze, the relieved sentries climbed down from the parapet at dawn on Thursday, *21 November*, it would be mid-morning before the sun was high enough to warm the frosty interior of the fort. After three weeks of being sealed inside, Goreham and his fencibles still held out despite rumours to the contrary in Halifax. Eddy's blockade had been successful in choking off supplies from the countryside and with many mouths to feed – two hundred defenders with "numerous Families" – dwindling reserves were strictly rationed.[3] Desertion was on the rise again which at least reduced the number of mouths to feed. In the past week four soldiers disappeared from the garrison, the latest to run being Private Benjamin Andrews who failed to answer this Thursday's muster.[4] In the circumstances it was surprising that morale was still relatively high. There was satisfaction at not having been overwhelmed by rebellion. The crumbling defenses had resisted Eddy's attacks. The over-crowding was not yet intolerable and the fencibles, regularly drilled on the tiny parade square, were improving. It was hoped that the worst might be over and reinforcements were expected to arrive any day.

The mood of cautious optimism in the garrison was not matched in Camphill where the atmosphere was uncongenial. Ethnic tensions and bickering among contingents, especially the Cumberland rebels and Machias men, increased after the fort attack. The committee only partially filled the leadership void in which soldiers defied regulation as Camphill verged on anarchy. A Micmac who apparently refused to join the raucous soldiers was prevented from leaving camp and in trying to do so was chased onto the marsh and drowned.[5] The cause of the tension was not evident at a glance. Certainly Camphill did not suffer the same irritants as the garrison. Supplies were no problem since the countryside lay open to plunder and the Acadian barns, stuffed with "salt provisions, flour, rice, and pease, besides grain of different kinds,"[6] were a handy commissary.

Unlike the garrison which suffered the claustrophobia of siege, Camphill offered perfect freedom of movement. Patriot pessimism stemmed from receding objectives and military setbacks. Eddy's goal of reducing the fort, not to mention the whole province, seemed farther away than ever; defeat in the fort attack plunged the camp into a depression from which it had not recovered. Worst of all was the inaction. The tactic of starving out the fort was slow and unexciting although it was actually working. Eddy could point to hardship reports coming out of the garrison but by the time the blockade succeeded the rebellion would collapse through inactivity. Revolutionary zeal like evangelical fervour is action-oriented, demanding a steady stream of easily measured results or enthusiasm flags. Tiresome tactics caused the hiatus in Camphill. A radical new tactic was needed to reactivate idle troops and shore up sagging leadership. The tactic must hold the promise of quick results and be dramatic yet require only a small force to execute. Here Eddy faced a dilemma: more support was required to storm the fort but only a dramatic success such as its capture could attract that support at this juncture.

Eddy's dilemma meant that naval delays were not as critical as they seemed and at any rate Commodore Collier was unaware of most of them. He had no idea where *Albany* and *Diligent* were or that *Vulture* had not sailed from Windsor this Thursday as expected. Surprised by *Hope*'s return to Halifax, he had ordered the ship's captain to re-embark at once for the Bay of Fundy with the *Nancy* transport in convoy. By noon *Hope* was at sea again in moderate breezes with *Nancy* astern and the familiar Sambro Head slipping by in the starboard haze.[7]

Along the Cumberland shore the weather continued to be cold in the afternoon and the northerly breeze that chilled the sentries in the morning increased to a sharp wind. The poorly clothed "soldiers were forced to wear the Barrack Ruggs and Blanketts, otherwise they must suffer greatly if not entirely perish." Resembling vagabonds more than garrison soldiers, the men lined up for their daily rum ration. To compensate for the lack of clothing, extra duty, and cold weather, Goreham now offered "not only an allowance of Rum by day but to the Guards and others by night."[8] He knew the excuses in Cumberland for drinking heavily all year around – in summer as a diversion from mosquitos, in winter as a shelter from the cold – as well as the weaknesses of such excuses just as his adversary Colonel Eddy knew them. From his experience as a British officer at the fort in 1759, Eddy knew that "Rum will not defend the Soldiers from the inclemency of the weather nor the attacks of Stinging insects ... as clothes would, and besides," he warned then, "too much strong water intoxicates the Brain"![9]

It felt like winter in Camphill in the damp quarters and uncomfortable wigwams. At Eddy's encouragement discussion of a new attempt on the fort resumed at Gardiner's farm. The elect of each group from Machias to Cobequid spoke on the issue. Many suggestions foundered on the reality of limited personnel until the idea of burning out the garrison was raised. There were those who had always thought that the best way to defeat the fort (without artillery) was to set it on fire. Goreham knew this and countered with the frieze of poles around the palisade to prevent burning bales of hay from being thrown inside. The pyrotechnical advisors formed the radical fringe of an already radical group, but so far the siege had proceeded along fairly standard military lines. Being a veteran British officer, Colonel Eddy had pinned his hopes on conventional tactics in capturing the fort, but after nearly two weeks of frustration a bold new initiative was required. Those advocating the burn-out option were listened to more seriously this Thursday than ever before in the revolutionary council.

Over a dozen buildings were clustered to the north of the fort and tonight they would be upwind of it. These were soldiers' huts and garrison buildings including the hospital, and other properties belonging to villagers. If only a few were set alight, it was argued, the wind would sweep the fire into the fort. Eddy conceded that some attempt ought to be made. The committee debated all day but in the end the north wind, which at dusk was fairly howling outside Gardiner's house, supplied the most compelling reason for swift action. This was the night to burn out the garrison. The decision was made. The raid would proceed tonight.

Just as in the fort attack nine days before, volunteers were scarce when Eddy's officers circulated to collect soldiers for the raid. By midnight a detachment of about eighty men mustered at Read's place and huddled in the lee of the barn out of the biting wind to await instructions. As usual the attack plan was sketchy with no attack options considered, contingency plans prepared, or special units formed. The volunteers were armed and buoyed by the prospect of some excitement at last. Sometime after midnight the operation began with the men marching down the road towards the fort, encouraged by their optimistic Colonel, and pushed on by the strong wind buffeting their backs.

While the second major attack of the siege was set in motion on this windy Thursday night, Judge Isaac Deschamps in Windsor folded his diary and fell asleep, supposing the relief force was on its way to Cumberland. However although Captain Feattus had "cleard Hawse[r], unmoord Ship and hove into 1/2 Cable" by noon, nothing else was done on *Vulture* except to take on fresh water during a leisurely afternoon and evening, and it was now evident that the warship and *Lavinia* would not sail for Cumberland until the next morning.[10]

"IN FULL SIGHT, AND MUCH EXPOSED"

The hour "between 3 and 4 in the morning" is the worst time for guard duty. Sentries at Fort Cumberland were in a state of chilled boredom at this hour on Friday morning, 22 *November,* "it being very dark, and a high Wind" whipped across the parapet, slicing through their inadequate clothing. Several minutes lapsed before the red glow that broke the veil of darkness registered on their consciousness. By the time the alarm sounded and the garrison turned out of barracks, the buildings set on fire by the patriots were fully ablaze and "shingles and pieces of wood on fire" were flying on the wind "over the Spur buildings" The fireworks were brilliant in the night sky. Fiery missiles descended in a shower on the dry shingles of the old wooden buildings crowded in the spur, and the fires ignited by the deadly storm "had got to a considerable length" before Goreham could organize to fight them. He had no choice but to order the Fencibles up on the rooftops where, above the elevation of the curtain walls and illuminated by the fires, they were exposed to the enemy. Already, the rattle of musketry could be heard above the firestorm, causing Goreham to fear for the garrison now more than at any time since the fort was first attacked. This was "their next tryal of any consequence," he thought, and could spare only a few soldiers for defence, "more than half the Garrison being employed in extinguishing the fire"[11]

This was the moment of crisis in an already critical period. After days of inactivity the awful purpose of the siege returned clearly to the terrified people now filling the constricted alley-ways and parade square. In the bright glow above the parapet they faced the spectre of the fort in flames and everyone – men, women and children – burned to death with the herd of cows, or fleeing into the waiting guns of the patriots. If the fires raced out of control or if Eddy compounded the attack with an effective musket volley, the fort would be lost. The crisis developed very quickly. Strong winds caught the blazing barns and swept the flaming debris in a trail of sparks over the spur just as the patriots hoped. When the Fencibles went up to fight the fires they presented perfect targets to Eddy's musket party. Everything went according to the patriot plan but the assault was not exploited. Goreham, who was directing his own musket party from the parapet, sensed this from the number of patriots out there firing in the darkness and he wondered why "the Enemy made but a very indifferent use of their expected confusion." He figured that Eddy "kept but Ten or a Dozen men firing at ours, who were placed on the tops of the houses in full sight and much exposed"[12]

The few patriots in the musket party stayed well hidden and displayed only token force. Eddy appeared not to notice, being fascinated with the fire. His simple objective was to burn out the garrison and, as he stood in the warmth of his arson, he was pleased to see the firebrands falling into the spur, hopeful as the conflagration intensified, and excited when he saw fires breaking out on the rooftops of the buildings. He waited for the entire fort to erupt in flames. But he had not reckoned on such a determined response from the soldiers and civilians inside. Perhaps it was because they had nowhere to run that they fought the fires so tenaciously. Vigorously, they beat away at the many little fires on the roofs and organized a bucket brigade to attack the larger ones. There was a great danger that the flames would race ahead and get into the dry roof timbers. If that should happen to just one of the buildings tightly-packed in the spur the whole fort would go and the garrison would be forced to evacuate and surrender to Eddy. "But the readiness and Activity of our Men on this difficult occasion was really surprising" to Goreham who watched the fires brought slowly under control, then extinguished one by one, after which each flaming missile was stamped out as it landed. Gradually, the buildings torched by the patriots burned down; perhaps Eddy discontinued the attack because the wind fell. Many buildings remained standing near the fort. The fires abated, the roar receded, and the red sky darkened again. Another threat to the fort passed. The patriots retreated in disgruntled groups to Camphill, the sentries returned to their lonely duty on the parapet, and the Tantramar night returned to impenetrable darkness.

At first light that Friday Goreham climbed the ramparts to survey the devastation of last night's raid. The roofs of several buildings in the spur were scarred and blackened while outside the fort, those that were set a fire to promote the attack were burnt-out hulks. Viewing the damage filled him with admiration for his corps. "No Troops," he thought, "could be more ready and alert at their posts nor more active in extinguishing the Fire." Charred shingles on barrack roofs that already leaked were not the real concern but a tough decision faced him concerning the remaining buildings near the fort. Well over a dozen still stood, among which were "some very good houses" intended for the use of the reinforcements and "our Hospital which was a very large building."[13] He decided to demolish them all. The fear of being burned out was always there and especially after the burning of Harper's place, but Thursday's escalation in the use of this tactic left him no choice. Workers commenced the unwelcome task that would take many days to complete; they were consoled only by the prospects of an increased fuel supply.

Had he known, Goreham would have been truly consoled by the news that the task force set sail that morning. At five o'clock *Vulture* "weighed in Company [with] *Lavinia* a sloop, with the Grenadier Company of Royal Emigrants."[14] They departed the Avon sailing north in strong gales and fair weather. The sun rose to starboard above the broad sweep of the basin while Cape Blomidon, around which they must sail to reach the Bay of Fundy, hoved up to port. On the bow horizon was the distant Cobequid coast.

The activity of Goreham's demolition crew disconcerted the Committee-of-Safety in Camphill and a hasty meeting was convened to decide what to do. Fire the buildings advised the pyrotechnical team; better to burn them than to watch Goreham solve his fuel crisis. Some of the buildings were owned by patriots; one – "a very Valuable House"[15] – belonged to the family of John Allan. Should not the huge fire that would result from burning so many buildings be used for another purpose as well? Weather conditions were not favourable for burning out the fort. Perhaps they should await a windy day. Neither concern for the property of "Friends to Liberty" nor the prospect of using the buildings to start a massive fire when conditions were favourable would stay the hand of the committee. Fuel was in short supply in the garrison. If those buildings were converted to firewood, the siege would go on indefinitely. The decision was made. Fire them tonight before Goreham could "carry the Timber into the Fort for Firing." Eddy agreed: "The Committee ordered me to Prevent it by firing them."[16]

The demolition crew finished work and withdrew to the fort late in the afternoon. Darkness descends early in November so the hour was not late nor were the sentries yet chilled to the bone when fires broke out among the remaining buildings. The garrison was roused for the second night in a row to fend off an attack. Fires raced quickly through the vacant houses and barns and the large hospital to join in one enormous blaze – the largest conflagration of the siege by far and probably the largest in the turbulent history of the county. The spectacle was especially awesome to the garrison. As walls and roofs of a dozen buildings burst open, exposing structural timbers to the flames, the crackling noise grew to a roar that was magnified to deafening proportions in the confines of the fort. Terrified families huddled on the parade square beneath a night sky turned to red daylight by the fire, the huge shadows cast by the flames raced wildly across the bastions and curtain walls that surrounded them. The blazing sky, gigantic shadows, and fierce roar of the inferno frayed the nerves of those trapped for so long. As spectacular and frightening as the fire was to those incarcerated in the fort it was not nearly as threatening as the previous night's fire because of the lack of wind. Also, there was no musket volley, the single goal being to deprive the garrison of fuel. In this respect the action merely reinforced the blockade, it was not a direct attack on the fort. Responsibility rested with the committee; Eddy simply followed orders. Perhaps because of the limited objective of the action, Eddy washed his hands of the whole affair. He confessed that the committee ordered him to burn the buildings and candidly admitted to the indiscriminate nature of the destruction: "We Destroyed a Number of Houses, the Property of Friends to each Side, which lay adjacent to the Fort."[17]

To those watching from a distance the fire seemed catastrophic. The flames on Cumberland Ridge were visible across the Tantramar, from Amherst in the southeast to Sackville in the northwest, and reflected far out over the waters of Cumberland Basin. From Amherst the Blacks saw the fire and supposed that Eddy had "burnt the town."[18] Far down the Bay of Fundy near Joggins Point, sailors and marines on *Vulture* saw the fire's red glow in the northern sky and speculated on the fate of the fort, while Thomas Dixson and Charles Dixon on the same vessel worried about their families. Contrary winds had delayed their voyage and "by the Pilot's advice" Captain Feattus was turning back to the shelter of Minas Basin, having "found we could not weather Cape Chignecto."[19] Unless the situation improved overnight, the relief force would not reach the fort on the following day. Eyre Massey, already sceptical about the size of the force, would have been furious had he known of the delay, "tho' Massey knew no more of Sea Matters than a Savage of the Woods," according to George Collier.[20] Back in Halifax, Massey conveyed his scepticism to Arbuthnot and other officials who assumed that the force would be larger. An air of unreality prevailed. The people were still alarmed by the invasion and critical of the army, and the Executive Council was still trying to add to the task force.

Executive Council held its weekly meeting in Halifax on Saturday, *23 November*, with the main agenda item being HMS *Amazon* in the harbour. Arbuthnot explained that when this ship, which was en route from Quebec to New York, arrived in town earlier in the week he asked its captain, Maximillian Jacobs, to "order the Marines on board the ship under his Command to be landed in order that they may be sent as a further reinforcement to dislodge and disperse the Rebels." He wanted *Amazon*'s marines to march to Windsor and join the Cumberland expedition but Jacobs refused and "answered by letter that he could not reconcile to his duty a step that would ... incapacitate the *Amazon*." Angered by the rebuff and with renewed concern for the size of the relief force since Massey's return, Arbuthnot raised the matter in Council. That body was suitably indignant and agreed to ask Massey to requisition *Amazon*'s marines "if he should think it proper and necessary."[21] Nothing came of this resolution and Collier took no part in the dispute, having concluded from Dixson's report that the task force was adequate. However, strained relations with Massey and Arbuthnot prevented him from airing the matter. In truth Eddy's army was smaller than even Dixson estimated and the nature of the siege itself had changed.

In Halifax the perception was that Cumberland was facing an American invasion which was augmented by local rebellion and focused on capturing the fort and eventually the province. To a degree this was true until the fort attack, but after that event the siege changed. Local rebellion stopped growing: it had lost its popular appeal in the face of military defeat. The patriots turned to lesser goals such as burning the fort's barracks and plundering loyalist property. This blurred focus weakened Eddy's force and Camphill became difficult to control with groups detaching themselves ostensibly to carry out special missions. The effort to find cannon was developing along those lines.

Some of Eddy's men had been in Baie Verte all week trying to float Clough's schooner with which they hoped to fetch cannon from Charlottetown. "They attempted often to get off the Schooner from a Marsh where she lay but did not succeed." The idea was about to be given up when someone mentioned that "down along" the coast at Pictou was a ship "loading Lumber for Scotland." It was the *Molly*, captained by William Lowden; why not capture that vessel? It seemed possible although retrieval of the cannon from Charlottetown would be further delayed. But there was no alternative and the siege was dragging on. The Earle family of Pictou, of which there were six members in Camphill, were in favour of the idea, and patriot sympathizers in Pictou, such as Doctor John Harris, could be counted on for support. The plan was approved by the Committee-of-Safety which appointed one of its members, Nathaniel Reynolds, to lead "fifteen or Sixteen" men to Pictou. Among them was Charles Swan, a mariner captured earlier by Eddy's men in Baie Verte. Should *Molly* be taken, Swan would be useful in sailing it back to Baie Verte for additional crew before crossing Northumberland Strait to "take what guns were in Charlotte Town lying Buried in the Sand." Guns were not the only object on Reynolds' mind. "Part of their plan," he admitted, "was to come to Charlottetown to Pillage everything of Value." And should the guns be too unwieldy to fetch, he would not return to Cumberland but go privateering in the Gulf of St Lawrence and "if opportunity served," he might "visit" Quebec. With these thoughts in mind the party left Camphill on the overland trek to Pictou.[22]

No British ships were stationed in Northumberland Strait to patrol the waters near Pictou or guard St Johns Island, and across the isthmus in the Bay of Fundy the Royal Navy could not advance. Venturing out of Minas Channel late Saturday morning, HMS *Vulture* tried again to sail around Cape Chignecto. Conditions were miserable. The ship pitched in gale force winds and heavy rains all afternoon while Captain Feattus tried to make his way north. At eleven o'clock in the evening he gave up, and after signalling *Lavinia* "to come under our stern," *Vulture* "bore away for Annapolis Royal"[23] in the opposite direction from Cumberland!

"LOST SIGHT OF THE *LAVINIA*"

"Fogg and rain" moved into the Bay of Fundy on Sunday, *24 November,* and a calm replaced the gales of recent days. In such weather and at this time of year there is a feeling of wild desolation in the Cumberland landscape. The Tantramar is subdued and wet, its golden autumn grass beaten flat by wind-driven rain and bleached to a dull tan. On Cumberland Ridge the forested horizon is a grey maze of bare hardwoods and evergreens so deeply green as to be almost black. Heavy clouds that fill the huge sky and descend to the dark surface of the basin accentuate the airy bleakness of the, now burnt, hilltop ruin. If the general view is nearly monochromatic in late November, the scene around the fort in that same month of 1776 was one of blackened devastation from the two recent fires. It seemed that calamity and nature had conspired to depress the garrison and all the residents of Cumberland suffering from the siege. The occasion of Sunday was unlikely to raise spirits or add colour to the drab scene as it would have done in normal times. Chaplain Eagleson was on his way to New England as a prisoner this Sunday, and the absence of public worship at the fort for the third week in a row only added to the bleakness of the garrison.

Still bleaker was the lot of the loyalist prisoners held in Camphill and elsewhere in Cumberland. Yorkshire settlers under house arrest were singled out for "bad treatment."[24] They "kept me confined," moaned Moses Delesdernier, and "in their power." He described the lot of Eddy's prisoners: "We laboured under the Greatest Calamities and distresses that nature can bear," living entirely on a few potatoes "which we were Obliged to beg from the Rebells" and threatened with the same fate as Eagleson and the others on their way to New England gaols. "In this horrid situation," they were presented with a paper in support of the rebellion, "called an Association," and told to sign it. Moses and others signed, "which nothing in the world but the Intolerable misery we were in could have prevailed us to do."[25]

The incarceration of Cumberlanders in homes, in Camphill, and in the fort would continue until the navy delivered reinforcements. In Windsor it was supposed that those reinforcements, who had left their village on Wednesday, had already landed in Cumberland and those attending church this Sunday in Windsor listened to William Ellis with a measure of satisfaction. They wore their Sunday best as was the practice across the province (except in Cumberland this Sunday); the men dressed for church in "the finest cloth and linen," many with ruffled shirts and the women in colourful "silks and calicoes with long ruffles." The Sunday attire of Nova Scotians was so different from their usual dress "that you would scarce know them to be the same people."[26]

Ellis's sermon on this date is unknown but the growth of unrestrained zeal in religious and civil affairs was a theme that so concerned him in late 1776 that he wrote a sermon on it. The boatloads of people at the nearby services of the untrained Henry Alline and the rebellion in Cumberland were manifestations of that zeal – "mistaken zeal" in Ellis's view. "Zeal is a Dangerous instrument," he warned, to "the ignorant especially." Zeal "sanctified the most atrocious villainies, which converted robberies and murder into acts of piety and devotion." Although few would link religious and political zeal as closely as Ellis, his hearers understood the critical times and had witnessed important events in Windsor during the previous week, including the departure of the task force. Ellis invoked divine blessing on the defence of Nova Scotia and on those who led it. "Bless we beseech thee his Majesty's Forces by Sea and Land," he prayed "and influence with thy Spirit the councils of those who are appointed to Direct their operations."[27] This prayer was pertinent to the problems between Massey and Collier, and especially to the delays at sea of *Vulture* and *Lavinia*.

The *Lavinia* was decrepit. On the ships' first day out of Windsor, before they ventured past Cape Blomidon, Captain Feattus "sent the Boatswain and Carpenter on board the *Lavinia* to repair her Main boom, rigging, and other things." On the second day he "supplied the *Lavinia* with a Hawser, some rigging, and blocks." Repairs to *Lavinia* and waiting for this vessel to limp along delayed the voyage as much as the bad weather. The delays caused food shortages which resulted in another delay while *Vulture* "supplied *Lavinia* with some Provisions." Communication was another problem until Feattus "sent a Midshipman on board her to observe signals." The last straw was the discovery that *Lavinia* was "leaky."[28] Already the voyage had taken twice as long as it should have, and Sunday was spent unproductively, marking time in "little wind" only three leagues from Annapolis Gut. Captain Feattus made no progress in the calm. As his commodore was fond of saying, "tho' we are Lords of the Ocean, we are not so of the Air"[29] Visibility deteriorated this Sunday evening. At eight o'clock *Vulture* "made the Sig[na]l and brought too on the Starboard tack." For the first time since leaving Windsor the warship "lost sight of the *Lavinia*."[30]

Considering Captain Feattus's troubles, there was a chance that Captain Dawson might overtake the relief force and that *Hope* could be the first ship to reach the besieged fort. On Monday, 25 *November*, *Hope* and *Nancy* were three days out of Halifax, proceeding on course and without distraction off the south coast near Yarmouth. At eleven in the morning Dawson tacked two leagues westward to avoid Seal Island in "Foggy Weather" (although it was not as thick as in the Bay of Fundy where *Vulture* still searched vainly for *Lavinia*). These waters were frequented by privateers and out of habit Dawson kept a watchful eye. Two hours later *Hope* and *Nancy* were abreast of Seal Island and, having raised the top gallant yards, were sailing northward in "Fresh Breezes" towards the Bay of Fundy. Dawson saw nothing and if he had he would have sailed on as he dared not deviate again from Collier's orders. He scanned the horizon wistfully almost hoping in the present situation to see no ships. But fate would not make it so easy for him and "in the southeast quarter," where the low line of Seal Island was still visible astern, *Hope*'s lookout "Saw a Sail"! Resolutely, Dawson maintained course, assuming the sail would soon disappear from view. *Hope* and *Nancy* sailed on but instead of diminishing the strange sail grew larger; the vessel was following.[31]

"THE CHACE"

Monday afternoon wore on. The "Strange Sail" off the southern tip of Nova Scotia that had been viewed from *Hope* and *Nancy* for a full three hours was slowly narrowing the distance between them. Its profile was discernible now despite the misty weather. It was a two-masted sloop like *Hope* but rigged as a brigantine. Dawson tried to ignore the ship. Having made good time on the voyage, he would not be distracted from his orders to escort *Nancy* to Fort Cumberland. He expected to enter the Bay of Fundy later today and was aware of the race with time, of the seasonal storms, and of the winter freeze-up that must soon end navigation in Cumberland Basin. As the strange sail came on, the ship's lines and features emerged. It was a Massachusetts warship! The *Independence* brig! Captain Simeon Sampson! It was "in all respects Equipped in Warlike manner" – Fourteen 6-pounder guns, ten 4-pounders, ten swivels, and "two Couhorns" – "also well and properly Man'd" at ninety-five sailors, making it stronger and better armed than Dawson's fourteen-gun sloop of seventy sailors.[32] The excitement spread through His Majesty's vessels with no doubt left that *Independence* intended to engage them. Fate, it seemed, would not permit James Dawson an uneventful voyage in Nova Scotian waters. An American warship could not be ignored no matter what his orders and Dawson, who for sometime had been manoeuvring *Hope* into a favourable position anyway, decided it was time to make his move. *Hope* tacked and ran boldly towards the larger ship in a fair wind. The two warships closed dramatically and "Came to Action."[33]

Maybe Captain Sampson felt at a temporary disadvantage when Captain Dawson made his abrupt attack; or maybe he was surprised and caught off guard, being unaware of Dawson's plotting for a fair wind. Perhaps the "Action" went against him; or perhaps Sampson had heard of *Hope*'s growing reputation. Whatever the reason, when the two ships "Came to Action," the Captain blinked. "I thought [it] prudent to shear off," he admitted, "which I did." *Independence* tacked and the amazed sailors on *Hope* watched as "the enemy made sail from us"[34] At this point another captain might have broken off the action, returned to his task of protecting *Nancy*, and resumed the voyage to Cumberland, but for Dawson the chase was everything. His response was predictable. "Out all Reefs"! *Hope*'s top gallant and stidding sails were let out as the ship strained forward in pursuit, decks heaving and rigging taut. The chase was on! Half a mile off the *Nancy* transport was left to fend for itself. Dawson looked at the time. It was five o'clock.

At the exact time the chase began off Nova Scotia's south coast *Vulture* got under way somewhere north of Annapolis Royal, having given up on finding *Lavinia*. A signal gun had been fired every quarter hour all afternoon with no reply so at five o'clock Captain Feattus "bore away in 2 reefs topsails" and directed his ship towards the inner reaches of the Bay of Fundy, "tho' at the most Hazardous Season of the year." The bad weather, the loss of his convoy, and *Vulture*'s company of "young and inexperienced officers" complicated Feattus' problems.[35] Under these conditions, he could not expect to reach Fort Cumberland until the next morning.

Less than 100 miles down the coast the chase turned into a deadly drama. The *Independence* raced on ahead of HMS *Hope*, dodging between the gaps in the fog and manoeuvring to catch the wind's advantage. On his black-hulled sloop, Dawson plotted the wind for his own run and computed in his head the complex strategies of pursuit in the capricious currents criss-crossing the southern tip of Nova Scotia. His crew reacted confidently to a steady stream of commands that kept the wind in every inch of sail. Slowly the distance between the warships narrowed. Occasional circles of orange and yellow flame now burst from the grey bulk of *Independence*, the sound of the ship's cannon following moments later. Dawson fed this new factor into his pursuit plan, trying to present a slim profile to his enemy without losing speed. The bow guns of *Hope* were also firing and smoke and powder stained the sea breeze and streamed back into the faces of the tense crew.

It was nearly seven o'clock in the evening. *Independence* and *Hope* had been tightly locked in the chase "for near two hours," thought Dawson, but seemed "about three glasses" to the hard- pressed Sampson. An aberrant gust of wind could have decided the race at any moment but both captains had calculated finely. The cannonade exacted a toll on both ships. On *Hope* initial excitement was overlaid with fatigue and fear as the sloop drew nearer to the larger brigantine. Overhead, enemy shot ripped jagged holes in *Hope*'s sails and shredded the sloop's rigging and "our M[ain] Mast [was] wounded in Several Places"! Mariner Hugh

Robinson lay dead on the deck while William Gregory, a marine, was injured.[36] *Independence* was also damaged: "my riggin' and sails in a shattered condition," was Sampson's assessment, and there was confusion and carnage. "Two men killed ... and seven wounded," the bodies and blood on a slippery rolling deck, "a miserable situation!" Sailor Andrew Baker was hideously maimed "by a Shot striking him on the Right Shoulder [that] carried away his Right Eye, and part of his Nose."[37]

Having outsailed his adversary, Dawson was ready to attempt the brig's capture. Calculations were made for the final run in, his plan compensating for shifting breezes and the desire to face the least cannon. Fog banks were nearly black but the calm surface of the ocean glistened in the pale light of day's end, and the reflected prize beckoned, the ship's sails in tatters. Satisfied with his position and after signalling *Nancy*, which had followed the chase all day, the boarding drill was worked out and *Hope*'s marines were concealed at the ship's rail with loaded muskets. In a breath-taking manoeuvre *Hope* swooped in, "running up along side" the brig and crowding its starboard beam while *Nancy* bore down on the larboard quarter. "The enemy outsailed me," admitted Sampson and "came up after making a running fight."[38] For brief moments the ships huddled together in the open ocean, a strange quiet descending. All of Dawson's naval skills had been employed to bring the *Independence* to bay and now, just before dark, the outcome would be decided by a singular act of bluff and daring. The two ships were posed virtually rail to rail, their "Sails and Rigging much Tore." A single command followed by a loud shout and the marines "instantly rose up and fired a volley of small arms into the Brig." It was enough. "The Chace Call'd for Quarters"! The prize was Dawson's.[39] At that moment, sailor John Gardener was probably sorry he "shipped aboard" *Independence* in May 1776. Standing on the littered deck and staring into a row of muskets, he and his mates faced confinement in the notorious prison hulk in Halifax Harbour but agreed they "were obliged to surrender."[40]

Although the "smart Engagement" with *Independence* was successful for *Hope*, valuable time had been lost in the voyage to Cumberland. The chase, lasting until dark, was the least cause for delay. The damage to *Hope* and the need to escort the prize for the rest of the way would cause the sloop to be many days late in docking in Cumberland Creek.

"MY BEST CURTAINS ... [AND] A SILVER BOWL"

When Olive How looked out the window of her Fort Lawrence home on Tuesday, *26 November*, her view of the bleak Tantramar was framed with fine new curtains. Outside the day was dark and "thick with Rain" but inside the room was brightened by a new silver bowl sparkling on the table. Olive had reason to be happy. Only four years ago her life was shattered when her husband Joseph Morse died, leaving her with a large family unsupported in a pioneer settlement. Hard times followed until she married William How and in 1776 they enjoyed a comfortable living.[41]

The most traumatic experience in William How's life was the violent death of his father Edward who was killed by Natives at nearby Missiguash River in October 1750 when William was a young man. The large How family lived at various times in Annapolis Royal, Grassy Island, and Cumberland, and moved with equal ease on the frontier and in town. William was the second oldest of eight children and the only member of the family who embraced the patriot cause.[42] His wife Olive had managed without him during his exile in America in the summer and she had not seen much of him during the siege either. As a senior officer in Eddy's army, in command of special patrols, William How carried out many assignments which kept him away from home a great deal. He was on patrol again this Tuesday. But Olive never complained; he was a good provider as the new curtains and silver bowl attested.

Eddy's special patrols carried out unusual assignments one of which was the collection of outstanding debts, a difficult chore in normal times but a lot easier during the siege as Thomas Robinson of Amherst found out. This Yorkshire farmer grew corn, wheat, and oats on his diked in marsh, with barley and oats on the upland, and he summer-tilled a plot of turnips, a rare crop in Nova Scotia in 1776.[43] "Some time in the month of November," recounted Robinson, Doctor Parker Clarke, Zebulon Roe, and William How came armed to his house. Clarke claimed he owed him some money, "about thirty-five shillings." The bill was "of a long Standing," resulting from the Doctor attending Robinson's son; "now was the time for payment," declared Clarke! Backed up by two of Eddy's senior officers, now indeed was the time to collect the debt.[44]

The surprised Yorkshire farmer answered that he thought William Bulmer had paid the bill. "He had not received anything from ... Bulmer," persisted Clarke and again he "demanded payment." Robinson still refused and a normal bill collector might have given up at this point, but business affairs were easier to settle during the siege and Clarke understood his advantage: "it was a time," he said, "when all debts must be paid."[45] William How stepped closer to Robinson, and Zebulon Roe, hero of the Cumberland Creek raid, clapped him on the shoulder and "demanded in a threatening manner," that he "pay that money" to Clarke in five minutes "or go along with them a prisoner." The futility of further protest was obvious even to the methodical Yorkshiresettler, but being short of cash and "fearing to be made their prisoner," he asked if he could "borrow it from his neighbour Mr. Black."[46] This repayment proposal was acceptable and Robinson went along to William Black's with Clarke who talked disparagingly all the way "on the Yorkshire people and on those who took commissions under [Michael] Francklin."[47] Since they were under house arrest the Blacks were sure to be home when Clarke knocked on their door. The Doctor, who had often made house calls to Yorkshire homes, looked strange "with a Bayonet tyed on his Gun." Robinson explained his dilemma: that Clarke had presented him with a bill and "he was come to borrow the money to pay it." Because he was a good neighbour and also because Clarke was threatening "that if he did not pay he should be a prisoner," Black loaned Robinson the money who in turn passed it over to Clarke, "which he would not otherwise have done had he not been forced."[48]

The disorderly repayment of debt was only one scheme carried out by Eddy's special patrols. Another party combed the countryside in search of firearms for Camphill and cash to finance the siege. Arriving uninvited at homes from Sackville to River Hebert, this party was neither a blockade patrol nor even a collection agency, being aptly labelled "the plundering Party." It was capably led by William How. In Sackville, How and his party stopped at the Dixon home while Charles was away carrying news of the siege to Windsor. His wife Susanna, on seeing them approach, had the presence of mind to hide the family silverware and other valuables in a barrel of pig feed. Nevertheless, on this raid How robbed the Dixons of a length of linen, some cash, a sword, "an excellent gun" with shot and 3000 gun flints, a pair of shoes, and "a fatt cow."[49]

How led another party that included Richard Jones, Joseph Leger, and other Acadians to the Barron home and store in River Hebert while Edward Sr was in the fort during the siege. Anne Barron was at home and she watched aghast while How and his men ransacked the place, removing "30 Beaver Hatts," two guns with 200 flints and forty pounds of gunpowder, tools, snowshoes, and many other items. Seven sheep were rounded up from the barnyard and the Barrons' supply of West India rum was certainly not missed by the acquisitive patriots.[50] While his men argued over the division of these goods, William How indulged a more refined taste. While in the house, he admired the Barrons' "Best Curtains ... [and] Silver Bowl." These articles, which he loaded on the wagon and reserved for himself as commander, were the same drapes and bowl that graced the home of Olive How on Tuesday 26 November.[51]

The stormy weather that Olive How saw through her new curtains blanketed the entire Fundy coast and stayed the progress of the *Vulture* warship. Feattus had expected to reach the fort this Tuesday but was forced to drop anchor at six in the morning just inside Cumberland Basin. After sitting idle for two hours and with visibility at zero, he "fir[e]d seven sig[na]l Guns that the Fort might observe our being in the River" but *Vulture* was too far away to be heard in the storm. That afternoon the vessel "weighed and run a little further to the N[orth]ward," only to be forced to another anchorage by the foul weather.[52] Because provisions had been supplied earlier to *Lavinia* and because of the long voyage, the ship's company dined that night on two-thirds rations. *Lavinia* had not appeared since it lost contact on Sunday night, but Feattus had every reason to believe the ship was making its way independently to the fort. Although the coast could not be seen to port or starboard, the fort was reckoned to be no more than seven or eight miles further north, and Feattus was determined to make contact the next morning by putting out boats with some Royal Marines, who were good at "boat work" and sending them on ahead to the fort no matter what the weather.[53]

When the Royal Marines landed the next day *Vulture*'s voyage would be over; having lasted six days it was far longer than usual. Foul weather and the *Lavinia* caused the delays and Feattus had to concentrate every league of the way. Certainly, to navigate a warship into narrow, fog-bound Cumberland Basin, hard-drinking was forgone. For a captain once accused of being "in Liquor coming into Halifax Harbour," that was a tall order, but other qualities were also ascribed to James Feattus who, his friends said, "by his Diligence and unremitted Activity got up ... to Fort Cumberland."[54] What the marines would find when they went ashore and when *Lavinia* and the Highland Emigrants would appear were questions on everyone's lips.

8 The Camphill Rout

Wednesday 27 November to Friday 29 November

The Schooner, after landing the Troops, found the[y] had sallied out, burnt several Villages and entirely routed the Rebels; loss not known.

Josiah Clossen, HMS *Vulture*[1]

By the last week of November, Jonathan Eddy had depleted his options. Bluff, military assault, fire: all were tried but the walls of Fort Cumberland had not come tumbling down. The old ranger Joseph Goreham could not be bluffed, the patriots had no stomach for another salvo from the 6-pounders, and there was nothing left to burn in proximity to the fort. In considering how the siege might yet be won Eddy returned to his most successful tactic, the blockade. This tactic was meant to work in two respects: it was intended to prevent goods from entering the fort and news from leaking out. The news had leaked out and the outside world knew of the siege, but in the first respect the blockade was working albeit too slowly.

After four weeks of stalemate time had become the decisive factor and time was on Goreham's side unless Eddy could accelerate the blockade. To do this he had not only to block supplies from reaching the fort but actually to capture existing stores. Such action might starve out the garrison before winter. The capture of the provision sloop fit with this strategy because it deprived Goreham of vital supplies. By cutting his fuel supply the second great fire had the same effect. With few options and while hoping for reinforcement, the patriots looked for ways to enhance the blockade as the siege entered its fifth week. Loyalist tactics were unchanged. Goreham's logic, if not very creative, was irrefutable. So long as Eddy was denied the main objective there was every reason to stay in the fort. Worry over supplies was balanced by a daily expectation of reinforcement. It might be argued that improvements in the Fencibles' soldiery warranted a bolder strategy, but Goreham would take no risks.

The final crisis was near. Victory would go to the side that was reinforced first, but if neither side was reinforced quickly winter would force
the issue. Freedom from mosquitoes was an advantage soon to be out-
weighed by freezing temperatures. Although food was plentiful the patriots were otherwise unequipped for a cold weather siege while the
garrison, already on reduced rations, could not endure the winter. As
the enthusiasm for rebellion waned some patriots concentrated on settling old scores and plundering loyalists. One way or another – by force
or the rapidly advancing season – the stalemate at Fort Cumberland
must soon end.

"A SMART SKIRMISH"

"A very thick Fogg" blanketed Cumberland Ridge on Wednesday morning, 27 November. Sentries could not see beyond the ramparts as daily
routines commenced: the guard changed, the Fencibles formed up on
a mist-layered parade square, and the cows were herded through the
palisade gate to graze in the hayfield. A guard party went on a regular
circuit of inspection outside the fort. It was barely dawn and all was
quiet except for the drill sergeant's commands reverberating off the
walls. Enveloped in fog, the party examined the low ditch around the
spur and the burnt ruins of the hospital before passing the field where
summer hay was stacked and cattle grazed. Being essentials of the commissariat the cows were secured nightly within the palisade, and why
they were taken out on a day when the fog obscured them as fully as the
night was a question only the officer in charge could answer. Something
was bothering them. The guard party made out a group of men driving
the cows – Eddy's men capitalizing on the garrison's lapse in animal
husbandry. The patriots were on another raid! Having crept along the
ridge under the cover of the early morning fog, they had the cows already on the move. A soldier raced back to the fort to raise the alarm. If
milk and beef supplies were cut the garrison would be in crisis. Goreham would have to risk his Fencibles outside the defence walls at last.
Propelled by necessity but with a growing confidence in their improved
skills and drawing his best trained and best equipped soldiers directly
from the drill square, "an officers' party was sent out to intercept
them," and a second party followed shortly after to support the first.[2]
Haystacks apparently floating on a thinning fog gave the early morning scenery a pale ethereal quality. Presently, patriots were spotted driving the cows towards the woods on the far side of the pasture. Charging
over damp ground the Fencibles opened fire at close range and in uni-
son and a "smart skirmish" ensued. A rising mist revealed an open field
of yellow stubble and haystacks – the latter offered little protection from

the concentrated musketry. Caught in a cross-fire, the bewildered cows milled about or ran off in terror while the patriots fell back among the haystacks before breaking for the woods with the Fencibles in pursuit. Not everyone left the battlefield. The patriots suffered their heaviest losses of the siege: "our men drove them into the woods and kill'd several," noted Goreham afterwards "but we had three privates wounded." It was still only nine o'clock in the morning.[3] The haystack skirmish was a brief tragedy and garrison hill was quiet again even as the fog lifted exposing patriot casualties where they had fallen: limp forms in homespun impaled on the hard stubble of the hayfield. Stray cattle were rounded up and the Fencibles returned carrying their wounded; one, Private Peter Calahan, died the same day.[4] Goreham was heartened by the performance of his troops. That the skirmish took place outside the fort underscored the improvement of the corps under his command. The patriots, on the other hand, were frustrated in an attempt to hasten the effects of the blockade.

From the ramparts at mid-morning sentries surveyed the broad sweep of the Tantramar, scanning the tree-lined ridge where the patriots were last seen only an hour before, the marsh where the mist was fast retreating, and Cumberland Basin where the fog lingers longest. In this last view – the direction of reinforcement – where the fog was only now thinning to a silvery vapour, the faintest of shapes caught the attention of hopeful sentries. A slightly darker form, a grey chimera, emerged ominously from the pale mist until the distinctive profile of a warship was etched ghost-like above the still unseen surface of the basin. "At 10 o'clock His Majesty's Ship *Vulture* appeared off the Harbour," as welcome to the garrison this cold November day as any songbird of spring![5]

The garrison exulted in the vision of reinforcement but on the *Vulture*, where preparations were under way to go ashore, there was no certainty that Colonel Goreham still held the fort. From aboard ship it seemed a landing party was equally likely to face a patriot attack as a loyalist welcome and until the true situation was known every precaution had to be taken by Captain James Feattus. Two boats were "mann'd and arm'd." Huntsbach Branson's company of marines along with provincial officers Thomas Batt and Gilfred Studholme set off at eleven o'clock to row the last few miles to the fort. Two hours later the boats landed in Cumberland Creek to a welcoming garrison. In calm weather marines, sailors, fencibles, and families mingled and the newcomers were told about the siege and how "the Rebels had made several attacks on the Fort, but were repuls'd!" Out on *Vulture* in the meantime the relieved captain heard the sound he was waiting for: three of the fort's cannon booming "a Sign'l agreed on if it was still in our possession." It would be six o'clock before the two boats returned to *Vulture*, too late for the other company of marines to go ashore that day.[6]

Nova Scotia was the clear winner of the reinforcement race; Massachusetts was still at the debating stage. This Wednesday while *Vulture* appeared like an apparition in Cumberland Basin, the Machias Committee considered the two Cumberland letters describing Eddy's failure to capture the fort and pleading for help. Members listened to the news from the besiegers, read out by Clerk William Tupper, enumerating "the extreme difficulties they have laboured under by means of joining with Captain Eddy's party." It was clear from the letters and the firsthand account of Josiah Throop that the Cumberlanders had "high expectations" (raised by Eddy) of help from Boston, "and that Colonel Shaw will soon arrive to their assistance with a sufficient armament." Surprise must have registered on their faces at this news before the clerk went on to read that Cumberlanders requested – "very importunately requested," some members were heard to grumble – "all possible aid ... and everybody able to afford them the least assistance!"[7]

After examining the letters and listening to Throop, the Machias Committee agreed that urgent action was needed. Boston must be asked for "speedy relief" but it was realized, even as Tupper was instructed to pen the request, that there was little likelihood of a timely response from that quarter. Francis Shaw was not pursuing the matter with the Council and John Allan, by his own admission "a zealous opposer of the Expedition,"[8] was ignoring Eddy and concentrating on becoming an American Indian agent; only the day before Council had agreed that he "might write as [he] saw proper to the Micmacs."[9] Once again the burden fell on the Machias Committee and despite misgivings about Eddy's party, "yet we are disposed to help them so far as we are able and shall encourage all the men we can spare to go."[10] James Lyon, the member most supportive of Eddy, offered to spearhead the recruiting drive. To set an example, he stepped down from his pulpit to volunteer as a soldier. On "being requested to send them all the assistance in our power," he explained, "forty- nine of us immediately set out in boats as a reinforcement."[11] Its size was larger than the invasion force Eddy had with him when he had entered Nova Scotia at Passamaquaddy, yet it was obviously insufficient. As the committee deliberated that Wednesday, Nova Scotian reinforcements had already anchored off Fort Cumberland.

Civilians and Fencibles were overjoyed with the arrival of the Royal Marines. Plans to lift the siege were immediately afoot and not even the whereabouts of *Lavinia* with its 120 Highland Emigrants seemed to matter. Captain Feattus had no idea of *Lavinia*'s fate but supposed the vessel was still on course in the Bay of Fundy and might appear at any moment. But Goreham would await only the landing of the remaining marines the next day and then, with or without the Emigrants, he would go on the attack with available forces no later than Friday morning. Even if he had been reluctant to go quickly on the offensive, or had judged the Emigrants a requirement for Eddy's defeat, the attack could not have been put off. The food shortage would simply not permit him to wait any longer for *Lavinia*. A break-out into the countryside was essential and the situation compelled an early attack on Camphill. In the meantime, the marines and the warship had brought peace of mind. The presence of marine surgeon James Silvers was of special comfort to a garrison without a doctor for nearly three weeks. The tension of the siege had dissipated by Wednesday evening and the positive mood persisted through the overcrowding caused by 100 extra bodies and the food shortage which the occupants from *Vulture*, on short rations themselves, could only aggravate.

Following a night of celebration a crowded but confident garrison came to life at dawn on Thursday, *28 November*, with the reassuring profile of a British warship in the Cumberland Basin. A brisk westerly animated the few clouds in a sky that promised a fine day. *Vulture's* masts could be seen from long distances on the Tantramar, by friend and foe alike. Patriots in Fort Lawrence were thrown "in great confusion" by the ships appearance, so great that the schooner captured there earlier in the siege was retaken at five o'clock that morning by loyalist prisoners who sailed the schooner out to anchor under the protective wing of *Vulture*.[12] Camphill patriots spotted the *Vulture*. "In the mean Time," observed Eddy, "on the 27th Nov'r, arrived in the Bay a Man-of-War from Halifax with a Reinforcement for the Garrison consisting of near 400 men." The ship's appearance might have signalled to loyalists that the end of the siege was near, but this was not Eddy's first response. He saw the warship, even overestimated the size of the reinforcement, yet he lingered at Camphill. Perhaps he believed that the troops would not be used offensively but only to strengthen the fort. He might have been lured into this conclusion by Goreham's cautious military tactics and by his low opinion of Nova Scotia's will to fight. If he was right it would mean that Camphill was safe for the time being and he could risk waiting a few more days for his own reinforcement. Naturally reluctant to abandon the siege and accept defeat, Eddy nevertheless did not remain in Camphill through inertia alone. He made a conscious decision to stand pat as indicated by the extra guards he placed around the camp that Thursday.[13]

"THE MARINES WERE ORDERED TO HOLD THEMSELVES IN READINESS"

The presence of *Vulture* meant that nothing moved unchallenged in Cumberland Basin. A cannon was fired to halt a boat on Thursday near the entrance to that narrow body of water. On learning it was a trading vessel out of Annapolis Royal en route to Cumberland, the ship was allowed to sail to port. The appearance earlier of the schooner recaptured in Fort Lawrence was fortuitous for James Feattus who pressed the vessel into service to transport the second company of Royal Marines more commodiously to the fort. The schooner also proved convenient in carrying as one cargo the arms and ammunition which the captain sent ashore to assist the garrison. The schooner and one of *Vulture's* boats headed for shore with this cargo at eleven o'clock, and the partly cloudy morning had given way to a clear and cold afternoon by the time William Pitcairn led his marines ashore to complete the reinforcement of Fort Cumberland. The marines landed over the two days comprised a force much smaller than Eddy estimated. It fell far short of the number General Massey wanted, and included less than half the number he had seen leave Windsor. As work began on Friday's plan of attack, Goreham must have wondered about the fate of *Lavinia*.

The fate of the reinforcement was on Michael Francklin's mind as he waited in Windsor for news of the siege. Imagine his surprise that cold Thursday, 28 November, when *Lavinia* sailed into the Avon River on a wind that "blows hard" out of the northwest. At sea a week yet hardly out of Minas Channel, the ship's captain abandoned the voyage and returned with a cargo of disgruntled Highland Emigrants and several excuses. "Meeting with a gale of wind in their passage,"[14] losing all contact with *Vulture* and "in want of provisions," the leaky *Lavinia* limped back to port "for further orders."[15]

Subtracting over half the troops from a task force Massey already considered too small was the subject of earnest debate in Windsor and later in Halifax. Perhaps another sloop should be hired so "the party of troops might return to Cumberland with the convoy of an armed vessel."[16] But a good deal had happened to make that now appear unnecessary. Collier finally had the navy on the move or so it seemed in Halifax. While *Hope* and *Nancy* were underway with troops aboard, the news trickling into Windsor continued to confirm the small size of Eddy's force. It was felt that the Royal Marines sent on *Vulture*, with the support of *Hope* and *Nancy*, would be enough to relieve the fort. Other moves on the naval front would provide backup. Orders "to proceed instantly to Fort Cumberland"[17] stood at Annapolis Royal for the expected early return of *Albany* and *Diligent*. In Halifax HMS *Lizard* (Captain Thomas MacKenzie) was preparing to sail "with a schooner and sloop under our convoy for Fort Cumberland."[18] But long before *Lizard* got there, assuming the vessel could make it so late in the season, Collier expected the siege to be over; for a week he had been saying "that we daily expect to hear of the flight of this marauding set of Rebels."[19]

Unknown to Collier, Captain Dawson was again behind schedule. After the action with *Independence* on Monday, time was spent "splicing and Knitting the Rigging" of the damaged *Hope*. That Thursday *Hope* lay with *Nancy* and the prize "wooding, booming and Drying Sails" and would not be "turning out of Yarmouth Harbour" to resume the voyage to Cumberland until the next day. Ignorant of this delay, Executive Council concluded there was "no danger to apprehend." The Highland Emigrants would therefore stay in Windsor and by Thursday evening, when the wind had fallen and in Isaac Deschamps's opinion there would be frost, they were back in Fort Edward.[20] The conclusion that they were no longer needed did not soften the blow to the officers, nor prevent recrimination. Some officers blamed James Feattus for *Lavinia's* problems: "I believe you'll find it absolutely Necessary," intoned a fellow officer to Ranald McKinnon, "for you to bring the Conduct of the Captain of the Man of War to public hearing." He wanted McKinnon, who had been on the *Lavinia*, to collect affidavits from "the Pilot and Midshipman." The charge probably stemmed more from disgruntlement at losing the chance to lift the siege than from any shortcoming of Feattus who appears to have done all he could to assist the decrepit *Lavinia.*[21]

The *Lavinia's* "not appearing in sight" in the basin neither deterred Goreham from going on the offensive, nor suppressed the carnival atmosphere in the garrison. An air of expectancy pervaded the congested parade square where Fencibles blended with civilians and the Royal Marines stood out because they wore uniforms. A bustle of men and women at the bakehouse and commissariat worked overtime to cope with the sudden influx. Doors to the magazine opened to carts coming up from the creek with 350 round shot for the 6-pounders, part of the supplies donated by Captain Feattus. News from Camphill put Goreham in an ebullient mood. "Some people came in which gave an account of there being but two or three hundred [patriots] only remaining in that Camp and in the houses adjacent." Confidently, he turned to selecting the troops and officers for the party he would send to "that Camp" the next morning.[22] The size of the strike force could not be large, not only because the reinforcement was smaller than planned, but because at least half the garrison must stay behind for defence, and could not participate anyway for lack of equipment. The quality of the Fencibles was always a question. Given a choice the Marines would have preferred to go into combat with the Highland Emigrants, for while opinion of both provincial regiments was low, they regarded the Fencibles as the bottom of the barrel. The Emigrants for "the most part are a good body of Men and may soon be brought into some kind of discipline," allowed a marine officer earlier in 1776, but he added sarcastically that the Fencibles "are training to be soldiers."[23] Such criticism was academic now. No matter what their state of military training, there was no choice but to proceed with a combined force of about "150 Rank and file" soldiers plus officers with a nearly equal division between Marines of the reinforcement and Fencibles of the garrison.[24] And the field commander of the force would be Major Thomas Batt of the Fencibles.

While Goreham laid plans for Friday's search-and-destroy mission, rumours circulating across Nova Scotia were pessimistic about his fate. Fuelled alike by those in sympathy with the rebellion and those who complained that the fort had not been adequately provided for by the army, these rumours spread fast and even supposed that the fort had fallen. "We are in the midst of confusion and alarm," wrote a Haligonian a few days before, "We expect the rebels every day and we hear they have actually invaded and taken Fort Cumberland, which our General here forgot to send provisions and ammunition to, and so it is lost"[25] In Liverpool, "fair weather" on the South Shore that Thursday found Jacob Jones and William Knoulton in Simeon Perkins's store with news from Halifax "that Fort Cumberland was taken by an army from New England ... and that many of the people of this province have joined them."[26]

"The whole of the Marines were ordered to hold themselves in readiness."[27] Details of the attack plan were filled in Thursday evening. Captains Branson and Pitcairn would lead their two Marine companies with four junior officers: lieutenants Philip Hoise, John Dyer, Thomas Sewings, and Robert Short. They would form the flanking parties and provide eighty-nine men to the force. The role of the Fencibles would be to carry the centre of the attack and charge directly into the patriot camp with Marines on either flank. Selecting Fencibles meant finding "those best shoed or cloathed" and these – "64 Rank and file" – were picked chiefly from the companies of Thomas Batt and Gilfred Studholme. The detachment would include two drummers, four sergeants, and three junior officers and be commanded by a captain for a total of seventy-four men. To lead them Goreham picked his most intrepid officer, the vigorous Captain Studholme. Junior officers would be first Lieutenant Lewis De Beauduoin and second Lieutenant Ambrose Sharman of Studholme's company and second Lieutenant Constance Connor of Batt's company (first Lieutenant John Walker had been taken prisoner in Shepody Point). Four sergeants were selected from the six in Studholme's and Batt's companies: James Innis, Matthew Magrath, John Traverse, Henry George, William MacLeod, and Pattrick Daniel. The drummers probably were John Austin and James Liddle.[28] Assembly of the Fencibles was complete. If by their variable dress these provincials cut a poor military figure and were the butt of Marine jokes, it was not Goreham's fault. He had fought with Halifax over uniforms but without success and now the Marines would realize their worst fears. "The Fencibles," howled a Marine, "not being all Cloth'd, look so much like Yankees that [the thought] of doing [service] with them gives me Horrors!"[29]

"GAVE A LOUD HUZZAH AND RAN LIKE LIONS"

Few secrets can be kept for long during civil strife in rural districts; any action planned by one side will soon be known to the other. Goreham's intentions leaked to Camphill even before his plan was complete. "Intelligence was given our [Eddy's] people in the Evening of the 28th that a Sally was determined in the Garrison."[30] If the message reached Eddy, he made no special effort to take advantage of it either by abandoning Camphill or strengthening defences other than by placing more guards around the perimeter. Seldom did all patriots sleep overnight in Camphill; some locals went home to their own comfortable beds every night. This pattern was known to Eddy and had been an obstacle when assembling men to attack the fort, but he did nothing that Thursday night to break the pattern and confine patriots to headquarters. This was not the only reason for reduced numbers in Camphill. The Committee-of-Safety explained that some of Eddy's men, "being stationed at different posts for the safety of the Inhabitants could not be collected."[31] For various reasons, not the least of which must have been the prospect of imminent attack, fewer people than usual slept in Camphill on that clear late autumn night. The wind dropped and temperatures plunged as frost entered the ground. The air was sharp and cold in the narrow alley-ways of the fort where unusual activity continued very late. The last of twenty half-barrels of powder was stowed gingerly in the magazine to complete the transfer of *Vulture*'s supplies. Yellow candle-light glowed from barrack windows as Goreham and his officers applied final touches to their plan for the strike force to be sent "the next morning to attack their Camp." The final composition was settled at eighty-nine Marines and seventy-four Fencibles for a total of 163 men, of whom 141 were private soldiers, and the remaining twenty-two were officers and other ranks.[32] All worries about the Highland Emigrants were set aside but while *Lavinia* had removed itself from reinforcement duty, other ships were vying to come to the aid of Fort Cumberland.

"Ran up the Harbour" of Annapolis Royal at the stroke of midnight Thursday and "came too with the Best Bower" a mile distant from the town: HMS *Diligent* arrived several days later than Collier would have liked, but then *Albany* did not arrive at all. Only *Diligent* followed the commodore's orders to proceed to Cumberland. After scraping the vessel off Old Man rock, Captain Hyndman was concerned about damage to *Albany*'s hull and decided not to accompany *Diligent* to Annapolis Royal as planned. The two ships "parted company" off the Maine coast on Tuesday afternoon; *Albany* was making directly for the naval yard in Halifax where the ship could have its bottom inspected.[33] The order to go to Cumberland might not have been in Captain Dodd's hands until Friday morning when he went ashore and it would take a day to get *Diligent* back under sail. Many miles to the south in Yarmouth Harbour HMS *Hope* would be unable to resume its voyage until the next day. It was uncertain Thursday night which of these two ships would reach Cumberland first. It was certain that no more reinforcements would arrive before Goreham attacked Camphill in less than six hours.

The pre-dawn Tantramar was black at half past four Friday morning, *29 November.* It was blacker still inside the walls of the fort. Peculiarly, the main source of light was the marsh itself where a heavy frost spread a sheen of vague paleness barely matched by the thin horizon line above Maccan. On the parade square the frost-encrusted grass was crunchy underfoot and cold to the 160-odd troops, who were turned out of spur barracks and officers' quarters stiff of limb and shivering in the sub-zero chill. To muffled orders the men formed a tight knot in the small space to be equipped and armed, some with flints, bayonets, and muskets supplied by *Vulture.* Major Thomas Batt received final orders from Commander Goreham amid a cold breakfast and tobacco smoke. At five o'clock the march to Camphill began.

The tight military knot unwound gradually into a single line of soldiers, an increasingly long and longer line that cut a swath in the frosty air, its 160 pairs of lungs puffing out a cloud of vapour as it snaked its way between buildings in search of the open Tantramar. The line lengthened and pushed through the east gate to the place-of-arms outside the main defence walls before bending left on the protected way. To the right was the old carpenter shop nestled up against the palisade; Prince Frederick Bastion loomed on the left. The heavily rutted track, a mud slick in daytime, was rock hard and treacherous to marching feet in early morning. Unwinding to its full length, the line reached the bakehouse where it curved sharply right to the palisade gate and marched out into the cold Cumberland countryside. Once clear of the fort Major Batt bore eastward, leading his men downhill and along "the right hand road" that skirted the edge of the marsh. Except for the crunch of frozen marsh mud they marched silently, passing on their left the homes of Benoni Danks and Jotham Gay where rested the gravely wounded Samuel Wethered.[34] Gay was loyal but Danks was in Eddy's camp. Keeping to the lowlands the Marines and Fencibles marched on until they reached the foot of Camphill where they huddled in a hollow in the pre-dawn chill, awaiting "sufficient day-light to enable us clearly to distinguish objects."[35] The sky was starting to turn grey as the veteran Batt adjusted his cramped legs and tried to make out the contours of Camphill emerging slowly from the gloom in front of him. Ragged hedgerows criss-crossed a gentle slope while higher up fog banks hung heavily on the wooded hill top. Rain was a certainty. The Major signalled his men to move out.

Silently the troopers ascended the hill and in a short time the advance guard heard "the Indians talking at their wigwams." Somewhere through the trees ahead was the road leading to Read's farm. The men paused again, on the brow of the hill now, at the edge of the fog banks. Finding that his force was still "wholly undiscovered," Batt reviewed the final orders. Captain Branson would sweep the right flank with half of the Marines while the remainder under Captain Pitcairn would take the left flank. Captain Studholme would press up the centre with the Fencibles. They would hit the Baie Verte Road, wheel north and head straight for the patriot encampment at Read's farm.[36] Marines moved off to the left and right while the Fencibles entered the light stand of trees that separated them from the road. To their right the tops of several wigwams were visible in the eerie light of half dawn. A break in the mist ahead marked the road they were looking for: a section of quiet country lane flanked by bare trees and tall evergreens with brown leaves strewn in the frozen ruts. That Friday the Baie Verte Road resembled the scene of an early morning partridge hunt more than a contested battle line. Suddenly, the silence was broken by a startled voice in the woods ahead, followed by other voices and muffled sounds of running feet in a gathering commotion. They were discovered. Studholme swung his men out into the lane. A drum roll from the heart of the patriot camp beat out an urgent call to arms.

Pandemonium broke over Camphill as the Fencibles went into action. They "gave a loud Huzzah and ran like lions"! Like a pack of crazed animals they charged down the lane in the direction of Eddy's stronghold. Studholme raced his courageous men past the levelled musketry of patriot outguards concealed in their hiding places. "The villains fired at us from right and left of the road leading to Eddy's headquarters" This wooded stretch was still so deeply shaded as to be nearly dark but a lighter patch ahead showed where the road merged with the open fields of Read's farm. On the right flank, Pitcairn's Marines swept through the Maliseet camp only minutes behind the Maliseets who had fled at the first sign of attack. Fires still burning in the circle of wigwams and equipment strewn on the ground attested to their hasty retreat.[37]

Amid a scene of profound confusion a young Black drummer at Read's farm thumped his drum to the same heightened rhythm as the attackers' heartbeats. Doors at Eddy's headquarters flew open and the barnyard filled with half-dressed patriots tumbling from tents and make-shift barracks. Camphill was caught nearly by surprise since the Nova Scotia loyalists "came out in the Night by a round about March [and] got partly within our Guards."[38] In the farmhouse, "in the midst of such a Tumult," patriot officers struggled to grasp the situation as well as their trousers. Why had there been so little warning? Where were the scouts? "We had Scouts out all Night,"[39] shouted Eddy. Little thought had been given to fortifying the farm with barricades and trenches and no patriots displayed the defensive creativity of Goreham. Whatever works were thrown up between the buildings were superficial and went unattended that morning as all efforts were directed towards evacuating the premises. Only moments could be spared. Marines appeared at the edge of the woods and near the farmyard Micmacs and Maliseets ran across the field in the general direction of Baie Verte. A Micmac[40] was struck in his flight by a musket ball and fell dead.

On the open road there suddenly appeared the main body of Fencibles for whom the way lay open to the farm. Fencibles and Marines combined and in full flight "began the attack on a number of the Rebels they found in Read's house."[41] The charge was directed at the cluster of farm buildings and led through a hail of musketry. "The rebels who occupied the house darted out of it at our approach and fired as they fled."[42] Batt's men "routed them and all the others who were in Hutts and Sheds."[43] A patriot soldier, Private Furlong, fell dead in this exchange while the rest fled to the nearby woods, among them Jonathan Eddy, escaping capture with only seconds to spare.[44] In his short dash to safety (at "about Sunrise") Eddy glimpsed the assault troops over his shoulder. They "furiously Rushed upon the Barracks where our Men were quartered" and there was "just Time Enough to Escape out of the Houses and run into the Bushes"![45] The farm was surrounded and on entering Read's house, the Fencibles found only the Black drummer who had earlier beat the call to arms and had been left behind by his comrades.[46] Camphill was captured. Patriot resistance was broken.

The action at Read's blunted Major Batt's momentum; "we pursued, however, as fast as we could" and elements of his "lions" were already past that farm: "The next house we entered was the rendezvous of their wretched Committee and owned by one Gardiner." It was from Ebenezer Gardiner's home that the patriot Committee-of-Safety wielded authority and out of Gardiner's that How's plundering party operated. If there was a prime target for loyalist wrath on this day of reckoning, it was this house. "This I burnt," announced Batt glibly, with no hint of remorse.[47]

Four miles further up the road at Bloody Bridge, Mary Allan was looking out her front door at a column of smoke billowing skyward above the trees far to the south. She was thunder-struck! Had not Jonathan Eddy assured her that the fort would fall? Did not William How control the countryside, and were not the "friends of government" frightened in their homes? Now it was her turn to be frightened. Converging in the roadway were Acadians, hurrying off towards Camphill. What was she to do? With husband John out of the country, she managed their *Inverary* farm, cared for the five children, and dealt with tenants as she always did when he was away politicking with the Native peoples or Acadians. He had been home so little recently, often after dark and frequently in secret, and now he had been away for over a month, since before the siege. Having fled a charge of treason and with a price on his head, he could not return as long as Nova Scotia remained loyal. At first the siege raised Mary's spirits but it had dragged on too long with Eddy immobile in Camphill. If the garrison was on the attack this morning as indicated by the smoke billowing in that direction, surely the soldiers would be stopped in Camphill. If not, they were unlikely to come all the way to Bloody Bridge and at any rate, they would never harm *Inverary* farm "esteemed to be one of the best farms," with the marsh dyked-in and nearly all "under Plow." Surely it was safe![48]

Leaving Gardiner's place in flames, the soldiers were moving out again in the direction of Bloody Bridge. It was broad daylight and the fog had lifted but the morning was overcast and threatened rain. The attack had turned into a rout and in their flight the remnants of Eddy's army fought rearguard actions house to house along the road. Batt proceeded methodically and his pattern of advance emerged: the Marine parties weaved in and out of the bush on either side of the road, breaking up ambushes and picking up stragglers; the Fencibles marched up the road and fanned out across the fields of each farm, searching houses and barns and separating patriots from loyalists. The burning of Gardiner's place added a strong element of retribution to the advance. Instead of being an exceptional event reserved for Committee-of-Safety headquarters it became a model of vengeance to be applied generally in lifting the siege. "The Enemy on this retreat, firing from some of the Houses, the soldiers, after beating them out, set fire and consumed ... the buildings."[49] The advance was strenuous and dangerous, requiring instant, often harsh decisions from Captain Studholme. Distinguishing friend from foe is never easy in civil war and with the Fencibles only too eager to apply the torch, the captain had only minutes to decide whether a complex of farm buildings would remain intact or be burned flat. In the heat of battle and with the swiftness of the advance, the tendency was to err on the side of vengeance. This incendiary aspect of the rout was copied by rear elements of Batt's force, who burned Eddy's command centre at Read's farm. This fire gave a graphic illustration of victory to a wide audience, including the garrison and the crew of *Vulture* standing out in the Cumberland Basin.

Terror preceded the Fencibles driving north. From scattered farm houses families watched the patriots running up the road, occasionally disappearing into the woods, sometimes clustering by a barn or outbuilding as if to make a stand, only to flee again. Some abandoned their weapons. Mothers gathered their children and watched the road anxiously, listening for the sound of musketry, awaiting the first view of the soldiers. All women living in the path of the advance had cause for concern but those with husbands in Eddy's army did not linger in their homes; they bundled their children into the woods, hoping for the best. And the Fencibles kept on coming, knocking down fences in their rampage, destroying "the Cattle and sheep ... others strayed in the confusion."[50]

Further north Mary Allan watched as a row of smoke columns billowing above the trees stretched down the road closer to the village, closer to her home. The signs were now unmistakable to this young mother of five. Having broken through at Camphill, the loyalists had not halted the attack but were continuing towards Baie Verte on a path of revenge, destroying farms as they went. Her own must also be a target of the King's wrath. Considering her husband's treason and that their Acadian tenants were with Eddy, she had reason to fear that a special vengeance was reserved for Bloody Bridge and *Inverary* farm. Her father Mark Patton might have already warned her that her home could be a target. Patton supported the rebellion in January but did not join Eddy in the siege although he knew of William How's plundering party and was aware of the potential for revenge if Eddy failed.[51] All November the traffic past Bloody Bridge was busier than usual with detachments of patriots on their way to attack the fort, heading in the opposite direction to patrol Baie Verte, or returning to homes in Jolicure. The Acadian barns nearby were Eddy's commissariat. The road was filled again this Friday morning with patriots fleeing the loyalist attack. Some stopped at her house to warn of "the approach of the Enemy."[52] She went back inside but the familiar interior offered no solace; her mind raced. Protect the children! Collect the valuables! Presently, she reappeared in the farmyard with her arms full. Surely there was time to hide possessions in the forest!

The frost was out of the ground and for a few hours the Baie Verte Road reverted to mud. Briefly this Friday the road was also a battlefield along which nearly all fronting properties were in flames: "every rebel's house and barn for six miles," calculated Major Batt.[53] The destruction, amounting to "12 Houses and 12 Barns" according to Eddy, but which actually exceeded those numbers, broke patriot resolve.[54] "The enemy burnt up almost all the stores our people had collected;

burnt many of the houses and barns and driven men, women and children almost naked into the woods."[55] The mist which increased to a light rain added to their misery on that cold November Friday. Batt was troubled by the burnings, by the tragedy and waste, by seeing the possessions of whole families go up in smoke, and glimpsing the horrified faces of women and children at the edge of the woods. "All the houses I destroyed," he explained, "contained the comforts and many of the luxuries of life." But at the same time he noticed they contained "numbers of spare arms and the barns of the French were receptacles [for provisions]: circumstances," Batt observed darkly, "which denoted mature ideas of war."[56] The burning continued.

The Baie Verte Road was long, muddy and dangerous, with stubborn pockets of resistance to overcome. Private Michael Dickie was killed and several fencibles and one marine were wounded in small intermittent skirmishes that did nothing to dampen the lust for property destruction. Among the resistance fighters were the Acadians, many of whose farms were in the path of the advance which by now was approaching Bloody Bridge. By no mere chance was the fiery wrath of Major Batt directed to this village which was infamous to loyalists as the home of John Allan and a centre of Acadian rebellion. Many of the Acadians lived as tenant farmers on Allan's estate, "every man belonging to which was this day in action against us."[57]

A pall of smoke hanging low on the southern tree line reminded Mary Allan of the urgency of her task. Several bundles were stacked at the edge of the field awaiting transfer to a hiding place in the woods beyond. Acadian families nearby were doing the same and some of the menfolk had returned to help. She had just returned for another bundle when a new pillar of smoke shot skyward so close that flames were visible above the trees. At the same time small groups of men began to appear where the road turned into the woods. Nothing in their dress distinguished them as soldiers. Neither red-coated nor uniformed in any military fashion, they were the variously clad troops of His Majesty's Royal Fencible Americans, not looking very royal but displaying a certain co-ordination of movement and unmistakably well-armed. Thoroughly terrified, Mary dropped everything and gathering the children fled towards the forest, breathlessly crossing her fields, urging little William, at eight her eldest, before her. He in turn helped two of the younger children, six-year-old Mark and four-year-old John Jr, while three-year-old Isobel, the only daughter, held tightly to her mother. Clasped in Mary's arms was her baby, seven-month-old George Washington Allan. On reaching the far side of the fields, they scarcely had time to glance back at their home before plunging into the woods. Everything had been abandoned, "even what was before secured."[58]

The Fencibles swept into Bloody Bridge with a special ferocity and, carrying torches, spread out among the Acadian houses. Here was the lair of Joseph Caisse, there the home of Isaiah Boudreau, captain of Eddy's Acadians! Before the buildings were set alight, beaver hats and other articles taken recently from Edward Barron's store in River Hebert were found inside.[59] Barns and granaries were torched without salvaging the stores inside. Livestock was rounded up or shot. Samuel Wethered's horse, requisitioned by Eddy, escaped and wandered off into the marsh.[60] On reaching Allan's farm, "the Troops soon set fire to the House and Plundered everything!"[61] Barns were burned with "Carts, Sleds, Plows, Harrows and other Utensils" inside. Crops were destroyed and livestock "taken: a Cow, 8 Oxen, 4 Horses, sundry Sheep, Swine and Poultry." The farm was ruined, the dooryard littered with "Furniture, Cloths and books, burnt and plundered!"[62] Too deep in the woods to witness the destruction, Mary and the children must have seen the smoke from the fiery inferno that was their home and village.

It had been a busy day for Batt and his military agenda was not complete. Beyond Bloody Bridge, in the direction of Baie Verte, was Jolicure. Also known as a centre of rebellion, this village was slated for the same grim fate as Bloody Bridge. But before the Marines and Fencibles could attack they had to pause. The reason for delay was not the fatigue of several hours of continuous warfare, not the need to consolidate gains, not even the tired old legs of their veteran commander. The reason was fundamental: it was tea-time. Jolicure would be spared for at least an hour. So at the edge of the marsh, by the ruins of Allan's farm, the soldiers sat down to eat. Behind them Bloody Bridge was a collection of smoke-blackened chimneys; ahead, only a mile away, Jolicure could be seen across the marsh. After his men had "taken a little refreshment," Batt intended to lead them across the marsh and lay that "other nursery of rebellion in ashes."[63] But for the moment the soldiers relaxed and enjoyed their tea break.

Colonel Eddy had suffered a crushing defeat which Committee-of-Safety member Nathaniel Reynolds had luckily or cleverly avoided. Having left Cumberland several days before, ostensibly in search of a ship, he was in Pictou on Friday and even as Eddy was routed from Camphill, Reynolds's goal was in sight and a trap was set. He and his men were concealed on the slopes of Pictou Harbour and were watching William Lowden, master of the ship *Molly*, wend his way through the village and disappear into a house with Daniel Earle Jr. The house belonged to Earle's father, Daniel Sr, and Doctor John Harris greeted the shipmaster at the door. Lowden came ashore to be paid for goods the younger Earle had purchased from him a few minutes before down at the ship. The transaction was a pretence for enticing him away from his ship and was the first phase in Reynolds's plan to seize the *Molly*. The doctor's presence confirmed the prevailing impression among loyalists "that Harris was concerned in the Plot along with Earl … to take the Ship." As soon as the door closed Reynolds and his party, including Charles Swan, James Watson, John Cornie, William Fulton, Isaiah Horton, and others, sprang up and surrounded the Earle home. After about fifteen minutes "some of them rushed into the room" where the unsuspecting Lowden was "in Company" with Harris. "Two of them presented Pistols to [the Captain's] Breast and desired he would surrender himself a Prisoner" Lowden surrendered and was immediately "confined," enabling phase two of the plot to be set in motion.

Back down to *Molly* went Daniel Earle Jr "under the Pretence of purchasing more goods," along with James Watson, another Pictou patriot. After waiting "a very short time" for the ship's mate to bring the goods, "a Boatfull of Armed men under the command of Nathaniel Reynolds" rowed along side. Most of the crew were in the woods cutting lumber for the cargo and no resistance was offered. In the name of the American Congress, Reynolds "made Prize of the Ship." After Captain Lowden was taken prisoner, Doctor Harris excused himself under the pretence of needing to visit a patient and left the Earle house with Charles Swan. This gave the impression that Harris was not one of the patriots, but as soon as he was gone the wily doctor resumed his co-operation with Reynolds. He encouraged the belief that Reynolds's party was four times larger than it really was in order to guard against a counter-action by loyal Pictonians, and he "boasted to Swan of their success in taking the Ship" *Molly*.

Charles Swan, the former prisoner of the patriots, was now ready to perform a valuable patriot service. "Swan took the Command and gave Directions for getting the Ship under Sail." *Molly*'s crew would be captured on returning from the woods and some would be pressed into sailing the ship on the voyage to Baie Verte. Finding supplies might have been a problem in a settlement only about seven years old but Pictonians were "mostly doing well" on land that was "pretty good," yielding a variety of crops; "one man has a fine plantation of tobacco." More importantly for Reynolds, the only store was owned by the ever-helpful Doctor Harris, who "voluntarily killed two Bullocks and ordered their carcasses on board the *Molly*, also a considerable quantity of his store goods." With captain, crew, and supplies ready the *Molly* would soon be fit to sail from Pictou to Baie Verte and beyond. For Reynolds "the operations" were successful. Having "laid their plot with Judgement," Harris agreed that it had "succeeded to their Wishes"! But their success was of no use to Eddy, even if they fetched cannon from Charlottetown.[64] While Reynolds's party celebrated the capture of *Molly*, Camphill was a smouldering ruins, the committee table at Gardiner's (around which Reynolds had sat in council day after day during November) was a bed of glowing embers, and the loyal garrison of Fort Cumberland was dining out by the ashes of Bloody Bridge.

Tea-time is an eminently sensible institution that exerts a civilizing effect on the fiercest warrior. It soothed Major Batt's nerves, gaining him valuable moments for reflection. His attack on the patriots illustrated plainly "the superiority of the detachment under my command and the correction the enemy had just received." The Major was not normally vindictive, nor was he an arsonist. "Indeed, notwithstanding the resentment which their conduct as rebels highly merits, I should not have added fire to the sword had they not introduced that calamity by wickedly burning all the buildings near the fort." Repelled by the tactic of burning private property and concluding that his eye-for-an-eye policy had been carried far enough, he decided to spare Jolicure. "I determined to return to the fort," resolved Batt, finishing his tea, "to give them time to reflect on their infamy and madness, to wait the operation of ... justice, and the offer of mercy."[65]

It was raining again when the soldiers turned back towards Fort Cumberland and marched past the scenes of havoc they had wreaked: burnt-out buildings in the centre of farm clearings. Women and children were digging through the charred ruins of what hours before had been comfortable homes. There was Levi's Ames' farm, which was leased to Samuel Wethered, burnt down and its fences shattered. Many homes were gone including those of William Chapman and William Wells. It was surprising to find these two Yorkshire settlers in support of Eddy; perhaps they had been coerced into helping the patriots, or just unlucky in living so close to Camphill, or perhaps Studholme's rough justice had been as inaccurate as it was swift.[66] The troops passed sullen-faced refugees lining the roadside in the cold drizzle, overtook ox carts hauling captured grain to the fort, and passed other carts carrying the dead and wounded, as well as prisoners captured in the rout. Precautions were taken against counter-attack but there was no sign of the enemy. It was concluded that "Major Batt ... struck such a Panic into the Rebels that they fled with the greatest Precipitation"[67] and were so scattered as to be incapable of counter-attack. This was not entirely true. John Allan heard later that they had "retreated, some into the woods ... others fled to save their Familys," but "a number of them joined together with Captain Eddy in the Rear of the Enemy, and For some Reason did not choose to attack."[68] They were lurking somewhere in the woods, probably nearby, but while they might have been in a position to attack they lacked the military skill and, after the shock of defeat, possibly also the will. Their purpose for regrouping more likely was to organize a retreat to Sackville and they were hiding until the troops had re-entered the fort.

A fortunate outcome of the Camphill rout was the short casualty list. On the loyalist side the Fencibles suffered the most. "Our regiment had one man killed and four wounded," disclosed Batt, and of those four, one died of his wounds. The Marines had only one man wounded. Patriot casualties were not so easily determined. "The loss of the enemy cannot be ascertained," concluded Batt. At any rate, "We did not search for their dead, the thickness of their cover rendering it exceedingly difficult to find them." He confirmed three patriot casualties. "In the pursuit," he recalled, "We saw two Indians and one white man, who had received the just wages of wanton and unprovoked rebellion."[69] Reports from all sources led Goreham to guess imprecisely that Batt's soldiers had "killed several Indians, French Acadians and Rebels."[70]

"The behaviour of officers and men was equal to the cause that inspired them,"[71] reported Major Batt; "both Corps behaved with great activity and resolution"[72] Goreham's regular drilling of the Fencibles had paid off "and," added Batt, "the cheerfulness with which the marine light companies underwent the fatigue of the service deserves the highest encomium"[73] Encomiums all around! Praise for the troops meant praise for their commanding officer. When news of victory reached Halifax one person exclaimed "that Major Batt has gained immortal honour on the Occasion"[74] And when King George III was advised of the victory in Camphill, His Majesty "expressed his approbation of Major Batt's conduct of the party under his command upon that occasion."[75]

"CONVINCED OF THEIR ERRORS"

Knowledge of Eddy's defeat was communicated instantly to a watchful populace. An air of expectancy had prevailed since *Vulture*'s arrival on Wednesday and on Friday the signs were easily read. The smoke on Cumberland ridge, visible across the Tantramar, signalled that the long-awaited assault was underway. Spectators followed Major Batt's progress by the chain of fires ignited along the ridge to Allan's farm. Joyous loyalists left their properties for the first time in nearly a month. William Black Sr set out immediately to visit friends in Fort Lawrence. Patriot sympathizers were shocked and many households were thrown into turmoil by a family member returning terror-stricken from Camphill. Black met Doctor Parker Clarke on the road, minus his gun and displaying none of the threatening posture of only a few days ago. "He would not be taken [in armms]," he confided to Black, "but would surrender" to the Fencibles.[76] Another result of the victory was the release of loyalist prisoners held in scattered locations across the isthmus. "As soon as the Rebells were dispersed," William Milburn "came to the Garrison,"[77] while another, "who had been a Prisoner to the Rebels," left Amherst immediately for Windsor.[78] The Delesderniers were among the first to show up at the fort. "I came in directly after the Defeat of the Rebels," Moses recalled, "as soon as they were beaten and drove away, we went to the Fort."[79] His incentive was to explain his signature on the "Association" that Eddy had circulated in support of the rebellion. Leaving the garrison when it was under siege, even with Goreham's approval, and the involvement of his relatives in the rebellion, implicated Moses in the eyes of his neighbours for whom the appearance of his name on the "Association" proved his guilt.

Very few of Eddy's men were captured in the rout so measures had to be taken to prevent further acts of rebellion by the many patriots still at large on the isthmus. It was heard that William How and others "had agreed with the Indians and French Acadians ... to burn all the houses belonging to the Yorkshire Familys and other Government friends, particularly at Fort Lawrence."[80] The vengeful How, it was said, threatened to go to Fort Lawrence and "Destroy the place"![81] So Goreham decided "to take post there."[82] Captain Branson's Marines, some Fencibles and militiamember Thomas Dixson were ordered on this service and set off this Friday afternoon in the rain. Other orders were issued to intercept patriots as they fled westward to Memramcook and the Petitcodiac River. "To cut off their Retreat and destroy a number of Boats and Canoes the Enemy had lain on the Bank of that River and Shepody Bay," Goreham ordered a party of 100 troops to march to Memramcook. However, by then it was late in the afternoon and it was deemed best that these troops remain in the fort because the rain had turned the Tantramar to mud and made "the Roads excessive bad."

The patrol ordered to Fort Lawrence marched in the rain "till about sundown" when two patriots were spotted on the road.[83] Thomas Dixson's party fired at them and they "endeavoured to escape by running away."[84] By chance they ran past the home that William Black had gone to visit as soon as the siege was lifted. Inside, Black "heard a cry, there were Rebells"![85] Rushing to the door, he saw Thomas Faulkner and James Avery running by with troops right behind. Faulkner looked "much terrified"! Dixson "called out to them to surrender which they did." The two were "taken in their flight" and deprived of "their Firelocks, powder horns and some Ball which they had about them." Dixson noticed that Faulkner "trembled much."[86] The capture of Avery, Eddy's commissary officer, and Faulkner, chief of the Cobequid contingent, prompted Parker Clarke, who also happened to be at Fort Lawrence, "to deliver himself up" and he went out to meet Dixson, his neighbour, who "told him he must come with him." Clarke was handed over to Captain

Branson, who would transfer all the prisoners to Fort Cumberland.[87]
The patrol then searched patriot properties in the vicinity. Goods plundered from Anne and Edward Barron were salvaged from the home of
William and Olive How before it was burned. But the climax of Friday's
arson was the destruction of Eddy's large farm in Fort Lawrence. This
spectacular fire consumed the effects of other patriots, including Elijah
Ayer Jr's "furniture and stores," which had been removed to Eddy's farm
early in the siege. The patrol camped that night on the property of patriots and drew rations from "a Quantity of provisions they had left."[88]

Both sides had to adjust quickly to the devastating rout. Repentance
came quickly to many patriots. With pragmatic contrition those at Westcock gathered hastily on Friday to write a letter that was passed to Charles
Dixon on his way home to Sackville. They were now "convinced of their
errors," they wrote, "and desirous of surrendering to the King's Mercy."
Loyalists also had concerns: "Most all the Yorkshire Familys and other
friends of Government" made representations to Goreham that evening.
Their concern was the escalation of arson. Some patriots had claimed
that Native people and Acadians would burn down loyalist homes "which
they could easily effect during the night." While the threat was real, it was
a ploy to stave off loyalist vengeance, and it worked. "The continuance of
this burning on both sides," argued the loyalists, "must soon terminate in
the destruction and ruin of the whole Country." They pleaded with Goreham to break the cycle of arson.[89]

A terrible day for the patriots was followed by a comfortless night.
Many were homeless refugees. Mary Allan and her five little children
huddled in the woods all night, cold and hungry, without food or blankets and in weather "severe with wind and rain."[90] Quite in contrast to
Mary's plight were the circumstances of her husband on that same Friday. While flames consumed their farm, John enjoyed a plentiful noonday meal in Boston. After a pleasant three-week stay he had decided to
go on to Philadelphia and Baltimore and was saying goodbye to friends.
In his quest for the job of Indian agent he hoped to meet General Washington and be presented to Congress. "After dinner I took horse and set
off," riding to Roxbury and on to Dedham and "about dark" found lodgings at Grey's Tavern.[91] Now while he luxuriated in the fireside warmth
and enjoyed the entertainment in this Massachusetts tavern, Mary and
the children suffered from exposure on the Tantramar.

The heavy rain that extinguished the fires on Cumberland Ridge and
drenched the homeless refugees, including the Allan family, was part of
an extensive weather system that blanketed the Fundy coast. In Mount
Denson on the Minas Basin this Friday it rained "very hard" on a solitary
horserider wending his way downhill into Kings County. The rider was
Henry Alline who had accepted an invitation to preach in Cornwallis.

Having ridden over the hill with more than a little trepidation, "being a stranger in the place," "being weary and very wet," and his horse being lame he decided to stop for the night at the edge of the village. Never before as a preacher had he left his home district and tomorrow was soon enough to face a strange audience.[92] While Alline rode to Cornwallis his neighbours in the militia stood guard in Windsor as they had since the relief expedition sailed to Cumberland. There was a strange parallel between this expedition (of which Alline would have been aware) that enabled the break out of the garrison and defeat of the King's enemies in Camphill, and Alline's break out from his home district on the same day. The religious awakening that followed his excursion to Cornwallis helped to fix Nova Scotia in the loyalist cause in much the same way as Goreham's victory in Cumberland.

Inside the congested fort in Cumberland, in dry if not comfortable quarters, Joseph Goreham savoured victory and wrestled with the problem of how to restore order to a shattered community. Illustrating how difficult this would be was the task of disarming the populace in a district where doctor, coroner, church treasurer, even ministers of the gospel owned guns and where the community was an armed camp with many of the guns supplied by the Americans still in circulation. Restraining the arm of vengence was another challenge. Goreham appreciated the points made to him by loyalists. Further arson would only "drive a number of people with their numerous Families to their last recourse of recovering their support and protection from the Garrison."[93] Throwing that burden on the depleted resources of the fort would be disastrous. The fort was already terribly overcrowded; even the guardhouse was filled with the prisoners captured that day, including Richard Uniacke and Benoni Danks. The bakehouse operated at full capacity, the burial party was at work, and Surgeon James Silvers treated the casualties. When he attended the one Marine wounded in the Camphill rout and "applied the bandage, the ball fell out."[94]

Amid the confusion the garrison celebrated victory, although Goreham knew that provincial arms had been barely sufficient to deal with the siege. Had the American reinforcement arrived ahead of *Vulture*, Nathaniel Reynolds been able to fetch cannon from Charlottetown, or the blockade been drawn a little tighter, the result might have been different. "I am sorry to say it," Massey would write in self-congratulation, "but am certain, by every Account I have heard, the Fort would have fallen, had I not been so quick in sending off assistance from Windsor."[95] On Friday Goreham still expected an American counter-attack and was unsure whether to deal harshly or leniently with the defeated rebels.

Complicating Goreham's task of restoring order was the break down of the community into a bewildering array of factions before Friday was out. The people did not divide along purely patriot and loyalist lines and in the struggle for preservation a confusing overlap of interests developed. Loyalists pointed fingers at loyalists while patriot sympathizers found common cause with certain loyalists and many families had members on both sides of the conflict. The struggle that ended on the battlefield continued that Friday night in the homes of Cumberland's extended families. In the garrison where Thomas and Katherine Dixson celebrated victory Thomas was feted for his role in carrying news of the siege to Halifax and in the capture that afternoon of Thomas Faulkner, James Avery, and Parker Clarke. Katherine's sister, Sarah Law, and Sarah's husband, barrack master James Law, probably joined these celebrations. But the joy of sisters Katherine and Sarah was tempered by thoughts of their brother, Samuel Wethered, who lay gravely wounded with half his buttocks shot away. A not untypical Cumberlander who had been caught dealing with both sides in the rebellion, Wethered lost his tavern to the patriots who burned it (after it was shelled by the garrison) and today his farm on the Baie Verte Road was burned by the loyalist soldiers. Tonight his life hung in the balance. It was a comfort to both the sisters and Samuel that a doctor was once again in their midst. One of the first visits James Silvers had made after his arrival on *Vulture* had been to the bedside of Samuel Wethered in the home of Jotham Gay. Although the prognosis was not good, Samuel was at last receiving medical attention, and at garrison expense. The presence of conflicting loyalties in the Dixson-Law- Wethered families, with relatives taking opposite sides and some taking both sides, was repeated in many Tantramar households.[96]

In searching for a solution to the confusion and bitterness all around him, Goreham was inclined towards mercy and he found inspiration in Major Batt's leniency on the battlefield. Tea-time had spared Jolicure from the wrath of fire and that example became Goreham's model although he was aware that the mayhem meted out by Batt on the Baie Verte Road that morning was probably more in tune with prevailing public opinion than his teatime dispensation to Jolicure. Nevertheless, Goreham resolved to extend the olive branch of mercy and to proclaim an amnesty for defeated patriots. This was probably the last decision the commander made on that Friday 29 November 1776, a day of loyalist victory in Nova Scotia. Goreham's choice of leniency set the tone for official responses to the rebellion both on the Isthmus of Chignecto and later in Halifax.

Epilogue

We cheerfully Engaged and bravely attacked. We gained at first; at last
were repulsed; it was the fortune of War.

Josiah Throop, patriot officer, 1777[1]

Optimistic by nature and philosophical in defeat, Josiah Throop reviewed the siege of Fort Cumberland in an engagingly succinct manner, but his summary (above) belies the hardships inflicted on all
parties and fails to gauge the depth of defeat suffered by the patriots.
The Camphill rout was the end of the patriot movement in Nova
Scotia. A month-long siege to capture a fort and conquer a province
served only to arouse a passive population to overt loyalty and provoke
a divided administration into concerted action. Jonathan Eddy ruined
any chance of success, if not by premature action as claimed by John
Allan, then by mismanagement of the siege itself. In defeat he brought
calamity to Cumberland and caused a patriot emigration comparable
in limited respects to the much larger loyalist immigration caused by
the American Revolution. Refugee patriots left behind a fractured
community, an outcome of civil war made worse in Cumberland by its
particular history of factional controversy and political dissent. The victory transformed provincial politics into an enduring pocket of loyalist
ideology although the war was far from over. Internal rebellion was
over but not the threat of invasion. Barely a month after the debacle,
even before news of it reached Baltimore where Congress was then in
session, that body approved a new and larger invasion and President
John Hancock extolled "the Glory" of attacking Nova Scotia.[2]

In the immediate wake of the siege was the spectre of the refugee – a
vision of Nova Scotians fleeing the colony, of starving children and
women begging for food. We were "obliged to leave," a committee member emphasized. Being "exiled from their habitations and proscribed,"

they were forced to abandon their families "to the Mercy of an Enraged Enemy."[3] The remnants of Eddy's force departed Sackville in small groups just days after the siege.[4] Their last view of the Tantramar was of a house in flames: Elijah Ayer Jr's home was torched in Sackville by a late patrol of Goreham's Fencibles.[5] Then, "travelling through the wilderness to take shelter in the United States," the refugees reached the St John River and rested (some in the Maliseet village of Aukpaque) before going on across the border to Machias and Boston in a journey lasting two months.[6] The conditions borne in this patriot exodus can be glimpsed in one refugee's account of struggling through "by-paths, over ponds of glare ice; snow knee deep; crossed over a river on floating cakes of ice in the night, suffering in body and mind all the time."[7]

The cross-border flow of refugees during the revolution was in both directions. Although loyalist refugees were far more numerous, patriot refugees from Nova Scotia and Quebec fled to the United States with equal political conviction, under the same compulsion, and in circumstances similarly trying. The 300 or more men, women, and children who fled Nova Scotia suffered property loss just like their American counterparts. In the United States they were eligible for rations, land grants, and eventually pensions in the same way loyalists were compensated by the British.[8] And like the loyalists, some returned to their former homes.[9]

Just as many loyalists stayed in the United States and adapted to republicanism after the war, many of Eddy's associates chose not to join him in the exodus. They remained behind and made peace with ascendent loyalism. In response to a conditional pardon issued the day after the Camphill rout, "upwards of one hundred" surrendered at the fort.[10] Goreham made the offer to all except the ringleaders; in their case a reward was offered for their capture. His promise of "the King's mercy" was a powerful incentive "in giving up their Arms" and at least publicly to "regret the part they [had] been taking." Acadians and Native peoples, with a reputation of being "very mischievous and revengeful in the Rebellion," laid down their arms only to take them up again at Goreham's persuasion to join in the hunt for patriot leaders. Doing it "for the sake of the Reward" produced mixed results.[11] They helped to capture the *Molly* when it sailed into Baie Verte from Pictou but the ship's new captain, Nathaniel Reynolds, escaped.[12] A policy of leniency that applied not only to those who stayed behind but to the families of those who fled, and included those who switched sides and joined garrison patrols, had the effect of overcrowding the fort and depleting supplies. The rapid advance of winter, the mood of revenge, and the almost daily appearance of naval vessels in the Cumberland Basin added to Goreham's burden in the immediate aftermath of the siege.

The pressure of the aftermath was relieved only by exceptional instances of charity. Despite the amnesty, some patriots who had complaints against them were arrested and held at the fort before being sent on as prisoners to Halifax. One was Alpheus Morse whose wife Theodora and their young children, having lost everything in the siege and suffering from hunger, came with other families through the deep snow to the fort. "She had not one Mouthful of Vitals to give her Children." In their distress one of the children begged Lieutenant James Innis for some flour. When this hardened veteran of the Camphill rout saw the mother and child in their plight his heart softened. He asked Theodora to bring him the biggest container she had and he filled it up for the grateful family, a small act of reconciliation remembered long after the bitterness of the aftermath had faded.[13]

Gradually a true picture of the siege emerged. The nature of Eddy's force and the scale of the provincial response was only revealed in the final month of 1776. In fact the relief effort continued to grow for more than two weeks after Eddy's defeat and did not reach its zenith until mid-December. As the several naval delays were rectified Commodore Collier filled Cumberland Basin with ships. Captain Feattus was anxious to depart on HMS *Vulture* the day after the Camphill rout, but Goreham persuaded him to stay longer because of the fear of a counter-attack. HMS *Hope* arrived on 2 December with *Nancy* and the captured American warship *Independence*. HMS *Diligent* arrived the same day and finally HMS *Lizard* appeared on 15 December. Six ships in all: the largest naval fleet ever assembled in Cumberland Basin so late in the season. The Marines on *Nancy* increased the garrison and the guns of the *Independence* were installed in the fort. Over the next few days the ships undertook missions in the basin and in Shepody Bay to capture stragglers before racing back down the Bay of Fundy ahead of the advancing ice.[14] On board *Nancy* were Goreham's principal prisoners who were off-loaded in Windsor.

News of the victory was slow to reach the capital and when it did Haligonians were surprised at how small Eddy's force was compared with the rumours. It was 19 December before "the fate of the interior part of this Province" was known to Eyre Massey.[15] The first patriot prisoners, marched overland from Windsor, claimed the invasion was comprised of "only thirty Ragged Rascalls from New England and ten wretched Indians."[16] Townspeople were incredulous. The scale of the rebellion and the number of Nova Scotians Eddy had recruited in Maugerville, Cobequid, and elsewhere were greater, but again not as large as had been rumoured. Eddy's force was weak and inept but then so was the garrison and if Major Batt did not quite merit the "immortal honour" one officer attributed to him on first hearing of the victory, it was also true that "the Noise about Fort Cumberland" was more than the "Meer Phantom" it had seemed to the same officer after interviewing the prisoners on their arrival in Halifax.[17] The truth lay between his two exaggerations. Batt's victory preserved a key military post, reinforced loyalty across the province, and improved security in the frontier by its effect on Native nations. Any doubt in Halifax about Micmac neutrality was erased by the success at Fort Cumberland. The Maliseets were still problematic, but St Aubin's appearance on the losing side was a setback for the revolutionary faction of that nation. Outsettlers were now more secure although initiatives would be required in the spring to guarantee neutrality in Aukpaque and enforce loyalty in Maugerville and Cobequid.

Victory in Cumberland did not result in peace for Nova Scotia. The aftermath of the siege was marked by intimidation, arson, and a litigious turmoil that undermined the justice system.[18] Nor was there peace in Halifax where cracks in the triumvirate of Massey, Collier, and Arbuthnot widened towards structural failure. And for another seven years the revolutionary war raged disquietingly in the background. The optimism that had accompanied the British army to New York in June 1776 faded quickly as the decisive victories anticipated never happened. That loyalism thrived despite civil antagonism, administrative chaos, and pessimism about the war meant that Nova Scotia's response to the revolution was no routine matter. The supply of the British in Boston was the initial test that set a pattern. The victory of Fort Cumberland reinforced the pattern and brought loyalty into focus as the course to follow in the cataclysmic times. After the siege the loyal militia expanded in every district. The religious reformation also continued to spread such that by 1782 its leader, Henry Alline, could speak of "unparallel blessing ... in almost every corner of the Province."[19] Religious revival was not an escape from the revolution but another piece in the pattern of loyal response.

The apocalyptic times actually favoured Alline's ministry. His message was conservative in tone and came closest to loyalist ideology when he reminded his fellow planters of the benefits of living in Nova Scotia. When he asked his hearers to "think but a moment ... what dangers you have escaped, what kindness received, what favours enjoyed," he was using loyalist rhetoric and echoed the official government line which held that the planters had been indulged by government: they had been granted free land and rations, subsidies in times of famine, religious freedom, and political representation. Far from being rebellious, they ought to be grateful.[20]

The American Revolution was no glorious struggle to Alline. He degraded it to a disease, a "lamentable disorder" to be referred to in metaphors of natural disaster: a calamitous flood, sweeping deluge, impending cloud, and terrible storm. All these terms for the revolution were used by

Alline in just one sermon. It was not simply the horror of war he had in mind but the revolution itself and the period of radical politics leading up to it. Hearers were reminded how they had been "screened" (a term he used twice in one sermon) from the impending crisis, "screened from the trials of our (once happy) Nation." In Nova Scotia, when threatened by the revolution and daily expecting "to share the bitter cup," Alline determined "heaven's indulgent hand has interposed and averted the blow."[21] This was more than a general reference to the revolution; Alline was referring to Eddy's attack and the expected invasion of the province in 1776, that is, to the rumours that Fort Cumberland had fallen and that rebellion was spreading.

His hearers would have understood how the blow was averted by the successful defence of the fort and the effective muster of the militia in King's and Annapolis Counties. Nova Scotians should be thankful for avoiding war and the evils of revolution and consider as God's blessing the planter emigration of the 1760s: "Your being called away from the approaching storm that was hanging over your native land and sheltered here" saved the planters according to Alline. Nova Scotia was a haven from war, revolution, and the radical politics of the previous decade. Leaving New England was God's plan. "Altho' you have often murmured that ever you came to those inhospitable wiles" and asked the question – and here he likened the planter emigration to the Israelites arriving in Canaan and asking the same question – "Has God brought us here to slay us?" No, preached Alline, but to be sheltered "in this peaceable corner of the earth."[22] In the stream of consciousness that was an Alline sermon, delivered day in and day out around Minas Basin, through the Annapolis Valley, in Yarmouth, Argyle, Liverpool, Cumberland and up the Petitcodiac and St John Rivers, lay the true sentiment of Nova Scotian planters – a people repelled by revolution and thankful to be in a beneficent land, as Alline maintained – "a people highly favoured of God."[23]

Cumberland was the exception. Not having "averted the blow," the people there were forced "to share the bitter cup" for many years. Recollections of the siege were almost too painful to record in formal history and violent acts related to it were perpetrated long after the event. Perhaps the last was an arson attack in Sackville in 1788, twelve years after the siege, which extended the legal aftermath into the New Brunswick courts.[24] When the last deliberately set fire burned out and the last legal proceeding lapsed, the bitterness lingered for a generation and longer. The part played by the Maugerville settlers, for example, was "used as a bitter sarcasm" against them for many years, especially in times of "political Strife."[25] In Shepody animosity towards the Peck family was detected as late as 1867.[26]

The long and bitter aftermath was ameliorated by the many patriots who renounced their past and became indistinguishable from loyalists. The best known of these transformations was managed by Richard Uniacke who in a few short years went from principal prisoner to principal law officer of the province.[27] This former revolutionary soldier published in 1805 a virulently anti-revolutionary political treatise that few loyalists could have matched.[28] Uniacke's escape from a charge of treason and success in post-siege Nova Scotia have never been fully explained, but his amazing progress bears testimony to the government's policy of leniency in the aftermath.[29] Even more dramatic but less well known than Uniacke's redemption was that of Hugh Quinton, a captain in Eddy's army and commander of the St John River contingent. Just one year after the siege Quinton was captain of the loyal militia of Sunbury County and during the remainder of the revolution "turned out sundry times and fought the rebel parties."[30]

The phoenix-like rise of many patriots from the ashes of the siege did not result in total memory loss by the general public – the events of November 1776 were too deeply seared in people's minds for that. Sometimes, when least expected, the redeemed patriots were confronted publicly with recollections of past exploits which they had tried studiously to bury.[31] Patriots who became community leaders were another manifestation of the confusing times, the very brilliance of their conversion contributing to the ambiguous reputation of those now known collectively as the pre-loyalists.

There was an impulse by the succeeding generation to forget the siege and the animosities it created. If the role of resident loyalists in the defence of the province was obscured by the appearance of refugee loyalists in overwhelming numbers, that of resident patriots was obliterated, and with the help of the patriots themselves. The evidence of purposeful forgetfulness is strong; it is a fact admitted by certain early historians, and history has paid the price. There is a lack of recollective documentation about the siege and the history remains skewed as a result. New Brunswick's first historian Peter Fisher, in his 1825 *Sketches of New Brunswick*, recounted briefly the burning of Fort Frederick but never mentioned the siege of Fort Cumberland nor the role of the Maugerville settlers in it.[32] The event was recalled with mild humour by Calvin Hatheway in his 1846 *History of New Brunswick*. He seems to have used recollective sources in his brief account but only noted the tendency of the first generation to forget unpleasant memories of the rebellion.[33] Charles Knapp came closest to recording recollections in his "Folklore About Old Fort Beausejour," but he was careful not to engage in close conversation and noted candidly that it would not "do" even to mention the names of Eddy's associates.[34] The most striking example of a truncated perspective is in Beamish Murdoch's 1866 *A History of Nova Scotia*. His two brief comments emphasize invasion, underplay rebellion, and in naming the parties who attacked the fort conveniently exclude the planters while mentioning Acadians and Native peoples, an omission not borne out by the two primary sources that Murdoch otherwise closely paraphrased.[35] With respect to the siege he chose not to use the important legal sources with which as a lawyer he would have been familiar.[36] Murdoch the historian ignored an excellent source at hand – Richard Uniacke, in whose office Murdoch the lawyer worked. His reference to Uniacke's role in the siege is gratuitously brief and misleading.[37]

Not only did early historians minimize the siege and suppress the exploits of patriots, they failed to note the role of local loyalists. Reinforced by a later more exclusive definition of the term loyalist, this failure persists in Canadian historiography. The misrepresentation of the militia by Brebner, already noted, has led other historians to infer wholesale disaffection at the beginning of the revolution. This conclusion has militated against analyses of the extent of resident loyalism. There is little which assesses the supply of the British in Boston, the loyal defenders of Fort Cumberland, or the residents issued loyalist land grants in Nova Scotia and New Brunswick. No notice has been taken of Nova Scotians compensated by the Loyalist Claims Commission. No study has been carried out of militia operations on land and sea, of the provincial regiments and naval force, of the coast guard, or of Nova Scotia privateering. Recognition of indigenous loyalism from the outset of the revolution could link the political and social development of planters in the 1760s and early 1770s with the post-revolutionary period.

The year 1776 ended in weary relief for Nova Scotians and winter, if nothing else, safeguarded the isthmus behind a frozen Cumberland Basin. To British officials winters in the colony were "dreary, long and severely cold" and variable in the capital. "At Halifax you seldom have the same weather for three Days together," exclaimed George Collier; "deep Snows are succeeded by Rains and those by Frosts." A sailor whose sealegs steadied him on the steepest deck in the heaviest sea, Collier was curious about how people got around on the hillside streets of Halifax in such weather. "Both Men and Women are obliged to have Galoshes over their Shoes and at the bottom, Spikes fix'd on (which they call creepers) to prevent them from falling on the slippery Ground." He seldom used the treacherous streets himself, remaining in his comfortable quarters on the *Rainbow* from which he conducted naval affairs and entertained an expanding circle of friends, dining on delicacies such as "Moose's Nose and the Tail of the Beaver."[38] After the shortages in the spring due to the presence of the British military, exotic cuisine and all supplies were again plentiful in Halifax. Prices were persistently high but at least this irritant was now a side effect of a booming wartime economy. Seldom had the pace of growth in the town been quicker or the waterfront been busier, and thanks to Collier, Halifax was guaranteed "perfect Security" through the winter. The brashly confident commodore would match his flagship *Rainbow* against "all the Force that the rebellious Colonys can set forth."[39] Perhaps to cover his delays in the Cumberland relief expedition, Collier dismissed the siege as "the imbecile Attempt of an inconsiderable Number of New England Banditti."[40]

The lieutenant-governor also thought Halifax secure ("from anything but fire") although his reason was Howe's engagement of the Americans in New York, not Collier's naval prowess.[41] And what was the siege of Fort Cumberland to Marriot Arbuthnot except a "small interruption" in administrative routines and a diversion from his patronage interests.[42] With the extravagant confidence of hindsight, victory was the outcome "I have had the honour to predict from the beginning."[43] His attention in December 1776 was taken by the live wild cat he had captured in the woods near Halifax and was preparing to send to Lord Sandwich in England as a present as soon as the *Lizard* returned from Cumberland.[44] Eyre Massey, the third member of the triumvirate also agreed that Halifax was secure but for a different reason again. Ice in the Bay of Fundy assured that "we must remain quiet until the Spring." Relations with Collier and the pain of old war wounds were Massey's aggravations: "my hand shakes too much" to write.[45] Strangely, of the three it was Massey who articulated the benefit of the siege of Fort Cumberland. "It was a very important Event and has changed the People's Sentiments here."[46] Sentiments changed. Loyalty confirmed. These were the results of the victory in Cumberland.

On the Chignecto Isthmus snow turned the Tantramar into a vast white plain and encased the earthworks of Fort Cumberland in an icy mantle from which the glare in sunlight nearly blinded Fencible sentries peering south across the frozen Cumberland Basin. Down on the parade square protective walls reduced the wind-chill but also blocked the rays of a low-angled sun. In the intense cold, frost crystallized in thick patterns on the tiny windows of Joseph Goreham's quarters, obscuring his vision. Inside, the commander was struggling within himself. So many problems were piling up – the boredom of garrison duty (in contrast to the excitement of the siege), the bickering among his officers, the desperation of families victimized by the siege, the mood of revenge and the nightmare of arson, the realization that creditors might find him even in a god-forsaken frozen fort, the pain in his leg from an old fracture – any one of which could ignite a return of his well-known drinking problem.[47] Nearby his comrade, tavern-keeper Samuel Wethered, was on his deathbed. There seemed to be no relief and winter had just begun. North of the fort the snow lay thick in the woods and completely covered the ruins of abandoned farms on the Baie Verte Road. Bare stone chimneys were all that projected above the deep drifts – signposts of the recent conflict.

All North America was in the grip of winter. The Susquehanna River on the Pennsylvania border was frozen "pretty hard" when John Allan crossed it in late December en route to Baltimore. He arrived there weary and with a bad cold but with no time to rest. Intense lobbying with generals and Congress representatives brought results. During the first week of the new year, 4 January 1777, he achieved the high point of his exile: an audience with the Continental Congress. That body, then in session in Baltimore, "most civilly and kindly" received Allan who gave "a full account" of matters in Nova Scotia: the military strength of the colony, the extent of disaffection and the Native situation.[48] Allan's oratorical skill was demonstrated by the extent to which he enthralled the American authorities. Just four days later Congress authorized a new attack on Nova Scotia and a week later elected Allan as its salaried agent to the eastern Native peoples.[49] Allan's ideas "appear to me to be feasible," thought one Congress representative;[50] another regarded their decision "of a very important nature,"[51] while President Hancock imagined "the vast Advantages" of an expedition against Nova Scotia.[52] Massachusetts was empowered to prepare the expedition to be mounted "in the Course of the Winter or early in the Spring." An army of 3,000 would be raised with all necessary stores and that state could "draw on Congress for Money for these purposes."[53]

An elated John Allan set out on the return journey to Boston and north to Machias to begin the duties of Indian agent. On the way he began developing plans for the new attack on Nova Scotia.[54] Unlike Eddy who had gone so far for conquest but left so much behind, Allan had the full backing from Congress. In Connecticut he read newspaper accounts "setting forth the disasters at Cumberland" (including the burning of his own home) and two days later met Jonathan Eddy and other refugees face to face.[55] Undeterred by their accounts of defeat (which he had predicted) he pressed on with his plans. In 1777 Allan hoped a new American invasion would defeat loyal Nova Scotians and "bring them under the American banner."[56] His dream, however, would not be realized.

The Patriots

The force that besieged Fort Cumberland in 1776 was small but remarkably diverse. It conversed in four languages and represented Native, Acadian and English-speaking communities in nine separate contingents from Massachusetts to Nova Scotia. The members of each contingent whose names can be verified are listed below for a combined total of 186 patriots.

1 AMERICAN CONTINGENT

The names of eleven of the "about Twenty" recruits from Machias, Maine, and adjacent communities can be verified.

1 Albee, John
2 Albee, William
3 Avery, James
4 Crediford, Nathaniel
5 Gooch, James
6 Longfellow, Nathaniel
7 Mills, William
8 Mitchell, John – from Chandler's River Maine; settled in Burton on the St John River, N.B.
9 Parsons, Richard – from Mount Desert Maine; settled in Burton on the St John River, N.B.
10 Stone, Daniel
11 West, Jabez – commander of the contingent.

2 PASSAMAQUODDY CONTINGENT

Only four of Eddy's nine Passamaquoddy recruits can be verified.
1 Crow(e), William – charged with treason.
2 Elvill, William (Elwell) – charged with treason.
3 Kenny, William
4 Wilson, Robert – from Campobello Island; charged with treason; drowned at Cobscook Falls, Maine in 1782.

3 ST JOHN RIVER CONTINGENT

Of the twenty-seven English-speaking recruits from Sunbury County in the St John River valley, the names of twenty-four can be verified. They were not just from Maugerville but from settlements all along the river.
1 Branch, Samuel
2 Bubar, Benjamin (Booby) – son of Joseph and Mary Bubar; remained in the St John Valley.
3 Burpee, Edward – son of Jeremiah and Mary Burpee; remained in Maugerville
4 Coy, Amasa – son of Edward and Amy Coy; remained in Gagetown.
5 Dow, David
6 Dow, John
7 Estabrooks, Elijah Jr – remained in the St John Valley.
8 Haite, Joseph
9 Jewett, Daniel – married Abigail Burpee; junior officer of the contingent; remained in Maugerville.
10 Lovet, Daniel – settled in Conway Township, N.B.
11 McKeen, William – son of Robert McKeen of Amesbury Township.
12 Miller, Henry
13 Nevers, Jonathan
14 Nevers, Phineas – granted 1,000 acres in Maine.
15 Noble, Seth – granted 300 acres in Maine and 500 in Ohio.
16 Peabody, Stephen
17 Pitchard, John – settled in Burton, N.B.
18 Price, Edmund – wife Jean and fifteen children settled in Gagetown.
19 Quinton, Hugh – innkeeper in Conway Township; senior officer of the contingent; remained in the St John Valley.
20 Roe, Zebulon (Rowe) – granted 750 acres in Maine.
21 Roe, Zebulon Jr – remained in the St John Valley.
22 Russell, John
23 Turner, William
24 Whitney, John – remained in Amesbury Township.

4 MALISEET CONTINGENT

Among the Maliseets on the St John River and in Passamaquoddy there were "computed to be about 140 fighting men, and much superior in every degree to the Micmacs." At least eighty families lived in the Maliseet capital of Aukpaque. The names of all sixteen Maliseet recruits are known.

 1 Abraham
 2 Baptiste, Jean
 3 Baptiste, Michel
 4 Coleau, John
 5 Coleau, Pierre
 6 Le Porte, Subatiste
 7 Newell, Jean
 8 Newell, Newelis
 9 Pazil (Parel, Bazil) – died near Woodstock, N.B. in 1789.
10 Prugway, Pierre
11 Quodpan, Thomas (Squapan, Squatpan) – living at the Mouth of the Becaguimec (Hartland) N.B. in 1790.
12 St Aubin, Ambrose – second chief of the Maliseet nation.
13 Tomah, Joseph – living at the Mouth of the of the Becaguimec in 1790.
14 Tomah, Joseph Jr – lived in the upper St John Valley after the revolution.
15 Tomah, Pierre – not Grand Chief Tomah.
16 Tuennis, Antoine (Att. Juennis) – living near Woodstock, N.B. in 1788.

5 MICMAC CONTINGENT

Eddy's four Micmac recruits came from Cocagne near Richibucto.
 1 Bear, Andrew
 2 Bear, Charles
 3 Nicholas
 4 Paul, Pierre

6 ACADIAN CONTINGENT

The twenty-one Acadian recruits came from the Memramcook River Valley and some were tenant farmers on the estate of John Allan on the Baie Verte Road.
 1 Allain, Benjamin
 2 Bastarache, Joseph
 3 Boudreau, Captain Isaiah – senior officer of the contingent.
 4 Boudreau, Joseph
 5 Bourg, Michel
 6 Caissie, Pierre

7 DesRoches, Jean
8 DesRoches, Mathurin
9 Doiron, Louis
10 Farrell, David
11 Gaudet, Jean
12 Gaudet, Joseph
13 Gaudet, Mathurin
14 Govin, Michel
15 LeBlanc, Jean
16 LeBlanc, Pierre
17 Leger, Joseph
18 Maillet, Charles
19 Mallet, Jean-Baptiste
20 Thiboudeau, Isaac
21 Throop, Jean-Baptiste

7 COBEQUID CONTINGENT

Only ten of the "about 25 men" of this contingent can be verified, the bulk of which came from Onslow.

1 Avery, James – charged with treason; gave King's evidence; escaped gaol and fled to the USA.
2 Bradford, Carpenter – from Onslow; granted 150 acres in Maine.
3 Faulkner, Thomas – commander of the contingent; granted 230 acres in Maine and 750 in Ohio.
4 Faulkner, Edward – from Truro; returned to N.S.; dead by 1785; estate granted 750 acres in Ohio.
5 Logan, Hugh
6 Miller, Henry
7 Miller, Noah – granted 750 acres in Ohio.
8 Morrison, John
9 Pashelms (?), John
10 Thomas, Isaac

8 CUMBERLAND CONTINGENT

Because other contingents had to form up and travel long distances to join the rebellion, they are more identifiable than the Cumberland contingent whose members already lived within the influence of the siege in the various settlements across the isthmus. Only those patriots whose record of service survives are named and for this reason the actual number of Cumberlanders who helped Eddy is likely to have been larger than the eighty-eight listed here. Sometimes a record of service exists without a name, such as in the case of Eddy's Black drummer whose name is unknown.

1   Austin, Simon – probably from Amherst; indicted for treason.
2   Ayer, Elijah – Sackville; granted 400 acres in Maine and 1,000 in Ohio; died in N.B.
3   Ayer, Elijah Jr – his house burned; granted 320 acres in Ohio; died in 1837 in Buctouche, N.B.
4   Ayer, Obadiah – dead by 1785; his widow Chloe granted 1,280 acres in Ohio.
5   Bent, Jesse – died in Fort Lawrence 6 December 1816.
6   Bent, John – indicted for treason; stayed in N.S.
7   Brien, John (Bryan)
8   Burk, Anthony – indicted for treason; granted 150 acres in Maine and was entitled to 250 acres in Ohio.
9   Campbell, Peter – Amherst; wife Martha.
10   Casey, John – charged with treason.
11   Chapman, William – his house burned.
12   Chester, Simeon – Amherst; granted 750 acres in Ohio.
13   Clarke, Parker – Fort Lawrence; convicted of treason; granted 500 acres in Maine and 1,000 acres in Ohio.
14   Cole, Ambrose – Sackville; granted 200 acres in Ohio.
15   Cole, Edward – dead by 1785.
16   Connor, Samuel – dead by 1785.
17   Converse, Jesse
18   Copp, Thomas – son of John and Isabel (Dixon) Copp.
19   Copp, Timothy – brother of Thomas.
20   Cornie, John (Corney)
21   Crath, Samuel – Amherst.
22   Crawford, James – probably from Amherst; granted 500 acres in Ohio.
23   Crawford, Nathaniel – returned to N.S. by 1785.
24   Cuzens, Joseph – his house burned.
25   Danks, Benoni – taken prisoner and died of his wounds in Windsor, N.S.
26   Delesdernier, Lewis Frederick – Shepody; granted 500 acres in Ohio, later increased to 960 acres.
27   Dickie, James – son of Matthew and Janet Dickie of Amherst.
28   Eackly, John (Eckley, Akley) – granted 150 acres in Maine.
29   Eddy, Elias – turned nineteen 30 November 1776; settled in Maine.
30   Eddy, Isbrook (Ibrook, IBrook) – died 1834 in Maine.
31   Eddy, Jonathan – Fort Lawrence; commander of the patriots; granted 1,500 acres in Maine and 1,000 in Ohio.
32   Eddy, Jonathan Jr – granted 150 acres in Maine; returned to Sackville; died at sea 1808.

33 Eddy, William – granted 350 acres in Maine; killed in action 3 May 1778.

34 Fales, Atwood – Amherst; indicted for treason; granted 450 acres in Maine and 750 acres in Ohio.

35 Fales, Samuel – son of Atwood; granted 1,000 acres in Ohio.

36 Fillmore, Asa – Jolicure; son of John and Leah Fillmore.

37 Fillemore, Spiller – brother of Asa.

38 Foster, Robert – Sackville; granted 550 acres in Maine.

39 Fulton, John – son of James and Anne (Colwell) Fulton; charged with treason; settled in Maine.

40 Fulton, William – brother of John.

41 Furlong, ——— – killed in Camphill rout, 29 November.

42 Gardiner, Ebenezer – wife Demaris; their house burned; granted 1,000 acres in Maine and 750 acres in Ohio.

43 Goodwin, Daniel – his house burned.

44 Haggart, Robert – his house burned.

45 Hampson, Edward – charged with treason; dead by 1785.

46 Harvey, Seth

47 How, William – Fort Lawrence; granted 150 acres in Maine and 750 acres in Ohio.

48 Jenks, David – Sackville; granted 250 acres in Ohio.

49 Jones, Richard – his house burned.

50 Jones, William – wife Mary (Dobson); their house burned.

51 Killam, Amasa – Sackville; wife Elizabeth (Emerson).

52 Killam, John – dead by 1785.

53 Lawrence, William – returned to N.S.

54 Marsh, John

55 Maxwell, William – Sackville; son of Hugh and Sarah Maxwell; granted 750 acres in Maine and 500 acres in Ohio.

56 Morse, Alpheus – wife Theodora (Crane); arrested after the siege; remained in N.S.

57 MacGowan, John – Amherst; granted 750 acres in Ohio.

58 MacGowan, Robert – father of John; charged with treason.

59 McGuire, Daniel – his house burned.

60 Newcomb, Simon

61 Oulton, Charles (Houlton) – wife Abigail (Fillmore); arrested after the siege; remained in N.S.

62 Paine, Christopher – dead before 1785.

63 Peck, Abiel – wife Ruth (Estabrooks); charged with treason; drowned in Shepody 16 December 1802, age 73.

64 Read, Eliphalet – son of Joseph and Hannah Read; his house burned; remained in N.S.

65 Reynolds, Nathaniel – wife Lydia; indicted for treason; granted 300 acres in Maine.

66 Reynolds, Nathaniel Jr

67 Rogers, George – Sackville; brother of Samuel; died 1778.

68 Rogers, James

69 Rogers, Samuel – granted 300 acres in Maine.

70 Sharp, Joseph – Amherst; indicted for treason; settled in Pennsylvania.

71 Sharp, Matthew – dead by 1785.

72 Sharp, Robert – arrested after the siege; eligible for land grant in Ohio.

73 Sharpe, Samuel – dead by 1785.

74 Sibley, John – settled in Maine.

75 Simpson, John – arrested after the siege.

76 Starr, John – indicted for treason; settled in Connecticut; granted 750 acres in Ohio.

77 Stewart, John – arrested after the siege.

78 Swan, Charles – arrested after the siege.

79 Terrill, David – settled in Maine.

80 Thomas, Nicholas

81 Thornton, Daniel – dead by 1785.

82 Throop, Josiah – his house burned; "liberally compensated" by a grant of 1,000 acres in New York.

83 Tumbull, Thomas

84 Uniacke, Richard – taken prisoner; charged with treason; gave King's evidence.

85 Ward, James

86 Watson, Robert – wife Hannah; killed during the siege.

87 Wells, William – his house burned.

88 Williams, John

9 PICTOU CONTINGENT

The Pictonians in Eddy's army were chiefly former Cumberlanders. The Earle family was heavily represented in this contingent, the service of which centred on the capture of the ship *Molly* in Pictou Harbour.

1 Day, John – granted 230 acres in Maine.

2 Earle, Daniel – granted 500 acres in New York.

3 Earle, Daniel Jr – granted 500 acres in New York.

4 Earle, Jonas – granted 500 acres in New York.

5 Earle, Jonas Jr – settled in New York.

6 Earle, Nathaniel – "liberally compensated" with 1,000 acres in New York.

7 Earle, Robert – granted land in New York.

8 Horton, Isaiah – one of Nathaniel Reynolds's party.

9 Watson, James – one of Nathaniel Reynolds's party.

The Royal Fencible Americans

The Royal Fencibles posted to Cumberland in 1776 are listed below. Excluded, therefore, are those who left the regiment before June 1776 or were recruited after 1776. All dates are for the year 1776 except as otherwise noted. Names should be checked against the primary source – the regimental muster rolls, NAC C Series, vol. 1893.

1 THE SHEPODY OUTPOST

1 Boardman, Andrew – private; captured 29 October.
2 Bryan, Samuel – private; captured 29 October.
3 Connor, Morris – private; captured 29 October.
4 Fielden, Abraham – private; captured 29 October.
5 Garland, James – private; captured 29 October.
6 Goggan, Thomas – private; captured 29 October.
7 King, Solomon – 2nd lieutenant; killed 29 October.
8 Lacey, John – private; captured 29 October.
9 Lloyde, David – private; enlisted 2 November 1775; captured 29 October; settled in N.B.
10 McCarthy, Patrick – private; captured 29 October.
11 Morrice, Rodman – private; captured 29 October.
12 Pagett, George – private; captured 29 October.
13 Phillips, James – private; captured 29 October.
14 Walker, John – 1st lieutenant; wounded and captured 29 October.
15 Welsh, John – private; captured 29 October.

2 THE GARRISON OF FORT CUMBERLAND

1 Acheson, Alexander – second lieutenant.
2 Adolph, Peter – private; deserted 11 November.
3 Agness, John – private; enlisted 18 April.
4 Andrews, Benjamin – private; deserted 21 November.
5 Apps, John – private; granted 100 acres in Remshag, N.S.
6 Austin (Ostin), John – drummer; settled in N.B.
7 Austin (Ostin), William – private; settled in N.B.
8 Bailey, Phillip – first lieutenant; settled in N.B.
9 Bampton, Paul – sergeant; settled in N.B.
10 Barrett, Richard – private; granted 100 acres in Remshag, N.S.
11 Barry, James Jr – private; enlisted 13 March; died 12 August.
12 Barry, James Sr – private; enlisted with his son; died 4 February 1777.
13 Barry, John – corporal; enlisted 13 March.
14 Bassett, Joseph – private.
15 Batt, Thomas – major; commissioned 21 May.
16 Belford, James – private.
17 Bernice, James – corporal.
18 Biggens (Biggin), Thomas – private; granted 100 acres in Remshag, N.S.
19 Blood, Thomas – second lieutenant; enlisted 24 December 1775; discharged 24 June 1777.
20 Bollard, John – sergeant.
21 Bowe, Patrick – private; deserted 3 June.
22 Bowan, James – sergeant.
23 Brenan, Martin – private; enlisted 25 May; taken prisoner 7 November.
24 Brinan, John – drummer.
25 Bryan, John – private; discharged 22 June.
26 Bryan, John – private; deserted 20 November.
27 Bryan, Patrick – private.
28 Bulcher, Henry – private.
29 Bulkley, John – private; discharged 1 July 1777.
30 Burk, Michael – private; enlisted 17 April; taken prisoner 7 November; granted 400 acres in Remshag, N.S.
31 Burns, George – captain-lieutenant; commissioned 11 May.
32 Burns, John – corporal; settled in N.B.
33 Burns, Moses – corporal; settled in N.B.
34 Calahan, Peter – private; died 27 November.
35 Carlile, Robert – corporal; settled in N.B.
36 Carmel, Patrick – private.
37 Carrol, Maurice – private.
38 Cashen, John – private; enlisted 1 December; settled in N.B.
39 Cavanagh, Daniel – private; taken prisoner 7 November.

40 Chapman, John – private; taken prisoner 7 November.

41 Christy, William – private.

42 Clark, Jeremiah – private.

43 Clinch, Peter – adjutant; commissioned 30 October; settled in N.B.

44 Coffee, Michael – private; taken prisoner 7 November.

45 Cogran, Daniel – private; taken prisoner 7 November.

46 Coleman, Thomas – private; died 27 December.

47 Coleman, William – private; enlisted 18 March; granted 100 acres in Remshag, N.S.

48 Collier, John – private.

49 Collins, Richard – private; deserted 1 July.

50 Condon, John – private.

51 Conelly, William – private; deserted 14 October.

52 Connor, Constance – second lieutenant.

53 Connor, Hugh – private; settled in N.B.

54 Conway, John – private; taken prisoner 7 November.

55 Conway, John – private.

56 Coony, John – private.

57 Corbett, Cornelius – private.

58 Corbett, John – private; granted 100 acres in Remshag, N.S.

59 Cordwell, Joseph – private.

60 Crabbe, George – private.

61 Creary (Cravey), Martin – sergeant; granted 300 acres in Remshag, N.S.

62 Cruset, John – private; discharged 9 June.

63 Cullen, Walter – surgeon; enlisted 24 May; taken prisoner 7 November.

64 Cummins, Edward – private; enlisted 29 November 1775; deserted 14 October 1777.

65 Cunningham, Miles – corporal; settled in N.B.

66 Curry, John – private; died 8 November.

67 Dangerfield, Thomas – sergeant.

68 Daniel, Patrick – sergeant; settled in N.B.

69 DeBeaudoin, Lewis – first lieutenant; killed by fellow officer Constance Connor in a duel 29 May 1777.

70 Dee, David – private; settled in N.B.

71 Dickie, Michael – private; died 29 November.

72 Dickson, William – private; enlisted 17 June.

73 Dillon, John – private; deserted 6 June.

74 Dinnie, James – private; enlisted 28 May.

75 Dixie, James – private; enlisted 8 May; died 6 July.

76 Dobson, David – private; enlisted 27 July; taken prisoner 7 November.

77 Dollard, Richard – private.

78 Dolloway, John – private; enlisted 28 March; died 29 June.

79 Donovan, Keady – private; deserted 3 June.

80 Downey, Michael – private; enlisted 3 March; discharged 20 June.

81 Doyle, James – private.

82 Driscoll, Jeremiah – private.

83 Dunagan, Francis – private.

84 Dunfield, Michael – corporal; settled in N.B.

85 Dunn, John – private; died 2 March 1777.

86 Durney, John – private; settled in N.B.

87 Eagan, Edward – private; settled in N.B.

88 Eagan, Timothy – private; taken prisoner 7 November.

89 Emerson, Thomas – corporal.

90 Etter, Peter – sergeant; enlisted after the evacuation of Boston; settled in Westmorland, N.B.

91 Evans, Daniel – private; settled in N.B.

92 Fenall, Thomas – private.

93 Finn, Darby – private; settled in N.B.

94 Fitzharris, Henry – private; taken prisoner 7 November.

95 Freeman, James – captain; resigned 24 June.

96 Gearish, Nathaniel – private; enlisted 10 August.

97 George, Henry – sergeant.

98 Gleeson, Patrick – private; enlisted 6 November 1775.

99 Goreham, Joseph – lieutenant-colonel and commander of the regiment.

100 Gorman, Joesph – private.

101 Graham, Barnabas – private.

102 Graham, William – private; discharged 24 June.

103 Grant, James – captain; enlisted after the evacuation of Boston; commissioned 11 May; died 18 July 1779.

104 Griffin, Michael – private; enlisted 15 April; taken prisoner 8 November.

105 Hammon(d), George – private; granted 100 acres in Remshag, N.S.; settled in N.B.

106 Hanagen, Michael – enlisted 15 April; deserted 5 June.

107 Harrigan, John – private; deserted 30 July.

108 Hatton, William – corporal; settled in N.B.

109 Hays, Hugh – private.

110 Helling, William – private.

111 Henby, Cornelius – private.

112 Henderson, Alexander – private; settled in N.B.

113 Henessy, Phillip – private; taken prisoner 7 November.

114 Hickey, Lawrence – private.

115 Hoakway, John – private.

116 Hoban, John – private; settled in N.B.

117 Hogarth, Aaron – corporal; settled in N.B.

118 Hogg, William – private.

119 Hooper, William – private; settled in N.B.

120 Hughs, John – private; deserted 19 November.

121 Hughs, Robert – private.

122 Hunter, Robert – private; deserted 15 November.

123 Hunter, William – private; deserted 15 November.

124 Ingurton, Peter – private; discharged 6 May 1777.

125 Innis, James – sergeant; settled in N.B.

126 Innis, John – private; settled in N.B.

127 Johnston, Anthony – private; enlisted 16 April.

128 Johnston, James – private; enlisted 11 November 1775.

129 Johnston, William – private.

130 Jones, Alexander – private; taken prisoner 8 November.

131 Jones, William – private enlisted 15 May; died 9 June.

132 Jordan, Thomas – private; enlisted 6 December 1775.

133 Joyce, Phinias – drum major.

134 Keefe, William – private; taken prisoner 7 November.

135 Kelley, Edward – private; deserted 7 June.

136 Kelley, John – private; taken prisoner 7 November.

137 Kelly, Michael – private; settled in N.B.

138 Kenny, Stephen – private; deserted 14 June.

139 Kerns, George – corporal; settled in N.B.

140 Kershaw (Kinshaw), William – private; granted 300 acres in Remshag, N.S.

141 King, Patrick – private; taken prisoner 7 November; settled in N.B.

142 Kinon, James – private; enlisted 3 May; deserted 5 June.

143 King, Thomas – corporal.

144 Kirby, James – private; settled in N.B.

145 Knowling, John – private.

146 Laffin, Pence – private; died 12 November.

147 Lane, William – private.

148 Lantz, John – private; enlisted 10 April; settled in N.B.

149 Lee, Joseph – private.

150 Lester, George – private.

151 Liddle, James – drummer.

152 Litton, John – private; taken prisoner 7 November.

153 Looby, John – private; deserted 1 June.

154 Looby, Thomas – private; settled in N.B.

155 Lovely, Benjamin – private; granted 300 acres in Remshag, N.S.; settled in N.B.

156 Lunsby, Gilbert – private; enlisted 10 August.

157 Madden, Michael – private; enlisted 30 May.

158 Magner, John – private; died 21 November.

159 Magrath, Matthew – sergeant.

160 Mahony, Daniel – private.

161 Mahony, Darby – private; died 12 July.

162 Maley, Patrick – private; discharged 30 June.

163 Malmoy, James – private; enlisted 27 May.

164 Maning, James – private.

165 Masters, William – private; settled in N.B.

166 Matthews, Edward – private.

167 McCarthy, Dennis – private; enlisted 23 January.

168 McCarthy, John – corporal.

169 McDonald, John – private.

170 McDonald, Patrick – private; taken prisoner 7 November; settled in N.B.

171 McKinnin, James – private; died 6 July 1777.

172 McLeod, John – drummer; enlisted 10 June; settled in N.B.

173 McLeod, William – sergeant.

174 McNaly, James – private; taken prisoner 7 November.

175 Merry, Patrick – private.

176 Metcalf, Ralph – private; taken prisoner 7 November.

177 M'Ginnis, Andrew – private.

178 Miller, Richard – private.

179 Moon, John – private; taken prisoner 7 November.

180 Moore, Christopher – private; died 15 December.

181 Moore, Peter – private; taken prisoner 7 November.

182 Morgan, William Sampson – private.

183 Morison, John – private.

184 Morrice, John – private; deserted 30 July.

185 Morrison, James – private; settled in N.B.

186 Morrison, William – private.

187 Murray, James – private; enlisted 18 February; settled in N.B.

188 Murray, John – private.

189 Nash, Joseph – private; settled in N.B.

190 Newitt, Joseph – private; died 23 July.

191 Noonan, Daniel- private.

192 Nouson, William – private; enlisted 27 July; taken prisoner 10 November.

193 O'Bryan, John – private.

194 O'Bryan, Luke – private; enlisted 22 March; granted 100 acres in Rem-
     shag, N.S.

195 Osman, William – drummer.

196 Oxford, John – private.

197 Pagett, Thomas – private.

198 Pattenton, John – private; taken prisoner 7 November.

199 Patterson, James – private; deserted 2 June.

200 Pendergast, Edward – private; enlisted 5 April.

201 Pendergast, Peter – private.

202 Player, William – private; settled in N.B.

203 Power, Edward – private.

204 Power, Morris – corporal; settled in N.B.

205 Power, Phillip – private; enlisted 13 January.

206 Power, William – private; deserted 14 June.

207 Procter, William – second lieutenant.

208 Purcell, Francis – deserted 1 June.

209 Quigley, William – private.

210 Raynes, Richard – private; taken prisoner 7 November.

211 Reynolds, Joseph – private.

212 Richards, Robert – private; settled in N.B.

213 Riely, James – sergeant; enlisted 19 March; settled in N.B.

214 Roach, John – private; taken prisoner 7 November; settled in N.B.

215 Robbins, Isaac – private.

216 Robinson, Thomas – private; deserted 11 November.

217 Ruth, George – private; settled in N.B.

218 Ryan, Bartholemew – sergeant.

219 Ryan, Cornelius – private; settled in N.B.

220 Ryan, James – private; enlisted 16 April.

221 Ryan, John – corporal; settled in N.B.

222 Ryan, Samuel – private; deserted 6 June.

223 Ryan, Timothy – private; deserted 1 June.

224 Seelig, Jacob – private; enlisted 21 May.

225 Scott, John – sergeant.

226 Shanahan, Michael – private.

227 Sharmon, Ambrose – second lieutenant; settled in N.B.

228 Shaw, John – private; taken prisoner 7 November; settled in N.B.

229 Sheehan, Morris – private; taken prisoner 7 November.

230 Shortly, William – private.

231 Shute, Samuel – private; deserted 14 June.

232 Simmons, James – private; taken prisoner 9 November.

233 Sirter, Stephen – private.

234 Small, John – private.

235 Smallpiece, John – private.

236 Smith, Alexander – sergeant.

237 Smith, Joseph (or Josiah) – corporal; granted 500 acres in Remshag, N.S.

238 Sollum, George – private; enlisted 15 April; died 2 March 1777.

239 Speare, Robert – sergeant.

240 Standard, John – private; settled in N.B.

241 Stanton, Philip – private.

242 Steel, Thomas – private; discharged 9 June.

243 Stone, John – private; settled in N.B.

244 Street, Samuel Denny – private; enlisted 1 May.

245 Studholme, Gilfred – captain; commissioned 15 July; settled in N.B.

246 Sutherland, Alexander – sergeant.

247 Thomas, Richard – private; enlisted 20 May.

248 Thompson, James – private; enlisted after the evacuation of Boston; died 24 April 1777.

249 Tibbets, Timothy – private.

250 Tierney, Thomas – private.

251 Tobin, Patrick – private.

252 Traverse, John – sergeant; settled in N.B.

253 Walker, Joseph – private; taken prisoner 7 November; settled in N.B.

254 Walsh, George – private; settled in N.B.

255 Wambolt, Adam – private.

256 Warren, George – private.

257 Watson, Joseph – private; granted 100 acres in Remshag, N.S.

258 Welsh, William – private; settled in N.B.

259 White, Peter – private.

260 White, Timothy – private; died 22 July.

261 Whiteman (Wightman), John – private; granted 100 acres in Remshag, N.S.

262 Wilkonson, Francis – corporal.

263 Wills, John – private.

264 Wilson, Richard – first lieutenant; discharged 24 June 1777.

265 Wolf, John – private; deserted 14 June.

266 Wood, Edward – private; died 24 August.

267 Wood, James – private; taken Prisoner 7 November.

268 Vaile, Nathaniel – private.

Notes

ABBREVIATIONS

AA *American Archives: Consisting of a Collection of Authentick Records Forming a Documentary History of the Origin and Progress of the North American Colonies; Of the Causes and Accomplishment of the American Revolution; And of the Constitution of Government for the United States* ed. Peter Force (Washington 1837–53) 9 volumes

BHQ British Headquarters Papers (formerly known as the Carleton Papers or the American Manuscripts)

CDQ *Canadian Defence Quarterly*

CHR *Canadian Historical Review*

DAB *Dictionary of American Biography*

DAR *Documents of the American Revolution, 1770–1783 (Colonial Office Series)*, ed. K.G. Davies (Shannon: Irish University Press)

DCB *Dictionary of Canadian Biography*

DL Dalhousie University Library (Killam)

DNB *Dictionary of National Biography*

DR *Dalhousie Review*

DUA Dalhousie University Archives

JCC *Journals of the Continental Congress, 1774–1789, from the Original Records in the Library of Congress*, ed. Worthington Chauncey Ford (Washington: Government printing office 1904–37)

JHA *Journals of House of Assembly* of Nova Scotia

LCC *Letters of Members of the Continental Congress*, ed. Edmund C. Burnett
(Washington: Carnegie Institution 1923)
MA Massachusetts Archives
MAUA Mount Allison University Archives
MHS *Massachusetts Historical Society*
NA National Archives of Canada
NBHS *New Brunswick Historical Society* Collections
NBM New Brunswick Museum
NDAR *Naval Documents of the American Revolution*
NEQ *New England Quarterly*
NGSQ *National Genealogical Society Quarterly*
NMM National Maritime Museum (Great Britain)
NSHR *Nova Scotia Historical Review*
NSHS *Nova Scotia Historical Society* Collections
NYHS *New York Historical Society* Collections
PANB Public Archives of New Brunswick
PANS Public Archives of Nova Scotia
PCC Papers of the Continental Congress
PRO Public Record Office (Great Britain)
SPG Society for the Propagation of the Gospel
SRO Scottish Record Office
UNBLJ *University of New Brunswick Law Journal*

PREFACE

1 Nathaniel Smith to his brother and sister, 25 January 1777, Anna Calabresi,
"Letters Home: The Experience of an Emigrant in 18th Century Nova
Scotia" (Ph.D thesis: Yale University 1986).
2 Throop to Massachusetts Council, 23 December 1776, PANS Record Group
(RG) 1, 364. Throop's comment had literal meaning in 1776. On
1 January, George Washington hoisted at Cambridge the first American
flag which bore thirteen stripes and the British union. See Trevor Dupuy
and Gay Hammerman, *People and Events of the American Revolution* (New
York: R.R. Bowker 1974), 87.
3 Nevertheless, this national historic site is officially known only as Fort
Beauséjour, a fact which complicates a study such as this one as it means the
identity of Fort Cumberland has to be established at the outset. The fort's
identity is already sufficiently complicated by the fact that at the time of the
siege it was located in the original County of Cumberland in Nova Scotia,
but is now in Westmorland County, New Brunswick.
4 Arbuthnot to Germain, 31 January 1777, NA Manuscript Group (MG) 11,
vol. 97, 114–5. At the end of the war the fort could still "be looked upon as
the key to Nova Scotia," S. Hollingsworth, *The Present State of Nova Scotia with*

a Brief Account of Canada and the British Islands on the Coast of North America (Edinburgh: Printed for William Creech 1787), 122.

5 Pierce Hamilton, "History of the County of Cumberland" 1880, transcript PANS; and James Snowdon, "Footprints in the Marsh Mud" (M.A. thesis: University of New Brunswick 1974).

6 J.B. Brebner, *The Neutral Yankees of Nova Scotia* (New York: Columbia University Press 1937), 275. Although Brebner's claim that patriots outnumbered loyalists in Nova Scotia is a corollary of his neutrality thesis, the evidence in this study leads to the opposite conclusion. On a comparative basis the claim is incredible. This question of numbers was considered at length in the American context by John Adams and Thomas McKean, and, according to them, patriots did not outnumber loyalists in any of the thirteen colonies. "Upon the whole," wrote John Adams, it would be generous to assume two-thirds of Americans "to have been with us in the revolution." Thomas McKean agreed and added his opinion that more than a third of influential Americans were opposed. The majority in Delaware "were unquestionably against the independence of America," wrote McKean after thoughtful analysis. The Southern States "were nearly equally divided," understood Adams, and New York and Pennsylvania were at best evenly divided. The majority in these two states may actually have opposed the revolution and without pressure from Virginia on one side and New England on the other, Adams believed "they would have joined the British." Even in Boston, the heart of the revolution, "the last contest ... in 1775 between whig and tory was decided by five against two." See correspondence between McKean and Adams, 31 August and 15 November 1813, and January 1814 (three letters), Charles F. Adams, *The Works of John Adams* vol. 10 (Boston: Little, Brown and Co. 1856), 62–3, 80–2, 87.

7 George A. Rawlyk, *Nova Scotia's Massachusetts: A Study of Massachusetts-Nova Scotia Relations 1630–1784* (Montreal: McGill-Queen's University Press 1973). See also Gordon T. Stewart and George A. Rawlyk, *A People Highly Favoured of God: the Nova Scotia Yankees and the American Revolution* (Toronto: McClelland and Stewart 1972), particularly chapter 4; and George A. Rawlyk, "J.B. Brebner and Some Recent Trends in Eighteenth-Century Maritime Historiography," in *They Planted Well*, ed. Margaret Conrad (Fredericton: Acadiensis Press 1988), 97–119.

8 Brebner placed great weight in his *Neutral Yankees* on what he concluded to be the militia's refusal to do loyal service in 1776, describing the incident twice (pages 248 and 274). In a momentary lapse of his usual iron grip on sources, he cited faulty and incomplete evidence as is shown in chapter 6; see note 51.

9 Mary Beth Norton, *The British-Americans: The Loyalist Exiles in England 1774–1789* (Boston: Little, Brown and Co. 1972), 7.

10 For evidence of Nova Scotians who received loyalist land grants see Esther Clark Wright, *The Loyalists of New Brunswick* (Moncton 1955).

11 J.M. Bumsted, *Understanding the Loyalists* (Sackville: Mount Allison University 1986), 18. The useful labels "refugee loyalist" and "resident loyalist" are Bumsted's, ibid., 43.

12 See Charles M. Andrews, "The Boston Merchants and the Non-Importation Movement," *Transactions* 19 (Boston: Colonial Society of Massachusetts 1917), 159–250; and Arthur Schlesinger Sr, *Colonial Merchants and the American Revolution, 1763–1776* (New York: Columbia University Press 1918).

13 See in particular Bernard Bailyn, "The Central Themes of the American Revolution," in *Essays on the American Revolution*, eds. S.G. Kurtz and J.H. Hutson (Chapel Hill 1973), 16. Such a Neo-Whig comment resembles patriot rhetoric. For example, in a vindication of congress written in 1774, Alexander Hamilton presumed that Nova Scotia and other colonies not then joined with congress would soon come to their senses. "I cannot believe," wrote Hamilton with nearly as much certainty as Neo-Whigs 200 years later, that "they will persist in such conduct as must exclude them from the secure enjoyment of those heaven-descended immunities we are contending for." See "A Full Vindication of the Measures of the Congress," in *The Papers of Alexander Hamilton* vol. I, ed. Harold C. Syrett (New York: Columbia University Press 1961), 62.

14 John W. Tyler, *Smugglers and Patriots: Boston Merchants and the Advent of the American Revolution* (Boston: Northwestern University Press 1986), 250–1.

15 Janice Potter, *The Liberty We Seek: Loyalist Ideology in Colonial New York and Massachusetts* (Cambridge: Harvard University Press 1983), 60.

16 Adams to Niles, 13 February 1818, John Adams, *The Works of John Adams*, 282–3. This point is also made in Stewart and Rawlyk, *A People Highly Favoured of God*, 3.

17 Bernard Bailyn, *Voyagers to the West, a Passage in the Peopling of America on the Eve of the Revolution* (New York: Alfred A. Knoff 1986), 373.

18 For more details on early Nova Scotian development see the pamphlet by "A Member of Assembly," *An Essay on the Present State of the Province of Nova Scotia, With Some Strictures on the Measures Pursued by Government from its First Settlement by the English in the Year, 1749* (1774).

19 Throop to Massachusetts Council, 29 May 1777, MA vol. 142, 66–77. For details on planter migration and settlement see, for example, W.O. Sawtelle, "Acadia: The Pre-Loyalist Migration and the Philadelphia Plantation," *Pennsylvania Magazine of History and Biography* 51 (1927); Jean Stephenson, "The Connecticut Settlement of Nova Scotia Prior to the Revolution," *National Genealogical Society Quarterly* 42 (June 1954): 53–60; C.B. Fergusson, "Pre-Revolutionary Settlements in Nova Scotia," NSHS 37 (1970): 5–22; and Esther C. Wright, "Cumberland Township: A Focal Point of Early Settlement on the Bay of Fundy," CHR 27 (1946): 27–32.

20 "Tantramar Revisited," in *The Collected Poems of Sir Charles G.D. Roberts*, ed. Desmond Pacey (Wolfville: The Wombat Press 1985), 78. The opening

lines of Roberts' elegiac poem of 1883 (see page 1) evoke an emotional contradiction of elemental exhilaration amid profound melancholy. Nature, so powerfully displayed on the Tantramar, is a dramatic backdrop to fading memories of past tragedy. Intuitively, the poet has understood the enigma of this unique region with its turbulent history. In prosaic terms, the author has also revisited the Tantramar and provides a similar vision of the community that witnessed the single instance of violent rebellion in colonial Nova Scotia during the American Revolution.

21 In four articles written between 1932 and 1936 Kerr was working towards a more balanced overview of Nova Scotia's response to the revolution than the one Brebner later produced. Kerr's viewpoint is outlined in W.B. Kerr, "Nova Scotia in the Critical Years 1775–1776," *DAL* 12 (1932): 97–107, the first of the four articles. Although in his book of 1941, written after Brebner's, Kerr resisted the neutrality paradigm, his work appears strangely incomplete, as if he had been discouraged from fully developing his own thesis.

INTRODUCTION

1 Letter from Boston, 2 November 1774, The Earl of Dartmouth Papers, NA H-992-4, 4352-3. Nearly a year later an official wrote: "The king's Authority is entirely at an End throughout the Continent, except in Canada, Nova Scotia, and the Floridas." But then he added: "The Spirit of Revolt begins also to be Discovered in Nova Scotia." Graves to Duff, 4 September 1775, *NDAR*, various eds., (Washington 1966) vol. 2, 9–11.

2 Legge Proclamation, 19 September 1774, Earl of Dartmouth Papers, 177–8.

3 This incident is related in Executive Council Minutes, 16 and 19 September 1774, PANS RG 1, vol. 212. See also Legge to Earl of Dartmouth, 20 September 1774, *DAR*, ed. K.G. Davies (Shannon: Irish University Press) vol. 8, 200–3. Analysis in W.B. Kerr, "The Merchants of Nova Scotia and the American Revolution," *CHR* 13 (1932): 29–31. See also J.B. Brebner, *Neutral Yankees* of Nova Scotia (New York: Columbia University Press 1937), 144–7. Fillis and Smith remained loyal and took steps to redeem their characters. The House of Assembly acknowledged their loyalty on 16 June 1775 and the *Nova Scotia Gazette* published the proceeding on 20 June 1775. Fillis resumed his duties as a member of the Assembly.

4 Legge to Dartmouth, 6 March 1775, *DAR* 9, 66–8.

5 Dr Isaac Winslow to John Allan, 5 April 1775, in George H. Allan, *Sketch of Col. John Allan of Maine* (New York: n.d.), 2–3. A copy of this eight-page pamphlet is in the Bangor Public Library. Others described the state of anarchy and confusion in Massachusetts; see Wallace to Haldimand, 26 April and 4 May 1775 (two letters), NA Haldimand Collection, B.19, 125, 127.

6 Letter from Halifax, *Scots Magazine* 8 May 1775. Accounts of the events at Lexington and Concord appeared in the *Nova Scotia Gazette*, 2 and 9 May 1775.

7 Letter to Washington, 8 February 1776, *AA*, ed. Peter Force (Washington: 1837–53) 4th Series, vol. 5, 936–8.

8 Proceedings of SPG, 30 June 1775, SPG Papers, no. 194, 575–6, mfm at PANS.

9 The two reviews were by lawyers Richard Gibbons and James Monk. See Barry Cahill, "Richard Gibbons' Review of the Administration of Justice in Nova Scotia 1774," *UNBLJ* 37 (1988): 34–58; and Cahill, "James Monk's Observations on the Courts of Law in Nova Scotia 1775," *UNBLJ* 36 (1987): 131–45.

10 See Graves to Carleton, 27 April 1775, *NDAR* 1, (1964): 230–1.

11 Letter from Halifax, *Scots Magazine* 8 May 1775. "Gage and Graves have sent for provisions to Nova Scotia and measures are in progress for forwarding them," Legge to Dartmouth, 30 April 1775, NA CO 217/9, 271. Nearly all the regular troops left in the province were rushed to Boston, sailing from Halifax on the evening of 30 April.

12 Graves to Legge, 24 April 1775, *NDAR* 1, 213. Three days later Graves requested supplies from Quebec, see Graves to Carleton, 27 April 1775, *NDAR* 1, 230–1. Supplies were also obtained from the West Indies and, of course, Great Britain.

13 The export ban is in *JCC* 17 November 1775. American privateering commenced soon after Boston was besieged in April 1775. Long before Congress officially authorized privateering on 23 March 1776 and began issuing letters of marque and reprisal, the practice had been sanctioned by Washington: "I fitted out at the Continental Expense, several Privateers; chiefly with design to Intercept their fresh Provision Vessels from Nova Scotia and Canada." Washington to Ramsay, 8 December 1775, *NDAR* 3, (1968): 5–6. Washington was doing this at least by October. See Washington to J.A. Washington, 13 October 1775, *NDAR* 2, (1966): 436. Massachusetts authorized privateering 1 November 1775, *NDAR* 2, 834–9.

14 Legge to Dartmouth, 19 August 1775, *DAR* 11, 78–80.

15 For delays see for example Graves to Stephens, 24 July 1775, *NDAR* 1, 961; Legge to Graves, 3 August 1775, *NDAR* 1, 1049; Gage to Graves, 9 August 1775, *NDAR* 1, 1103; and Legge to LeCras, 11 August 1775, *NDAR* 1, 1116–7.

16 Letter from Halifax, 5 September 1775, *London Chronicle* 14–16 November 1775; Harold A. Innis ed., *The Diary of Simeon Perkins, 1776–1780* (Toronto: The Champlain Society 1948), 30 August 1775, 99; and extract of a letter from Boston, 13 December 1775, *NDAR* 3, 84–5.

17 Graves to Wallace, 17 September 1775, *NDAR* 2, 129–30. Falmouth was destroyed 18 October 1775.

18 For examples of how the escort service worked, follow the journals of HM Sloops *Merlin* and *Tartar,* PRO Adm 51/604 and 972. From Nova Scotia see Executive Council Minutes, 15 and 16 August 1775, PANS RG 1, vol. 212; from Boston see Hutcheson to Haldimand, 19 August and 25 December 1775 (two letters), NA Haldimand Collection, B.20, 26, 74; and Gage to Dartmouth, 25 May and 12 June 1775 (two letters), *The Correspondence of General Thomas Gage with the Secretaries of State* vol. I, ed. Clarence E. Carter (Archon Books 1969), 401–3.

19 The extent to which the Nova Scotian's supplied of the British Army during the siege of Boston can be calculated from the ships' logs of the British escort, the Gage and Howe orderly books, official correspondence, and newspaper reports.

20 Nathaniel Smith to his brother and sister, 30 July 1775, Calabresi, "Letters Home."

21 Legge to Dartmouth, 19 August 1775, *DAR* 11, 78–80; and Allan to Massachusetts Council, 19 February 1777, MA vol. 144, 169–71, a transcript in PANS MG 100, vol. 129.

22 John Stanton to Legge, 5 December 1775, NA MG 11, vol. 94, 272–9.

23 Throop to Massachusetts Council, 29 May 1777, MA vol. 142, 66–77.

24 For uncertainty about the origin of one of the dockyard fires (a naval officer was inclined to think it an accident), see Graves to Stephens, 19 August 1775, *NDAR* 1, 1178–9. Descriptions of the incidents in Legge to Dartmouth, 31 July 1775, *DAR* 11, 60–1; letter of an American officer at Cambridge, 18 May 1775, *AA* 4, vol. 2, 639; and letter from Halifax, 23 September 1775, *AA* 4, vol. 3, 780.

25 Legge to Dartmouth, 31 July 1775, *DAR* 11, 60–1. See also "State of the Troops now Actually in Garrison of 65th Regiment, Halifax, 14 June 1775," Earl of Dartmouth Papers, 293, mfm at PANS.

26 Legge to Dartmouth, 19 August 1775, *DAR* 11, 78–80. "The batteries are dismantled, the carriages of the guns all decayed, and they lying on the ground," he elaborated.

27 Letter to Washington, 8 February 1776, *AA* 4, vol. 5, 936–8.

28 Legge to Dartmouth, 31 July 1775, *DAR* 11, 60–1.

29 Legge's biography in *DCB* 4. For an excessively uncritical view, see Viola F. Barnes, "Francis Legge, Governor of Loyalist Nova Scotia, 1773–1776," *NEQ* 4 (1931): 420–47.

30 Gibbons Observations, Earl of Dartmouth Papers, 2930–8. The most complete description of the burning of Fort Frederick is Lyon to Massachusetts Council, 11 October 1775, MA vol. 138, 238–41, in *NDAR* 2, 445–8. For other contemporary mention see *Nova Scotia Gazette,* 5 September 1775; *London Chronicle,* 14–16 November 1775; James Warren to Samuel Adams, 28 September 1775, *Warren-Adams Letters* I (The Massachusetts Historical Society 1917), 49–50; Executive Council Minutes, 4 September 1775, PANS RG

1, vol. 212; and Petition of James Simonds and William Hazen, *JHA* 15 JUNE 1779. For recollections see Peter Fisher, *Sketches of New Brunswick: An Account of the First Settlement of the Province ...* (Saint John: Chubb and Sears 1825), 121–2.

31 *Sketches of New Brunswick* 121–2. For the capture of the attorney-general, see Phillips Caulbeck to Dartmouth, 5 January 1776, *NDAR* 3, 625–30; and same to Shuldham, 10 January 1776, *The Despatches of Molyneux Shuldham, Vice-Admiral of the Blue and Commander-in-Chief of His Britannic Majesty's Ships in North America, January–July, 1776*, ed. Robert W. Neeser (New York: De Vinne Press 1913), 69–73.

32 *The Despatches of Molyneux Shulham* 69–73. For the raid at Cape Sable and other points on the coast, see Executive Council Minutes, 15 December 1775, PANS RG 1, vol. 212; Legge to Graves, 15 December 1775, *NDAR* 3, 109; Legge to Dartmouth, 20 December 1775, *NDAR* 3, 179–80; Eleazer Butler et al. of Yarmouth to Legge, 5 December 1775, Earl of Dartmouth Papers, 2889–90; and deposition of Joshua Snow, 13 December 1775, Earl of Dartmouth Papers, 3788–9.

33 Cumberland Remonstrance, 23 December 1775, PANS RG 1, vol. 45.

34 The Massachusetts plan, known as Colonel Thompson's proposal, envisaged a force of 1,000 men, four armed vessels, and eight transports that would have proceeded from Machias to attack Nova Scotia at Windsor, *AA* 4, vol. 3, 90. The invasion of Canada was entrusted to General Philip Schuyler, *JCC*, 27 June 1775. The British garrison at Fort Ticonderoga, New York, surrendered on 10 May 1775 to a small force led by Ethan Allen, who two days later captured the nearby outpost of Crown Point. Allen's account, 10 May 1775, *AA* 4, vol. 2, 807–9.

35 Washington to Massachusetts Council, 11 August 1775; same to Schuyler, 15 August 1775; and same to same, 20 August 1775, *The Writings of Washington from the Original Manuscript Sources, 1745–1799*, ed. John C. Fitzgerald (Washington: Government Printing Office 1931–44) 3, 414–16, 423–4, and 436–9. Two letters concerning the resolution to attack Quebec were sent to Washington in June: Hancock to Washington, 28 June 1775, and Lee to same, 29 June 1775, *Letters of Members of the Continental Congress*, ed. Edmund C. Burnett (Washington: Carnegie Institution 1921), 1, 146 and 147.

36 Gage to Graves, 8 September 1775, *NDAR* 2, 47; and Graves to Duddingston, 10 September 1775, *NDAR* 2, 68–9. For rumours brought by travellers see deposition of Phineas Lovet, 15 July 1775, NA MG 11, vol. 94; deposition of Thomas Lowden, 7 August 1775, *NDAR* 1, 1080–1; and declarations of Susannah Sheppard and William Shey, 16 August 1775, Executive Council Minutes, PANS RG 1, vol. 212.

Just how widespread the rumours were in October is indicated by the concern in Montreal about the fate of Halifax. "I was much alarmed on Receiving news from Boston that Halifax was taken," wrote Brook Watson (who had once lived in Cumberland and was then visiting Montreal from England) to John Butler, 19 October 1775, manuscript, PCC, 153, vol. I.

37 Breynton to Mauger, 22 July 1775, Earl of Dartmouth Papers, 317.

38 Legge to Dartmouth, 27 November 1775, DAR 11, 197–8; and Ellis to SPG, 4 October 1775, SPG Papers, no. 196, 582–5. This show of loyalty was noticed by the patriots: letter to Washington, 8 February 1776, AA 4, vol. 5, 936–8.

39 Mauger to Pownall, 16 October 1775, NA MG 11, vol. 96. For reaction to the Stamp Act of 1765 see W.B. Kerr, "The Stamp Act in Nova Scotia," NEQ 6 (1933): 552–66.

40 Francklin to Dartmouth, 2 January 1776, NA MG 11, vol. 96.

41 Ellis to SPG, 4 October 1775, SPG Papers, no. 196, 582–5.

42 Legge to Dartmouth, 17 October 1775, CO 217/52, 3.

43 The recruiting officers arrived in June hoping "to raise a number of Men, particularly Highlanders," Gage to Legge, 7 June 1775, NA MG 11, vol. 94, 131–4. Two examples of Nova Scotians in the military in 1775 were Lieutenant Edward Barron Jr of River Hebert who was "lately wounded at Boston," (Arbuthnot to Shuldham, 15 February 1776, Shuldham Despatches, 145); and Tamberlane Campbell of Falmouth (and later of the upper St John River valley of New Brunswick), one of the defenders of Quebec City where the Americans were defeated on New Year's Eve 1775. For this service Campbell received General Carleton's "thanks for good conduct." Petition of Tamberlane Campbell, 1785, Land Papers, PANB.

44 The request for these men in Gage to Legge, 29 July 1775; the replies in Legge to Gage, 7 August 1775, and Legge to Gage, 16 August 1775, NDAR 1, 1002–3, 1080, and 1159.

45 Letter to Washington, 8 February 1776, AA 4, vol. 5, 936–8.

46 For lack of sentries see Legge to Dartmouth, 31 July 1775, DAR 11, 60–1. The House opened Monday 12 June and prorogued 20 July 1775. For an insight into the make-up of the House in 1775, see James Monk's notations on a list of members on 20 October 1775. Journal of the House of Assembly with Monk's notes, Special Collections, Vaughan Library, Acadia University, CD 3620, A4, N7.

47 "Extracts of the proceedings, Sufferings, etc. of Sam'l Rogers of Nova Scotia," 10 April 1779, manuscript, PCC 41, vol. 8.

48 A committee of the House consisting of John Day of Halifax and Newport (one of the most capable members of the Assembly), Henry Denny Denson and Winckworth Tonge of King's County, Charles Morris Jr of Sunbury County, and Jotham Gay of Cumberland County drew up this document, a Nova Scotia example of loyalist ideology. See J.B. Brebner's analysis of the document in "Nova Scotia's Remedy for the American Revolution," CHR 15 (1934): 171–81.

49 Letter to Washington, 8 February 1776, *AA* 4, vol. 5, 936–8.

50 John McDonald to Germain, 30 October 1776 to 22 March 1777, NA CO 217, vol. 52, 302. Alexander McDonald, for example, had to deal with one magistrate who was "as great a rebel as any in New England," McDonald to Gage, 1775, "Letterbook of Captain Alexander McDonald of the Royal Highland Emigrants 1775–1779," *NYHS* (1883): 205.

51 The expense of entertaining the Americans was approved by officials of Maugerville township. See authorization to pay David Burpee, 30 October 1775, Gerald Keith, "The Pickard Papers," *NBHS* 15 (1959): 67–8. See also Keith's analysis of this key document.

52 *JCC* 3, 316. Congress received the petition 2 November 1775. For follow-up see 9 and 10 November, *JCC* 3, 344, 348; and 16 February 1776, *JCC* 4, 155. Nothing resulted from the Passamaquoddy petition and the committee lapsed. When Washington sent the spies, Aaron Willard and Moses Child, into Nova Scotia to gather intelligence near the end of 1775, they went no further than Passamaquoddy. They felt it was too dangerous to penetrate further and made no mention of the committee. See Report of Willard and Child in Washington's letter to Congress, 14 February 1776, *AA* 4, vol. 4, 1149–50.

53 *DCB* 5; Joseph W. Porter, *Memoir of Col. Jonathan Eddy of Eddington, Me. With Some Account of the Eddy Family, and of the Early Settlers on Penobscot River* (Augusta: Sprague, Owen and Nash 1877); Charles Eddy, *Genealogy of the Eddy Family* (Brooklyn, New York: Nolan Brothers 1881); and Ruth Eddy, *The Eddy Family in America* (Boston 1930). Also see G.O. Bent, "Jonathan Eddy and Grand Manan," *Acadiensis* 6: (1906) 165–71.

54 For Allan's report on the Native people, 1793, see Frederic Kidder, *Military Operations in Eastern Maine and Nova Scotia During the American Revolution* (Albany: Joel Munsell 1867), 309. See also John S. Sprague, "Colonel John Allan, A Maine Revolutionary Patriot," *Journal of Maine History* II, (n.d.) no. 5; *DCB* 5; and *DAB*.

55 Dixon to Butler, 14 January 1776, NA MG 11, vol. 95, 108–11.

56 Suffolk to Legge, 16 October 1775, CO 217/51, 473.

57 Ibid.

58 Arbuthnot appointment, *NDAR* 1, 1341–3. For Arbuthnot's arrival and events at Halifax, see *The Hamond Naval Papers*, Virginia State University Library.

59 Suffolk to Legge, 16 October 1775, CO 217/51, 473. Massey's arrival in *Nova Scotia Gazette*, 5 December 1775.

60 Howe to Massey, 19 December 1775, BHQ, NA MG 23, 22–3.

61 Goreham's biography in *DCB* 4. See also Goreham's entry in Alfred E. Jones, *The Loyalists of Massachusetts: Their Memorials, Petitions and Claims* (London: Saint Catherine Press 1930), 150–1.

62 McDonald to Ogilvie, 6 January 1776, and same to McAdams, 22 July 1778, McDonald Letterbook, 234–6 and 430. Massey's biography in *DNB*. Massey, who was in charge of the army in Nova Scotia for three critical years during the American Revolution, is missing from the *DCB*.

63 Butler to Mauger, 1 January 1776, CO 217/52, 165. Arbuthnot's biography in *DCB* 4 and *DNB*.

64 Graves to Collins, 17 September 1775, *NDAR* 2, 130–1.

65 The House convened 20 October 1775. Legge explained in his opening speech that the "alarming … Affairs in America has made it necessary to call you together at this Time" to consider measures "which will most conduce to the Safety and Protection of the Province," *JHA*, 1775.

66 Josiah Throop charged that Legge "took the advantage of the Small pox being in Halifax [and] Called the Assembly together." Throop to Massachusetts Co., 29 May 1777, MA vol. 142, 66–77. The same point was made in a letter to Washington, 8 February 1776, *AA* 4, vol. 5, 936–8. See also Charles Morris Jr to DesBarres, 18 August 1775, PANS DesBarres Papers.

67 *JHA*, 30 October 1775.

68 Gibbons observations, 1775, The Earl of Dartmouth Papers, 2931–8.

69 Morris to DesBarres, 21 October 1775, PANS DesBarres Papers.

70 Gibbons observations, 1775, The Earl of Dartmouth Papers, 2931–8.

71 Legge to Dartmouth, 21 January 1776, *DAR* 7, 49–50.

72 Gibbons observations, 1775, The Earl of Dartmouth Papers, 2931–8.

73 *JHA*, 11 November 1775.

74 Gibbons observations, 1775, The Earl of Dartmouth Papers, 2931–8.

75 Letter to Washington, 8 February 1776, *AA* 4, vol. 5, 936–8.

76 Legge to militia officers, 12 January 1776, The Earl of Dartmouth Papers, 742.

77 Legge to Dartmouth, 21 January 1776, *DAR* 7, 49–50.

78 Letter to Washington, 8 February 1776, *AA* 4, vol. 5, 936–8.

79 Legge to Dartmouth, 18 March 1776, *DAR* 7, 79–81.

80 Ibid.

81 Dixon to Butler, 14 January 1776, NA MG 11, vol. 95, 108–11.

82 Legge to Dartmouth, 21 January 1776, *DAR* 7, 49–50. In Annapolis and Kings Counties "the people in General refuse to be embodied," Legge to Dartmouth, 1 January 1776, CO 217/52, 93. And while a third of the militia of LaHave on the South Shore mustered "for readiness in case of need, all refused to be drafted or to enlist," Innis ed., *The Diary of Simeon Perkins*, 5 October 1775, 102.

83 Legge to Dartmouth, 18 March 1776, *DAR* 7, 79–81.

84 Dixon to Butler, 14 January 1776, NA MG 11, vol. 96, 108–11.

85 Gibbons observations, 1775, The Earl of Dartmouth Papers, 2931–8.

86 Dixon to Butler, 14 January 1776, NA MG 11, vol. 95, 108–11.

242 Notes to pages 15–16

87 Ibid.
88 Gibbons observations, 1775, The Earl of Dartmouth Papers, 1931–8. Gibbons was an associate of the governor and his observations on the Cumberland remonstrance provide an excellent insight into the perspective of the Legge administration.
89 The Cumberland remonstrance with signatures is in Dartmouth Papers, 2891–5. A more legible copy without signatures is in PANS RG 1, vol. 45.
90 Dixon to Butler, 14 January 1775, NA MG 11, vol. 95, 108–11.
91 The proclamation is in the *Nova Scotia Gazette*, 5 December 1775. "Montreal is in the hands of the rebels," having fallen on 13 November; see Legge to Dartmouth, 5 December 1775, *DAR* 6, 200–1.
92 Inhabitants of Hopewell, Hillsborough, and Memramcook to Legge, 1775, The Earl of Dartmouth Papers, 3802–3; and Inhabitants of Yarmouth to Legge, 8 December 1775, *NDAR* 3, 3–4. The remonstrances of Truro and Onslow with signatures are in The Earl of Dartmouth Papers, 2922–4 and 2927–8.
93 Inhabitants of Yarmouth to Legge, 8 December 1775, *NDAR* 3, 3–4. The single use of the term "Neuter" in this one document was all Brebner needed to ascribe political neutrality, in the Acadian sense of that term, not only to Yarmouth but generally to the planter community in Nova Scotia. A review of the document does not support such a conclusion and when considered in the context of other relevant documents, different conclusions emerge. Other key items include: Citizens of Yarmouth to Legge, 5 December 1775, *NDAR* 2, 1281–2; Goold to Legge, Yarmouth, 19 September 1775, The Earl of Dartmouth Papers, 372–5; Eleazer Butler et al., Yarmouth to Legge, 15 September 1775, Dartmouth Papers, 2889–90; Executive Council Minutes, 15 December 1775, PANS RG 1, vol. 212; Bulkeley to inhabitants of Yarmouth, 16 December 1775, PANS RG 1, vol. 136; and Inhabitants of Barrington to Massachusetts Council, 19 October 1776, Edmund D. Poole, *Annals of Yarmouth and Barrington Nova Scotia in the Revolutionary War* (Yarmouth: J. Murray Lawson 1899), 10–11.
94 Arbuthnot to Sandwich, 26 December 1775, G.R. Barnes and J.H. Owens eds., *The Private Papers of John, Earl of Sandwich, First Lord of the Admiralty, 1771–1782,* (London: Navy Records 1932) 1, 113–15.
95 Innis ed., *The Diary of Simeon Perkins,* 17 January 1776, 109. Perkins did not hear about the suspension of the Militia Acts until February. It had been asserted that twenty persons from Liverpool had "joined the Rebels in New England," so the House appointed a committee to make an enquiry. The committee found the assertion false and cleared the town, *JHA,* 6 and 13 November 1775. Perkins may have initiated the move to clear his constituents of the charge, and at their urging. See entries for 23 October and 2 November in Innis ed., *The Diary of Simeon Perkins,* 103–4.

96 The precarious state of the Congregational Church had been evident since at least 1769 when a committee of the Cornwallis Church speculated that "in a Few years [we] Shall all be Churchmen or Nothing." Cornwallis Church to the Reverend Andrew Elliot, 8 November 1769, MHS 4/ 2 (1887–9), 67–9. The same letter appears in Gordon T. Stewart, "Documents Relating to the Great Awakening in Nova Scotia 1760–1791," *Publications of the Champlain Society* (Toronto 1982), 4–5, but the quotation is missing from the transcription.

97 Ellis to SPG, 4 October 1775, SPG papers, no. 196, 583–4.

98 Arbuthnot to Shuldham, 15 February 1776, *Shuldham Despatches*, 145–7. See also Hamond's journal of the American Revolution 1775–77, Hamond Naval Papers, Virginia State University Library.

99 AA 4, vol. 6, 223. In 1760 Halifax had 100 licensed drinking establishments and as many again that were unlicensed, according to an observer who concluded that "the business of one-half of the town is to sell rum and of the other half to drink it," Grant to Stiles, May 1760, Charles I. Bushnell ed., *The Narrative of John Blatchford, His Sufferings in the Revolutionary War, while a Prisoner with the British, as Related by Himself,* (New York: privately printed 1865), 71–2.

100 From "Satire on Halifax in Nova Scotia," poem by John Maylem, 1758, *Transactions of the Colonial Society of Massachusetts* 32 (Boston: published by the Society 1937), 104.

101 The House of Assembly was located at the northwest corner of Barrington and Sackville Streets. A heritage plaque marks the site.

102 *JHA*, 18 November 1775.

103 The Assembly prorogued 18 November.

104 From Maylem's "Satire on Halifax in Nova Scotia."

105 Rogers Extracts, PCC 41, vol. 8.

CHAPTER ONE

1 Rogers Extracts, 10 April 1779, PCC, 41, vol. 8. A native of Providence Rhode Island, Rogers was settled at Sackville by 1770. He was elected to the House of Assembly 3 November 1773.

2 Nathaniel Smith to his family, 15 August 1775, Anna Calabresi, "Letters Home: The Experience of an Emigrant in 18th Century Nova Scotia." Thesis: Yale University Press 1986.

3 Rogers Extracts, PCC, 41, vol. 8.

4 Unsigned letter and petition to Washington, 8 February 1776, AA 4, vol. 5, 936–8.

5 Eagleson to Butler, 27 January 1776, NA MG 11, vol. 95, 112–17.

6 Edward Barron junior of River Hebert quoted in Arbuthnot to Shuldham, 15 February 1776, *The Despatches of Molyneux Shuldham, Vice-Admiral of the Blue and Commander-in-Chief of His Britannic Majesty's Ships in North America, January-July 1976*, ed. Robert W. Neeser (New York: DeVinne Press 1913), 145–7.

7 Francklin to Legge, 22 February 1776, The Earl of Dartmouth Papers, mfm at PANS 3842–3. Michael Francklin had received "some letters" from Cumberland in January describing the rebellion.

8 Eagleson to Butler, 27 January 1776, NA MG 11, vol. 95, 112–17.

9 Allan to Massachusetts Council, 21 November 1776, F. Kidder, *Military Operations in Eastern Maine and Nova Scotia During the American Revolution* (Albany: Joel Munsell 1867), 168.

10 There is no record of religious reformation in Cumberland that winter but at Maugerville there was "a considerable shaking of the dry bones," according to Seth Noble, the settled Congregational minister. See Noble to Dewey, 7 February 1776, Lucius Boltwood, *The Descendants of Thomas Noble* (Hartford 1878), 203.

11 Procter to Legge, 6 March 1776, The Earl of Dartmouth Papers, 4178–83.

12 Ibid. Postilions are outriders who mount the lead horses when more than four are used to draw a sleigh.

13 McDonald to Ogilvie, 2 January 1776, McDonald Letterbook, NYHS, 233–4. Executive Council, 8 January 1776, PANS RG 1, vol. 212. Legge referred at the same time to "the great advances of the Rebels … investing Quebec which is supposed before this time to be in their hands." Legge to Dartmouth, 1 January 1776, PRO CO 217, vol. 52, 93.

14 Legge to Dartmouth, 15 February 1776, CO 217, vol. 52, in NDAR 3, 1298–9; and Legge to Shuldham, 25 February 1776, *The Despatches of Molyneux Shuldham*, 147–9.

15 Legge to Shuldham, 25 February 1776, *The Despatches of Molyneux Shuldham*, 147–9. In his plan for conquering Nova Scotia, John Allan recognized the importance of patrolling Northumberland Strait near Baie Verte, see "Proposals For Attack on Nova Scotia," NSHS II, 11–16.

16 Arbuthnot to Shuldham, 15 February 1776, *The Despatches of Molyneux Shuldham*, 145–7; and Eagleson to Butler, 27 January 1776, NA MG 11, vol. 95, 112–17. Mrs Cossins divulged Earle's and Dawson's plan to Edward Barron Jr, a loyalist who passed it to a corporal of the 65th Regiment who, in turn, brought it express to Halifax.

17 "Extract of a letter from Halifax communicated to Mr. Pownall by Joshua Mauger Esq.," 1 January 1776, PRO CO 217, vol. 52, 165. The letter was written by John Butler.

18 Band and bandleader Morgan are mentioned in the *Nova Scotia Gazette*, Tuesday 5 December 1775.

19 Legge to Dartmouth, 11 January 1776, PANS RG 1, vol. 45.

20 Legge to Dartmouth, 1 January 1776, PRO CO 217, vol. 52, 93.

21 Letter to Pownall, 1 January 1776, PRO CO 217, vol. 52, 165.

22 Andrew S. Hamond, Journal of the American Revolution 1775–77, Virginia State University Library, entry for December 1775.

23 Letter of George III, 6 February 1776, G.R. Barnes and J.H. Owens, eds., *The Private Papers of John, Earl of Sandwich, First Lord of the Admiralty, 1771–1782* (Navy Records 1982), 113.

24 Letter to Pownall, 1 January 1776, PRO CO 217, vol. 52, 165.

25 A Petition to the King by some "Principal Gentlemen and Inhabitants" of Nova Scotia, 2 January 1776, The Earl of Dartmouth Papers, 2905–12.

26 Letter to Pownall, 1 January 1776, PRO CO 217, vol. 52, 165.

27 "Petition of several Members of your Majesty's Council for the Province of Nova Scotia," 1 January 1776, by Jonathan Belcher, Henry Newton, Jonathan Binney, Arthur Goold, and John Butler. Also, "Petition of the Principal Gentlemen and Inhabitants of Your Majesty's faithful and loyal Province of Nova Scotia," 2 January 1776, by William Nesbitt, Benjamin Green, Jonathan Binney, Joseph Fairbank, William Smith, Francis Boyd, Andrew Wallace, John Breynton, James Brenton, John Newton, John Fillis, James Stevens, Phillip Hammans, James Browne, Joseph Butler, John Fillis Jr, Joseph Scott, Winckworth Tonge, and John Prince. The Earl of Dartmouth Papers, 2897–2911.

28 Executive Council, 8 January 1776, PANS RG 1, vol. 212; and Legge to Dartmouth, 11 January 1776, PANS RG 1, vol. 45.

29 Procter to Legge, 6 March 1776, The Earl of Dartmouth Papers, 4178–83.

30 Eagleson to Butler, 27 January 1776, NA MG 11, vol. 95, 112–17.

31 Procter to Legge, 6 March 1776, The Earl of Dartmouth Papers, 4178–83; and Eagleson to Butler, 27 January 1776, NA MG 11, vol. 95, 112–17.

32 Bulkeley to Law, 20 February 1776, PANS RG 1, vol. 136.

33 Francklin to Legge, 22 February 1776, The Earl of Dartmouth Papers, 3842–3; Legge to Francklin, 28 February 1776, The Earl of Dartmouth Papers, 559–60.

34 Legge to Dartmouth, 11 January 1776, PANS RG 1, vol. 45; and Executive Council, 8 January 1776, PANS RG 1, vol. 212. Legge circulated a letter to militia officers in an effort to limit the damage. See Legge, "to Commanding officers of the Militia in Various Counties," 12 January 1776, PRO CO 217.

35 Eagleson to Butler, 27 January 1776, NA MG 11, vol. 95, 112–17.

36 Ibid.

37 For repair instructions see Howe to Massey, 19 December 1775, BHQ. Also see, Bulkeley to Law, 20 February 1776, PANS RG 1, vol. 136. For Law's relationship to Wethered see Louise W. Throop, "Early Settlers of Cumberland Township, Nova Scotia," NGSQ 67, December 1979, 270.

38 Rogers Extracts, PCC, 41, vol. 8.

39 Washington to Congress, 30 January 1776, *The Writings of Washington from the Original Manuscript Sources, 1745–1799*, ed. John C. Fitzgerald (Washington 1931–44) 4, 292; "Talk of one of the St. John's Tribe, attended by two of the Passamaquoddy Indians, with ... Washington," 31 January 1776, AA 4, vol. 4, 894; "Keahawit and Pierre Toma, heads of the St. John's, and in behalf of the Miccamac Tribe" to Massachusetts Council, 5 February 1776, AA 4, vol. 4, 946; Allan to Massachusetts Council, 21 November 1776, Kidder, *Military Operations*, 166–79; Massachusetts Resolves, 16 October 1775.

40 Memorial of John Cort, 8 Apr. 1777, CO 217, vol. 27, 298; Allan to Massachusetts Council, 21 November 1776, Kidder, *Military Operations*, 166–79. Cort from Scotland and William Davidson were business associates on the Miramichi. They shared a large land grant and were interested in the salmon fishery. See Davidson, DCB 4.

41 Petition to Washington, 8 February 1776, by twelve inhabitants of Cumberland: Elijah Ayer, Nathaniel Reynolds, Mark Patton, John Allan, William Lawrence, Amasa Killam, Jesse Bent, William Maxwell, George Forster, Simon Newcombe, Robert Foster, and Simeon Chester in AA 4, vol. 5, 523–4. It is published a second time in vol. 5, 938–9, but Patton's name is missing from the list of signatures. The unsigned letter to Washington by an inhabitant of Cumberland, 8 February 1776, AA 4, vol. 5, 936–8; also in George A. Rawlyk, *Revolution Rejected, 1775–1776* (Scarborough: Prentice-Hall 1968), 19–23.

42 Rawlyk, *Revolution Rejected*, 19–23. News of "the Slaughter of their [American] General Montgomery and his Aid-de-Camp and the capture of 300 of their forces" was sent from Boston to Halifax on 2 February. See Graves to Arbuthnot, 2 February 1776, NDAR 3, 1096. By 19 February McDonald in Halifax had read in the *Massachusetts Gazette* "of the Fate of General M[on]tgomery and his Army," but official word may not have arrived until the end of February, McDonald Letterbook, NYHS (1883): 245, 281.

43 Petition to Washington, 8 February 1776, AA 4, vol. 5, 523–4 and 938–9. Of the twelve signatories, nine are known to have participated in the siege. Eight served on Eddy's siege committee (Ayer, Reynolds, Killam, Bent, Maxwell, Newcombe, Foster, and Chester) and William Lawrence was tried for his part in the siege. Of the remaining three, John Allan fled Nova Scotia before the siege, George Forster is not known to have played any role in the siege, and Mark Patton was acquitted of rebellious practices.

44 Ibid. Also, Josiah Throop to Massachusetts Council, 29 May 1777, MA vol. 142, 66–77.

45 Procter to Legge, 6 March 1776, The Earl of Dartmouth Papers, 4178–83.

46 Allan to Massachusetts Council, 19 February 1777, PANS MG 100, vol. 129.

47 Procter to Legge, 6 March 1776, The Earl of Dartmouth Papers, 4178–83. "Lieutenant Thomas Procter" is listed in "Return of the Officers of His Maj-

esty's Provincial Regiment of Loyal Nova Scotia Volunteers," 25 February 1776, The Earl of Dartmouth Papers, 3844. A proclamation of Governor Legge, dated 8 December 1775, refers to Thomas Procter as a justice-of-the-peace for Halifax County, *AA* 4, vol. 4, 222.

48 Thomas Procter was a grantee in the townships of Cumberland and Fort Lawrence. His land in Cumberland (Letter A, lot 60) was next to that of Simeon Chester, member of the Committee-of-Safety. PANS RG 20 C, vol. 86, 1.

49 Procter to Legge, 6 March 1776, The Earl of Dartmouth Papers, 4178–83.

50 Dixon to Butler, 14 January 1776, and Eagleson to Butler, 27 January 1776, NA MG 11, vol. 95, 111–17. Procter to Legge, 6 March 1776, The Earl of Dartmouth Papers, 4178–83.

51 Legge to Dartmouth, 15 February and 18 March 1776 (two letters), *NDAR* 3, 1298–9 and *DAR* 12, 79–81. See also Executive Council, 15 February 1776, PANS RG 1, vol. 212. "My orders," stressed Massey, "are to defend the Dockyard and Halifax only." Massey to Germain, 22 November 1776, NA MG 11, vol. 96, 342–7.

52 Allan to Massachusetts Council, 19 February 1777, PANS MG 100, vol. 129.

53 Besides Procter, those known to have visited Cumberland during this period include John Stanton of the 14th Regiment, James McDonald and Robert Campbell of the Highland Emigrants, one MacLean (possibly Murdoch MacLean, also an Emigrant officer), and a corporal of the 65th Regiment.

54 Legge to Dartmouth, 15 February 1776, CO 217, vol. 52, in *NDAR* 3, 1298–9.

55 John Knox Laughton ed., (London: Navy Records Society 1896), 23.

56 Arbuthnot to Shuldham, 15 February 1776, *The Despatches of Molyneux Shuldham*, 147–9.

57 Arbuthnot to Sandwich (three letters), 26 December 1775, 14 January 1776, and 1 February 1776, in Barnes and Owen, *The Private Papers of John, Earl of Sandwich* 1, 113–19.

58 A note from the king, 6 February 1776, commended Arbuthnot's reports, Barnes and Owen, *The Private Papers of John, Earl of Sandwich* 1, 113.

59 Legge's recall in Germain to Legge, 24 February 1776, PRO CO 217, vol. 52, 89. Arbuthnot's appointment in Germain to Arbuthnot, 24 February 1776, PRO CO 217, vol. 52, 91.

60 Francklin to Legge, 10 March 1776, The Earl of Dartmouth Papers, 3858–9. For the weather on 9 March see the diary of Isaac Deschamps, DUA.

61 Francklin to Legge, 3 March 1776, The Earl of Dartmouth Papers, 565–7.

62 Francklin to Legge, 26 February 1776, The Earl of Dartmouth Papers, 3846–8.

63 Francklin to Legge, 10 March 1776, The Earl of Dartmouth Papers, 3858–9.

64 Ibid.

65 Bulkeley to Francklin, 16 March 1776, PANS RG 1, vol. 136. Also, see Executive Council for March, PANS RG 1, vol. 212.

66 Francklin to Legge, 19 March 1776, The Earl of Dartmouth Papers, 3861. Same to Same, 10 March 1776, The Earl of Dartmouth Papers, 3858–9. Same to John Pownall, 4 May 1776, NA MG 11, vol. 95, 320–8.

67 "Extract of a letter from Boston," 21 March 1776, Margaret W. Willard ed., *Letters on the American Revolution 1774–1776* (New York: Kennikat Press 1925), 288–9. See Shuldham to Stephens, 8 March 1776, *NDAR* 4, 230, and George Gillespie to Dr Gillespie, 23 March 1776, *NDAR* 4, 471. See also Stuart to the Earl of Bute, 28 April 1776, *NDAR* 4, 1290–3, and "Extract of a Letter from a Midshipman on board the *Chatham*, 23 March 1776, *NDAR* 4, 473.

68 "Extract of an authentic letter, Boston Harbour," 22 March 1776, Willard, *Letters on the American Revolution*, 290. For accounts of the evacuation and retreat to Halifax, see Charles Stuart to his father, the Earl of Bute, 28 April 1776, *NDAR* 4, 1290–3; John T. Barker, *The British in Boston, Being a Diary of Lieutenant John Barker of the king's Own Regiment from 15 November 1774 to 13 May 1776; With Notes by Elizabeth Ellery Dana* (Cambridge: Harvard University Press 1924); "A British Officer in Boston in 1775 [and 1776]," *Atlantic Monthly* 39 (April-May 1877), 389–401, 544–54;

69 "Extract of a letter from Boston," 21 March 1776, Willard, *Letters on the American Revolution*, 288–9. Also, see Nepean to Graves, 25 March 1776, *NDAR* 4, 500–1.

70 Dr Henry Caner to SPG, 10 May 1776, in William S. Perry ed., *Historical Collections Relating to the American Colonial Church* (New York: Ams Press 1969), 585–6.

71 "Extract of a letter from Boston Harbour," 17 March 1776, Willard, *Letters on the American Revolution* 284–6.

72 Mercy Warren to John Adams, 3 April 1776, Robert J. Taylor ed., *Papers of John Adams* (Cambridge: Belknap Press 1983) 4, 108–9.

73 "From an Officer ... at Boston to a Person in London," 17 March 1776, Willard, *Letters on the American Revolution*, 279–80. Also, see Samuel Cooper to Benjamin Franklin, 27 March 1776, *NDAR* 4, 534–5.

74 Rogers Extracts, PCC 41, vol. 8. For Washington's activities, see Washington to Hancock (three letters), 9, 19, and 24 March 1776, *NDAR* 4, 254–7, 405–7, and 485–7.

75 Washington to Hancock, 9 March 1776, *NDAR* 4, 254–7. The American uncertainty over Howe's destination was set to verse:

> Some say they're sail'd to Halifax,
>   And others for New York;
> Howe let none know where he was bound,
>   When the soldiers did embark.

Where they are bound there's none can tell,
  But the great God on high;
May all our heads be cover'd well,
  When cannon balls do fly.

From one of "two favourite Songs, made on the Evacuation of the Town of Boston," NDAR 4, 491.

76 JCC 16 February 1776, 155.

77 Washington to Hancock, 27 March 1776, AA 4, vol. 5, 522–3.

78 Mary Allan was the daughter of Mark Patton and Anne McGowan. Her uncle, Robert McGowan, of Amherst was charged with treason in connection with the siege. Robert's son, John McGowan (Mary Allan's first cousin), was a patriot soldier who fled with Eddy after the siege. Mary Allan's younger sister, Martha Patton, married Peter Campbell, a member of Eddy's siege committee. See the Allan genealogy in Kidder, *Military Operations*, 25–32, and Throop in NGSQ 67, September and December 1979.

79 Delesdernier to Haldimand, 1778, PANS RG 1, vol. 367 1/2; and Morris to Desbarres, 21 October 1775, PANS Desbarres Papers, series 5, vol. 3.

80 Bulkeley to Law, 20 February 1776, PANS RG 1, vol. 136.

81 Notice of reward for the apprehension of William How, 2 July 1776, PANS RG 1, vol. 170, 206–7.

82 Allan to Massachusetts Council, 21 November 1776, Kidder, *Military Operations*, 166–79.

83 Ibid.

84 Bennett's mission to the Micmacs in 1776 is described in Bennett to SPG, 5 June and 10 December 1776 (two letters), SPG Papers, 604–6 and 623–5; Bennett to Germain, 7 January 1777, PRO CO 217, vol. 28, 11; Bennett to Legge, 21 March 1777, The Earl of Dartmouth Papers, 3963–4.

85 Washington to Hancock, 1 April 1776, AA 4, vol. 5, 755.

86 Washington was voted the degree of Doctor of Laws by the Corporation and Overseers of Harvard on 3 April 1776. The general's diploma was taken to him the next morning (4 April) but he had already departed for New York. The wording of the diploma reflected academic relief at seeing the army depart the campus: "our University had the agreeable Prospects of being restored to its ancient Seat." Clifford K. Shipton, *Sibley's Harvard Graduates* (Boston: MHS 1970), class of 1749, 502–3.

87 Rogers Extracts, PCC 41, vol. 8. On the return journey Eddy visited his cousin, John Eddy, at Chatham Connecticut, J.W. Porter, *Memoir of Col. Jonathan Eddy of Eddington, Me., with some Account of the Eddy Family and of the Early settlers on Penobscot River* (Augusta: Spraque, owen and Nash, 1877), 10.

88 "Journal of Chief Justice Peter Oliver," in *Diary and Letters of His Excellency Thomas Hutchinson Esq.*, ed. Peter O. Hutchinson (Boston: Houghton, Mifflin 1886), vol. 2, 49. "Extract of a letter to a Gentleman in London,"

24 March 1776, *NDAR* 4, 490. "Extract of a letter from an Officer on board a man of war in Halifax Harbour," 7 May 1776, Willard, *Letters on the American Revolution,* 310–11. Francis Hutcheson to Frederick Haldimand, 24 March 1776, *NDAR* 4, 487–9. "Extract of a letter from Halifax, Nova Scotia," 22 November 1776, in *The Remembrancer, or Impartial Repository of Public Events, 1775–1784,* ed. John Almon (1776): 267.

89 Arrival of the fleet in *Nova Scotia Gazette,* Wednesday 3 April 1776. The Reverend Jonathan Scott of Yarmouth was in Halifax at the same time; Henry E. Scott ed., *The Journal of the Reverend Jonathan Scott* (New England Historic Genealogical Society 1980), 81.

90 See "Extract of a letter from an Officer on board a man of war in Halifax Harbour," 7 May 1776, *NDAR* 4, 310–11. *Nova Scotia Gazette,* 3 April 1776; "Extract of a letter from Halifax, Nova Scotia," 22 November 1776, The *Remembrancer* III, 267; Andrew Eliot to Isaac Smith, 9 April 1776, Henry W. Foote, *Annals of Kings Chapel* from the Puritan Age of New England to the Present Day, vol. 2 (Boston: Little Brown and Co. 1896), 93–4.

91 Breynton to SPG, 13 January 1777, SPG Papers, 212. The Reverend Henry Caner confirmed Breynton's benevolence towards the refugee clergy which included the Reverend Mather Byles Jr, the Reverend Walter, and the Reverend McBadger. See Caner to SPG, 10 May 1776, SPG Papers.

92 "Extract of a letter from Halifax, Nova Scotia," 22 November 1776, Almon, The *Remembrancer* III, 267. Journal of Peter Oliver, *Diary and Letters of His Excellency Thomas Hutchinson,* 47. Byles to SPG, 4 May 1776, SPG Papers, 92.

93 Gardiner to Oliver Whipple, 9 May 1776, H.W. Foote, *Annals of Kings Chapel* II (Boston: Little, Brown 1896), 354. Journal of Peter Oliver, *Diary and Letters of His Excellency Thomas Hutchinson,* 50. Gardiner to Whipple, 9 May 1776, Foote, *Annals of Kings Chapel,* 50.

94 Captain John Bowater to Lord Denbigh, 12 April 1776, Marion Balderston and David Syrett eds., *The Lost War: Letters from British Officers during the American Revolution* (New York: Horizon Press 1975), 74–6.

95 Benjamin F. Stevens, *General Sir William Howe's Orderly Book at Charlestown, Boston and Halifax, 17 June 1775 to 26 May 1776* (London: Kennikat Press 1890), 243. See also General Orders of Thomas Gage, PANS MG 12, HQ. O A. The Howe and Gage orderly books are similar but not identical. Yet another is the "Orderly Book of the Detachment of the 14th Regiment Halifax 1776," 4 June – 9 June, National Army Museum (Great Britain), 5904/175, file 41 (6).

96 McDonald to Small, 3 October 1775, McDonald Letterbook, *NYHS* 227. On Tuesday 2 April there arrived at Windsor two officers of the 17th Regiment of Light Dragoons "to look for Quarters." Isaac Deschamps was appointed barrack master and commissary of Fort Edward and his son, George, who was employed to make repairs, worked all that week and on Sunday to get things ready. Two troops of Light Horse arrived the next Wednesday,

10 April, two more troops on Thursday, and another troop on Friday. More officers arrived on Saturday, and an engineer was also sent up from Halifax to supervise repairs. The first supplies were landed in Windsor by the *Neptune* transport ship on the following Saturday, 20 April. See George Deschamps diary, DUA.

97 Bowater to Denbigh, 12 April 1776, Balderston and Syrett, *The Lost War*, 74–6.

98 "Extract from a letter from Halifax, Nova Scotia," 22 November 1776, Almon, The *Remembrancer* 3, 267.

99 Shuldham to Stephens (two letters), 24 April 1776, *The Despatches of Molyneux Shuldham*, 187–8. "Everything was uncommonly scarce in this port at this time," wrote Bartholomew James, "but infinitely more so on the arrival of Lord Shuldham and General Howe from Boston with the fleet and army, when we were immediately put to half allowance." Laughton, *Journal of Rear-Admiral Bartholomew James*, 25.

100 Bowater to Denbigh, 12 April 1776, Bladerston and Syrett, *The Lost War*, 74–6.

101 Scott, *The Journal of the Reverend Jonathan Scott*, 81–2.

102 James Beverley and Barry Moody eds., *The Journal of Henry Alline* (Hantsport: Lancelot Press 1982), 74. Prayer, Discourses and Sermons of the Reverend William Ellis, Dalhousie University Archives (DUA) MS 2, 25, A 1–7. Weather was recorded by Isaac Deschamps, DUA.

103 Arbuthnot to Germain, 26 April 1776, NA MG 11, 309–12.

104 *JCC*, Saturday 27 April 1776, 314.

105 Rogers Extracts, PCC 41, vol. 8.

106 Eddy to Massachusetts Council, 5 January 1777, Kidder, *Military Operations*, 67–72.

107 Executive Council, 30 April 1776, PANS RG 1, vol. 212.

108 Howe to Germain, 7 May 1776, *DAR* 12, 126–30.

109 Orderly Book of Thomas Gage, PANS MG 12, HQ. O A.

110 The governor never returned to Nova Scotia although he clung to office (at full salary) for six more years during which the province was administered by a series of lieutenant-governors. The royal commission of enquiry reported on Legge's conduct 25 July 1776. The charges against him were "of a very general nature" and only one instance of "impropriety" pointing to "a dangerous tendency" was found, but the commissioners could not ignore the discontent caused by his administration. They agreed with the king that "so general a foment and dissatisfaction spread through the province that it became necessary for Your Majesty to call him home to answer to the complaints exhibited against him." Legge's shortcoming was revealed in lengthy understatement. "We shall not conceal from Your Majesty … that your governor, through the course of his administration, hath been wanting in that gracious and conciliating deportment which the

delicacy of the times ... demanded." Haligonians had already concluded (and more succinctly) that Legge was "an Ignorant Tyrant" and that was why, according to the commissioners, "those upright intentions which he carried with him into government became in great part fruitless and abortive." In short Legge was a failure and henceforth Nova Scotia would be spared his leadership. "When we consider the peculiar predicament of this faithful Colony ... we cannot under these circumstances think it will be for Your Majesty's service that Mr. Legge should be allowed (for the present at least) to return to Nova Scotia." See "Commissioners for Trade and Plantations to the King," 25 July 1776, DAR 12, 171–4.

111 *Tamer* Log, PRO ADM 51/968.

112 Orderly Book of Thomas Gage, PANS MG 12, HQ. O A. For the Royal Fencible Americans and the Royal Highland Emigrants see Harry Piers, "Regiments Raised in Nova Scotia," NSHS 21 (1927), 149–58; W.O. Raymond, "Loyalists in Arms," NBHS 2 (1904), 217–19; and Jonas Howe, "The Royal Emigrants," *Acadiensis* 7, 50–75.

113 Employment was so high and materials in such short supply that Ellis was forced to postpone renovation of the Falmouth Church; Ellis to SPG, 14 Sept. 1776, SPG Papers, no. 208, 614–19.

114 Alline did not refuse an officer's commission because of reluctance to defend Nova Scotia or to fight New Englanders. He made clear in his journal that a military career was attractive and would have been an acceptable alternative had he proved inadequate for the ministry. Indeed, at times Alline "began to wish that I had taken it [the officer's commission]." Any reluctance Alline may have had to bear arms was general in nature and may have stemmed from the Quaker influence in his district. Beverley and Moody, *The Journal of Henry Alline*, 71–2.

115 Sermon "On Mistaken Zeal" delivered in Windsor in the summer of 1776, Ellis Papers, DUA. Ellis to SPG, 14 September 1776, SPG Papers, no. 208, 614–19.

116 Beverley and Moody, *The Journal of Henry Alline*, 74.

117 *Tamer* Log, PRO ADM 51/968.

118 Rogers Extracts, PCC 41, vol. 8.

119 Jacob Barker to James Simonds, James White, and Jervis Say, 20 June 1776, MA vol. 181, 248–9.

120 Noble to Dewey, 7 February 1776, Boltwood, *The Descendants*, 203.

121 "Reminiscences of Mrs. Mary Bradley," New England Historical and Genealogical Society, Boston, n.d. As David Bell notes in his *Newlight Baptist Journals of James Manning and James Innis* (Saint John: Lancelot Press 1984), 132–3, the Bradley manuscript differs materially from her published work: *A Narrative of the Life and Christian Experience of Mrs. Mary Bradley of Saint John, New Brunswick* (Boston: Strong and Broadhead 1849). Mrs Bradley was the former Mary Coye whose father, Edward Coye, was a

member of the Sunbury Committee-of-Safety and whose elder brother, Amasa Coye, was a soldier in Eddy's army.

122 Noble to Dewey, P.S. dated 20 May 1776 in letter of 7 February 1776, Boltwood, *The Descendants*, 203–4. See also G.O. Bent, "Parson Noble," *Acadiensis* 7, 46–57.

123 Petition of Sunbury committee to Massachusetts, 21 May 1776, *AA* 5, vol. 1, 703–4. The absurdity of calling to arms those who were not trusted to bear them was apparent to one Halifax official. Arbuthnot to Sandwich, 26 December 1775, *The Private Papers of John, Earl of Sandwich*, 113–15.

124 Ibid.

125 Perley, Noble, Nevers, and Burpee to Goold, 16 May 1777, NA MG 11, vol. 97, 200–3.

126 Arbuthnot to Germain, 8 July 1776, NA MG 11, vol. 96, 92–7.

127 Perley, Noble, Nevers, and Burpee to Goold, 16 May 1777, NA MG 11, vol. 97, 200–3. Also memorandum to Massachusetts attached to the Petition of 21 May 1776 and the petition itself.

128 Resolves of the Committee, 21 May 1776, *AA* 5, vol. 1, 705–6.

129 Ibid.

130 Ibid.

131 Claim of Charles Jadis, 24 October 1776, NA AO 13. See also Jadis to Treasury, 30 March 1787, PRO T1/644. The best descriptions of the Maugerville rebellion belong to Charles Godfrey Newland Jadis. Both are coloured by Jadis' outrageous opinions and are not entirely consistent with each other. His chief problem was his belief that everyone in the valley who opposed him (and nearly everyone did) was a patriot. When he applied this faulty analysis to such genuine loyalists as Gervas Saye and James Simonds, Jadis was incredible. Nevertheless, when used carefully with other sources the Jadis accounts are invaluable.

132 Ibid.

133 Claim of Charles Martin, agent of the late John Anderson, NA AO 13.

134 Memorandum to Massachussets attached to the petition of 21 May 1776, *AA* 5, vol. 1, 706.

135 "The Petition of Jacob Barker, Israel Perley, Phineas Nevers, Daniel Palmer, Moses Pickard, Edward Coye, Thomas Hartt, Israel Kenney, Asa Kimball, Asa Perley, Hugh Quinton, and Oliver Perley, a Committee chosen in behalf of the Inhabitants of the River St. John's, in Nova Scotia," 21 May 1776, *AA* 5, vol. 1, 703–4.

136 Noble to Dewey, 7 February 1776, Boltwood, *The Descendants*, 203.

137 Jadis to Treasury, 30 March 1787, PRO T1/644.

138 Noble to Dewey, P.S. dated 20 May 1776 in letter of 7 February 1776, Boltwood, *The Descendants*, 204. Claim of Charles Jadis, 24 October 1776, NA AO 13.

139 Rogers Extracts, PCC 41, vol. 8.

CHAPTER TWO

1 Bulkeley to Desbarres, 8 November 1776, PANS Desbarres Papers, Series 5, vol. 3.

2 The records are filled with references to this Tantramar nuisance. These examples are from Luke Harrison to William Harrison, 30 June 1774; and John Metcalf to Ann Gill, August 1772, Harrison Family Papers, PANS MG 1, vol. 427. Nathaniel Smith to his brother and sister, 20 June 1774, A. Calabresi, "Letters Home: The Experience of an Emigrant in 18th Century Nova Scotia." Thesis, Yale University 1986.

3 *Tamer* Log, PRO Adm 51/968.

4 Smith to his brother and sister, 30 July 1775, Calabresi, *Letters Home.* Veterans ages: Dixson's from his tombstone at Fort Cumberland (Beauséjour); Eddy's in Porter, *Memoir of Colonel Jonathan Eddy* (Augusta: Sprague, Owen and Nash 1877), 36; and Danks' in DCB.

5 *Tamer* Log, PRO Adm 51/968. The *Tamer* suffered damage: "The *Tamer* has been on shore and is otherwise in so bad a Condition that I am apprehensive she must be Careen'd before she can leave this place." Arbuthnot to Howe, 30 June 1776, NDAR 5, 833–5.

6 "A Journal Kept by Henry Dearborn," *The Magazine Of History with Notes and Queries*, Extra no. 135 (1928): 146–50 (N.S. portion). Dearborn was an American who was captured in Quebec, brought to Halifax, and put aboard HMS *Scarborough* before repatriation.

7 For a detailed analysis of the fort that Goreham viewed that day, see Barbara Schmeisser, "A Narrative and Structural History of Fort Cumberland, 1776–1835," report prepared for Parks Canada, 1983; and her two unpublished reports on the same subject in earlier periods: 1751–1755 and 1755–1768.

8 Allan to Massachusetts Council, 19 February 1777, MA vol. 144, 169–71.

9 Dixon to Butler, 14 January 1776, NA MG 11, vol. 95, 108–11.

10 Delesdernier to Haldimand, 1778, PANS RG 1, vol. 367 1/2.

11 Allan to Massachusetts Council, 21 November 1776, F. Kidder, *Military Operations in Eastern Maine and Nova Scotia During the Revolution* (Albany: Joel Munsell 1867), 166–79.

12 Ibid.

13 Expenditure records of Fort Cumberland show that in the period 4 April to 24 June (Goreham arrived 1 June) an amount of only 204 pounds was spent on the fort; in the next period, 25 June to 24 September, nearly five times that amount was spent (about 1002 pounds); and in the next period, 25 September to 24 December (which period included the siege), nearly twice as much again was spent (about 1850 pounds). NA MG 14, AO 1, Bundle 2531, Roll 664, 48–9.

14 RFA Muster Roll, NA C Series, vol. 1893. See Appendix 2.

15 McDonald to Ogilvie, 24 April 1 1776, "Letterbook of Captain Alexander McDonald of the Royal Highland Emigrants, 1775–1779," *NYHS* (1883). 266–8; Batt to Patterson, 10 July 1777, BHQ Papers; and Arbuthnot to Sandwich, 26 December 1775, *The Private Papers of John, Earl of Sandwich, First Lord of the Admiralty 1771–1782*, vol. 1, eds. G.R. Barnes and J.H. Owen (Navy Records, 1932), 113–15.

16 Allan to Massachusetts Council, 21 November 1776, Kidder, *Military Operations*, 166–79.

17 Morris to Legge, 18 November 1776, The Earl of Dartmouth Papers, mfm in PANS 3953.

18 "Extract of a Letter from Cumberland Nova Scotia," 23 June 1776, *AA* 4, vol. 6, 1043.

19 Ibid.; Arbuthnot to Howe, 30 June 1776, *NDAR* 5, 833–5.

20 Francklin's instructions are in Executive Council, 16 March 1776, PANS RG 1, vol. 212; Bulkeley to Francklin, 21 March 1776, PANS RG 1 vol. 136; and Arbuthnot to Howe, 30 June 1776, *NDAR* 5, 833–5.

21 Arbuthnot to Howe, 30 June 1776, *NDAR* 5, 833–5; and Francklin to Germain, 2 January 1777, B. Murdoch, *A History of Nova Scotia or Acadie* vol. 2 (Halifax: James Barnes 1865), 589–90.

22 Arbuthnot to Germain, 31 January 1777, NA MG 11, vol. 97, 114–15.

23 Shuldham to Sandwich, 9 June 1776, *Sandwich Papers* I, 129.

24 See Clarke, "The Error of Marriot Arbuthnot," *NSHR* 8, 94–107. Admiral Shuldham, Lord Percy, and Bartholomew James sailed on the *Chatham*; Howe sailed on the *Greyhound*, John Knox Laughton, ed., *Journal of Bartholomew James 1752–1828*, (Navey Records 1846) 27. For an account of the retreat, the stay in Halifax, and the journey to New York, see "Kemble's Journal," *NYHS* (1883), 70–9.

25 Edward H. Tatum ed., *The American Journal of Ambroise Serle, Secretary to Lord Howe, 1776–1778* (California: The Hungtington Library 1940), 21.

26 See report of John MacDonald to Germain, 30 October 1776 to 22 March 1777, PRO CO 217, vol. 52.

27 Executive Council Minutes, 3 June 1776, PANS RG 1, vol. 212; and Legge to Dartmouth, 12 July 1774, *DAR* VIII, 148–9. For the women and children who came to Halifax on the evacuation of Boston, see Walter H. Blumenthal, *Women Camp Followers of the American Revolution* (New York: Arno Press 1974), 16.

28 Clarke, "The Error Of Marriot Arbuthnot," 94–107.

29 Ellis to Legge, 2 September 1776, The Earl of Dartmouth Papers, 3944–7. Arbuthnot's charges are confirmed in a memorial of officers of the Nova Scotia Volunteers to General Howe, The Earl of Dartmouth Papers, 3910.

30 Denson to Legge, 7 July 1776; and Gibbons to Legge, 8 June 1776, 14 June 1776, 8 July 1776 (three letters), The Earl of Dartmouth Papers, 3901–7, 3920–5.

31 Ellis to Legge, 2 September 1776, The Earl of Dartmouth Papers, 3944–7.

32 Assembly Proceedings, 20 June 1776, PANS RG 1, vol. 217.

33 William Shaw to Legge, 26 June 1776; Gibbons to Legge, 8 July 1776; and Morris to Legge, 8 July 1776, and 12 July 1776 (two letters), The Earl of Dartmouth Papers, 708, 3916, 3922–7.

34 Assembly Proceedings, 17 June 1776, PANS RG 1, vol. 217.

35 Thomas Brown to Samuel Peters, 30 April 1778, Peters Papers, mfm in PANS.

36 See Clarke, "The Error of Marriot Arbuthnot," 94–107.

37 Member Simeon Perkins attended the dinner: Harold A. Innis, ed., *The Diary of Simeon Perkins 1766–1780* (Toronto: The Champlain Society 1948), 124. Gibbons to Legge, 8 July 1776; and Denson to Legge, 7 July 1776, The Earl of Dartmouth Papers, 3920–5. Arbuthnot to Germain, 8 July 1776, NA MG 11, vol. 96, 92–7.

38 Denson to Legge, 7 July 1776, The Earl of Dartmouth Papers, 3920–1.

39 Ibid.; Gibbons to Legge, 18 June 1776, The Earl of Dartmouth Papers, 3912–13.

40 Bennett to SPG, 5 June 1776, SPG Papers, 604–6; and Bennett to Legge, 21 March 1777, The Earl of Dartmouth Papers, 3963–4.

41 Memorial of John Cort, 8 April 1777, CO 217, vol. 27, 298.

42 Allan to Massachusetts Council, 21 November 1776, Kidder, *Military Operations*, 166–79.

43 Ibid.

44 Ibid.

45 Ibid.

46 They "fell in" with six Fencible deserters, see Rogers Extracts, PCC 41, vol. 8.

47 Allan to Massachusetts Council, 19 February 1777, PANS MG 100, vol. 129.

48 Allan to Massachusetts Council, 21 November 1776, Kidder, *Military Operations*, 166–79.

49 Rogers Extracts, PCC 41, vol. 8, transcript in NA.

50 Rogers Extracts, PCC 41, vol. 8. William D. Williamson, *The History of the State of Maine from its First Discovery, 1602, to the Separation, 1820* vol. 2, (Glazier, Masters and Smith 1839), 451.

51 A resolution for independence was introduced in Congress on 7 June and was approved by Congress in committee on 1 July. It was signed by President John Hancock on 4 July 1776. Copies of the declaration of independence were sent to various state and colonial assemblies the next day. Nova Scotia's copy arrived in Halifax about mid-August but only a portion of it was published in the local *Gazette*.

52 Bulkeley to Harper and Black, 1 July 1776, Claim of Christopher Harper, NA AO 13, Bundle 92. Also Commission Book, PANS RG 1, vol. 168.

53 McDonald to Ogilvie, 24 April 1776, McDonald Letterbook, 266–8. McDonald was responding to an enquiry about property owned by John Hus-

ton, one-time resident of Cumberland. "I don't think it advisable to Lay out money immediately," he warned, but offered to look after the enquirer's interest until the political troubles were past and to consult William Allan about its value. Like any good real estate agent, McDonald exuded optimism: "The affairs in America Must be settled Sometime or another," and he added philosophically, "Land cannot be carried away." Another agent would speculate on land for his client only "when the present storm subsides," see Morris to Desbarres, 27 November 1776, PANS Desbarres Papers, Series 5, vol. 3. William Allan was concerned enough in July to go to Cumberland "immediately to secure his Property," see Morris to Legge, 12 July 1776, The Earl of Dartmouth Papers, 708.

54 Allan to Massachusetts Council, 19 February 1777, PANS MG 100, vol. 129.

55 Throop to Massachusetts Council, 29 May 1777, MA vol. 142, 66–77.

56 Washington to Massachusetts Council, 11 July 1776, and same to Congress, 4 July 1776, John C. Fitzpatrick, ed., The *Writings of George Washington from the Original Manuscript sources 1745–1799*, vol. 5, (Washington: Government Printing Office), 261–2, 220–1. Maugerville Committee to Massachusetts Council, 21 May 1776, *AA* 5, vol. 1, 706.

57 Washington to Massachusetts Council, 11 July 1776, and same to Congress, 4 July 1776, *Writings of Washington* 5, 261–2, 220–1. *JCC*, July 1776, 527. The Maliseet news item in *American Gazette*, 19 June 1776.

58 Memorial of John Cort, 8 April 1777, CO 217, vol. 27, 298.

59 Record of a Conference of the St John and Micmac Native peoples with the Americans, 10 to 17 July 1776, James P. Baxter, *Documentary History of the State of Maine* 24 (Portland: LeFavor-Tower Co. 1910), 165–93.

60 Diary of Caleb Gannett, 1776–77, Houghton Library, Harvard, MS AM 516.3. This portion of the diary is published, see Maurice W. Armstrong, "The Diary of Caleb Gannett for the Year 1776," *The William and Mary Quarterly* 3 (1946), 117–22.

61 Ibid. This royal artifact, which hung in the Massachusetts Council Chamber, now hangs in Trinity Church, Saint John, New Brunswick. For another account of the celebrations in Boston, including the bonfire of royal artifacts, see Edward M. Griffin, *Old Brick Charles Chauncey of Boston 1705–1787* (Minneapolis: University of Minnesota Press 1980), 162.

62 Conference Record, July 1776, Baxter, *History of Maine* 24:165–93.

63 Micmac Chiefs to Massachusetts Council, 19 September 1776, Kidder, *Military Operations*, 57–8.

64 Conference Record, July 1776, Baxter, *History of Maine* 24:165–93.

65 Ibid.

66 Bowdoin to Washington, 30 July 1776, Baxter, *History of Maine* 14:361–2. Washington to Massachusetts Council, 11 July 1776, *Writings of Washington* 5, 261–2.

67 Bowdoin to Washington, 30 July 1776, Baxter, *History of Maine* XIV: 361–2. Regarding Shaw's part, see Massachusetts Council to Captain Lambert, 27 July 1776, *NDAR* 5, 1238.

68 Smith to Massachusetts Council, 22 June 1776, *AA* 5, vol. 1, 703.

69 Jadis to Treasury, 30 March 1787, PRO T1/664, and Claim of Charles Jadis, 24 October 1776, NA AO 13.

70 Allan to Massachusetts Council, 19 February 1777, PANS MG 100, vol. 129.

71 Jadis to Treasury, 30 March 1787, PRO T1/664, and Claim of Charles Jadis, 24 October 1776, NA AO 13.

72 Ibid. See the certificate of the *Viper*'s Captain Samuel Graves, 19 September 1785, PRO T1/664.

73 Jacob Barker to James Simonds, James White And Jarvas Say, 20 June 1776, and appendix dated 24 September 1776, MA vol. 181, 248–9.

74 Ibid.

75 *Massachusetts Resolves*, 26 June 1776, no. 89, 468, mfm at MA.

76 The July rumour of an attack on Nova Scotia was amply mentioned: Executive Council Minutes, 29 June 1776, PANS RG 1, vol. 212; McDonald to Small, early July 1776, McDonald Letterbook, 278; Massey to Germain, 5 July 1776, NA MG 11, vol. 96, 82–6; Arbuthnot to Germain, 8 July 1776, NA MG 11, vol. 96, 92–7; Gibbons to Legge, 8 July 1776, The Earl of Dartmouth Papers, 3922–5; and Feilding to Denbigh, 10 July 1776, Marion Balderston and David Syrett, eds., *The Lost War, Letters from British Officers during the American Revolution* (Horizon Press: New York 1975), 90–2.

77 Arbuthnot to Germain, 8 July 1776, NA MG 11, vol. 96, 92–7.

78 Rogers Extracts, PCC 41, vol. 8; Throop to Massachusetts Council, 29 May 1777, MA vol. 142, 66–77.

79 Allan to Massachusetts Council, 21 November 1776, Kidder, *Military Operations*, 166–79.

80 For the lieutenant-governor's presents to the earl, see Arbuthnot to Sandwich, 11 October 1777, *Sandwich Papers* 1:304–6.

81 Arbuthnot to Germain, 15 August 1776, *DAR* 12, 183–4. See also Arbuthnot to Germain, 8 July 1776, NA MG, vol. 96, 92–7.

82 Diary of Isaac Deschamps, DL.

83 Supreme Court, the King versus Thomas Faulkner, 15 July 1776, PANS RG 39 J, no. 143.

84 Diary of Isaac Deschamps, Dalhousie Library. Further reference to *Little Dyke* farm in Supreme Court, the King versus John Morrison, 31 July 1777, PANS RG 39 C, Box 17.

85 Depositions of Sampson Moore, Peleg Card and Thomas Stevens, PANS RG 1, vol. 342.

86 Population estimates for the Cobequid district are from "Abstract of the Numbers of Families Settled in Nova Scotia," August 1775, The Earl of Dartmouth Papers, 3749–50.

87 Patrick M'Robert, *A Tour Through Part of the North Provinces of America: Being a series of Letters wrote of the spot in the Years 1774 and 1775* (Edinburgh: Printed for the Author 1776), 21; Arbuthnot to Germain, 15 August 1776, *DAR* 12, 183–4.

88 Arbuthnot to Germain, 15 August 1776, *DAR* 12, 183–4. For early studies of the Cobequid district see Israel Longworth, "A Chapter in the History of the Township of Onslow, Nova Scotia," *NSHS* 9 (1895), 41–71; and Thomas Miller, *Historical and Genealogical Record of the First Settlers of Colchester County* (Halifax: A. and W. MacKinlay 1873).

89 Caleb Gannett Diary, Ms Am 516, Houghton Library, Harvard.

90 For the Penobscot refusal see Massachusetts Council to John Taylor, 7 September 1776, Baxter, *History of Maine* 14:378. Council was informed of the Penobscot decision on 27 July and Eddy's intervention was on 2 August: Massachusetts Council to Congress, 2 August 1776, *MA* vol. 195, 165.

91 Charles Baker to Captain Edward Barron, 8 August 1776 enclosed in Massey to Germain, 20 August 1776, *NA MG* 11, vol. 96, 135–40. Barron was assistant engineer at Fort Cumberland. For more on the August rumour see: "New York," 22 August, and "Extract of a Letter from Long Island," 5 September 1776, *The Remembrancer,* Part 2, 343; Feilding to Denbigh, 17 August 1776, *The Lost War,* 96–8; Massey to Germain, 5 September 1776, *NA MG* 11, vol. 96, 143–4; and *New England Chronicle,* 5 September 1776. Cannons would be brought in boats along the shore "for the purpose of attacking the Fort at Cumberland"; see Arbuthnot to Captain Barclay, 15 August 1776, *PANS RG* 1, vol. 136.

92 Claim of Charles Jadis, 24 October 1776, *NA AO* 13; and Jadis to Treasury, 30 March 1787, *PRO* T1/664. For rumours of a loyalist expedition to the St John River and New Hampshire see: "Extract of a Letter from Halifax," 15 August 1776, Almon, John, ed., *The Remembrancer, or Impartial Repository of Public Events* (London 1775–84), part 2, 343; and later in Part III, 140. Reports were also "in the Halifax newspapers," and involved the ship *Tamer.*

93 Jadis to Treasury, 30 March 1787, *PRO* T1/664.

94 For reaction of the Royal Marines to staying in Halifax that summer see Feilding to Denbigh, 23 May 1776, Balderston and Syrett, eds., *The Lost War,* 80–1.

95 Shirley B. Elliott ed., *The Legislative Assembly of Nova Scotia 1758–1983: A Biographical Directory* (Halifax 1984).

96 Washington to Massachusetts Legislature, 2 August 1776, J.C. Fitzgerald, ed., *Writings of Washington* 5, 365.

97 Eddy, How, and Roe to Massachusetts Council, 28 August 1776, *MA* vol. 181, 168–9.

98 Shaw to Massachusetts Council, 28 August 1776, *MA* vol. 195 ,211–13.

99 The Diary of Isaac Deschamps, Dalhousie Library. Morris to Legge, 18 November 1776, The Earl of Dartmouth Papers, 3952–4.

100 Letter to Washington, 8 February 1776, *AA* 4, vol. 5, 936–8; Throop to Massachusetts Council, 29 May 1777, MA, vol. 142, 66–77; Allan to Massachusetts Council, PANS, MG 100, vol. 129. Besides Elijah Ayer Sr, committee-man William Maxwell sold goods to the fort as did Elijah Ayer Jr, George Rogers, and William Eddy (Jonathan's son); see King versus George Rogers et al, PANS, RG 39 C, Box 17, 1777.

101 Allan to Massachusetts Council, 21 November 1776, Kidder, *Military Operations*, 166–79.

102 Throop to Massachusetts Council, 29 May 1777, MA, vol. 142, 66–77. Morris to Legge, 18 November 1776, The Earl of Dartmouth Papers, 3952–4.

103 *Massachusetts Resolves*, 2 September 1776, no. 247, 533. Regarding American authorization, see Eddy to Massachusetts Assembly, 12 November 1776; Lyon to Congress, 26 December 1776, *AA* 5, vol. 3, 626 and 1435–6; and Massachusetts General Court to Hancock, 30 December 1776, PANS, MG 100, vol. 129.

104 *Massachusetts Resolves*, 4 September 1776, no. 258, 538; Eddy to Massachusetts Council, 5 January 1777; and Memorial of Eddy, 1783, Porter, *Memoir of Colonel Jonathan Eddy*, 11–16 and 17. Weather on Wednesday 4 September is from Caleb Gannett's diary, Houghton Library, Harvard. In view of the confusion regarding the timing of Eddy's progress from New England – Kerr, for example placed Eddy in Machias "early in August" – the following chronology is reiterated from sources already cited: 1) Eddy petitions Massachusetts Council 28 August; 2) Eddy visits Caleb Gannett in Boston 4 September; 3) Eddy's supply list is revised same day, 4 September; 4) Eddy receives supplies 5 September; 5) thereafter, Eddy sailed to Machias where he arrived "about the first of October," according to Samuel Rogers. Supporting this, Eddy said he took "about three weeks" to reach Machias. See W.B. Kerr, "The American Invasion of Nova Scotia 1776–7," *CDQ* 8 (October 1935–July 1936), 433–45.

105 Micmac Chiefs to Washington, 19 September 1776, and Allan to Massachusetts Council, 21 November 1776, Kidder, *Military Operations*, 166–79.

106 Ibid. For the phrase "indigent Indians," see L.F.S. Upton, *Micmacs and Colonists: Indian-White Relations in the Maritimes, 1713–1867* (Vancouver: University of British Columbia Press 1979), 71.

107 Ibid.

108 Allan diary, PANS RG 1, vol. 364, no. 96.

109 Rogers Extracts, PCC, 41, vol. 8.

110 *Rainbow* log, PRO Adm 51/761.

111 Ibid.

112 "The War in America 1776. Original Manuscript Journal by Admiral Sir George Collier," NMM, JOD/9, published as Appendix C in *NDAR* 6, 1513–26. Also "A detail of some particular services performed in America

during the years 1776–79 by Sir George Collier," NMM, BGR/28, published in "Biographical memoir of Sir George Collier, Knt., Vice-Admiral of the Blue," *Naval Chronicle* 32 (1814): 265–96 and 353–400.

113 Ibid.

114 *Hope* log PRO Adm 52/1794. Collier even brought American prisoners with him on the *Rainbow.* For instructions on prisoner exchange at Halifax see Howe to Stephens, 31 August 1776; also see Collier's instructions to Thomas Stone "appointed to settle the exchange of Prisoners at Newbury Port," 15 October 1776, both in *NDAR* 6, 373 and 1268–9.

115 Logs of HMS *Hope* and *Diligent,* PRO Adm 52/1794 and 1669; *Whitehall Evening Post,* 12–14 November 1776, *NDAR* 6, 1076; Journal of HMS *Lizard,* *NDAR* 6, 1286; *Perkins Diary*, 133–4; *Independent Chronicle,* 24 October 1776, *NDAR* 6, 1395; Collier Memoir, *Naval Chronicle* 32:400; and Collier entry in *DNB*.

116 Rogers Extracts, PCC, 41, vol. 8.

117 Lyon to Washington (two letters), 25 December 1775, and 16 May 1776, and Lyon to Congress, 26 December 1776, *AA* 4, vol. 4, 460–1, vol. 6, 484–5, and 5th Series, vol. 3, 1435–6; Lyon to Massachusetts Council, September 1776, Baxter, *History of Maine* 14:379– 84. Lyon was in Nova Scotia six years (1765–71), residing in Halifax, Onslow, and Pictou. Lyon's claim that he knew the men of influence in Nova Scotia is partially borne out by Executive Councillor Arthur Goold who knew Lyon when he was in Halifax and who thought him "a man of humane feeling." Goold to Lyon, 20 May 1777, PANS RG 1, vol. 409.

118 Ibid.

119 Eddy to Massachusetts Council, 5 January 1777, Porter, *Memoir of Colonel Jonathan Eddy,* 11–16; Rogers Extracts, PCC, 41, vol. 8; Tupper to Massachusetts Assembly, 27 November 1776, *AA* 5, vol. 3, 881–2. John Mitchell and Richard Parsons later settled on the St John River in Burton, see Studholme's Report, *NBHS* I, 100–18. For others in the American contingent see Muster Roll of Jabez West's Company, 1776, MA, vol. 37, f11, 59; and Appendix 1. Both James Hanney and W.O. Raymond incorrectly placed Mitchell and Parsons in the St John River contingent: see Hanney, "The Maugerville Settlement," *NBHS* 1 (1894): 76; and Raymond, "At Portland Point," series of papers, *The New Brunswick Magazine* 1 and 2 (Saint John 1898, 1899), 276.

120 Lyon to Congress, 26 December 1776, *AA* 5, vol. 3, 1435–6.

121 Rogers Extracts, PCC, 41, vol. 8. Whoever should lead an expedition against Nova Scotia, the Reverend Lyon promised on 25 December 1775 to "pray for his success, as I ever do that God may smile on all the American arms." Coastal trade between Machias and Boston resumed after the British evacuation of Boston in March; see for example the recollection of Ephraim Chase, John C. Dann ed., *The Revolution Remembered, Eyewitness*

Accounts of the War for Independence (Chicago: University of Chicago Press 1980).

122 Allan diary, PANS, RG 1, vol. 364, no. 96.

123 Eddy to Massachusetts Council, 5 January 1777, Porter, *Memoir of Colonel Jonathan Eddy,* 11–16. Known members of the Passamaquoddy contingent (listed in Appendix I) are from treason indictments, PANS RG 1, vol. 342, and Muster Roll of Jabez West's Company, MA vol. 37, f11, 59. Michael Francklin heard that Eddy's force included Penobscot and Passama-quoddy Native members but nowhere else is this mentioned, not even in Eddy's first-hand account. See Francklin to Pernette, 9 December 1776, PANS MG 100, vol. 143, no. 22.

124 Executive Council Minutes, 16 October 1776, PANS RG 1, vol. 212; peti-tion of inhabitants of Barrington to Massachusetts Council, 19 October 1776, *NDAR* 6, 1328–9; see also Bulkeley to magistrates of Liverpool, Yarmouth, and Barrington, 16 October 1776, PANS RG 1, vol. 136.

125 Eddy to Massachusetts Council, 5 January 1777, Porter, *Memoir of Colonel Jonathan Eddy,* 11–16.

126 Sunbury Committee to Massachusetts Council, 24 September 1776, MA, vol. 181, 247–7a.

127 Known members of the St John River contingent (listed in Appendix I) are in Muster Roll of Jabez West's Company, MA, vol. 37, f11, 59 and Stud-holme's Report, *NBHS* 1, 100–18. The Roe family was also living in Sun-bury in 1775, see census, W.O. Raymond, *The River St. John, Physical Features, Legends and History, from 1604 to 1784* (Saint John: J.A. Bowes 1910), 279. Indications are that the Reverend Seth Noble was a member of the contingent; however, it should be noted that his first child was born to his teenaged wife 5 August 1777, precisely nine months from Novem-ber, the siege month, L. Boltwood, *The Descendants of Thomas Noble* (Hart-ford 1878), 211.

128 For what may have been the last time that Maliseets returned to Meductic with New England prisoners see Edward P. Hamilton, tr. and ed., *Adven-ture in the Wilderness, The American Journals of Louis Antoine de Bougainville 1756–1760,* (University of Oklahoma Press), 137.

129 *New England Chronicle,* 5 September 1776.

130 Chief Tomah's policy reported in Hawker to Collier, 4 July 1777, NA MG 11, vol. 97, 221–30.

131 The idea of financing an invasion on "Tory" plunder is outlined in Throop to Massachusetts Council, 29 May 1777, MA, vol. 142, 66–77. Committee support of Maliseet families is in Preble to Massachusetts Council, 27 January 1777, Baxter, *History of Maine* 14:405–7. Shaw's reaf-firmation of Native service pay is also in this Preble letter.

132 Preble to Massachusetts Council, 27 January 1777, Baxter, *History of Maine* 14:405–7.

133 The members of the Maliseet contingent (listed in Appendix I) are in
"Return of Indians present in the Expedition against Fort Cumberland,"
17 December 1776, AA 5, vol. 3, 1269. The Pierre Tomah in this return
was not Grand Chief Pierre Tomah. A clue lies in the return in which the
name "Pierre Tomah" is not prefaced by any title. Patriot references to
Chief Tomah and other Native leaders invariably used the title "Chief,"
"Governor," or "Captain" to signify position. The fact that Ambroise
St Aubin, second chief of the Maliseets, is cited as "Governor" in the same
return makes it even less likely that Chief Tomah would have appeared
untitled in the same return. St Aubin was the leader, or "Governor," of the
Native contingent which included another Pierre Tomah. At least one
other Pierre Tomah capable of bearing arms lived in the region and this
Pierre Tomah and Chief Pierre Tomah both appear in a "Return of Indians and their Familys," prepared by John Allan 28 July 1780, Kidder, *Military Operations*, 284–5.

134 Conference Record, July 1776, Baxter, *History of Maine* 24:165–93.

135 A report in the *Boston Gazette*, 27 December 1776, indicates that Eddy left
Maugerville on 22 October, seven days before capturing Walker's outpost
on 29 October. The role of the St John River inhabitants in the revolution
is described in James Hanney, *History of New Brunswick* (Saint John: J.A.
Bowes 1909); William O. Raymond, "The Fall of Quebec to the American
Revolution" (24), "The Maliseets" (25), "The English on the River
St. John" (26), "The Forest Primeval" (27), "The Revolutionary War"
(28): a serial, *The Woodstock Dispatch*, 1896; William O. Raymond, *Glimpses
of the Past: History of the River St. John, A.D. 1604–1784* (Saint John 1905);
and Raymond, *The River St. John*.

136 Rogers Extracts, PCC, 41, vol. 8. For the seaworthiness of Native canoes
see Henry Grace, *The History of the Life and Sufferings of Henry Grace*, "written by Himself," (Reading: 1764).

CHAPTER THREE

1 Deposition of Sampson Moore, 16 November 1776, PANS RG 1, vol. 342.

2 Petition of thirty-three "dutiful and loyal subjects" of the townships of
Hopewell, Hillsborough, and Memramcook River, The Earl of Dartmouth
Papers, 992–4.

3 Allan's Journal, PANS RG 1, vol. 364. The Shepody Outpost was probably
established between 18 September when John Allan "set off for Cocagne"
and 25 September when he returned and "Received advice that Col.
Gorham had gone to Chepody with a party of Soldiers."

4 Joseph Goreham's Journal, NA *Report* 1894, 355.

5 "An authentic List of the Naval and Military force in the Province of Nova
Scotia, 13 August 1776," *The Remembrancer* 1776, 265–6.

6 Claim of John Walker, 1783, PRO AO 13.

7 Walker was in a ranger detachment (led by Captain Benoni Danks) that killed and scalped three Frenchpeople in a raid on an Acadian village on the Petitcodiac River, 1 July 1758. Arthur G. Doughty, ed., *An Historical Journal of the Campaigns in North America for the years 1757, 1758, 1759 and 1760 by Captain John Knox* vol. 1, (Toronto: The Champlain Society 1914), 196–8. For his military service, Walker received a land grant in Cumberland but might never have lived there. See "A State of the Township of Cumberland, November 1767," PANS RG 20 C, vol. 86.

8 Petition of thirty-three inhabitants, The Earl of Dartmouth Papers, 992–4.

9 Delesdernier to Haldimand, [1778], PANS RG 1, vol. 367 1/2.

10 Charles Baker to Edward Barron, 8 August 1776, NA MG 11, vol. 96, 139–40.

11 *Juno* log and journal, PRO Adm 52/1811.

12 "The War in America by Sir George Collier," NMM JOD/9.

13 Collier to Sandwich, 21 November 1776, *NDAR* 7, 228.

14 "The War in America by Sir George Collier," NMM JOD/9.

15 For sails in Native canoes, see *Life and Sufferings of Henry Grace*, 29, 30.

16 Eddy Account, F. Kidder, *Military Operations in Eastern Maine and Nova Scotia During the Revolution* (Albany: Joel Munsel 1867), 67. Peck family, Wright, *Planters and Pioneers*, 219. Ruth Peck was an Estabrooks whose sister Sarah married the Reverend Job Seamons (see Seamons' diary). The marriage of Sarah Estabrooks and Job Seamons, 10 August 1769, is recorded in the Sackville Township Book (mfm at PANS).

17 Abiel Peck was one of the thirty-three "dutiful and loyal subjects," who signed the Hopewell petition, The Earl of Dartmouth Papers, 992–4. Despite its title, this document can hardly be regarded as a loyalty test since Richard Uniacke, one of Eddy's patriot soldiers, also signed it.

18 Goreham Journal, 355.

19 Isbrook Eddy recollection, William D. Williamson, *The History of the State of Maine from its First Discovery, 1602, to Separation, 1820* vol. 2, (Glazier, Masters and Smith 1839), 451.

20 Goreham Journal, 355. The land between the Petitcodiac and Memramcook Rivers is known as Fort Folly Point, a name derived either from the French fortification located there in the 1750s or from Joseph Goreham's 1776 outpost. According to local tradition the point was also used as a supply depot by Eddy. Alan Rayburn, *Geographical Names of New Brunswick* (Ottawa 1975), 109.

21 Claim of John Walker, PRO AO 13.

22 Ibid. King's death is in RFA Muster Roll, NA RG 8, vol. 1893.

23 For the names of the RFAs captured at the Shepody Outpost see Appendix 2 and RFA Muster Roll, NA RG 8, vol. 1893. Eddy claimed that he captured fourteen men (including Walker) and his son Isbrook thought they had captured sixteen men.

24 Williamson, *History of Maine,* 452. Eddy's account does not record the date
   of the Shepody landing; neither do accounts of other patriots. The best
   source is Goreham's Journal in which the Colonel stated (entry
   4 November) that Eddy landed "on Tuesday the 29th [October]" and the
   information was given him that day (4 November) by those who visited
   Ruth Peck the day before. Supporting this date is the fact that the soldiers
   of the Shepody Outpost were captured 29 October (RFA Muster Roll) and
   Eddy said that he attacked the outpost "immediately." In the second part of
   his journal written over a week later and in which he merely summarized
   early events of the siege, Goreham recorded 25 October as the date of the
   landing. Considering all factors, the most likely date of the patriot landing
   in Cumberland County is Tuesday 29 October.
25 Goreham Journal, 359.
26 Eddy Account, 67.
27 Baxter, *Documentary History of Maine* 24:165–93.
28 Delesdernier to Haldimand, [1778], and same to Goreham, 30 October
   1778 (two letters), PANS RG 1, vol. 367 1/2.
29 Eddy to Massachusetts Council, 3 November 1776, Baxter, Documentary
   History of Maine XIV, 394–5. Walker and the other prisoners were probably
   transported to New England on 3 November and some had reached Boston by early December. "Last Monday [2 December] two prisoners were
   brought to town, who were lately taken near Fort Cumberland, and committed to gaol." *Boston Gazette,* 9 December 1776.
30 Claim of John Walker, PRO AO 13.
31 *Juno* log, PRO Adm 52/1811.
32 Goreham Journal, 355. The name of provision sloop *Polly* is in John Allan's
   Daybook (original in Bangor Public Library).
33 Arbuthnot to Germain, 30 March 1777, NA MG 11, VOL. 97, 143–4. HMS
   Secretary had earlier assumed (Germain to Arbuthnot, 14 January 1777)
   that the provision vessel was armed; this prompted Arbuthnot to provide
   this description.
34 Goreham Journal, 359. The Fencibles did not get their uniforms until after
   the siege. A consignment of 1,000 uniforms reached Halifax from England
   late in September but they were for the Loyal Nova Scotia Volunteers.
   None was sent out for the Fencibles. However, the Volunteers had achieved
   only about half of their quota leaving Arbuthnot with a surplus of 500 uniforms on his hands and since he knew that "it is with the utmost difficulty
   that I can procure a place to store them [except] at an extravagant rate,"
   he asked to reassign them to Goreham's regiment. These extra uniforms
   were placed on ships that did not reach Fort Cumberland until after the
   siege. "The Uniforms are green turned up with White," described Arbuthnot, "and White Waistcoats and Breeches." Arbuthnot to Howe,
   11 November 1776, NA MG 11, vol. 96, 372–5. The uniforms arrived in the

Newcastle Jane, Captain Murdoch Maclaine to a Gentleman, *Public Advertiser*, London, 8 January 1777.

35 *Juno* log, PRO Adm 52/1811.

36 Eddy Account, 67. For Acadian recruits see Appendix I and "An Abstract of Pay Roll of a Company of Frenchmen raised in the County of Cumberland ... of Nova Scotia by Captain Isaiah Boudreau under the Command of Colonel Jonathan Eddy in 1776." MA 55, folio 52.

37 Unsigned letter from Newburyport, Massachusetts, 19 December 1776, AA 5, vol. 3, 1305. Also, *Boston Gazette*, 27 December 1776.

38 Eddy Account, 67.

39 Charles Dixon and William Black, "Justices of the Peace and Officers of the Volunteer Militia In behalf of themselves and 150 Yorkshire and other well affected Inhabitants of the County of Cumberland" to Massey, 9 January 1777, NA MG 11, vol. 97, 122–5.

40 Matthew Richey, *A Memoir of the Late Rev. William Black, Wesleyan Minister, Halifax, N.S.* (Halifax: William Cunnabell 1839), 11.

41 Dixon and Black to Massey, 9 January 1777, NA MG 11, vol. 97, 122–5.

42 Ibid.

43 Richey, *A Memoir of the Late Rev. William Black*, 11.

44 Allan to Massachusetts Council, 19 February 1777, PANS RG 1, vol. 365, 1–11.

45 Committees of Cumberland and Sunbury to Massachusetts Council, 17 December 1776, PANS RG 1, vol. 365, 1–4.

46 Allan to Massachusetts Council, 19 February 1777, PANS RG 1, vol. 365, 1–11.

47 Committees of Cumberland and Sunbury to Massachusetts Council, 17 December 1776, PANS RG 1, vol. 365, 1–4.

48 Allan to Massachusetts Council, 19 February 1777, PANS RG 1, vol. 365, 1–11.

49 Ibid.

50 *Juno* log, PRO Adm 52/1811.

51 For the names of the four Micmacs who joined Eddy see Appendix I and MA 37, folio 149, published in *Les Cahiers* 7, no. 1, Mars 1976.

52 Micmac nation to Massachusetts Council, 21 November 1776, Kidder, *Military Operations*, 57–8.

53 *Juno* log and journal, PRO Adm 52/1811. For Dalrymple's orders see Collier to Sandwich, 21 November 1776, NDAR 7, 228. *Juno*'s features are in "Disposition of His Majesty's Ships & Vessels..," 18 September 1776, NDAR 6, 894. *Juno* had a complement of 220 men.

54 *Lizard* journal, PRO Adm 51/550.

55 Beverley and Moody, *The Journal of Henry Alline*, 182. The activities of some American privateers, according to John Allan, "will occasion more Torys

than 100 Such Expeditions Will make good." Letter of John Allan, 17 August 1778, Kidder, *Military Operations*, 256.

56 The Council member advocating privateering was Charles Morris; see Morris to Desbarres, 19 November 1776, PANS Desbarres Papers, Series 5, vol. 3.

57 Eagleson to SPG, 15 September 1770, SPG Papers, no. 158, 461.

58 For Eagleson' Presbyterian background see Esther C. Wright, *The Petitcodiac* (Sackville: Tribune Press 1945), 44, 45, and *Samphire Greens: The Story of the Steeves* by the same author, 8–17.

   For Eagleson's travels while stationed at Cumberland see Eagleson to SPG, 27 December 1773 and 16 January 1775 (two letters), SPG Papers, no. 182, 541, and no. 186, 548–9; Halifax SPG Board, 11 April 1775 and 1 May 1775, SPG Papers, no. 194, 569, 571–2; and Journals of the SPG, 15 August 1772, vol. 19, 361.

   Eagleson's support of schools is found in his letter to SPG, 15 September 1770, SPG Papers, no. 158, 461. Also, Halifax SPG Board, 11 April 1775, SPG Papers, no. 194, 569, and 1 May 1775, 572. Two schoolmasters hired in 1774–75 by Eagleson under the auspices of the SPG were a Mr Throop and a Mr Porter. The former probably was Josiah Throop.

59 Journals of the SPG, letter of Eagleson, 4 July 1778, vol. 21, 330.

60 Proceedings of SPG, 25 March 1771, SPG Papers, no. 152, 427.

61 Eagleson to SPG, 16 January 1775, SPG Papers, no. 186, 552.

62 Eagleson to Butler, 27 January 1776, NA MG 11, vol. 95, 117.

63 Eagleson vs. Oulton et al., Halifax County Supreme Court, PANS RG 39 C, Box 20, 1779.

64 Eagleson to SPG, 25 March 1771, SPG Papers, no. 152, 427.

65 Breynton to SPG, 23 October 1767, SPG Papers, no. 121, 318.

66 *Juno* log and journal, PRO Adm 52/1811. The accurate dates of *Juno*'s arrival (31 October) and its departure (3 November) are from the ship's logbook and journal. The other source is Goreham's Journal in which he recalled in his entry of 4 November that *Juno* arrived 29 October and "sailed soon after." Sometime after 11 November he thought it had arrived 25 October and "soon after sailed."

67 Eddy to Machias Committee, 3 November 1776, AA 5, vol. 3, 627.

68 Beverley and Moody, *The Journal of Henry Alline*, 77.

69 Ellis to SPG, 14 September 1776, SPG Papers, 617.

70 Goreham Journal, 355. The source of the date of 3 November for sending the command boat to Shepody is Goreham's Journal. On 4 November he stated that he sent the boat "yesterday" when he clearly had no knowledge of Eddy's invasion or the capture of his outpost. He also stated then (4 November) that the boat "returned immediately" with the news. Sometime after 11 November when he was summarizing these early events in the second instalment of his journal, he recalled that the boat was sent to Shepody on 4 November and returned immediately. From his remarks and their

context, and because of the distance to Shepody, it can be reasonably de-
duced that the boat was sent 3 November and returned the following day.
71 Ibid.

CHAPTER FOUR

1 John Hall to his brother, 12 December 1778, E. Poole, *Annals Of Yarmouth
And Barrington, Nova Scotia, in the Revolutionary War* (Yarmouth: J. Murray
Lawson 1899), 94–5.
2 Diary of Thomas Calhoun 1771, serialized in *Chignecto Post*, 26 October
1876 to 8 February 1877.
3 Ibid.
4 Goreham Journal *NA Report* 1894, 355. The soldier may have been Private
David Dobson, RFA Muster Roll, NA RG 8, vol. 1893.
5 Goreham Journal, 355.
6 John Robinson and Thomas Rispin, *Journey Through Nova Scotia Containing a
Particular Account of the Country and Its Inhabitants* (York, England: "Printed
for the Authors by C. Etherington" 1774), 11.
7 *Albany* and *Rainbow* logs, PRO Adm 51/23 and 517/61.
8 Arbuthnot to Howe, 11 November 1776, NA MG 11, vol. 96, 373.
9 Executive Council Minutes, 5 November 1776, PANS RG 1, vol. 212, 328;
and Bulkeley to Collier, 5 November 1776, PANS RG 1, vol. 136.
10 Collier's orders to Michael Hyndman, HMS *Albany*, 6 November 1776, NA
MG 11, vol. 96, 326–8.
11 Goreham Journal, 356.
12 Eddy Account, F. Kidder, *Military Operations in Eastern Maine and Nova Scotia
During the Revolution* (Albany: Joel Munsell 1867), 68.
13 Goreham Journal, 356.
14 Eagleson vs. Oulton et al., Halifax Supreme Court, PANS RG 39 C, Box 20,
1779.
15 Eagleson to SPG, 16 January 1775, SPG Papers, 73, no. 186, 552; and Proceedings of SPG, 11 April 1775, SPG Papers, no. 194, 576.
16 Eagleson vs. Oulton et al., 1779.
17 Ibid.
18 Journals of the SPG, vol. 21, 330.
19 Delesdernier to Haldimand, 1778, PANS RG 1, vol. 367 1/2.
20 Robinson and Rispin, *Journey Through Nova Scotia*, 15, 27. Description of the
Harper home in Nathaniel Smith to his brother and sister, 20 June 1774,
Calabresi, *Letters Home.*
21 Harper was appointed magistrate 1 July 1776, Arbuthnot to Harper and
Black, in Harper Claim, PRO AO 13, Bundle 92.
22 Harper vs. Clarke et al., Halifax Supreme Court, PANS RG 39 C, Box 22,
1780.

23 Eagleson vs. Oulton et al., 1779.

24 Goreham Journal, 356.

25 Ibid.

26 Arbuthnot to Shuldham, 15 February 1776, Neeser, *Shuldham Despatches*, 145–7.

27 Eddy Account, 68. James Brenton Bench Book PANS. The *Boston Gazette*, 27 December 1776, reported several boats captured.

28 Hall to his brother, 12 December 1778, Poole, *Annals Of Yarmouth And Barrington*, 94. Hall was a member of the Assembly for Annapolis until 1776 when he was expelled for non-attendance, the same day and for the same reason as John Allan. He was also a rum dealer: in the years 1776 and 1777 respectively, he purchased 350 gallons and 435 1/2 gallons of rum in Halifax; see W.A. Calnek, *History of the County of Annapolis* (Ontario: Mika Studio 1972), 336–7.

29 Eddy Account, 68.

30 Ibid.

31 Goreham Journal, 356.

32 Eddy Account, 68.

33 Ibid.

34 Committees of Cumberland and Sunbury to Massachusetts Council, 17 December 1776, PANS RG 1, vol. 365.

35 Collier to Sandwich, 21 November 1776, PRO Adm 1/1611–12, (*NDAR* 7, 228–30). Collier was really criticizing the army in this passage of his letter to the naval lord. These remarks were expurgated from his similar letter of the same date to secretary Germain.

36 Goreham Journal, 356.

37 Eddy Account, 68.

38 Ibid.

39 Eddy to Massachusetts Council, 12 November 1776, AA 5 vol. 3, 626.

40 Committees of Cumberland and Sunbury to Massachusetts Council, 17 December 1776, PANS RG 1, vol. 365.

41 Goreham Journal, 356.

42 Eddy Account, 69.

43 Goreham Journal, 356.

44 Eddy Account, 69.

45 Goreham Journal, 359, 356.

46 Ibid., 360.

47 Ibid., 356, 360.

48 Delesdernier to Haldimand, [1778], PANS RG 1, vol. 367 1/2.

49 Goreham Journal, 356.

50 Massey to Germain, 17 January 1777, NA MG 11, vol. 97, 96–9.

51 James Brenton Bench Book, mfm at PANS.

52 Goreham Journal, 360.

53 Ibid.

54 In 1759, during the struggle for Quebec, atrocities were committed on both sides and Joseph Goreham, then a young captain in Goreham's Rangers, did not remain on the sidelines.

July 1759, Quebec: "We were alarmed by a smart firing of musketry in the woods ... occasioned by a party of Indians coming down to annoy our camp, for whom Captain Goreham and his Rangers laid in ambush and scalped nine of them."

August 1759, Quebec: "Captain has sent an express to the General to acquaint him that he has burned a large settlement and made some prisoners; that his Rangers met with some Canadians dressed like Indians; had routed them, and took a few scalps."

September 1759, Quebec: "The detachments ... under ... Captain Goreham who went down the river ... are returned: they took a great quantity of black cattle and sheep; an immense deal of plunder, such as household stuff, books and apparel; burned above 1100 houses, and destroyed several hundred acres of corn, besides some fisheries; they made 60 prisoners." Arthur G. Doughty, ed., *An Historical Journal of the Campaigns in North America for the years 1757, 1758, 1759 and 1760 by Captain John Knox* vol. 1, (Toronto: the Champlain Society 1914), 394–5; vol. 2, 26, 136.

55 Goreham Journal, 361, 363.

56 Eddy to Massachusetts Council, 12 November 1776, James P. Baxter, *Documentary History of the State of Maine* 14 (Portland: LeFavor-Tower Co. 1910), 395.

57 Recollection of Isbrook Eddy, William D. Williamson, *The History of the State of Maine from its First Discovery, 1602, to Separation, 1820* vol. 2, (Glazier, Masters and Smith 1839), 452.

58 Josiah Throop to Massachusetts Council, 23 December 1776, PANS RG 1, vol. 364.

59 Eddy Account, 68.

60 John Hall to his brother, 12 December 1778, Poole, *Annals of Yarmouth and Barrington*, 94–5. Hall eventually got his boat back, but James Law never did. His boat, which was taken at the same time, was burned by Eddy's men, see James Brenton Bench Book, mfm at PANS.

61 Eddy Account, 69.

62 Certification of the claim of Christopher Harper by officers of the garrison, PRO AO 13, Bundle 92.

63 Delesdernier to Goreham, 3 October 1778, PANS RG 1, vol. 367.

64 Claim of Christopher Harper, 16 February 1784, PRO AO 13.

65 James Brenton Bench Book, mfm at PANS.

66 Claim of Edward Barron, PRO AO 13, Bundle 26.

67 Isaac Deschamps Court Book, PANS RG 39 C.

68 Goreham Journal, 360.

69 Ibid., 356, 360.

70 Goreham Manifesto, 7 November 1776, NA *Report* 1894, 363–4.

71 Goreham Journal, 356.

72 Ibid. Names of the soldiers are from RFA Muster Roll, NA RG 8, vol. 1893, see Appendix 2.

73 Throop to Massachusetts Council, 23 December 1776, PANS RG 1, vol. 364.

74 The Pictonians with Eddy were chiefly former Cumberlanders. The Earle family was heavily represented in this contingent, the size of which is unknown. The date of their arrival in Camphill and whether they arrived as a group, are also unknown. For known members see Appendix I.

75 The Cobequid contingent amounted to about twenty-five men who probably arrived in Camphill at different times. William Milburn arrived in Camphill on 12 November, after which "another [contingent] arrived from Cobequid in the Rebell Army's Camp, about 25 men who joined the Rebells." Milburn Deposition, 10 January 1777, Bulmer, "Trials for Treason in 1776–7," NSHS 1, 115–16. James Yuall claimed that "two or three" Onslow men went to Camphill as early as 8 November. Yuall Deposition, 16 November 1776, PANS RG 1, vol. 342. The chief source for the Cobequid names is the Muster Roll of Jabez West's Company 1776, MA vol. 37, f.11, 59. For the ten names that can be verified, see Appendix I. Their leader "Devil Tom" Faulkner was the son of Edward and Martha (Stewart) Faulkner. Gertrude G. Sanborn, "Genealogies on Families Settling Both in New England and Nova Scotia" (unpublished 1961), copy at PANS.

76 Delesdernier to Haldimand, 1778, and same to Goreham, 3 October 1778, PANS RG 1 vol. 367 1/2.

77 *Lizard* log, PRO Adm 51/550.

78 Francklin to Pernette, 9 December 1776, PANS MG 100, vol. 143.

79 Goreham Journal, 356.

80 Delesdernier to Goreham, 3 October 1778, PANS RG 1 vol. 367 1/2.

81 Tupper to Massachusetts Council, 27 November 1776, Baxter, *Documentary History of Maine* 14:399.

82 "[I] have been in several vessels that was in his Majesty's service Guarding the Coast in the Bay of Fundy out of Windsor in the province of Nova Scotia and had the misfortune to be Lame with the hurts and Coalds Received there": one naval militiamember's description of such service in Fundy waters. Petition of James Yorke to Thomas Carleton, 1785, PANB Land Papers. Yorke, who was from Falmouth (and a neighbour of Henry Alline), moved to the St John River after the revolution where he was compensated for his loyal service and later settled near Woodstock, New Brunswick.

83 Francklyn to Pernette, 9 December 1776, PANS MG 100, vol. 143. Without the benefit of the additional sources J.B. Brebner concluded incorrectly that Francklin's volunteer militia had refused to go to Cobequid to retake the ferry and that army regulars had to do the job; see John B. Brebner, *The Neutral Yankees of Nova Scotia, a Marginal Colony during the Revolutionary Years* (New York: Columbia University Press 1937), 248. This would have been a minor error had he not compounded it by inferring that the militia refused generally to provide any assistance during the siege of Fort Cumberland. See note 51, Chapter 6 above.

84 Francklyn to Pernette, 9 December 1776, PANS MG 100, vol. 143.

85 Depositions of James Yuall, Mary and Robert Morrison, and Sampson Moore, 16 November 1776, PANS RG 1, vol. 342.

86 For details of the visit of Captain William Carleton and the privateers to Cobequid, see the interrogation of Charles Dickson, 23 November 1776 and his indictment; the deposition of John Cole, 31 October 1776; the deposition of Peleg Card, 7 November 1776; and the depositions of Emmus McNutt, Sampson Moore, Robert Morrison, Abner McNutt, Thomas Stevens, and James Yuall, all sworn in Windsor 16 November 1776, PANS RG 1, vol. 342.

87 Arbuthnot to Germain, 17 November 1776; Collier's orders to James Feattus, *Vulture*, 9 November 1776, NA MG 11, vol. 96, 369, and 329; Collier to Sandwich, 21 November 1776, *NDAR* 7, 229.

88 Collier's orders to Feattus, 9 November 1776, NA MG 11, vol. 96, 329–31.

89 Feattus Papers, PRO Adm 1, 1790.

90 Collier's orders to Feattus, 9 November 1776, NA MG 11, vol. 96, 329–31; *Vulture* journal, NMM Adm L/V/126.

91 Goreham Journal, 357. This letter was in the handwriting of Edward Barron Jr.

92 Delesdernier to Haldimand, [1778], and same to Goreham, 5 October 1778, PANS RG 1, vol. 367 1/2.

93 Goreham Journal, 357.

94 The Wethered incident is from Charles E. Knapp, "Folklore About Old Fort Beausejour," *Acadiensis* 8, October 1908, 300; and Will R. Bird, *A Century At Chignecto: The Key To Old Acadia* (Toronto: Ryerson Press 1928), 227–8. Although Kerr said that this incident "need not be taken seriously" (see Kerr, "The American Invasion of Nova Scotia," *CDQ* [October 1936], 444) and later historians have generally followed his advice, it is fully corroborated by primary evidence from at least two sources: Francklin to Pernette, 9 December 1776, PANS MG 100, vol. 143; and Halifax County Probate, Wethered Papers, PANS RG 48, Reel 425. Not only is there no doubt that Wethered was wounded in the manner described by Knapp and Bird, other details, such as Wethered's deal with the garrison, are supported by the primary evidence.

95 Goreham Journal, 361.
96 Richey, *Memoir of William Black*, 11–12. See also "An Account of Mr. Will-iam Black, Written by Himself," a series in eight parts, *Arminian Magazine*, 1791.
97 Robinson and Rispin, *Journey Through Nova Scotia*, 15.
98 Goreham Journal, 357.
99 Claim of Christopher Harper, PRO AO 13, Bundle 92.
100 Allan Journal, PANS RG 1, vol. 364; Gannett Diary, Houghton Library, Harvard.

CHAPTER FIVE

1 William D. Williamson, *The History of the State of Maine from Its First Discov-ery, 1602, to the Separation, 1820* (Glazier, Masters, and Smith 1839), 452.
2 A colonel's commission for Eddy was granted by the Massachusetts Coun-cil 28 December 1776, a month after the siege ended. PANS RG 1, vol. 364.
3 In 1750 Henry Grace, a soldier at Fort Lawrence, wrote that "The Coun-try in Summer is very delightful but People who are not used to it are al-most devoured by the Musquitos and black Flies ... Whoever goes to the Side of the Woods cannot see twenty Yards before their Faces in calm Weather, there are such Clouds of Musquitos and black Flies." Henry Grace, *The History of the Life and Sufferings of Henry Grace* (Reading, Eng. 1764), 7.
4 Harold A. Innis, ed., *The Diary of Simeon Perkins, 1766–1780* (Toronto: The Champlain society 1948), 125. Arbuthnot called Smith "one of the most distinguished and Popular Clergymen in the whole District." Ar-buthnot to Smith, 4 December 1776, PANS RG 1, vol. 136.
5 I.F. MacKinnon, *Settlements and Churches in Nova Scotia, 1749–1776* (Mon-treal: Walter Press 1930), see in particular 97.
6 *Perkins Diary*, 136–7.
7 Clifford K. Shipton, *Sibley's Harvard Graduates* (Boston 1970), vols. 12 and 17.
8 Goreham Journal, NA Report 1894, 357.
9 Francklin to Joseph Pernette, 9 December 1776, PANS MG 100, vol. 143. The information in Francklin's private letter is confirmed by the public record. Probate records for Halifax County verify that Wethered was "wounded by a Cannon Ball from the Garrison of Fort Cumberland when the Rebells invaded the Country in the Fall of 1776." Thus another of Charles Knapp's stories is proven true.
10 Goreham Journal, 357.
11 Eddy to Goreham, [10 November 1776], NA Report 1894, 364.
12 Ibid.; Goreham to Eddy, 10 November 1776, NA Report 1894, 364.

13 Ibid.; Goreham Journal, 361.

14 Ibid.; [Throop] to Goreham, [11 November 1776], 365.

15 Deposition of William Milburn, 10 January 1777, J.T. Bulmer, "Trials For Treason," NSHS 1 (1879):115.

16 Goreham Journal, 361. James Brenton's Bench Book, mfm. at PANS. Thomas Dixson's role in carrying news of the siege to Windsor and Halifax has been immortalized with a bronze plaque at the restored fort but that of Charles Dixon is unknown, and is not mentioned in the Dixon Papers or in the book about Charles Dixon written by his descendent. See Justice Brenton's notes of the sworn testimony of Charles Dixon in the case of Allan vs. Law, 1782.

17 Goreham Journal, 361.

18 Ibid. Materials from at least one adjacent farm were confiscated for use in the last minute repairs to the fort. Fences, timber, rails, posts, bricks, and boards were taken from the farm of William Allan (not Inverary Farm also owned by William Allan and occupied by John Allan) who was living in Halifax at the time and who later sued to recover the loss. See Halifax County Supreme Court cases, William Allan vs. Thomas Batt, Joseph Goreham, and James Law (three separate suits), PANS RG 39 C, Box 19, 1779.

19 Deposition of Major Matthew Winniett and George Thompson, 23 July 1777. See also the attached sworn statements, particularly that of Thomas Harris, and the "Return of men raised by Col. Shaw of the Annapolis Militia," PANS RG 1, vol. 222, no. 56 and no. 60.

20 Deposition of William Milburn, Bulmer, "Trials For Treason," 115.

21 Eddy Account, 72. Eddy's theory that if he had more officers many "disorderly actions" could have been prevented was undermined by the excesses of his senior officers, notably How and Roe.

22 Deposition of William Milburn, Bulmer, "Trials For Treason," 115.

23 Eddy Account, 69.

24 Ibid. Josiah Throop likewise underestimated the strength of the garrison at "about a Hundred men." Throop to Massachusetts Council, 23 December 1776, PANS RG 1, vol. 364, no. 30.

25 Goreham Journal, 360. One civilian worker was John Anderson of Cumberland (not the John Anderson of the St John River), "who was Employed as Principal Carpenter ... in the Engineers' branch of Works in this Garrison," and who "when the Fort was Invested by the Rebels, acted as a good and Loyal subject in its Defence." Certificate of John Anderson given by Joseph Goreham, 5 July 1779, MAUA, Webster Collection, 7001, no. 198.

26 Goreham Journal, 361.

27 Isbrook Eddy's recollection, Williamson, *History of Maine*, 452.

28 Goreham Journal, 361–2.

29 Lewis Delesdernier's recollection, "The Delesdernier Family," *Lubec Herald*, 15 October 1931.

30 Goreham Journal, 361.

31 Delesdernier, "The Delesdernier Family."

32 Goreham Journal, 361–2.

33 The earliest published reference to this action is in Howard Trueman, *The Chignecto Isthmus And Its First Settlers* (Toronto: William Briggs 1902), 61, in which Trueman claimed the Maliseet man was "maimed for life." The story is partially corroborated. Eddy and Goreham noted that a Native man was wounded in the fort attack but neither gives any details. The story is lent credence by the fact that one of the Maliseet contingent, Pierre Tomah (not Grand Chief Tomah who did not participate in the siege), was later listed as having "1 arm," see John Allan's "Return of Indians and their Familys," 28 July 1780, Frederic Kidder, *Military Operations in Eastern Maine and Nova Scotia during the Revolution* (Albany: Joel Munsell 1867), 284–5.

34 Goreham Journal, 362.

35 Eddy Account, 70; Delesdernier, "The Delesdernier Family"; and Isbrook Eddy's recollection, Williamson, *History of the State of Maine*, 452. Eddy's recollection, which was gleaned by Williamson more than fifty years after the event when Eddy was seventy-eight years old is remarkably accurate especially in its mention of such details as the log rollers, the construction of which was described in Goreham's Journal. It is particularly important to cite this high degree of accuracy in view of Frederic Kidder's contrary opinion. In his invaluable *Military Operations*, Kidder thought it "strange that his [Isbrook's] story is so completely erroneous" (see p. 74); of course, Kidder laboured under a double handicap – an unfeigned bias to the American side in the revolution, and a paucity of Nova Scotian sources.

36 Goreham Journal, 361.

37 Eddy Account, 69–70.

38 Goreham Journal, 362.

39 Isbrook Eddy's recollection, Williamson, *History of Maine*, 452.

40 Johnathan Eddy account in Kidder, *Military Operations*, 69; Elijah Ayer Jr claim in *Letter from the Commissioners, Inclosing Certain Documents Relative to the Claims of Elijah Ayer, Deceased, and Elijah Ayer, Junior, Both Nova Scotia Refugees* (Printed by order of the House of Representatives 1802), 19; and Josiah Throop memorial to Massachusetts Council, 23 December 1776, PANS RG 1, vol. 364, no. 30, and memorial to the governor of New York, v10 January 1780 in *Public Papers of George Clinton, First Governor of New York* (Albany: James B. Lyon 1901), vol. 6, 452.

41 Allan to Massachusetts Council, 19 February 1777, PANS RG 1, vol. 365, no. 23.

42 Throop to Massachusetts Council, 23 December 1776, PANS RG 1, vol. 364, no. 30.

43 Cumberland Committee to Massachusetts Council, 13 December 1776, *AA* 5, vol. 3, 626; also Kidder, *Military Operations*, 76. There are minor differences in the transcriptions but the advantage of the *AA* version is the inclusion of the names of committee members.

44 Eddy Account, 70.

45 Cumberland Committee to Massachusetts Council, 13 December 1776, *AA* 5, vol. 3, 626.

46 Eddy to Massachusetts Council, 12 November 1776, *AA* 5, vol. 3, 626.

47 Throop to Massachusetts Council, 23 December 1776, PANS RG 1, vol. 364, no. 30.

48 Ibid. It is likely that Josiah Throop sailed to Boston in the provision sloop with the prisoners captured in the Cumberland Creek raid: "Last Friday [20 December] 37 Prisoners, lately taken by Captain Eddy at Fort Cumberland, were brought to Town, and committed to safe keeping – Among whom are a Captain [Barron], a Chaplain [Eagleson], and a Doctor [Cullen]." *Independent Chronicle*, Thursday, 26 December 1776. Throop went before the Massachusetts Council on Monday, 23 December. See also the *Boston Gazette*, 27 December 1776, which states that all those captured in the Cumberland Creek raid, together with the provision sloop, "were … carried into Newburyport the beginning of last week. On Friday last, 20 of the … persons were committed to gaol in this town."

49 Allan Journal, PANS RG 1, vol. 364, no. 96.

50 Allan to Massachusetts Council, 19 February 1777, PANS RG 1, vol. 365, no. 23.

51 Ibid.

52 Throop to Governor of New York, 10 January 1780, *Public Papers of George Clinton*, 452.

53 Eddy to Massachusetts Council, 12 December 1776, *AA* 5, vol. 3, 626.

54 Deposition of Charles Swan, 21 February 1777, P.E.I. State Papers, NA CO 229/1.

55 Deposition of William Milburn, Bulmer, "Trials For Treason," 116.

56 Collier to Dawson, HMS *Hope*, 14 November 1776, NA MG 11, vol. 96, 332–4; Collier to Sandwich, 21 November 1776, *NDAR* 7, 228–30; and Collier to Germain, 21 November 1776, NA MG 11, vol. 96, 316–24. Although of the same date and similar in content, both letters should be consulted.

57 Ibid.

58 Ibid.

CHAPTER SIX

1 Feilding to Denbigh, 19 August 1776; Marion Balderston and David Syrett, *The Lost War, Letters from British Officers during the American Revolution* (New York: Horizon Press 1975), 104–5.

2 Thomas Brown to Samuel Peters, 30 April 1778, Peters Papers, mfm at PANS.

3 John Robinson and Thomas Rispin, *Journey Through Nova Scotia, Containing a particular Account of the Country and Its Inhabitants* (York, England 1774), 55.

4 A Sketch of the Province of Nova Scotia written by Judge Isaac Deschamps in 1782, PANS RG 1, vol. 284, 6.

5 Ellis to SPG, 4 October 1775, SPG Papers, no. 196, 583–4, and 14 September 1776, no. 208, 614–15.

6 "An Exact Account of the Inhabitants in the townships of Windsor, Falmouth and Newport taken by the Reverend Joseph Bennett in the month of June 1770," Bennett to SPG, 12 August 1770, SPG Papers, no. 157, 442–4. In the chart, Fam. = Families; Ang. = Anglican; Pres. – Presbyterian; Cong. = Congregational; Bap. = Baptist; Qua. = Quaker; Q-B = Quaker-Baptist.

| Township | Fam. | Ang. | Dissenters | | | | |
			Pres.	Cong.	Bap.	Qua.	Q-B
Windsor	46	23	22		1		
Falmouth	36	11	9	8	3	4	1
Newport	54	17	11	2	18	6	
Total	136	51	42	10	22	10	1
Per cent	100	38	31	7	16	8	

38

7 Ellis to SPG, 14 September 1776, SPG Papers, no. 208, 614–19.

8 As early as 1776 consideration was given to a direct overland route between Cumberland and Truro. Robinson and Rispin, *Journey Through Nova Scotia*, 15.

9 Arbuthnot to "My Lord," 20 November 1776, PRO Adm 1/3820. Return of Annapolis Royal Militia, PANS RG 1, vol. 222.

10 Francklin and Batt to "The Commanders of any of His Majesty's Ships at Annapolis," 15 November 1776, NA MG 11, vol. 96, 380–1.

11 Francklin to Arbuthnot, 15 November 1776, NA MG 11, vol. 96, 376–9.

12 Ibid.

13 Collier to "the Captains and Commanders of His Majesty's Ships and Vessels in the Bay of Fundy," 15 November 1776, NA MG 11, vol. 96, 336–7. *Vulture* log, PRO Adm 51/1044.

14 Harold A. Innis, ed., *The Diary of Simeon Perkins 1766–1780 (Toronto: The Champlain Society 1948), 137.*

15 Francklin and Batt to Captains of ships in the Bay of Fundy, 15 November 1776, NA MG 11, vol. 96, 380–1.

16 Francklin to Arbuthnot, 15 November 1776, NA MG 11, vol. 96, 376–9.
17 Ibid.
18 Arbuthnot to "My Lord," 20 November 1776, PRO Adm 1/3820.
19 Memorial of Gilfred Studholme, 25 January 1783, BHQ, NA MG 23, B1, vol. 61, no. 6812.
20 Feilding to Denbigh, 23 May 1776, Balderston and Syrett, *The Lost War*, 80–1.
21 John MacDonald Report, October 1776 to March 1777, PRO CO 217, vol. 52.
22 Certificate of Eyre Massey, 10 May 1779, SRO 174/2128/4.
23 Massey to Germain, 22 November 1776, NA MG 11, vol. 96, 342–6. See also Arbuthnot to Germain, [17] November 1776, NA MG 11, vol. 96, 364. The November date of this letter was not given by Arbuthnot but it can be calculated to be the 17. Massey was explicit in his letter that the grenadiers left Halifax 16 November. Arbuthnot elaborated in his letter that Massey added the grenadiers to the reinforcement and had "marched them yesterday to Windsor." Hence, Arbuthnot's letter should be dated 17 or, if they stayed overnight at Fort Sackville before marching on to Windsor the next day, his letter could be dated 18 at the latest. NDAR and DAR incorrectly impute the date to be 26 November, over a week too late.
24 *Vulture* log, PRO Adm 51/1044. Feattus Papers, PRO Adm, 1790.
25 *Diligent* log, PRO Adm 52/1669.
26 Extract of a letter from Halifax, 22 November 1776, John Almon, ed., *The Remembrancer, or Imperial Repository of Public Events, 1775–1784* vol. 3, (London 1776), 267.
27 Massey to Germain, 22 November 1776, NA MG 11, vol. 96, 342–7.
28 In privateer hunting, the vessel pursued was called simple "the chace".
29 *Hope* logs, PRO Adm 52/1794 and 6469.
30 *Albany* journal, PRO Adm 51/23, and *Diligent* log, PRO Adm 52/1669.
31 Collier to Sandwich, 21 November 1776, PRO Adm 1/1611, in NDAR 7, 229. After leaving Fort Cumberland 3 November, Captain Dalrymple called at Annapolis Royal before sailing on to the Maine coast. According to the NDAR transcription (also DAR's), *Juno* left Annapolis Royal on the 17 November. But *Juno* captured an American ship on the 16 November! And if *Juno* had not departed Annapolis Royal until 17, why would Dalrymple not have received Francklin's appeal of two days earlier? In fact the transcriptions are wrong; *Juno* sailed on the November as is clear from an examination of the original text (see PRO Adm 1/1611) and confirmed by *Juno*'s log (PRO Adm 52/1811).
32 "An Account of Vessels Seized as Prizes by His Majesty's Ships (under Sir Geo. Collier's orders) Stationed on the Coasts of Nova Scotia and New England between the 21st Sept. 1776 and the 14th June 1777," in Collier's correspondence, PRO Adm 1/1611.
33 Notation in Massey's hand in Goreham's Journal, NDAR 7, 99.

34 Massey to Germain, 22 November 1776, NA MG 11, vol. 96, 343.

35 Certificate of Eyre Massey, 10 May 1779, SRO 174/2128/4.

36 Extract of a letter from Halifax, 22 November 1776, *The Remembrancer 1776*, 267.

37 Collier to Sandwich, 21 November 1776, PRO Adm 1/1611, in *NDAR* 7, 230.

38 Arbuthnot to Germain, [17] November 1776, NA MG 11, vol. 96, 366.

39 Ethan Allen, *A Narrative of the Captivity of Col. Ethan Allen from the Time of His Being Taken by the British, Near Montreal, on the 25ᵗʰ Day of September 1773 to the Time of His Exchange on the 6th Day of May 1778* (Albany: Pratt and Clark 1814), 69.

40 Ellis to SPG, 14 September 1776, SPG Papers, no. 208, 614–17.

41 Discourses to Seamen, Ellis Papers, DUA MS 2, 25.

42 *Albany* journal, PRO Adm 51/23 and *Diligent* log, PRO Adm 52/1669.

43 Francklin to Arbuthnot, 15 November 1776, NA MG 11, vol. 96, 377.

44 *Albany* journal, PRO Adm 51/23 and *Diligent* log, PRO Adm 52/1669.

45 Ibid.

46 Certificate of Eyre Massey, 10 May 1779, SRO 174/2128/4.

47 For other information about Captains McKinnon and MacLaine see McDonald to McAdams, 11 January 1778; McDonald to Ogilvie, 6 January 1778; McDonald to Small, 27 January 1776, McDonald Letterbook, 393, 235 and 247. For the exploits of Captain MacLaine on the *Newcastle Jane*, see "Extract of a letter of Murdoch MacLaine of the Royal Highland Emigrants to a gentleman in Halifax," 15 November 1776, *Public Advertiser*, 8 January 1777. Also, Massey to Alderman Baker of Corke, 5 November 1776, *NDAR* 7, 45.

48 Massey to Germain, 22 November 1776, NA MG 11, vol. 96, 344.

49 *Albany* journal, PRO Adm 51/23 and *Diligent* log, PRO Adm 52/1669.

50 Collett to Germain, 7 January 1777, NA CO 217, vol. 5, no. 63. For a biography of Collet, see Janet Schaw, *Journal of a Lady of Quality; Being the Narrative of a Journey from Scotland to the West Indies, North Carolina, and Portugal in the Years 1774 to 1776*, ed. Evangeline W. Andrews (New Haven: Yale University Press 1923), 330–3.

51 Arbuthnot to Germain, 31 December 1776, NA MG 11, vol. 96, 392. The militia received commendation from London for their assistance during the siege of Fort Cumberland; see Germain to Arbuthnot, 14 January 1777, NA MG 11, vol. 97, 84–6. This emphasis is important since J.B. Brebner drew the conclusion (with incomplete sources) that Francklin's militia refused "to give even minor assistance when Fort Cumberland was attacked," John B. Brebner, The *Neutral Yankees of Nova Scotia, a marginal Colony during the Revolutionary Years* (New York: Columbia University 1937), 274. It is certain that the militia provided substantial assistance. The crucial document is the statement of "Expenses incurred for Militia employed on Sundry Services between the 10 November 1776 and 30 July 1777," NA MG

11, vol. 97, 299–300. The militia of Kings County, Annapolis County, and Halifax were paid for "doing Duty during the Invasion of Fort Cumberland." Even in his allowance that the only "probable exception" was Halifax, Brebner was off base if the amounts paid are any indication of the extent of service; the Kings and Annapolis County militias were paid substantially more than that of Halifax.

52 Feilding to Denbigh, 19 November 1776, Balderston and Syrett, *The Lost War*, 105; Massey to Germain, 22 November 1776, NA MG 11, vol. 96, 342–7; Executive Council Minutes, 22 November 1776, PANS RG 1, vol. 212.

53 Francklin to Arbuthnot, 15 November 1776, NA MG 11, vol. 96, 378. Massey would later say that the Windsor Militia had refused to go to Cobequid, but this is another example of his propensity for exaggeration. The militia had gone to Cobequid to retake the ferry, but Massey wanted to post the militia there for an extended tour of duty and was ready to so order them. After arriving in Windsor, however, and finding the Partridge Island ferry already retaken and learning about Francklin's intelligence-gathering in Cobequid, Massey allowed Francklin to change his mind and left the militia in Windsor.

Even more bizarre was the claim made by an army officer in Halifax that the Windsor militia had refused to go to Fort Cumberland. Massey never ordered the militia to go there nor included them in the larger 420-member contingent first planned. However he may have contemplated sending them to Cumberland before going to Windsor since there was an impression in Halifax that the militia had been used in the relief force. It is possible, after it was learned they were not used, that the rumour circulated that they had refused to leave their home district, and indeed if they had been ordered either to Cobequid or Cumberland for an extended period, they might well have refused. As it was, the role of the militia was to assist the depleted Fort Edward garrison and defend home districts, a job for which they received the commendation of London. See Massey to Germain, 22 November 1776, NA MG 11, vol. 96, 343–7; MacDonald to Governor Tryon, 26 November 1776, McDonald Letterbook, 298; Feilding to Denbigh, 19 November 1776, Balderston and Syrett, *The Lost War*, 104.

54 Arbuthnot to Smith, 19 November 1776, PANS RG 1, vol. 136.

55 Bulkeley to the Magistrates in the District of Cobequid, 19 November 1776, PANS RG 1, vol. 136.

56 Arbuthnot was forced to retreat from his blanket condemnation of Cobequid. In a follow-up letter to Smith he explained that "I meant not to be understood to lay the crime of succouring Carleton and the other Pirates to the charge of the Inhabitants of Londonderry because I well knew where it was Committed and by whom as far as Affidavits will Ascertain any-

thing." In the meantime, the people of Londonderry apparently had protested through their minister to the lieutenant-governor that they had not been in rebellion and it is significant that this was their stand. Arbuthnot to Smith, 4 December 1776, PANS RG 1, vol. 136.

57 *Albany* journal, PRO Adm 51/23.

58 Collier to Sandwich, 21 November 1776, *NDAR* 7, 230.

59 Collier to Sandwich, 21 November 1776, *NDAR* 7, 230; and *Hope* logs, PRO Adm 52/1794 and 6469.

60 Feilding to Denbigh, 23 May 1776, Balderston and Syrett, *The Lost War,* 80–2. Arbuthnot to Sandwich, 1 February 1776, *Sandwich Papers,* vol. 1:118.

61 Massey to Germain, 22 November 1776, NA MG 11, vol. 96, 345.

62 Francklin and Batt to "The Commanders of any of His Majesty's Ships at Annapolis," 15 November 1776, NA MG 11, vol. 96, 380–1.

63 Arbuthnot to "My Lord," 20 November 1776, PRO Adm 1/3820.

64 Prayer in Ellis' handwriting, Ellis Papers, DUA MS 2, 25.

65 Arbuthnot to Germain, [17] November 1776, NA MG 11, vol. 96, 363–4. For more on Michael Francklin see W.B. Kerr, "The Rise of Michael Francklin," *DR* 13 (1934):389–400; James S. MacDonald, "Memoir Lieut-Governor Michael Francklin, 1752–1782," *NSHS* 16 (1912): 1–40; and *DCB* IV.

CHAPTER SEVEN

1 Allan memorial to Congress, 26 March 1800, PANS RG 1, vol. 364. His claim was certified by eleven residents of Cumberland including Alpheus Morse, one of Eddy's soldiers. Ironically, Morse could have been one of the "wanton individuals" referred to in the memorial who "ungenerously" burned this property.

2 Even those confined to their homes seemed to accept the helplessness of the garrison. "As there were but a handful of men in the garrison," explained William Black Jr, "and they knew not the weakness of the rebels, they did not attempt to come out to relieve the country." Matthew Richey, *A Memoir of the Late William Black, Wesleyan Minister, Halifax, N.S.* (Halifax: William Cunnabell 1830), 11.

3 Goreham Journal, *NA Report* 1894, 360.

4 RFA Muster Roll, NA RG 8, vol. 1893. The other three deserters were Privates William Hunter (15 November), John Hughs (19 November), and John Bryan (20 November).

5 Francklin to Pernette, 9 December 1776, PANS MG 100, vol. 143.

6 Batt to Goreham, 29 November 1776, John Almon, ed., *The Remembrancer or Imperial Repository of Public Events, 1775–1784,* vol. 3 (London 1776), 298.

7 *Hope* log, PRO Adm 52/6469. N.S. Court of Vice Admiralty, 21 November 1776, PANS RG 1, vol. 495.

8 Goreham Journal, 361.

9 Eddy's Order Book, J.W. Porter, *Memoir of Col. Jonathan Eddy of Eddington, Me., with Some Account of the Eddy Family, and of the Early settlers on Penobscot River* (Augusta: Spraque, Owen and Nash 1877), 6.

10 Diary of Isaac Deschamps, DAL. *Vulture* journal, NMM Adm L/V/126.

11 Goreham Journal, 361–2.

12 Ibid.

13 Ibid.

14 *Vulture* journal, NMM Adm L/V/126.

15 Report on Allan's property, 16 September 1798, Frederic Kidder, *Military Operations in Eastern Maine and Nova Scotia During the Revolution* (Albany: John Munsell 1867), 319. The Allan homestead was owned by John's father, William Allan of Halifax. It was "near Fort Cumberland," and contained at least four houses for tenants with a number of barns and outbuildings, not all of which appear to have been burned by the patriots in the fire of 22 November. Remnants of the estate may have been burned later by the garrison. Materials were confiscated by the garrison at various times during the siege, including bricks from the house chimneys after the fire. William Allan vs. Thomas Batt, Joseph Goreham, and James Law, PANS RG 39 C, Box 19, 1779.

16 Eddy Account, 71.

17 Ibid.

18 Richey, *Memoir Of William Black*, 11.

19 *Vulture* journal, NMM Adm L/V/126. After conversing with veterans of the siege, Charles Knapp wrote that "when the transports entered the Joggins, the country at Cumberland was lit up by flames." The story that those on the relief ships saw the red sky from the fire at the head of the basin was evidently passed down in Cumberland; thus another of Knapp's stories appears to have a basis in fact, Charles E. Knapp, "Folk-Lore About Old Fort Beauséjour," *Acadiensis* 8, no. 4 (October 1908): 301.

20 "The War in America by Sir George Collier," NMM JOD/9.

21 Executive Council Minutes, 23 November 1776, PANS RG 1, vol. 212. See also Arbuthnot to Germain, [17] November 1776, NA MG 11, vol. 96, 365. HMS *Amazon* was in Halifax Harbour by at least 13 November, *Hope* log, PRO Adm 52/1794.

22 P.E.I. State Papers, NA CO 229/1, 139–68.

23 *Vulture* journal, NMM Adm L/V/126.

24 Nathaniel Smith to his brother and sister, 2 May 1778, Anna Calebresi, "*Letters Home*: The Experience of an Emigrant in 18th Century Nova Scotia," Thesis, Yale University 1986.

25 Delesdernier to Haldimand, [1778], and same to Goreham, 5 October 1778, PANS RG 1, vol. 367 1/2.

26 John Robinson and Thomas Rispin, *Journey Through Nova Scotia, Containing a Particular Account of the Country and Its Inhabitants* (York, England: 1774), 26–7.

27 Prayer and sermon, "On Mistaken Zeal," 1776, Ellis Papers, DUA MS2 25, A 1–7.

28 *Vulture* journal, NMM Adm L/V/126.

29 "The War in America by Sir George Collier," NMM JOD/9.

30 *Vulture* journal, NMM Adm L/V/126.

31 *Hope* logs, PRO Adm 52/1794 and 52/6369.

32 Order to Simeon Sampson, Journal of Massachusetts Council, 26 July 1776, MA vol. 37; *Hope* logs, PRO Adm 52/1794 and 52/6369.

33 *Hope* logs, PRO Adm 52/1794 and 52/6369.

34 Ibid.

35 Feattus Papers, PRO Adm 1, 1790. *Vulture* journal, NMM Adm L/V/126.

36 *The Independent Chronicle*, 16 January 1777. *Hope* logs, PRO Adm 52/1794 and 52/6369.

37 Simeon Sampson to Massachusetts Council, 20 January 1777, MA vol. 196, 148–8a. Petition of Andrew Baker, mariner on *Independence*, 18 February 1777, MA vol. 183, 417. See also the petition of Charles Dyer, another mariner, 6 February 1777, MA vol. 183, 398–9; and that of Laben Lynds, MA vol. 37, 161–3.

38 *The Freeman's Journal*, 7 January 1777, in NDAR 7, 619. *Hope* logs, PRO Adm 52/1794 and 52/6369. Sampson to Massachusetts Council, 20 January 1777, MA vol. 196, 148–8a.

39 *Hope* logs, PRO Adm 52/1794 and 52/6369. *The Independent Chronicle*, 16 January 1777, reported that it was not *Hope* but the *Nancy* transport, "having 100 soldiers on board," that fired into the Brig, "which obliged her to give over the contest." These conclusions are not supported by *Hope*'s log or by Captain Henry Mowat quoted in *The Freeman's Journal*, 7 January 1777. The same issue of *The Independent Chronicle* also reported that "Captain Sampson would undoubtedly have taken Dawson before the ship came up had his men stood to their quarters; two or three of whom, he [Sampson] shot for deserting their Post."

40 Deposition of John Gardner (nd), *Dubros Times, Selected Depositions of Maine Revolutionary War Veterans*, ed. Sylvia J. Sherman (Augusta 1975), 16. Both Gardner and his Captain (Simeon Sampson) were kept on the *Boulongue* prison ship in Halifax Harbour, and "when first taken, put in Irons." See Journal of Massachusetts Council, 7 February 1777, MA vol. 37.

41 Morse Genealogy, William C. Milner, *The Basin of Minas and its Early Settlers* (Reprinted from the *Wolfville Acadian* 1937), 121–2.

42 Letter to George Washington, 8 February 1776, AA 4, vol. 5, 936–8. No signature is provided in the publication, but from its contents the author can

be reasonably assumed to have been William How. See also Calnek, *History of the County of Annapolis*, 529–33.

43 Robinson and Rispin, *Journey Through Nova Scotia*, 14.

44 Depositions of Thomas Robinson, J.T. Bulmer, "Trials For Treason in 1776–7," *NSHS* vol. 1 (1879): 111–14. Quotations are also taken from the notes of the testimony of William Black Sr and Thomas Robinson in Judge Isaac Deschamps's Notebook, PANS RG 39 C, Box A.

45 Deschamps's Notebook, PANS RG 39 C, Box A.

46 Depositions of Thomas Robinson, Bulmer, "Trials For Treason," 111–14.

47 Deschamps's Notebook, PANS RG 39 C, Box A.

48 Depositions of Thomas Robinson, Bulmer, "Trials for Treason," 111–14.

49 Mention of this incident by historians (i.e., Howard Truman, *The Chignecto Isthmus and its First settlers [Toronto: William Briggs 1902], 63; and Will R. Bird, A. Century of Chignecto, the key to Old Acadia [Toronto 1928], 222–3)* appears to be based on family tradition as recorded by a descendant, James D. Dixon, in *History of Charles Dixon: One of the Early English Settlers of Sackville, N.B.* (Rockford: Forest City Publishing 1891). None cites the primary source: "Sundries taken by W. How and others of Eddy's Party from the House of Charles Dixon in Sackville at the Investment of the Garrison in November 1776," PANB MC 251, MS1, 65.

50 Claim of Edward Barron, NA AO 13, Bundle 26. The Claims Commission refused Barron's application for compensation, not because he was a Nova Scotian but, like many other loyalists, because of deficiencies in his case.

51 Ibid. Among the "goods recovered immediately after the Defeat of Eddy and his Associates," explained Edward Barron, were "My Best Curtains, found in William How's House the day after the Defeat." Also retrieved from Olive How (William had already fled) was the Barronses' silver bowl.

52 *Vulture* journal, NMM Adm L/V/126. Also *Vulture* log, PRO Adm 51/1044.

53 Ibid. These marines were "of infinite service" when "boat work" was needed according to an officer in Halifax. Feilding to Denbigh, 23 May 1776, Balderston and Syrett, *The Lost War,* 80–2.

54 Feattus Papers, PRO Adm 1, 1790. The Feattus testimonial was signed by the entire Executive Council of Nova Scotia.

CHAPTER EIGHT

1 *Vulture* journal, NMM Adm L/V/126.

2 Goreham Journal, NA *Report* 1894, 362.

3 Ibid. Goreham's is the only account of the haystack skirmish but the event is corroborated. Elijah Ayer described how just before the *Vulture* arrived the patriots "continued to distress the enemy by taking their cattle." Ayer and Barker to Massachusetts Council, 17 December 1776, PANS RG 1, vol. 365.

"This anecdote has been told over and over, and its authenticity has never been doubted," stressed Charles Knapp, when referring to the cattle near Fort Cumberland in 1776 and the attempt "by Eddy to drive them within the rebel lines." Knapp's information about the incident, which he said "came from many who lived in the time of the Eddy and Allan rebellion," was published in his "Folklore About Old Fort Beausejour," *Acadiensis* (1908): 300–1, and his letter to the *Saint John Globe*, 10 December 1898.

As in so many of Knapp's stories his account of the haystack skirmish is riddled with errors, in particular that the central figure in the incident was Brook Watson, a Lord Mayor of London who once lived in Cumberland but who had moved away by 1776. In "this anecdote," however, Knapp's errors are understandable and an explanation is available. Another incident, also involving cattle, occurred in Cumberland in April 1755 while the French still held Fort Beauséjour. Cattle belonging to the British at Fort Lawrence wandered across to the French side of the Missiguash River and Brook Watson, then residing in the district, succeeded in diverting them back to the English side before the French could intervene.

Evidently, both incidents – the Brook Watson incident of 1755 and the haystack skirmish of 1776 – became local legends. Probably because of their similarity they merged into a single story while retaining elements of each incident. J. Clarence Webster, who in 1921 found Brook Watson's account of the earlier incident inscribed (in Watson's hand-writing) on the back of a painting of the same incident, published the account in his booklet, *Sir Brook Watson, Friend of the Loyalists* (Sackville: Mount Allison University 1924), in which he demolished Knapp's account, calling it "ridiculous" and pointing out the discrepancies between it and Watson's account of the incident of 1755. Webster was obviously unaware of the haystack skirmish of twenty-one years later which was equally well documented by Goreham. While pouncing on the inaccuracies in Knapp's blended tale, he missed the useful elements relating to the later incident.

4 RFA Muster Roll, NA RG 8, vol. 1893.
5 Goreham Journal, 362.
6 *Vulture* Journal, NMM Adm L/V/126.
7 Tupper to Massachusetts Council, 27 November 1776. AA 5, vol. 3, 881–2.
8 Allan Memorial to Congress, 26 March 1800, PANS RG 1, vol. 364.
9 Allan Journal, PANS RG 1, vol. 364. The support of the Massachusetts Council was a prerequisite to an appointment by Congress to the post of agent to the eastern Native nations. It is clear from his journal that Allan lobbied Council members from the time he arrived in Boston.
10 Tupper to Massachusetts Council, 27 November 1776. AA 5, vol. 3, 881–2.
11 Lyon to Congress, 26 December 1776. AA 5, vol. 3, 1435.
12 *Vulture* log, PRO Adm 51/1044.

13 Eddy Account, Frederic Kidder, *Military Operations in Eastern Maine and Nova Scotia during the Revolution* (Albany: Joel Munsell 1867), 70.

14 Arbuthnot to Germain, 31 December 1776, NA MG 11, vol. 96, 388.

15 Executive Council Minutes, 30 November 1776, PANS RG 1, vol. 212.

16 Ibid.

17 Collier to Sandwich, 21 November 1776, *NDAR* 7, 229.

18 *Lizard* journal, PRO Adm 51/550.

19 Collier to Sandwich, 21 November 1776, *NDAR* 7, 230.

20 *Hope* log, PRO Adm 52/1794. Executive Council Minutes, 30 November 1776, PANS RG 1, vol. 212. Windsor weather from Deschamps's diary, DAL.

21 McDonald to Ranald McKinnon, 14 December 1776, Letterbook of Captain Alexander McDonald of the Royal Highland Emigrants, 1775–1779," *NYHS* (1882): 301–2.

22 Goreham Journal, 362.

23 Feilding to Denbigh, 23 May 1776, Marion Balderston and David Syrett, eds., *The Lost War, Letters from British Officers during the American Revolution*, (New York: Horizon Press 1975), 82.

24 Goreham Journal, 362.

25 Extract of a letter from Halifax, 22 November 1776; John Almon, ed., *The Remembrancer or Impartial Repository of Public Events, 1775–1784*, vol. 3 (London 1776), 267.

26 Innis, *Perkins Diary*, 138. Weather on the South Shore is confirmed in *Lizard* journal, PRO Adm 51/550.

27 Goreham Journal, 362.

28 For the composition of the strike force see Goreham Journal, 362; Batt to Goreham, 29 November 1776, *The Remembrancer*, 297; and RFA Muster Roll, NA RG 8, vol. 1893. Names of marine officers are in Christopher Harper's claim, PRO AO 13.

29 Feilding to Denbigh, 23 May 1776, Balderston and Syrett, *The Lost War*, 82.

30 Allan to Massachusetts Council, 19 February 1777, PANS RG 1, vol. 365.

31 Committees of Cumberland and Sunbury, 17 December 1776, PANS RG 1, vol. 365.

32 Goreham Journal, 362.

33 *Albany* journal, PRO Adm 51/23; and *Diligent* log, PRO Adm 52/1669.

34 Batt to Goreham, 29 November 1776, *The Remembrancer*, 297.

35 Ibid.

36 Ibid.

37 Ibid., 298.

38 Eddy Account, 70.

39 Ibid.

40 Lyon to Congress, 26 December 1776, *AA* 5, vol. 3, 1435.

41 Goreham Journal, 362.

42 Batt to Goreham, 29 November 1776, *The Remembrancer,* 298.

43 Goreham Journal, 362.

44 There is ample evidence that a patriot died in the assault on Read's farm: "We lost only one man," said Elijah Ayer, "who was killed in the Camp," added Jonathan Eddy. John Allan heard that "all fled except one white [who] was killed," while the Reverend Lyon was told "we lost one man, an inhabitant of Cumberland." Only Knapp provides a name. No one named Furlong appears in the muster rolls of Eddy's men, but this is not unusual since the names of many Cumberlanders who were known to have assisted Eddy (especially those who remained in Nova Scotia) also do not appear on these lists. A family of Furlongs did live in Cumberland during this period. Harrison Papers, PANS MG 1, vol. 427.

45 Eddy Account, 70.

46 Batt to Goreham, 29 November 1776, *The Remembrancer,* 298. The identity of the Black drummer can only be guessed. Slave owning and trading were common in eighteenth-century Nova Scotia; Jonathan Eddy owned slaves, and in 1765 sold Abial Atwood, "a negro wench," in Cumberland. In 1776 Eddy owned a slave named Blackjack who fled with Eddy to Machias after the siege and was still residing in the Eddy household in Maine in 1788. J.W. Porter, *Memoir of Col. Jonathan Eddy of Eddington, Me., with Some Account of the Eddy Family, and of the Early Settlers on Penobscot River,* (Augusta: Spraque Owen and Nash 1877), 39.

47 Batt to Goreham, 29 November 1776.

48 Allan Estimate of Losses, 26 March 1800, PANS RG 1, vol. 364.

49 Goreham Journal, 362.

50 Levi Ames Papers, NA MG 40.

51 Mark Patton was one of eight people arrested and tried for plundering Christopher Harper's farm on 6 November and other occasions during the siege. Six were found guilty: Samuel Smith, William Jones, William Lawrence, Parker Clarke, Simeon Chester, and Elijah Ayer. Two were acquitted: David Forrest and Mark Patton. A ninth person, John Sim(p)son, was charged but not tried. Harper vs. Clarke et al., PANS RG 39 C, Box 22, 1780. Patton was one of twelve petitioners who recommended Jonathan Eddy to George Washington, 8 February 1776, when the twelve prayed for the success of American arms. NDAR 3, 1165–6.

52 Allan Memorial to Congress, 26 March 1800, PANS RG 1, vol. 364.

53 Batt to Goreham, 29 November 1776, *The Remembrancer,* 298.

54 Eddy Account, 70.

55 Lyon to Congress, 26 December 1776, AA 5, vol. 3, 1435.

56 Batt to Goreham, 29 November 1776, *The Remembrancer,* 298.

57 Ibid.

58 Allan Memorial to Congress, 26 March 1800, PANS RG 1, vol. 364.

59 Claim of Edward Barron, PRO AO 13.

60 Nathaniel Fales later found the horse "in the Marsh where he had been left by the Rebels, very poor." Wethered Estate, Halifax County Probate, PANS RG 48.

61 Allan Memorial to Congress, 26 March 1800, PANS RG 1, vol. 364. The village of Bloody Bridge (now Upper Point de Bute, N.B.) was aptly named for a massacre which occurred there in January 1759. A sergeant, three rangers, and seven soldiers from Fort Cumberland were out gathering firewood. As they descended to a ravine and approached a bridge on the trail to Baie Verte they were ambushed and killed by a party of French and Native peoples. The locale became known as Bloody Bridge and John Allan's farm was sometimes referred to as Bloody Bridge farm. See J. Clarence Webster, *The Forts of Chignecto, a Study of the Eighteenth Century Conflict Between France and Great Britain in Acadia* (published by the author 1930), 74.

62 Allan Estimate of Losses, 26 March 1800, PANS RG 1, vol. 364.

63 Batt to Goreham, 29 November 1776, *The Remembrancer,* 298.

64 Depositions of William Lowden, William Ball, James Glover, and Charles Swan, 21 February 1777, and accompanying correspondence, P.E.I. State Papers, NA CO 229/1; PANS MG 100, vol. 209. The description of Pictou is from a letter dated September 1774 in Patrick M'Robert, *A Tour Through the North Provinces of America: Being a Series of Leters wrote on the spot in the Years 1774 and 1775* (Edinburgh: printed by the author 1776), 21. For a description of the *Molly* incident based on oral tradition, see George Patterson, *A History of the County of Pictou, Nova Scotia* (Montreal: Dawson Brothers 1877), 98–105, and for further information on Doctor John Harris see R.F. Harris, "A Pioneer Harris Family and the Pre-Loyalist Settlement of Pictou," NSHS 33 (1961): 103–5. Neither Patterson nor Harris admits that Dr Harris was a willing helper of the patriots.

65 Batt to Goreham, 29 November 1776, *The Remembrancer,* 298.

66 *Independent Chronicle,* 2 January 1777. "The following Gentlemen's Estates were all destroyed, and their families drove into the woods": John Allan, Josiah Throop, Ebenezer Gardiner, Eliphalet Read, Joseph Cuzzins, William Chapman, Richard Jones, William Jones, Robert Haggard, Daniel Gooden, William Wells, Daniel McGuire, "together with a French village, inhabited by 8 Families." At least one other property on the Baie Verte Road was destroyed by the troops; that of Levi Ames, who was living in England in 1776. The farm was purchased by Ames from Benoni Danks and at the time of the siege was leased to one Wethered, probably Samuel or his son. Either lessee could have made the property a target for Captain Studholme.

The bad news was relayed promptly to Ames by John Huston, his Nova Scotian agent: "about the House and Barn being burnt on your Farm in

Cumberland ... some of the Cattle and Sheep belonging to the Farm had
been destroyed and others strayed in the Confusion." It was Jotham Gay
who later explained to Ames that his farm had been laid waste not by the
patriots, nor by vengeful civilian loyalists, but by the troops in the course of
their duty. "I am very sorry for the Great Loss you sustained as well as Many
Others in this Place," commiserated Gay, "by this Garrison being Invested
in the fall of 1776. Your House and Barn was Burnt (not by the Enemy) But
by the King's Troops when they Attacked and Drove the Enemy out of the
Country." Levi Ames Papers, NA MG 40.

67 Collier to Stephens, 8 January 1777, *NDAR* 7, 883.

68 Allan to Massachusetts Council, 19 February 1777, PANS RG 1, vol.
365.

69 Batt to Goreham, 29 November 1776, *The Remembrancer,* 298.

70 Goreham Journal, 362.

71 Batt to Goreham, 29 November 1776, *The Remembrancer,* 298.

72 Goreham Journal, 362.

73 Batt to Goreham, 29 November 1776, *The Remembrancer,* 298.

74 McDonald to Ranald McKinnon, 14 December 1776, "Letterbook of Captain Alexander McDonald", 301.

75 Germain to Arbuthnot, 6 March 1777, NA MG 11, vol. 97, 136.

76 Deschamps's Notebook, PANS RG 39 C, Box A. This notebook contains the
testimony of William Black, Thomas Dixson, and Thomas Robinson in the
trials of Parker Clarke and Thomas Faulkner.

77 Deposition of William Milburn, J.T. Bulmer, "Trials for Treason in 1776–7,"
NSHS vol. 1, (1879): 116.

78 Francklin to Pernette, 9 December 1776, PANS MG 100, vol. 143.

79 Delesdernier to Goreham, 3 October 1778, and same to Haldimand,
[1778], PANS RG 1, vol. 367 1/2.

80 Goreham Journal, 363.

81 Deschamps Notebook, PANS RG 39 C, Box A.

82 Goreham Journal, 363.

83 Deschamps Notebook, PANS RG 39 C, Box A.

84 Deposition of William Black Sr, Bulmer, "Trials for Treason," 1: 113.

85 Deschamps's Notebook, PANS RG 39 C, Box A.

86 Ibid.

87 Ibid.

88 *Letter from the Commissioners Appointed Pursuant to the Act, Entitled "An Act for
the Relief of the Refugees from the British Provinces of Canada and Nova Scotia," Inclosing Certain Documents Relative to the Claims of Elijah Ayer, Deceased, and Elijah Ayer, Junior, Both Nova Scotia Refugees* (Printed by order of the House of
Representatives 1802), 12.

89 Ibid.

90 Allan Memorial to Congress, 26 March 1800, PANS RG 1, vol. 364.

91 Allan Journal, PANS RG 1, vol. 364. On the second day of his horseback ride to Philadelphia (Saturday 30 November) Allan "called at Job Seamans' at Attleborough." Seamans was a former Baptist minister in Sackville Nova Scotia and Abiel Peck's brother-in-law.

92 *Alline Journal*, 78.

93 Goreham Journal, 363.

94 Batt to Goreham, 29 November 1776, *The Remembrancer*, 298.

95 Massey to Germain, 20 December 1776, NA MG 11, vol. 96, 382.

96 The garrison not only paid Samuel Wethered's medical bill and the expense of boarding and lodging him and his family at Jotham Gay's from 9 November to February 1777 when he died of his wounds, but the military also paid a much larger sum to his estate for an indeterminate reason. The authorization of these expenses first by the Cumberland commissary then by Halifax suggests that Goreham had indeed made a deal with Wethered. Wethered Estate, Halifax County Probate, PANS RG 48.

   The Dixson-Law-Wethered connections are in Throop, "Early Settlers of Cumberland Township," NGSQ 67, (December 1979). In addition, Thomas and Katherine Dixson's daughter, Sarah, married William Allan Jr, brother of John Allan; another of the Dixsons' daughters, Anne, married William Harper, son of Christopher Harper; and the Dixsons' son, Robert, married Rachel Peck, daughter of Abiel Peck.

EPILOGUE

1 Throop to Massachusetts Council, 29 May 1777, MA vol. 142.

2 Hancock to Massachusetts Assembly, 10 January 1777, LCC 2, 213.

3 Petition of Elijah Ayer, 6 December 1782, James Phinney Baxter, *Documentary History of the State of Maine*, vol. 20 (1914): 136–7; and of other refugees, 25 February 1784, PCC no. 42, 12.

4 Eddy "retreated with his men to the town of Sackville and in a day or two after retreated to the River St. John." Allan to Massachusetts Council, 19 February 1777, PANS MG 100, vol. 129. A list of those who fled (forty-six of whom are named) is in Frederic Kidder, *Military Operations in Eastern Maine and Nova Scotia during the Revolution* (Albany: Joel Munsell 1867), 76–7. Twenty-eight went on from Machias to Boston.

5 As Ayer's wife escaped from the house with her infant daughter in her arms, a piece of burning wood fell from overhead and injured the baby's wrist. The baby grew up and lived eighty-seven years, and always bore a scar from the Cumberland rebellion. William H. Kilby, *Eastport and Passamaquoddy a Collection of Historical and Biographical Sketches* (Eastport: E.E. Shead 1888), 436.

6 Memorial of Robert Foster, 15 April 1782, Baxter, *History of Maine* vol. 19 (1914): 467–8. Samuel Rogers began his march on 3 December "with my brother George." They arrived in Machias about 1 January and in Boston

in February, and found Cumberlanders already there. Rogers extracts, 10 April 1779, PCC 41, vol. 8.

7 Delesdernier Narrative, *Lubec Herald,* 15 October 1931. Refugees can sometimes be traced in obscure local histories; for example, Nathaniel and Atwood Fales, two refugees of Amherst, are described in Cyrus Eaton, *History of Thomaston, Rocklin, and South Thomaston, Maine* 2 vols. (Hallowell: Masters, Smith and Co. 1865), 152.

8 The case for American compensation was made by John Hancock and John Adams in support of Eddy's petition: "It certainly would not be showing a more just adherence to *our* unfortunate friends than has been shown by the British to *theirs.*" Hancock and Adams to Massachusetts Council, 24 February 1784, PCC 42/2, 416.

9 Works on patriot refugees include the following: Elyzabeth S. McCorkle, "Canadian and Nova Scotia Refugees to New York," *NGSQ* 53/2 (June 1965): 116–18; Clifford N. Smith, "Revolutionary War Refugees from Canada and Nova Scotia," *NGSQ* 59/4 (December 1971): 266–73; Alice Arneson, "New York's Canadian and Nova Scotia Refugees in the Revolution," *Tree Talks: Central New York Genealogical Society* 4/3 and 4 (September and December 1964, March and June 1977); Carl Wittke, "Canadian Refugees in the American Revolution," *CHR* (December 1922): 320–38; and Allan S. Everest, *Moses Hazen and the Canadian Refugees in the American Revolution* (Syracuse: Syracuse University Press 1976).

10 Arbuthnot to Germain, 31 December 1776, NA MG 11, vol. 96, 388–93. Goreham's proclamation of 30 November was an undertaking "to obtain His Majesty's most gracious Pardon to all such of the Inhabitants of this Part of the Province or others that have lately been in Arms." The time limit was four days and the offer excluded Eddy, Rogers, How, and Allan. On 3 December a second proclamation was issued adding Zebulon Roe to the proscribed list. *NA Report* (1894): 365–6.

11 Goreham Journal, *NA Report* (1894): 363.

12 For accounts of the *Molly*'s recapture see the log of HMS *Hunter,* Adm 52/1799, and P.E.I. State Papers, NA CO 229/1.

13 David G. Bell ed., *Newlight Baptist Journals of James Manning and James Innis* (Saint John: Lancelot Press 1984), 245.

14 These naval manoeuvres, that included boat patrols to the Petitcodiac River, probably a visit to the home of Abiel and Ruth Peck, intelligence-gathering from Acadians in Memramcook, and the capture of two patriots in Hopewell, can be followed chiefly in the logs of *Hope* and *Diligent,* Adm 52/1794, 6469, and 1669.

15 Massey to Germain, 20 December 1776, NA MG 11, vol. 96, 382–7.

16 McDonald to McLean, 13 January 1777, McDonald Letterbook, 314–17.

17 McDonald to McKinnon, 14 December 1776; and same to McKenzie, 25 January 1777, McDonald Letterbook, 301–2 and 320–2.

18 For aspects of the aftermath see Clarke, "Cumberland Planters and the Aftermath of the Attack on Fort Cumberland," *They Planted Well*, ed. Margaret Conrad (Acadiensis: Fredericton 198): 42–60.

19 "A Sermon On a Day of Thanksgiving Preached at Liverpool by Henry Alline," 21 November 1782, George A. Rawlyk ed., *The Sermons of Henry Alline* (Hantsport: Lancelot Press 1986), 94.

20 Ibid., 99.

21 Ibid., 94.

22 Ibid., 100.

23 Ibid., 95. Beverley and Moody, editors of *The Journal of Henry Alline*, observed that Alline barely mentioned the revolution in his private journal; this was not the case in his public sermons. Of the hundreds he delivered only three were published and in one of these the revolution is referred to repeatedly. But it was not simply referred to, it was woven into the fabric of the exhortation, presented in vivid imagery, and employed dramatically for tactical purposes. In this sermon, preached "On a Day of Thanksgiving," Alline's theme of the revolution and Nova Scotia's response to it is so full blown and richly expressed that it could only have been refined through the course of many sermons. Nova Scotian planters would have understood every nuance of this sermon. Alline's ability to explain their predicament and give voice to their inner dilemmas was his great appeal. In *The Sermons of Henry Alline*, 28, Rawlyk states that Alline "undoubtedly used many of the same points raised in these three sermons and much of the actual language in many of the other sermons that he preached as he crisscrossed Nova Scotia from 1777 to 1783."

24 Stephen Millidge to Ward Chipman, 23 January 1788, NBM Hazen Collection, F 1, pkt. 6. See also Clarke "Cumberland Planters and the Aftermath of the Attack on Fort Cumberland," 58; and for a traditional reference to this incident see W.C. Milner, *History of Sackville, New Brunswick* (Sackville: Tribune Press 1934), 115.

25 Calvin L. Hatheway, *The History of New Brunswick, from its First Settlement* (Fredericton: J.P.A. Phillips 1846), 11–14.

26 Esther Clark Wright, *The Petit codiac, a study of the New Brunswick River and of the People Who Settled along it* (Sackville: Tribune Press 1945), 56; and *Samphire Greon: The Story of the Steeves* (1961), 27.

27 Uniacke's career after his appointment as solicitor-general in 1781 is thoroughly chronicled in Brian Cuthbertson, *The Old Attorney General, Biography of Richard John Uniacke* (Halifax: Nimbus 1980), and L.G. Power, "Richard John Uniacke, A Sketch," *NSHS* 9 (1895): 73–118. His role as a patriot has been underplayed thereby diminishing the scale of his transformation. Cuthbertson says Uniacke "did not play even a minor role" in the rebellion although Goreham ranked him among the principal prisoners.

28 The preface in Richard Uniacke's *The Statutes at Large passed in the several General Assemblies held in His Majesty's Province of Nova-Scotia, 1758–1804* (Halifax, 1805).

29 One historian thought the government's motive in rewarding former patriots like Uniacke was "to keep them out of mischief in the future, many of them were placed in good offices," Charles E. Knapp, "Folklore About Old Fort Beausejour," *Acadiensis* vol. 8, no. 4, (1908): 302.

30 Studholme Report, NBHS vol. 1, (1894):114. Quinton was appointed a captain in the Sunbury Militia, 6 December 1777, PANS RG 1, vol. 168, 524.

31 An incident in which Attorney General Uniacke was confronted with his patriot past while cross-examining a witness in court in Cumberland is in Howard Trueman, *The Chignecto Isthmus and its First Settlers* (Toronto: William Briggs 1902), 233–4. See also Milner, *History of Sackville*, 31–2, for notice of Uniacke at a case in Windsor and a reminder of his role in the siege.

32 Peter Fisher, *Sketches of New Brunswick* (Saint John: Chubband Sears 1825), 121–2.

33 Calvin L. Hatheway, *The History of New Brunswick From its First Settlement, Containing a Geographical Description of the Province* (Fredicton: J.P.A. Phillips 1846), 12–13. This account appears to derive in part from the recollections of veterans of the siege. He evidently learned some interesting details about the capture of the provision sloop in the Cumberland Creek raid. Several of Eddy's soldiers settled in the St John Valley, including Zebulon Roe Jr whose father led that raid.

34 Knapp, "Folklore About Old Fort Beausejour," 299. There are no recorded recollections of local patriots who stayed in Nova Scotia to compare, for example, with that of Isbrook Eddy recorded by William D. Williamson in the 1830s, and no autobiographical accounts comparable with those of Josiah Throop or Samuel Rogers.

35 Beamish Murdoch, *A History of Nova Scotia, or Acadie* 3 vols. (Halifax: James Barnes 1866), vol. 2, 577–8. The presence of Nova Scotian planters among the attackers is amply documented in the two chief sources used by Murdoch, the Executive Council Minutes and the Colonial Correspondence.

36 These legal sources were known to other lawyers. Pierce Hamilton and J.T. Bulmer used them at a later date.

37 Murdoch, *A History of Nova Scotia*, 584.

38 Collier Journal, NMM JOD/9.

39 Collier to Sandwich, 21 November 1776, NDAR 7, 228–30.

40 Collier to Stephens, 8 January 1777, NDAR 7, 883–4.

41 Arbuthnot to Germain, [17] November 1776, DAR 7, 254–6.

42 Arbuthnot to Germain, 31 January 1777, NA MG 11, vol. 97, 111–13.

43 Arbuthnot to Germain, 31 December 1776, NA MG 11, vol. 96, 388–93.

44 Arbuthnot to Sandwich, 11 October 1777, G.R. Barnes and J.H. Owen, *The Private Papers of John, Earl of Sandwich, First Lord of the Admiralty 1771–1782*, vol. 1 (Navy Records 1932), 304–6.

45 Massey to Germain, 17 January 1777, NA MG 11, vol. 97, 96–9.

46 Massey to Germain, 30 January 1777, NA MG 11, vol. 97, 108–10.

47 The broken leg is referred to in Goreham's memorial, The Earl of Dartmouth Papers, 4321–4; the drinking problem in *DCB*.

48 Allan Journal, PANS RG 1, vol. 364, no. 96.

49 *JCC* 7, 20, and 34.

50 Elbridge Gerry to John Adams, 8 January 1777, Robert J. Taylor, ed., *Papers of John Adams*, vol. 5 (Cambridge: Belknap Press 1983), 64–7.

51 Samuel to John Adams, 9 January 1777, Charles F. Adams, *The Works of John Adams Second President of the United States*, vol. 9 (Boston: Little Brown 1856), 448–9.

52 Hancock to Massachusetts Assembly, 10 January 1777, Edmund C. Burnett ed., *Letters of Members of the Continental Congress* vol. 2, (Washington: Carnegie Institution 1923), 213.

53 Gerry to Adams, 8 January 1777, *Papers of John Adams* 5, 64–7.

54 "Some Proposals for an attack on Nova Scotia," Allan to Massachusetts Council, MA vol. 144, 172–4. This long and detailed attack plan is published in *NSHS* 1, 11–16.

55 Allan Journal, PANS RG 1, vol. 364, no. 96.

56 Allan Proposals, *NSHS* 1, 14.

Index